THE FIRST EVER

WOMEN'S FOOTBALL YEARBOOK

2017/18

THE FIRST EVER WOMEN'S FOOTBALL YEARBOOK 2017/18

EDITED BY
CHRIS SLEGG & TOM GARRY
FOREWORD BY
JACQUI OATLEY

ISBN: 978-1-78324-072-2

Published by Wordzworth
www.wordzworth.com

FRONT COVER IMAGES

Alex Scott of Arsenal, Karen Carney of Chelsea, Steph Houghton of Manchester City (all © PA images), and Jess Clarke of Liverpool (© Liverpool Ladies)

INTERIOR IMAGES

Alex Scott of Arsenal, Jess Carter of Birmingham City (© Birmingham City Ladies), Jas Matthews of Bristol City (© Bristol City Women), Gilly Flaherty of Chelsea, Gabby George of Everton, Jess Clarke of Liverpool (© Liverpool Ladies), Georgia Stanway of Manchester City (© Manchester City Women's), Jo Potter of Reading (© Neil Graham), Melanie Reay of Sunderland (© Sunderland Ladies), and Annie Heatherson of Yeovil Town (© Yeovil Town Ladies)

BACK COVER IMAGES

Gillingham celebrate their WPL South East One title win (© Gillingham Ladies), Bolton Wanderers are crowned North West Premier League champions (© Bolton Wanderers Community Trust), the promotion-winning Barnsley squad (© Barnsley FC Ladies), Chichester City uncork the champagne following their WPL South West One title triumph (© Chichester City Ladies), Durham celebrate a goal in the 2017 WSL2 Spring Series (© Durham Women's), Lewes hold aloft the 2017 WPL Plate (© Lewes FC) and Rinsola Babajide in action for Watford (©Ed Henderson)

CONTENTS

A TRIBUTE TO NETTIE J.	IX
ACKNOWLEDGEMENTS	XI
FOREWORD	XIII
HOW TIMES HAVE CHANGED	1
A BRIEF HISTORY	5
THE NEWS 2016/17	13
LEAGUE TABLES	27
TOP SCORERS	33
CHAMPIONS LEAGUE 2016/17	39
FA CUP 2016/17	49
WSL CONTINENTAL CUP 2016	59
WPL CUP 2016/17	61
WPL PLATE 2016/17	65
WOMEN'S FOOTBALL PYRAMID 2017/18	69

WSL1 71
Arsenal – WSL1 72
Birmingham City – WSL1 79
Bristol City – WSL1 86
Chelsea – WSL1 93
Everton – WSL1 100
Liverpool – WSL1 107
Manchester City – WSL1 114
Reading – WSL1 122
Sunderland – WSL1 129
Yeovil Town – WSL1 136

WSL2 143
Aston Villa – WSL2 144
Brighton & Hove Albion – WSL2 149
Doncaster Rovers Belles – WSL2 155
Durham – WSL2 160
London Bees – WSL2 165
Millwall Lionesses – WSL2 171
Oxford United – WSL2 177
Sheffield FC – WSL2 182
Tottenham Hotspur – WSL2 188
Watford – WSL2 192

WOMEN'S PREMIER LEAGUE (WPL) 197
Actonians 199
AFC Wimbledon 200
Barnsley 201
Basingstoke Town 202
Birmingham & West Midlands 203
Blackburn Rovers 204
Bolton Wanderers 205
Bradford City 206
Brighouse Town 207
Brislington 208
Burton Albion 209
C&K Basildon 210
Cambridge United 211
Cardiff City Ladies 212
Charlton Athletic 213

Cheltenham Town	214
Chester-Le-Street Town	215
Chichester City	216
Chorley	217
Coventry United	218
Crewe Alexandra	219
Crystal Palace	220
Denham United	221
Derby County	222
Enfield Town	223
Exeter City	224
Fleetwood Town Wrens	225
Fylde	226
Gillingham	227
Guiseley Vixens	228
Haringey Borough	229
Huddersfield Town	230
Hull City	231
Ipswich Town	232
Keynsham Town	233
Larkhall Athletic	234
Leeds United	235
Leicester City Ladies	236
Leicester City Women	237
Lewes	238
Leyton Orient	239
Liverpool Marshall Feds	240
Long Eaton United	241
Loughborough Foxes	242
Loughborough Students	243
Lowestoft Town	244
Luton Town	245
Maidenhead United	246
Middlesbrough	247
Milton Keynes Dons	248
Morecambe	249
Mossley Hill Athletic	250
Newcastle United	251

Norwich City 252
Nottingham Forest 253
Plymouth Argyle 254
Poole Town 255
Portsmouth 256
Queens Park Rangers 257
Radcliffe Olympic 258
Rotherham United 259
Shanklin 260
Sheffield United 261
Solihull Moors 262
Southampton Saints 263
Southampton Women's 264
Sporting Khalsa 265
St Nicholas 266
Steel City Wanderers 267
Stevenage 268
Stoke City 269
Swindon Town 270
The New Saints 271
Tranmere Rovers 272
West Bromwich Albion 273
West Ham United 274
Wolverhampton Wanderers 275

EURO 2017 **277**

ENGLAND 2016/17 **285**

A TRIBUTE TO NETTIE J.

The British Ladies' Football Club (circa 1895).
Nettie J. Honeyball is second from left of photo, top row

The glitz and glamour of the WSL; crowds of 35,000-plus at Wembley for the FA Cup final; England's semi-final appearances at the 2015 World Cup and Euro 2017; television audiences of more than four million viewers. Would any of this have been possible without Nettie J. Honeyball, founder of the British Ladies' Football Club in 1894? Fearing the consequences of revealing her true identity, due to the anger directed, by some, at women playing football, Nettie J. Honeyball was a pseudonym. Many believe her to have been Dublin-born London resident Mary Hutson. This first ever Football Yearbook for women's football is dedicated to its greatest pioneer. Thank you Nettie J. Honeyball.

A note on the text: Throughout this book we have omitted Women's or Ladies wherever possible since it seems superfluous. It is only used where there could be confusion with the men's game and to distinguish Cardiff City Ladies (who compete in English football) from Cardiff City Women (who compete in Welsh football), Leicester City Ladies from Leicester City Women and to give a clearer distinction between Southampton Saints and Southampton Women's.

ACKNOWLEDGEMENTS

We would like to say a huge thank you to Jacqui Oatley for agreeing to write the foreword, to former England internationals Gill Coultard, and Pru Buckley and to current WSL1 players Jess Carter (Birmingham City), Jess Clarke (Liverpool), Gilly Flaherty (Chelsea), Gabby George (Everton), Annie Heatherson (Yeovil Town), Jas Matthews (Bristol City), Jo Potter (Reading), Melanie Reay (Sunderland), Alex Scott (Arsenal), and Georgia Stanway (Manchester City), for their time giving interviews.

This book would not have been possible without the thorough additional research carried out by Khalid Karimullah, the assistance given by Alex Rice and the proof reading of Frances Prior-Reeves.

Thanks also to all the WSL and WPL clubs for their co-operation. We made efforts to contact every club to verify information and we are extremely grateful to those who responded. If our voicemails and emails did not find the appropriate people who are currently at some of the clubs, then we do apologise. We made our very best attempts to track people down.

Thank you to Birmingham City, Bristol City, Everton, Liverpool, Manchester City, Sunderland and Yeovil Town for providing photos for use in this book and to Neil Graham for permission to use the photo of Reading's Jo Potter. Also thank you to Barnsley, Bolton Wanderers, Chichester City, Durham, Gillingham, Lewes, Millwall Lionesses, Watford and Wolverhampton Wanderers for providing photos. Due to design reasons we may not have been able to use them all.

We have also had much assistance from Naomi Loveless, Sarah Levy and Gary Mellish at the FA regarding information on team sheets and League tables.

There are many more people to thank than those who appear on this list, but we are particularly grateful to: Dorita Agius (Malta FA); Mercedes Antrobus (Manchester City); Neil Bailey (QPR, Maidenhead and Portsmouth); David Baker (Luton Town); Nick Barrett (Morecambe); Katie Bent (Bolton Wanderers Trust); Will Boye (Ashford Town); David Brenchley (Charlton Athletic); Mark Broadhurst (Aston Villa); Will Brown (Long Eaton United); Joe Burlison (Chester-le-Street Town); Hannah Burnett-Kirk

(Millwall); Amanda Burroughs (Southampton Women's); Helen Carver (Birmingham & West Midlands); Daniel Chitty (Actonians); Amy Colson (London Bees); Joanne Currivan and Alan Pines (Denham United); Janet Dawson (Chorley); Karen Dean and Owen Evans (MK Dons); Donna Dodds (Sheffield United); Lisa Dootson-Gill (Poole Town); Mark Donnelly (Durham); Sheila Edmunds (Doncaster Rovers Belles); Louise Edwards (Tranmere Rovers); Steven Edwards (Cambridge United); Brian Eley & Tracey Wheeler (Southampton Saints); Claire Ford and Julie Square (Enfield Town); Sue Foulkes (Leicester City Ladies); Lisa Fulgence (formerly Brighton & Hove Albion); Christopher George (Fylde); Duncan Gibb (Derby County); Lauren Haynes (Oxford United); Ash Head (Lewes); Ed Henderson (Watford); James Hilsum (Brighton & Hove Albion); Leah Hinchcliffe (Fleetwood Town Wrens); John Ivers (AFC Wimbledon); Rachel Jardine (Barnsley); Trevor Jenkins (Yeovil Town); Karen Jones (Cardiff City Ladies); Peter King (C&K Basildon); David Leek (Coventry United); Andy Liddle (Cheltenham Town); David Mallin (Huddersfield Town); Josh Miller (Lowestoft Town); Helen Mitchell (Sheffield FC); Nicki O'Connell (Larkhall Athletic); Nick Pearce (Crewe Alexandra); Shirley Pollock (Rotherham United); Dave Potter (Stevenage); Iain Prior (St Nicholas); John Shirt (Guiseley Vixens); David Smith (Leicester City Women); Mark Snell (Scottish FA); Richard Spokes (Crystal Palace); Alex Saulter (Radcliffe Olympic); Chantelle Thompson (Liverpool Marshall Feds); Hannah Thompson, Rossana Frith-Salem and Jamie Barlow (Loughborough Students); Kath Tranter (Stoke City); Robert Wells (Mossley Hill Athletic); Sharon Whelan (Brislington Town); Jenny Wilkes (Wolverhampton Wanderers); Steve Wilkinson (Loughborough Foxes); Kelly Williams (Sporting Khalsa); Julie Woodhouse (Shanklin), and many, many more.

FOREWORD

BY JACQUI OATLEY

My love for football is perhaps a non-conventional one. My dad wasn't at all into football; my brother hates sport with a passion, so I didn't get taken to games. I was at home ill one day, lying on the sofa and a football match was on. We didn't have remote controls in those days, so I couldn't have turned the channel over even if I'd wanted to. I watched this game and it was like it flicked a switch in my head that it was the sport for me. I think I was born football-ready, if that makes sense. Since that day I have been completely and utterly obsessed with football, with no sense that that passion will wane in any way.

I went to an all-girls' school and my friends thought it was the weirdest thing in the world. They soon realised I was serious when I started going to games, buying kit and buying footballs and teaching myself keepy-uppies at lunch-time. There was no club for me to play at though. It wasn't until I got to university that I had the chance to play organised football.

It is heartening to see just how much opportunity there is for young girls now. The FA is pushing hard to get more football for girls into primary schools. That's so important. There is still a lot of work to do. My six-year-old daughter recently told me that at a sports club she was at, the girls were told to pick up hula-hoops while the boys kicked a ball around! We need to make sure that all coaches and teachers realise that it is just as normal for girls to play football as it is for boys.

The greater exposure that women's football is getting thanks to England's success in reaching the semi-finals of the 2015 World Cup and Euro 2017 is brilliant. Now we need to capitalise on that with the domestic game. We need to make sure people are aware of their local club, how they can get tickets, and what great value it is to go and see the teams play. The top teams have international players you can go and watch, with tickets at most of them very reasonably priced when compared to other means of a family day out. You can take a family of four to some clubs for under £16.

Even if you do not live close to a WSL club there are so many WPL clubs and teams lower down the football pyramid, that are held together by volunteers doing incredible work for their local community. They would be so appreciative of the support, and of more fans coming through the gate. Domestic women's football remains an unknown quantity to many. This **Football Yearbook** tells everyone a bit more about the club on their doorstep and uncovers the fascinating history of the game in England. Hopefully it will play its own small role in bringing the sport to a wider audience as women's football continues to go from strength to strength.

HOW TIMES HAVE CHANGED

BY GILL COULTARD AND PRU BUCKLEY

GILL COULTARD

Twice League champion: 1991/92, 1993/94
Six-time FA Cup winner: 1983, 1987, 1988, 1990, 1992, 1994
Won 119 caps for England

I was the youngest of eight siblings; four brothers and three sisters. The brothers really looked after me and I was playing football from the age of three or four. I played through primary school and middle school, and then when I got to high school they banned me at the age of 13. They said there were physical differences with the boys and they couldn't let me play. My world was shattered. Luckily the PE teacher at the school put me in touch with Doncaster Rovers Belles and the rest is history.

Belles were the top team in the country. They weren't exactly on my doorstep – I had to travel ten miles to get there by bus – but I'm lucky I was fairly local. If I hadn't had Belles I think my career would have been over. It was, and still is, a great family club. The older girls would be there to meet me at the bus stop. I was in their first team at the age of 13, but playing with women 10 or 20 years older than me wasn't daunting. I had an advantage, because I was a young whippersnapper. I went on to have some magical days there. We won six FA Cups and two League titles. I was training with the England team from 13 as well and made my debut at the age of 18 in a 5-0 win against the Republic of Ireland at Dalymount Park in May 1981. I have many great memories, but that international debut is the one that really stands out. In total I went on to amass 119 caps – which remained a record for a long time – and captained my country on numerous occasions. We didn't play anywhere near as many internationals as they do nowadays, so I sometimes wonder how many caps I would have won in this day and age. In 1984 we reached the European Championship final and lost on penalties to Sweden on what was a mudbath of a pitch in Luton. I was next up to take a penalty, but I never got the chance. Defeat was hard to take, but because I was so young I was able to cope with it. I think it is later on in your career that you realise how precious every moment is, and then losing big matches gets harder to deal with.

To see the strength of women's football today makes me feel really proud of what my generation, and the generation before mine, did. We played for the love of the game, we weren't paid anything, not even expenses. We all had to combine our training and playing, with work. I was one of the lucky ones. I did a couple of factory jobs and the hi-fi company I worked for – Pioneer – were happy to sponsor me so I could get the time off to play. Some of the girls though, had to take holiday two years in advance to have enough time to play and they weren't getting paid. It's great to see there are many more clubs and much more opportunity for women to play today.

Of all the goals I scored the one I will most remember is the one I scored to win the FA Cup final for Belles against Friends of Fulham at the Baseball Ground in 1990. It was the only goal of the game. It was from just outside the box, I was about 20 yards out and it just came to me. I threw a dummy one way and then just hit it and it went in. It was a dream goal to win the FA Cup.

PRU BUCKLEY

FA Cup winner: 1997
League Cup winner: 1997
Won 3 caps for England
Ten-time Millwall Player of the Year

The way that women's football has changed since I played is impressive and also quite hard to believe. I am so proud of everything I achieved. I can look back on being an FA Cup winner, a League Cup winner and 10-time Millwall Player of the Year, and I also have real pride in having won my three caps for England.

It was hard work though. We couldn't make money from the game even though I was playing for one of the best teams in the country. I worked for Lloyds Bank when I left school. I would have to go from work straight to training. So I was working full-time and training Tuesdays and Thursdays. I lived in Essex and I would have to drive through the Blackwall Tunnel to get to training which is always a nightmare. I then had the opportunity to go and play semi-pro in Finland, so I quit the bank job. I couldn't settle abroad and I lasted about two weeks because I was so homesick. I came back and got a job in the Millwall ticket office where I am still working today. I played for Millwall Lionesses for about 15 years and, in my 20-year association with the club, I have filled nearly every role. I was captain, then Under-16s manager and even first-team manager. I really enjoyed my time as youth coach and would recommend it to anyone. Youngsters can be really receptive and take your ideas on board. They are willing to learn.

The FA Cup final I played in, 20 years ago, was very different from how it is now. I think there were probably about 4,000–5,000 people there when we played against a team called Wembley at Upton Park and it was shown live on a channel called UK Living, which perhaps a lot of people don't remember. We won 1-0 and it was a great occasion, but it's incredible to see the teams nowadays walking out in front of 30,000 at Wembley and to a huge audience watching live on the BBC. Nothing beats playing. I treasured every minute of it and I'm really pleased to have played a small part in helping the game evolve to the level it has reached.

A BRIEF HISTORY

1881: The first recorded women's international takes place in Edinburgh, in May, with Scotland beating England 3-0. Lily St Clair scores the opening goal. Four days later, in Glasgow, another match between the teams is abandoned when hundreds of male spectators run on to the pitch and fighting breaks out. Some reports suggest the majority of those fans did not approve of women playing.

1894: Nettie J. Honeyball and Florence Dixie place newspaper adverts for players, which leads to the foundation of the British Ladies' Football Club (BLFC) the following year. Its primary aim is to provide football-playing opportunities for girls and women, but it also aspires to make money from the game. Nettie J. Honeyball was a pseudonym and her true identity is still not certain though many believe her real name to have been Mary Hutson.

1895: The first official women's football match takes place under the auspices of the BLFC with North London (red) beating South London (light and dark blue) 7-1 in front of an estimated crowd of 10,000 at Crouch End in London on 23 March.

1917: A Preston-based munitions factory called Dick, Kerr and Co. (named after William Dick and John Kerr), sets up a women's team called Dick, Kerr's Ladies.

1920: Dick, Kerr's Ladies (representing England) beat a France XI 2-0. A crowd of 25,000 watches on at Deepdale, the home of Preston FC men's side. The two teams meet three more times in quick succession with Dick, Kerr's again winning, 5-2 at Stockport, before a 1-1 draw in Manchester. The final match is played at Stamford Bridge with France winning 2-1. Later in the year Dick, Kerr's play a four-match series against a France XI. The first three matches in Paris, Roubaix and Le Havre finish in draws with Dick, Kerr's winning the final match in Rouen. The tours generate huge interest and on Boxing Day 1920, a crowd of 53,000 comes to Goodison Park – home of men's team Everton – to witness Dick, Kerr's Ladies beat St Helen's 4-0. To this day the attendance is still a record for a domestic women's match in England. There are reports that a further 14,000 fans have been locked out due to overcrowding. More than

£3,000 (well in excess of £100,000 in today's money) is believed to have been raised for charity.

1921: The FA bans associated clubs from allowing women to play matches on their grounds. Their edict reads: 'The game of football is quite unsuitable for females and ought not to be encouraged.'

1922: With women's teams continuing to play wherever they can, Dick, Kerr's take a tour to Canada. On arrival the Dominion Football Association tells them they will not be allowed to play anywhere because it objects to women's football. The team instead heads to the US and takes on nine US men's teams. They lose to Paterson FC in the first match with US goalkeeper Peter Renzulli recalling in an interview given years later: 'We were national champions and we had a hell of a job beating them.'

1926: The name of Dick, Kerr's Ladies is changed to Preston Ladies following a disagreement between the team's manager Alfred Frankland and the owners.

1937: Preston Ladies beat the best team in Scotland, Edinburgh Ladies, 5-1 to earn the title of the first unofficial World Champions. Preston Ladies are believed to have continued to attract crowds of 5,000 throughout the 1930s despite having to play their matches away from Football League grounds because of the FA ban.

1965: Preston Ladies fold due to a lack of players. The difficult decision is taken by Kath Latham who has served as the club's first female manager since the death of Alfred Frankland in 1957. She had previously been helping Frankland with the secretarial duties.

1969: The Women's Football Association (WFA), a separate entity from the FA, is founded with 44 member clubs. An unofficial European Championship – known as the European Competition for Women's Football – takes place for the first time. The tournament features four teams with all the matches played in Italy. The hosts beat France 1-0 in their semi-final in Novara with England losing the other semi-final 4-3 to Denmark in Aosta. In the third-place match England beat France 2-0 in Turin. Italy take the title as they defeat Denmark 3-1 in the final which is also played in Turin.

1971: The FA lifts the ban on women playing on Football League grounds, 50 years after it was enforced. The first Women's FA Cup final takes place that same year with Southampton beating Scottish side Stewarton and Thistle 4-1 at the Crystal Palace National Sports Centre in South London. At the time the competition is known as the Mitre Challenge Trophy.

1972: The first official women's international in Great Britain takes place with England beating Scotland 3-2 at Greenock.

1979: A second, still unofficial, European Competition for Women's Football is held a decade after the first. Italy are again hosts, but this time 12 teams take part. The winners of each of four groups of three contest the semi-finals. Italy beat England 3-1 in the last four and Denmark are 1-0 victors against Sweden. England finish fourth, losing the third-place match on penalties to Sweden after a goalless draw. Just as they did in 1969 Italy and Denmark meet in the final, but this time the Danes are 2-0 winners.

1983: The FA forms links with the WFA, inviting it to affiliate on the same basis as County Football Associations.

1984: The first official European Championship takes place. It is still known as the European Competition for Women's Football, but the 1984 edition is played under UEFA auspices. There is no single host nation. England reach the final against Sweden which is played over two legs. The Three Lionesses lose 1-0 in Gothenburg but win by the same score-line at Kenilworth Road in Luton only to lose 4-3 on penalties.

1987: Hosts Norway win the second official UEFA European Competition for Women's Football beating Sweden 2-1 in the final. England lose the third-place match 2-1 to Italy.

1988: FIFA stages a test event to help gauge whether an international tournament for women is viable. The 1988 FIFA Women's Invitational Tournament takes place in China from 1–12 June. The 12 teams compete in three groups of four prior to quarter-finals, semi-finals, a third-place match and the final. Norway beat Sweden 1-0 in the final in Guangzhou.

1989: Hosts West Germany win the third official UEFA European Competition for Women's Football thanks to a 4-1 win over Norway in the final.

1991: The FA launches its first National League with 24 clubs involved. The first FIFA Women's World Cup takes place in China. The format is the same as the 1988 test event with 12 teams competing in three groups of four prior to quarter-finals, semi-finals, a third-place match and the final. USA become the first world champions, beating Norway 2-1 in the final in Guangzhou. The competition is regarded as the first official FIFA Women's World Cup and is known as the 1st FIFA World Championship for Women's Football for the M&M's Cup. Earlier in the year Denmark host the fourth official European Championship, but the first to be known by that name. Germany beat Norway 3-1 after extra-time in the final.

1993: The FA takes over the running of the main national cup competition for women and rebrands it as the Women's FA Challenge Cup. A Women's Football Committee, and the post of women's football coordinator are also introduced at the FA. Italy host Euro 1993 and lose the final 1-0 to Norway in Cesena.

1994: The Women's National League is also brought under the control of the FA and is known as the FA Women's Premier League (FAWPL).

1995: The second official World Cup, and the first to be known as the FIFA Women's World Cup, takes place in Sweden. England are present for the first time and reach the quarter-finals where they lose 3-0 to Germany. Norway beat Germany 2-0 in the final. Earlier in the year England reach the semi-finals of Euro 1995. With no single host nation for the competition, the Three Lionesses lose a two-leg semi-final 6-2 on aggregate to Germany who go on to beat Sweden 3-2 in the final in Kaiserslautern.

1996: Women's football is introduced to the Olympic programme for the first time for Atlanta 1996. Hosts USA beat China in the final.

1997: Norway and Sweden co-host Euro 1997 with Germany beating Italy 2-0 in the final in Oslo.

1998: The FA appoints its first full-time coach for the England women's international team – Hope Powell. The FA also sets up the first 20 centres of excellence for girls and attains sponsors for the League and Cup competitions.

1999: USA hosts the World Cup which is expanded to 16 teams and draws huge crowds. A world record crowd for a women's match of 90,185 attends the final at the Rose Bowl in Pasadena, California, where the hosts beat China 5-4 on penalties following a goalless draw. Brandi Chastain converts the winning penalty kick. What becomes an iconic celebration follows as she spontaneously takes off her jersey, clenches her fists and drops to her knees in her black sports bra.

2000: Norway beat defending champions USA 3-2 with a golden goal in the Olympic final in Sydney.

2001: Germany host Euro 2001 and beat Sweden 1-0 with an extra-time golden goal scored by Claudia Muller in the final.

2002: The FA celebrates football becoming the top participation sport for girls and women in England three years ahead of schedule. The first women's Champions League final, at the time bearing the name the UEFA Cup, sees German side Frankfurt beat Umea of Sweden 2-0.

2003: USA stands in to host the World Cup for the second finals in succession. China had been due to stage the tournament, but a switch is required after the outbreak of the SARS virus. The hosts finish third with Germany beating Sweden 2-1 with an extra-time golden goal in the final.

2004: USA regain their Olympic title by beating Brazil after extra-time in the final in Sydney. The golden goal has been replaced by the silver goal in all FIFA competitions whereby if the teams are separated after 15 minutes of extra-time then no second period of extra-time is played. However Abby Wambach's winner comes seven minutes into the second period of extra-time.

2005: England host the European Championship. A television audience of 2.9 million watches the hosts' opening match against Finland live on BBC Two. A crowd of 29,092 is also present at the City of Manchester Stadium for a thrilling match. England let a 2-0 lead slip and appear to have thrown away two points when Sweden's Laura Kalmari makes it 2-2 with two minutes to play. But 17-year-old Karen Carney hits a dramatic injury-time winner. Unfortunately England fail to make it to the knockout stages as they lose their next two group games to Denmark and Sweden. Germany eventually beat Norway 3-1 in the final in front of 21,105 people at Blackburn's Ewood Park.

2007: Arsenal become the first English team to win Europe's most prestigious prize as they beat Swedish side Umea 1-0 on aggregate over two legs in the UEFA Cup final (later to become the UEFA Women's Champions League). China host the World Cup. England – who have qualified for the first time since 1995 – reach the quarter-finals where they are beaten 3-0 by USA who eventually finish third. Germany are 2-0 victors against Brazil in the final in Shanghai.

2008: Arsenal suffer their first defeat in more than 50 games as Everton pull off a huge shock in the FA Women's Premier League Cup final with a 1-0 win at Brisbane Road. The Gunners do complete the League and FA Cup double though. A then-record FA Cup final crowd of 24,582 watches the match at Nottingham Forest's City Ground where Arsenal beat Leeds 4-1. On the international front USA make it three gold medals from the four Olympic football tournaments played to date. They beat Brazil 1-0 after extra-time in the final in Beijing. The first Cyprus Cup – a global invitational tournament – is held. Canada beat USA 3-2 in the final in Nicosia.

2009: Arsenal continue their dominance of English football by winning the Treble of League, FA Cup and Premier League Cup. It's their sixth consecutive League title. England enter the Cyprus Cup for the first time and win it, beating Canada 3-1 in the final. Finland host Euro 2009 where England reach the final only to lose 6-2 to Germany. The Germans have now won seven of the last eight European Championships. The UEFA Cup is rebranded the UEFA Women's Champions League from the start of the 2009/10 season.

2010: It's a seventh straight League title for Arsenal, but there are different winners of the Cup competitions with Everton claiming the FA Cup and Leeds (then known as Leeds Carnegie) lifting the Premier League Cup. The FA announces that a new competition for the top sides in English football will launch next spring. It will be known as the Women's Super League and will run throughout the summer.

2011: The first Women's Super League contains just eight teams. Arsenal beat Chelsea 1-0 in the first ever match which is played in Tooting and eventually go on to be the inaugural WSL champions. Having also won the 2010/11 FA Cup, the Gunners make it three domestic trophies in a calendar year by winning the first WSL Continental Cup. Germany stage the World Cup where England reach the quarter-finals but they lose on penalties to France after a 1-1 draw. Japan win the tournament for the first time as they beat USA on penalty kicks following a 2-2 draw in the final.

2012: Team GB reach the quarter-finals of the Olympics where they are beaten by Canada. A crowd of 80,203 – a record for a women's Olympic football match – watches the final at Wembley where USA beat Japan 2-1. It's a successful year for England as they qualify unbeaten for Euro 2013. On the domestic front Arsenal retain their WSL title, Birmingham City win the FA Cup for the first time as they beat Chelsea on penalties following a 2-2 draw. Arsenal and Birmingham contest the WSL Continental Cup final with the Gunners prevailing 1-0.

2013: England win the Cyprus Cup for a second time beating Canada 1-0 in the final. Optimism ahead of Euro 2013 in Sweden soon dissipates as the team finishes bottom of the group. After the tournament Hope Powell – who has overseen 162 matches during her 15 years as manager – leaves her post and is replaced by Bristol Academy manager Mark Sampson. Germany claim their eighth continental title with a 1-0 win over Norway in the final. On the domestic front there are new winners of the WSL as Liverpool are crowned champions. Arsenal beat Bristol Academy 3-0 in the FA Cup final and complete a Cup double thanks to a 2-0 success over Lincoln in the WSL Continental Cup final. The FA, Sport England, the Premier League and the Football League Trust launch their first national participation programme for girls' football.

2014: Liverpool midfielder Fara Williams claims a record-breaking 130th cap for England when she starts a 4-0 friendly win over Sweden in Hartlepool on 3 August. A few months later, on a rainy afternoon in November, a record crowd for an England women's international turns up as the team plays at Wembley for the first time. The home fans among the 45,619 are left disappointed as the hosts lose a friendly 3-0 to two-time World champions Germany. Karen Carney wins her 100th cap on the night. The WSL ends in thrilling fashion with three teams still in with a chance of the title going into the final game. Liverpool, who start the day in third place, ultimately defend their title on goal difference with a 3-0 win over Bristol City. Chelsea are in the driving seat ahead of the final match but lose 2-1 at Manchester City to finish second. Birmingham City, who are two points behind Chelsea at kick-off, draw 2-2 with Notts County to finish third. Arsenal beat Everton 2-0 in the FA Cup final but lose the WSL Continental Cup final 1-0 to Manchester City. The year 2014 also sees the introduction of a second division in the WSL: WSL2 contains 10 teams with Sunderland becoming its first ever champions.

2015: England win the Cyprus Cup for the third time beating Canada 1-0 in the final. They then enjoy their best World Cup performance as they finish as the top European nation. In a tournament which is expanded to 24 teams for the first time, the Three Lionesses finish second in their group behind France before beating Norway 2-1 in the Round of 16. A 2-1 win over hosts Canada follows in the quarter-finals before the heartbreak of an injury-time own goal by Laura Bassett sees them lose the semi-final 2-1 to Japan. In the third-place match Mark Sampson's side beat Germany for the very first time with Fara Williams' extra-time penalty giving them a 1-0 win and the bronze medal. USA win their third World Cup with a 5-2 triumph over Japan in the final. The FA Women's Cup is renamed the Women's FA Cup with the final held at Wembley for the first time. A then-record FA Cup final crowd of 30,710 watches Chelsea claim their first trophy of any sort by beating Notts County 1-0. The Blues complete the Double by winning the WSL1 title. Arsenal are 3-0 winners over Notts County in the WSL Continental Cup final. Reading are champions of WSL2.

2016: MBEs are awarded to England captain Steph Houghton and most-capped player Fara Williams in the New Year's Honours list. Baroness Sue Campbell is named as the new Head of Women's Football. Manchester City dominate the League as they win their first trophy by claiming the WSL1 title in September. May's FA Cup final between Arsenal and Chelsea at Wembley draws a new record crowd of 32,912 as the Gunners beat the holders 1-0. In October, Manchester City also collect the WSL Continental Cup courtesy of a 1-0 extra-time win over Birmingham City. Yeovil Town win WSL2 on goal difference ahead of runners-up Bristol City. The FA announces that from next season WSL1 and WSL2 will revert to a winter calendar being played from autumn 2017 to spring 2018. To fill the void a Spring Series will be held in 2017 when the teams will play the other sides in their division just once. There will be no promotion or relegation at the end of the Spring Series. At the Olympics in Rio, hosts Brazil are under huge pressure to win a first Olympic football gold medal. While the men prevail, the women miss out on a place on the podium. They are beaten on penalties by Sweden in the semi-finals and then lose the bronze medal match 2-1 to Canada. Germany are crowned Olympic champions for the first time as they beat Sweden 2-1 in the final. For the first time in the six Olympic women's competitions played to date USA fail to reach the final, losing on penalties to Sweden in the quarter-finals.

2017: Manchester City make it three domestic trophies in a row as they beat Birmingham City 4-1 in the FA Cup final. A new FA Cup record crowd of 35,271 is present at Wembley. The WSL1 Spring Series is won by Chelsea on goal difference ahead of Manchester City on the final day of the season. The WSL2 Spring Series, which concludes a few weeks earlier, sees Everton beat runners-up Doncaster to the title. A record television audience for a women's football match, which peaks at more than four million, watches Channel 4's coverage of England's Euro 2017 semi-final against the Netherlands. The hosts win 3-0 and go on to claim the title three days later when they beat Denmark 4-2 in a thrilling final.

THE NEWS *2016/17*

Sun, 17 Jul 2016: England forward Natasha Dowie joins NWSL side Boston Breakers in the USA, having left Doncaster Rovers Belles earlier in the month.

Mon, 8 Aug: Scans reveal England and Liverpool full-back Alex Greenwood is likely to miss the rest of the season with ankle ligament damage sustained during training.

Tues, 30 Aug: England Under-19 and Fylde player Zoe Tynan, 18, tragically dies after being hit by a train at West Allerton station. Tynan started playing when she was six at Liverpool Marshall Feds and also spent six years at Everton's centre of excellence before joining Manchester City in the summer of 2015.

Thur, 1 Sep: The draw for the 2016/17 UEFA Champions League Round of 32 takes place. Chelsea are paired with German side and 2016 runners-up Wolfsburg while Manchester City will take on Russian outfit Zvezda Perm.

Tues, 6 Sep: Chelsea's Millie Bright, 23, is called up to the England senior squad for the first time. Manager Mark Sampson names her in a 23-player squad for the upcoming Euro 2017 qualifiers against Estonia and Belgium. Chelsea defender Claire Rafferty and Arsenal striker Danielle Carter are also recalled.

Sun, 11 Sep: In WSL1 Manchester City are 1-0 winners at Arsenal and remain seven points clear of Chelsea who beat Reading 3-0. It means City will win the WSL title for the first time if they can avoid defeat when they meet Chelsea on 25 September.

Thur, 15 Sep: England beat Estonia 5-0 at Meadow Lane meaning a draw away to Belgium at the Den Dreef Stadium in Leuven next week will be enough for them to secure top spot in Euro 2017 qualifying Group 7.

Mon, 19 Sep: England left-back Claire Rafferty (concussion) and goalkeeper Rebecca Spencer (back) are forced to pull out of the squad to face Belgium tomorrow. Reading's Mary Earps is called up to replace Spencer having trained with the Next Gen squad at St George's Park last week.

The FA announces England will play France in a friendly at the Keepmoat Stadium in Doncaster on Friday, 21 October.

Tues, 20 Sep: Goals from Nikita Parris and Karen Carney see England win their Euro 2017 qualifier away to Belgium 2-0 to finish top of Group 7.

Fri, 23 Sep: It's confirmed that England will play a friendly away to the Netherlands in Tilburg on Tuesday, 29 November.

Sun, 25 Sep: Manchester City are crowned 2016 WSL champions, it's their first national League title in women's football. A Katie Chapman own goal and a Toni Duggan penalty secure a 2-0 win at home to Chelsea. A WSL record crowd of 4,096 attends the match at the Academy Stadium, Manchester.

Wed, 5 Oct: Chelsea Ladies, who usually use Staines Town's Wheatsheaf Park for home matches, play at Stamford Bridge for the first time. A crowd of 3,783 is there for their Champions League Round of 32 first-leg tie at home to Wolfsburg. Unfortunately they witness a 3-0 defeat.

Wed, 12 Oct: Chelsea are out of the Champions League after a 1-1 draw away to Wolfsburg in the Round of 32 second leg sees them defeated 4-1 on aggregate. Manchester City are 4-0 winners away to Russian side Zvezda Perm and thus prevail 6-0 on aggregate.

Sun, 16 Oct: Doncaster Rovers Belles are relegated from WSL1 following a 2-1 defeat at Notts County. The result also ensures that Reading – who weren't in action this weekend – stay up with two games to spare.

Tues, 1 Nov: England-born coaches Jillian Ellis (USA) and John Herdman (Canada) are named on the shortlist for Best FIFA Women's Coach 2016. The other candidates are Silvia Neid (Germany), Pia Sundhage (Sweden), Philippe Bergeroo (France), Vera Pauw (Netherlands), Gerard Precheur (France), Vadao (Brazil), Martina Voss-Tecklenburg (Germany), and Thomas Worle (Germany).

Thur, 3 Nov: USA striker Carli Lloyd leads the way in the nominations for Best FIFA Women's Player 2016. Also on the shortlist are Melanie Behringer (Germany), Marta (Brazil), Camille Abily and Amandine Henry (France), Sara Daebritz and Dzsenifer Marozsan (Germany), Saki Kumagai (Japan), Lotta Schelin (Sweden), and Christine Sinclair (Canada).

Sun, 6 Nov: A WSL2 record crowd of 1,483 watches already-promoted Yeovil Town beat Sheffield FC 3-0 at Huish Park to win the title. The goals come from Lucy Quinn, Annie Heatherson and Nicola Cousins. It's a nail-biting finish to the season with the Glovers only beating Bristol City to the title on goal difference. City are 5-0 winners away to Oxford United. Both Yeovil Town and Bristol City finish the season on 39 points with Yeovil's goal difference +25 and City's +21. City will also be promoted.

Mon, 7 Nov: The FA announces average crowds for WSL1 matches for 2016 were 1,128 – up 5% on 2015 (1,076). WSL2 crowds are up 30% to 443 from 341 in 2015. Oxford United enjoyed the greatest upsurge with crowds increasing by 85%. It's also confirmed that the 2017 season will move to a winter calendar and run from September 2017 to May 2018. A WSL Spring Series – in which teams will play each other just once – will also take place to fill the void in the first half of 2017.

Wed, 9 Nov: Arsenal confirm that England defender Casey Stoney is leaving the club. Stoney won two FA Cups and one League Cup during her second spell with the Gunners having rejoined in 2014. Her first spell at Arsenal came between 1999 and 2002. Meanwhile, Liverpool announce that New Zealand international striker Rosie White is leaving to join NWSL side Boston Breakers in the US. White – who joined from University of California in July 2015 – scored four times during her Reds career.

Mon, 14 Nov: Reading announce the signing of 26-year-old defender and Netherlands captain Mandy van den Berg from Liverpool. Swedish striker Emma Lundh also leaves the Reds.

Tues, 15 Nov: Arsenal striker Jodie Taylor and Liverpool defender Gemma Bonner are recalled to Mark Sampson's England squad for the upcoming friendly against the Netherlands. Casey Stoney and Fran Kirby are left out due to injury, as are long-term absentees Alex Greenwood, Ellen White and Carly Telford.

Fri, 25 Nov: The draw for the UEFA Champions League quarter-finals pairs Manchester City with Danish side Fortuna Hjorring. City will be at home in the second leg. Should they win they will take on defending champions Lyon or Wolfsburg in the semi-finals.

Tues, 13 Dec: Liverpool announce the signing of England defender Casey Stoney who recently left Arsenal. Stoney reveals she hopes playing regular football will boost her chances of being included in the England squad for Euro 2017.

Fri, 16 Dec: Ray Trew, owner of Notts County and Notts County Ladies, refuses to comment after publication of a document lodged at Companies House which suggests the ladies team will be dissolved in two months' time.

Fri, 23 Dec: The final FIFA world rankings for 2016 are released with England ending the year in fifth place, one point behind fourth-placed Canada.

Tues, 3 Jan 2017: Chelsea sign USA winger Crystal Dunn, 24, from NWSL side Washington Spirit. She is the Blues' fourth signing of the transfer window, following the arrivals of Ramona Bachmann, Maren Mjelde and Erin Cuthbert. Dunn won the NWSL Golden Boot and MVP award in 2015 but narrowly missed out on her country's World Cup-winning squad that year.

Wed, 4 Jan: Notts County striker Rachel Williams returns to the England squad for the first time since April 2013 as manager Mark Sampson names a 28-player party for friendlies against Norway and Sweden in Spain later this month. Her club-mates Ellen White and Carly Telford also return to the squad as do Chelsea pair Millie Bright and Claire Rafferty.

Mon, 9 Jan: USA midfielder Carli Lloyd wins the Best FIFA Women's Player of the Year award 2016, it's the second year in a row that she has won it. Germany coach Silvia Neid wins the Best FIFA Women's Coach award 2016.

Tues, 10 Jan: Fixtures for the 2017 Spring Series are released. The 2016 WSL Champions Manchester City will kick-off at home to Chelsea on Sunday, 23 April. The competition will get under way the day before with newly-promoted Bristol City hosting Reading on Saturday, 22 April.

Wed, 11 Jan: England's all-time record goalscorer Kelly Smith announces her retirement from football at the age of 38. The Arsenal striker – who retired from international football two years ago having scored 46 goals in 117 games for her country – will take up a coaching role at her club. During her playing days with the Gunners she won the Champions League (then known as the UEFA Cup) in 2007 and five FA Cups. Elsewhere, businessman Alan Hardy, who became owner of Notts County men's team in December 2016, completes his takeover of Notts County Ladies.

Fri, 13 Jan: England striker Ellen White, 27, joins Birmingham City from Notts County on an 18-month deal with the option of a further year. Meanwhile, Reading sign Northern Ireland winger Rachel Furness, 28, from Sunderland on a full-time contract which runs until June 2018.

Wed, 18 Jan: Arsenal sign former USA midfielder Heather O'Reilly. The 32-year-old joins from FC Kansas City. She retired from international football in 2016 having won 231 caps, three Olympic gold medals and the 2015 World Cup.

Sun, 22 Jan: England lose the first of their two winter friendlies in Spain. They go down 1-0 to Norway in La Manga.

Tues, 24 Jan: England's second friendly – which takes place in Murcia – ends in a goalless draw against Sweden with Lionesses keeper Siobhan Chamberlain saving a penalty.

Fri, 3 Feb: Former England and Arsenal striker Kelly Smith, who announced her retirement from football last month, reveals she is pregnant. As a result she will not play in her own celebratory match on 19 February, but the game between Arsenal and Smith's All-Star XI will still go ahead.

Mon, 6 Feb: HMRC's winding-up petition against Notts County is adjourned for 49 days until 27 March after a court hears new owner Alan Hardy aims to clear the debt.

Wed, 15 Feb: The 2016 WSL Champions Manchester City sign USA World Cup-winning captain and 2016 FIFA Player of the Year Carli Lloyd for the upcoming Spring Series and their Champions League campaign. Meanwhile, Arsenal's Asisat Oshoala leaves the Gunners. The 2015 BBC Women's Footballer of the Year joins Chinese side Dalian Quanjian. The Nigerian international played 11 times for Arsenal and was part of the 2016 FA Cup-winning team.

Sun, 19 Feb: Having announced she wouldn't play because of her pregnancy, Kelly Smith makes a late cameo appearance in her farewell match. She scores a penalty for her All-Star XI side, but it isn't enough to stop them losing 4-2 to Arsenal in a game played at Boreham Wood.

Wed, 1 Mar: England lose their first match of the SheBelieves Cup 2-1 against France in Pennsylvania. Jordan Nobbs puts the Three Lionesses ahead just after the half-hour mark, but two goals in the final ten minutes from France turn the match on its head. The tournament is the second edition of a US-based invitational event which was held for the first time in 2016.

Sat, 4 Mar: Ellen White scores the only goal of the game with one minute to play as England beat hosts and World Cup holders USA 1-0 in their second match of the SheBelieves Cup at Red Bull Arena, New Jersey.

Tues, 7 Mar: England's final SheBelieves Cup match ends in a 1-0 defeat to Germany at Robert F. Kennedy Memorial Stadium in Washington DC. Anja Mittag grabs the only goal of the game a minute before half-time. France win the round-robin tournament ahead of Germany in second place, England third and hosts USA fourth.

Mon, 13 Mar: The FA announces its football 'For All' brand which aims to champion its provision and support of football for all people at all levels. It also launches a new strategy for women's and girls' football with an aim to double participation by 2020.

Thur, 16 Mar: Sunderland confirm head coach Carlton Fairweather has left the club. Former player Melanie Reay, who has been with the club in a playing and coaching capacity for two decades, will succeed him.

Sat, 18 Mar: FIFA Best Women's Player 2016 Carli Lloyd makes her Manchester City debut in the FA Cup fifth round win at home to Reading. Lucy Bronze scores the only goal to put City into the quarter-finals.

Sun, 19 Mar: The FA Cup fifth round programme is completed with Arsenal thrashing Tottenham 10-0 in a North London derby and Chelsea hammering Doncaster Rovers Belles 7-0. Victories for Bristol City, Birmingham City, Liverpool, Notts County and Sunderland mean the quarter-finals will be an all-WSL1 affair.

Mon, 20 Mar: Holders Arsenal are drawn away to Birmingham City in the FA Cup quarter-finals. Chelsea will host Sunderland, Liverpool will take on Notts County, and Manchester City will make the trip to Bristol City with all ties taking place on Sunday, 26 March.

Fri, 24 Mar: England move back up to fourth place – equalling their best ever position – in the latest FIFA world rankings. Germany oust USA in the number one spot.

Sat, 25 Mar: Blackburn win the WPL Northern title thanks to a 3-2 victory over Derby. Faye McCoy scrambles home a late winner to put Rovers nine points ahead of second-placed Middlesbrough who only have two matches left to play. Lynda Shepherd had earlier put Blackburn ahead from the spot before Leanne De Silva equalised for Derby. Melissa Johnson then fired the visitors into a 2-1 lead but Saffron Jordan tied it up at 2-2 for Blackburn before McCoy's late winner.

Sun, 26 Mar: Birmingham City knock holders Arsenal out of the FA Cup with a 1-0 win in the quarter-finals. In the other matches, 2015 Cup winners Chelsea beat Sunderland 5-1, Liverpool prevail 2-0 at home to Notts County and a last-minute goal secures a 2-1 victory for Manchester City at Bristol City.

Tues, 27 Mar: HMRC's winding-up petition against Notts County is adjourned for a second time with the club given until 3 July to pay their debts.

Mon, 3 Apr: England manager Mark Sampson takes the decision to name his Euro 2017 squad early. His 23-player party includes four players who have been selected for their first major tournament: Manchester City trio Demi Stokes (defender), Nikita Parris (striker), Izzy Christiansen (midfielder); and Chelsea midfielder Millie Bright. Big names to miss out include Eni Aluko, who finished as top scorer in the 2016 WSL, Chelsea pair Claire Rafferty and Gemma Davison and Houston Dash forward Rachel Daly.

Thur, 6 Apr: The FA confirms England will play a Euro 2017 warm-up match away to Switzerland at the Tissot Arena in Biel on Saturday, 10 June.

Fri, 7 Apr: Arsenal announce striker Beth Mead has successfully undergone surgery on her broken collarbone. England draw 1-1 with Italy in a friendly at Vale Park. Jodie Taylor nets for the Three Lionesses.

Mon, 10 Apr: Goals from Ellen White, Lucy Bronze and Izzy Christiansen see England beat Austria 3-0 in a friendly at Stadium MK.

Wed, 19 Apr: Tottenham play their first ever competitive match at White Hart Lane – due to be demolished this summer – and clinch the WPL Southern title with a 4-0 win over West Ham. A crowd of 2,140 watches on as goals from Josie Green, Wendy Martin (2) and Nikita Whinnett seal the title for Spurs with three games to spare.

Fri, 21 Apr: Women's football is shaken by the news that WSL1 side Notts County have gone out of business two days before they are due to face Arsenal in their first match of the WSL Spring Series. A club statement reads: '(Local businessman) Alan Hardy has reluctantly admitted defeat in his bid to save Notts County Ladies Football Club after facing a near-£1m bill to keep the club afloat this season.'

Sat, 22 Apr: Manchester City lose the first leg of their Champions League semi-final 3-1 at home to French side Lyon. Paris Saint-Germain win 3-1 away to FC Barcelona in the other semi-final.

Sun, 23 Apr: WPL Southern side Lewes beat Huddersfield of WPL Northern in the WPL Plate final. The competition is a consolation prize for those teams who were defeated in the WPL Cup Determining Round back in September. The match takes place at Brackley FC's St James Park. Lewes win 4-0 with two goals from Georgia Bridges and efforts from Danielle Lane and Rachel Palmer. It's the first national Cup final Lewes have competed in, and as such, the first national trophy they have won.

Guiseley Vixens secure the WPL Northern Division One title thanks to a 3-2 win away to Blackpool Wren Rovers. Two goals from Sarah Danby and one from Alarna Fuller see the Vixens clinch the title with three games to spare.

Thur, 27 Apr: The FA confirms Notts County's players have been given special dispensation to join new clubs with immediate effect, outside of the transfer window.

Sat, 29 Apr: Manchester City are out of the Champions League despite a 1-0 win away to Lyon. Carli Lloyd scores the winner after 57 minutes, in front of a crowd of 19,214 at the Parc Olympique Lyonnais, but City go down 3-2 on aggregate. PSG win the other semi-final 2-0 at home to FC Barcelona for a 5-1 aggregate triumph which sets up an all-French final in Cardiff next month.

Sun, 30 Apr: Gillingham are confirmed as WPL South East Division One winners with two games to spare as they crush Norwich City 13-0 at home.

Mon, 1 May: Two of the England players left without a club when Notts County folded sign for top-flight Reading. Midfielder Jade Moore and defender Jo Potter are snapped up by the Royals as is striker Kirsty Linnett who herself also played for County in the past.

Tues, 2 May: Chelsea sign England goalkeeper Carly Telford who was left without a club following the collapse of Notts County.

Thur, 4 May: Chichester City win the WPL South West Division One title with a game to spare thanks to a 10-0 win against St Nicholas in front of their own fans at Oaklands Park. The result means they have racked up 23 goals in two games, having won 13-0 away at Exeter on Sunday.

Sun, 7 May: Tottenham win the WPL Cup for the second year in a row. Having also claimed the 2016/17 WPL Southern title and Boux Avenue Cup, the victory sees Spurs clinch a treble of trophies. The match against Charlton Athletic, held at Stevenage FC's Lamex Stadium, finishes goalless after extra-time and goes to penalties. Spurs keeper Toni-Anne Wayne saves two penalty kicks from Kim Dixson and Grace Coombs as her side prevail 4-3.

Fri, 12 May: Spanish side Barcelona announce they intend to have a women's side playing in America's NWSL in 2018.

Sat, 13 May: Manchester City win the 2017 FA Cup. It's their first time FA Cup triumph. They beat fellow WSL1 side Birmingham City 4-1 in the final at Wembley in a match watched by a record FA Women's Cup crowd of 35,271. The goals are scored by Lucy Bronze, Izzy Christiansen, Carli Lloyd and Jill Scott. Charlie Wellings' 73rd minute goal for Birmingham briefly gave them hope at 3-1. Having won the WSL1 and Continental Cups in 2016, Manchester City currently have possession of all three domestic trophies.

Sun, 14 May: Wolverhampton Wanderers win the WPL Midlands Division One title on the final day of the season. Player of the season Emma Cross scores the only goal of the match away to Leicester City Ladies. The victory sees Wolves pip Loughborough Foxes to the title. Manager Tim Duddings' side lost just two League matches all season and clocked up 18 wins from their 22 games.

Tues, 16 May: With Notts County having gone out of business, the FA announces that WSL2 sides can apply to replace them in WSL1. Clubs are given until midday on Tuesday, 30 May to apply with the intention being that the winning applicant will be named at the next AGM on Wednesday, 28 June. The five elements of the application will be weighted for assessment purposes as follows: finance and business management (30%), players, staff and youth development (30%), facilities (20%), marketing and commercial (15%), 2016 Spring Series on-pitch performance (5%). WSL2 2017/18 was due to have 11 teams in it, with the winners of the WPL play-off between Blackburn and Tottenham on 28 May due to join the existing 10. But with one team now going up to replace Notts County, WSL1 and WSL2 will both have 10 teams in them for 2017/18.

Birmingham City sign England midfielder Rachel Williams who has been a free agent since Notts County folded. Two other former Notts County players also join new clubs. England defender Amy Turner signs for Liverpool and Wales international Angharad James is snapped up by Yeovil Town.

Wed, 17 May: England defender Laura Bassett, who has been left without a club since Notts County folded, says she won't sign for a new team before the Euro 2017 Championship.

Isle of Wight-based club Shanklin, who are bottom of WPL South West, resign from the WPL having failed to fulfil a number of recent fixtures. All their League results for this season are expunged.

Sat, 20 May: Everton win the WSL2 Spring Series on the final day of the season after a 4-0 win over London Bees at The Hive. The Toffees only needed a point to claim the title. Doncaster finish four points back in runners-up position after a 4-0 win at Oxford. It was agreed ahead of the Spring Series that there would be no promotions or relegations. The League positions achieved in the 2016 full WSL season will determine who will start in what division for the next full season of 2017/18.

Tues, 23 May: Arsenal sign Bayern Munich and Netherlands international striker Vivianne Miedema. The 20-year-old was part of her country's 2015 World Cup squad and had previously been linked with 2017 Champions League finalists PSG. She finished the 2016/17 Frauen-Bundesliga season as top scorer with 14 goals in 22 League games for Bayern who were runners-up behind champions Wolfsburg.

Thur, 25 May: Chelsea manager Emma Hayes criticises the FA on BBC Radio 4's Today programme. Hayes says women's football is a 'mere afterthought' to the game's governing body citing the lack of preparation time and development opportunities afforded to match officials. Later in the evening Hayes' side lose their WSL1 Spring Series match 1-0 away to Manchester City. There is a sombre atmosphere at the match at Manchester's Academy Stadium which takes place 72 hours after the Manchester Arena bomb attack which killed 22 people. Both sets of players wear black armbands and a minute's silence is held before kick-off.

It's confirmed Arsenal and Scotland international Kim Little will need to undergo surgery to repair a ruptured anterior cruciate ligament injured in training earlier in the week. The news comes seven-and-a-half weeks before the start of Euro 2017.

Sun, 28 May: WPL Southern champions Tottenham seal promotion to WSL2 for the first time. Spurs beat their WPL Northern counterparts Blackburn 3-0 in a promotion play-off held at The Valley. Bianca Baptiste hits a brace and Wendy Martin completes the scoring with a fine 30-yard lob in injury-time.

Tues, 30 May: Norway and Olympique Lyonnais striker Ada Hegerberg wins the BBC Women's Footballer of the Year award. It's the third year of the award, which is based on fans' votes from around the world. The 21-year-old pushes Brazil and Orlando Pride forward Marta into second place with Canada and Portland Thorns' forward Christine Sinclair finishing third. The other nominees were Chelsea and Sweden goalkeeper Hedvig Lindahl and Germany and Bayern Munich midfielder Melanie Behringer. Hegerberg played a key role in her club's 2016 Treble-winning season with 33 League goals and 13 more in the Champions League.

Thur, 1 Jun: Lyon win an all-French Champions League final by beating PSG 7-6 on penalties after a goalless draw at the Cardiff City Stadium. The victory sees Lyon equal Frankfurt's record of four Champions League triumphs and also means they are the first team to twice retain the trophy.

Sat, 3 Jun: Chelsea claim the WSL1 Spring Series title courtesy of a 2-0 win away to Birmingham City on the final day of the season. Nearest challengers Manchester City win 3-1 at fourth-placed Liverpool to clinch the runners-up spot. Arsenal finish third after a 5-0 win at Bristol City. Chelsea's title triumph ends Manchester City's run of three consecutive domestic trophies. Yeovil Town finish bottom but pick up their first point of the Series courtesy of a goalless draw away to Birmingham. It was decided before the Spring Series that final positions would not result in promotion or relegation.

Wed, 7 Jun: Manchester City announce that Danish international defender Mie Jans will join the club from Brondby on 1 July. Jans played against City in the 2016/17 Champions League.

Fri, 9 Jun: Everton are named as the FA's preferred option to take the WSL1 position left vacant by Notts County following their liquidation. Doncaster Rovers Belles were the only other club to apply and are given seven days to appeal against the decision should they so wish.

Sat, 10 Jun: England win a Euro 2017 warm-up match 4-0 away to Switzerland. The goals come from Jordan Nobbs, Fran Kirby and Jodie Taylor who nets a brace.

Tues, 20 Jun: Scotland have to delay the announcement of their squad for Euro 2017 because of a dispute between the SFA and the players who are refusing to carry out their media commitments while they seek agreement over undisclosed terms and conditions. The SFA say they 'are disappointed (the players) have chosen not to undertake their media responsibilities which are designed to help promote the game.'

Wed, 21 Jun: England goalkeeper Karen Bardsley agrees a new two-year contract with her club, Manchester City. Meanwhile, the FA announces that Marieanne Spacey will leave her role as England women's assistant manager with immediate effect before Euro 2017 to become England women's player and coach developer. In her new position she will help players transition from youth teams into the senior set-up.

Mon, 27 Jun: Arsenal agree a new 10-year deal with men's non-League team Boreham Wood to continue playing their first-team and youth matches at Meadow Park.

Tues, 28 Jun: Everton's election to WSL1 to take up the position left vacant by the liquidated Notts County is ratified. The club also announces that Gabby George has become their first full-time professional player. The 20-year-old defender signs a two-year deal.

Wed, 29 Jun: Arsenal sign 25-year-old Scotland winger Lisa Evans from Bayern Munich. The former St Johnstone trainee, who has also played for Glasgow City and Turbine Potsdam, won the Frauen-Bundesliga with Bayern in 2015/16 and finished as a runner-up in 2016/17. Meanwhile, England Under-20 forward Carla Humphrey leaves Arsenal for Bristol City. She scored three goals in 23 appearances for the Gunners after coming through their academy.

Sat, 1 Jul: Ellen White is named as captain and scores both goals as England win their final Euro 2017 warm-up game 2-1 against Denmark in Copenhagen. The FA announces that Gemma Grainger will join the England Women senior coaching staff with immediate effect on an interim basis. Grainger has worked with the FA's development teams since 2007. She received her UEFA Pro Licence in 2016.

Mon, 3 Jul: Arsenal captain Alex Scott signs a new contract at the club two days after making her 139th England appearance against Denmark.

Thu, 6 Jul: Toni Duggan leaves Manchester City for FC Barcelona on a free transfer, becoming the first English player to join the Catalan club since Gary Lineker in 1986. The England striker signs a two-year contract and leaves the Academy Stadium having scored 31 goals in 74 appearances for City.

Sun, 9 Jul: England are crowned European Women's Beach Soccer champions after beating Switzerland 4-3 in the final of the six-team tournament on the sands of Nazare, Portugal. An England side containing WSL1 striker Lucy Quinn of Yeovil Town, and coached by Portsmouth Ladies boss Perry Northeast, reached the final thanks to group stage wins over previous holders Spain (6-1) and the Netherlands (4-3).

Fri, 14 Jul: The FA confirms that England's opening 2019 World Cup qualifier against Russia on 19 September will take place at Tranmere Rovers' Prenton Park.

Sun, 16 Jul: Euro 2017 gets under way with hosts the Netherlands beating two-time champions Norway 1-0 in the opening game in front of a crowd of 21,732 in Utrecht. Liverpool's Shanice van de Sanden heads the only goal of the game. Denmark are 1-0 winners against Belgium in the other Group A encounter in Doetinchem.

Wed, 19 Jul: England's Euro 2017 campaign begins with their biggest finals win of all-time. They trounce Scotland 6-0 in Utrecht. Arsenal's Jodie Taylor follows Sir Geoff Hurst (1966 World Cup) and Gary Lineker (1986 World Cup) as only the third senior player to score a hat-trick for England in a major tournament. Ellen White, Jordan Nobbs and Toni Duggan are also on target. The other Group D match ends Spain 2-0 Portugal. In domestic news, former England head coach Hope Powell is confirmed as the new manager of Brighton & Hove Albion ahead of what will be their first full season in WSL2. They finished the Spring Series in sixth place.

Sun, 23 Jul: England's second Group D match ends in a 2-0 win over Spain in Breda. Fran Kirby and Jodie Taylor get the goals. Scotland's hopes of progress are hanging by a thread as they lose again, this time slipping to a 2-1 defeat to Portugal in Rotterdam.

Thu, 27 Jul: Toni Duggan and Nikita Parris are on target as England beat Portugal 2-1 in their final Group D game. Mark Sampson's side are the first England senior team to take maximum points in the group stage of a major tournament since the men's World Cup in 1982. Scotland's elimination is confirmed despite a 1-0 win over Spain. A second Scotland goal would have sent them through.

Sat, 29 Jul: Hosts the Netherlands beat Sweden 2-0 in the first Euro 2017 quarter-final but the match between Germany and Denmark is postponed after torrential rain leaves the pitch in Rotterdam unplayable. The fixture is immediately rescheduled for the following day.

Sun, 30 Jul: A huge television audience, which peaks at 3.3 million (a record for a women's football match), tunes in to Channel 4 to watch England beat France 1-0 in their Euro 2017 quarter-final in Deventer. Jodie Taylor nets her fifth goal of the tournament as the Lionesses beat France for the first time since 1974. The victory is marred by a serious-looking injury to goalkeeper Karen Bardsley (later confirmed as a broken leg) who has to be replaced by Siobhan Chamberlain with 17 minutes to play. England hang on to book a semi-final against hosts the Netherlands. In the rearranged quarter-final there is a huge shock as Denmark beat holders Germany – who have won the last six Euros – 2-1. Austria will complete the semi-final line-up thanks to a 5-3 penalty shootout win over Spain following a goalless draw. England are installed as new favourites to win the tournament.

Thu, 3 Aug: England's Euro 2017 campaign ends in a comprehensive 3-0 defeat to hosts the Netherlands in the semi-finals. The record is again broken for a television audience for a women's football match in the UK with a peak of more than 4 million watching Channel 4's coverage. Denmark beat Austria 3-0 on penalties after the other semi-final ends in a goalless draw.

Fri, 4 Aug: Former Arsenal goalkeeper Emma Byrne announces her retirement. Byrne served the Gunners for 16 years, winning nine top-flight titles, 11 FA Cups, the UEFA Cup (now Champions League), three WSL Continental Cups, and five WPL Cups. She also made 127 appearances for the Republic of Ireland, making her the country's most-capped female player. She most recently played for Brighton & Hove Albion, starting all nine of their 2017 WSL2 Spring Series matches.

Sun, 6 Aug: Hosts the Netherlands are crowned European champions as they beat Denmark 4-2 in a scintillating Euro 2017 final. It's the country's first major women's title and they follow Sweden, Norway and Germany as only the fourth team to win an official European Championship. England's Jodie Taylor is confirmed as the Golden Boot winner having struck five goals in her four appearances.

Mon 7 Aug: The fixtures for the 2017/18 WSL season are announced. On the opening weekend of 23/24 September WSL1 Spring Series champions Chelsea are at home to Birmingham City while Manchester City – who won the last full WSL1 season in 2016 – will visit Yeovil Town. In WSL2, newly-promoted Tottenham will go to Durham while Brighton – who are beginning their first full WSL2 season – will head to Aston Villa.

Wed 9 Aug: The FA announces its intention to launch a bid for England to host the 2021 European Championship. Chief executive Martin Glenn also says he's confident that a British women's team will be able to compete at the 2020 Olympics in Tokyo.

LEAGUE TABLES

2016 WSL SEASON AND 2017 WSL SPRING SERIES

2016 WSL 1 (TIER 1)

Pos	Team	P	W	D	L	F	A	GD	Pts
1.	Manchester City	16	13	3	0	36	4	32	42
2.	Chelsea	16	12	1	3	42	17	25	37
3.	Arsenal	16	10	2	4	33	14	19	32
4.	Birmingham City	16	7	6	3	18	13	5	27
5.	Liverpool	16	7	4	5	27	23	4	25
6.	Notts County	16	4	4	8	16	26	-10	16
7.	Sunderland	16	2	4	10	17	41	-24	10
8.	Reading	16	1	6	9	15	26	-11	9
9.	Doncaster Rovers Belles (R)	16	1	0	15	8	48	-40	3

2016 WSL 2 (TIER 2)

Pos	Team	P	W	D	L	F	A	GD	Pts
1.	Yeovil Town (P)	18	12	3	3	41	16	25	39
2.	Bristol City (P)	18	12	3	3	37	16	21	39
3.	Everton	18	10	4	4	35	18	17	34
4.	Durham	18	10	3	5	30	19	11	33
5.	Sheffield FC	18	7	5	6	25	18	7	26
6.	Aston Villa	18	7	3	8	26	27	-1	24
7.	London Bees	18	6	4	8	28	39	-11	22
8.	Millwall Lionesses	18	3	7	8	24	31	-7	16
9.	Oxford United	18	4	1	13	20	42	-22	13
10.	Watford	18	2	1	15	13	53	-40	7

2017 WSL 1 SPRING SERIES (TIER 1)

Pos	Team	P	W	D	L	F	A	GD	Pts
1.	Chelsea	8	6	1	1	32	3	29	19
2.	Manchester City	8	6	1	1	17	6	11	19
3.	Arsenal	8	5	3	0	22	9	13	18
4.	Liverpool	8	4	2	2	20	18	2	14
5.	Sunderland	8	2	3	3	4	14	-10	9
6.	Reading	8	2	2	4	10	15	-5	8
7.	Birmingham City	8	1	4	3	6	10	-4	7
8.	Bristol City	8	1	1	6	5	21	-16	4
9.	Yeovil Town	8	0	1	7	6	26	-20	1

2017 WSL 2 SPRING SERIES (TIER 2)

Pos	Team	P	W	D	L	F	A	GD	Pts
1.	Everton	9	7	1	1	25	7	18	22
2.	Doncaster Rovers Belles	9	5	3	1	19	9	10	18
3.	Millwall Lionesses	9	5	2	2	12	8	4	17
4.	Aston Villa	9	5	2	2	19	16	3	17
5.	Durham	9	5	1	3	14	10	4	16
6.	Brighton & Hove Albion	9	2	4	3	8	13	-5	10
7.	London Bees	9	3	1	5	13	21	-8	10
8.	Watford	9	2	2	5	12	17	-5	8
9.	Sheffield FC	9	2	0	7	9	18	-9	6
10.	Oxford United	9	0	2	7	7	19	-12	2

WPL 2016/17 SEASON

2016/17 WPL NORTHERN PREMIER (TIER 3)

Pos	Team	P	W	D	L	F	A	GD	Pts
1.	Blackburn Rovers	20	17	3	0	59	20	39	54
2.	Middlesbrough	20	14	1	5	60	31	29	43
3.	Leicester City Ladies	20	10	4	6	44	37	7	34
4.	Stoke City	20	8	6	6	43	37	6	30
5.	Derby County	20	9	2	9	39	35	4	29
6.	West Bromwich Albion	20	8	3	9	33	37	-4	27
7.	Fylde	20	8	5	7	36	30	6	26*
8.	Bradford City	20	7	1	12	40	40	0	22
9.	Huddersfield Town	20	5	5	10	37	53	-16	20
10.	Nottingham Forest	20	5	3	12	27	49	-22	18
11.	Newcastle United (R)	20	2	1	17	16	65	-49	7

*Fylde docked 3 points for fielding ineligible player

2016/17 WPL SOUTHERN PREMIER (TIER 3)

Pos	Team	P	W	D	L	F	A	GD	Pts
1.	Tottenham Hotspur (P)+	20	17	1	2	58	13	45	52
2.	Coventry United	20	15	3	2	55	15	40	48
3.	Cardiff City	20	14	2	4	72	19	53	44
4.	Charlton Athletic	20	13	3	4	55	25	30	42
5.	Crystal Palace	20	9	6	5	48	23	25	33
6.	C&K Basildon	20	8	3	9	29	42	-13	27
7.	Lewes	20	7	4	9	31	36	-5	25
8.	Portsmouth	20	5	2	13	31	66	-35	17
9.	West Ham United	20	1	6	13	12	59	-47	9
10.	Swindon Town	20	2	2	16	20	60	-40	8
11.	QPR	20	2	2	16	11	64	-53	8

+Promoted to WSL2 after beating WPL Northern champions Blackburn 3-0 in play-off

2016/17 WPL NORTHERN DIVISION ONE (TIER 4)

Pos	Team	P	W	D	L	F	A	GD	Pts
1.	Guiseley Vixens (P)	22	19	2	1	72	20	52	59
2.	Liverpool Marshall Feds	22	13	5	4	66	29	37	44
3.	Hull City	22	14	1	7	54	38	16	43
4.	Chester-le-Street Town	22	13	2	7	58	42	16	41
5.	Chorley	22	12	2	8	51	44	7	38
6.	Brighouse Town	22	11	4	7	50	34	16	37
7.	Morecambe	22	10	2	10	51	50	1	29*
8.	Leeds	22	7	2	13	51	59	-8	23
9.	Mossley Hill	22	6	1	15	45	72	-27	19
10.	Crewe Alexandra	22	4	6	12	31	59	-28	18
11.	Blackpool Wren Rovers (R)	22	5	3	14	37	68	-31	18
12.	Tranmere Rovers (R)	22	1	4	17	19	70	-51	7

*Morecambe docked 3 points for fielding unregistered player v Crewe

2016/17 WPL MIDLANDS DIVISION ONE (TIER 4)

Pos	Team	P	W	D	L	F	A	GD	Pts
1.	Wolverhampton Wanderers (P)	22	18	2	2	57	18	39	56
2.	Loughborough Foxes	22	18	0	4	111	31	80	54
3.	Sporting Khalsa	22	13	2	7	57	33	24	41
4.	Radcliffe Olympic	22	13	1	8	58	36	22	40
5.	Birmingham & West Midlands	22	13	1	8	59	45	14	40
6.	The New Saints	22	12	3	7	65	44	21	39
7.	Long Eaton United	22	9	3	10	54	45	9	30
8.	Steel City Wanderers	22	9	1	12	46	62	-16	28
9.	Solihull	22	6	5	11	41	55	-14	23
10.	Leicester City Ladies	22	5	2	15	27	88	-61	17
11.	Rotherham United	22	5	1	16	45	70	-25	16
12.	Loughborough Students (R)	22	0	1	21	19	112	-93	-1*

*Loughborough Students docked two points

2016/17 WPL SOUTH EAST DIVISION ONE (TIER 4)

Pos	Team	P	W	D	L	F	A	GD	Pts
1.	Gillingham (P)	22	18	3	1	104	14	90	57
2.	Milton Keynes Dons	22	16	1	5	63	21	42	49
3.	AFC Wimbledon	22	13	5	4	57	28	29	44
4.	Cambridge United	22	13	2	7	55	35	20	41
5.	Luton Town	22	11	4	7	44	39	5	37
6.	Actonians	22	10	6	6	51	37	14	36
7.	Enfield Town	22	7	4	11	31	51	-20	25
8.	Denham United	22	8	1	13	38	59	-21	25
9.	Ipswich Town	22	7	4	11	36	58	-22	25
10.	Norwich City	22	4	4	14	31	81	-50	16
11.	Stevenage	22	3	6	13	19	45	-26	15
12.	Lowestoft Town (R)	22	2	0	20	21	82	-61	6

2016/17 WPL SOUTH WEST DIVISION ONE (TIER 4)

Pos	Team	P	W	D	L	F	A	GD	Pts
1.	Chichester City (P)	20	19	1	0	100	8	92	58
2.	Plymouth Argyle	20	18	0	2	104	19	85	54
3.	Southampton Saints	20	12	5	3	52	32	20	41
4.	Keynsham Town	20	12	2	6	71	32	39	38
5.	Larkhall Athletic	20	11	3	6	45	42	3	36
6.	Brislington	20	6	4	10	44	63	-19	22
7.	Maidenhead United	19	5	2	12	26	54	-28	16*
8.	St Nicholas	20	4	3	13	31	74	-43	15
9.	Basingstoke Town	20	3	5	12	29	57	-28	14
10.	Cheltenham Town	20	4	1	15	25	74	-49	13
11.	Exeter City (R)	19	0	4	15	16	88	-72	4

*Maidenhead United docked one point. Maidenhead v Exeter City unfulfilled fixture.

NB: Shanklin withdrew from the League on 17 May while occupying 12th position. All their results were expunged from the records.

TOP SCORERS

2016 WSL1 TOP GOALSCORERS

	Goals	Apps
Aluko, Eniola (Chelsea)	9	16
Ross, Jane (Manchester City)	8	16
Weir, Caroline (Liverpool)	7	16
Carter, Danielle (Arsenal)	6	13
Kirby, Fran (Chelsea)	5	7
Chapman, Katie (Chelsea)	5	13
Duggan, Toni (Manchester City)	5	15
Clarke, Jess (Notts County)	5 (2 pens)	16
So Yun, Ji (Chelsea)	5	16
Mead, Beth (Sunderland)	5	16

2016 WSL2 TOP GOALSCORERS

	Goals	Apps
Umotong, Ini-Abasi (Oxford United)	13	17
Wilson, Jo (London Bees)	13	16
Wiltshire, Sarah (Yeovil Town)	11	12
Emslie, Claire (Bristol City)	10	11
Farrow, Millie (Bristol City)	9	13
Hepple, Beth (Durham)	9 (2 pens)	18
Merrick, Bethan (Aston Villa)	9	18
Heatherson, Ann-Marie (Yeovil Town)	7	16
Michalska, Jodie (Sheffield FC)	7	18

2017 WSL1 SPRING SERIES TOP GOALSCORERS

	Goals	Apps
Kirby, Fran (Chelsea)	6	5
Weir, Caroline (Liverpool)	5	8
Duggan, Toni (Manchester City)	4	4
Cuthbert, Erin (Chelsea)	4	5
Carter, Danielle (Arsenal)	4	7
So-Yun, Ji (Chelsea)	4	7
Spence, Drew (Chelsea)	4	7
Harding, Natasha (Liverpool)	4	8
Nobbs, Jordan (Arsenal)	4	8

2017 WSL2 SPRING SERIES TOP GOALSCORERS

	Goals	Apps
Sweetman-Kirk, Courtney (Doncaster Rovers Belles)	9 (1 pen)	9
Walker, Claudia (Everton)	7	9
Magill, Simone (Everton)	5	7
Ness, Zoe (Durham)	5	9
Umotong, Ini-Abasi (Oxford United)	4	7
Baptiste, Natasha (Aston Villa)	4	9
Goddard, Ashleigh (London Bees)	4	9
Wilson, Jo (London Bees)	4	9

2016/17 WPL SOUTHERN TOP GOALSCORERS

	Goals	Apps
Graham, Kit (Charlton Athletic)	37	32
Bryan, Gemma (Crystal Palace)	32	24
Baptiste, Bianca (Tottenham Hotspur)	27	34
Martin, Wendy (Tottenham Hotspur)	26	34
Chivers, Chloe (Cardiff City)	23	25
Bartlett, Kerry (Cardiff City)	21	26
Shepherd, Gemma (Charlton Athletic)	18	15

2016/17 WPL SOUTHERN TOP GOALSCORERS CONT.	Goals	Apps
Hall, Alison (Coventry United)	18	22
Quayle, Samantha (Portsmouth)	17	24
Kempson, Sarah (Portsmouth)	14	13
Williams, Cori (Cardiff City)	14	26

2016/17 WPL NORTHERN TOP GOALSCORERS

	Goals	Apps
Mallin, Kate (Huddersfield Town)	32	32
Heckler, Emily (Huddersfield Town/Fylde)	27	29
Owens, Bianca (Middlesbrough)	22	24
Jordan, Saffron (Blackburn Rovers)	22	31
Ella Toone (Blackburn Rovers)	21	25
Hayes, Ashleigh (Stoke City)	20	18
Cottam, Abigail (West Bromwich Albion)	20	26
Campbell, Hannah (Bradford City)	19	26
Elford, Laura (Bradford City)	17	21
Johnson, Melissa (Derby County)	16	24
Bell, Andrea (Nottingham Forest)	16	27

2016/17 WPL SOUTH WEST DIVISION ONE TOP GOALSCORERS

	Goals	Apps
Knapman, Natasha (Plymouth Argyle)	34	25
Bath, Rebecca (Southampton Saints)	32	20
Wilson-Blakely, Charley (Chichester City)	21	17
Lorton-Radburn, Justine (Keynsham Town)	21	22
Khassal, Cherelle (Chichester City)	19	20
Leandro, Cristina Vega (Keynsham Town)	18	14
Marks, Tori (Plymouth Argyle)	18	14
German, Kate (Larkhall Athletic)	18	22
Lewry, Jess (Chichester City)	17	23
Arkell, Jodie (St Nicholas)	16	21

2016/17 WPL SOUTH EAST DIVISION ONE TOP GOALSCORERS

	Goals	Apps
Gibbons, Felicity (Gillingham)	48	28
Gurr, Charlotte (Gillingham)	39	20
Perschky, Nicole (Cambridge United)	23	31
Barrett, Hannah (Milton Keynes Dons)	19	26
McDonnell, Heather (Milton Keynes Dons)	19	26
Barreca, Alessandra (Actonians)	15	18
Cudone, Leah (Milton Keynes Dons)	15	21
Gallop, Evangeline (Cambridge United)	15	25
Jung, Melissa (Actonians)	14	17
Low, Laura (AFC Wimbledon)	14	29
Taylor, Becky (Cambridge United)	14	30
Bowers, April (Gillingham)	14	32

2016/17 WPL MIDLANDS DIVISION ONE TOP GOALSCORERS

	Goals	Apps
Newton, Cara (Long Eaton United)	38	25
Pilling, Emma (Loughborough Foxes)	33	25
Cooper, Charlotte (Loughborough Foxes)	31	25
Hamilton, Precious (Long Eaton United)	26	18
Cross, Jade (Wolverhampton Wanderers)	26	32
Ridge, Emily (The New Saints)	24	23
Young, Chloe (Loughborough Foxes)	20	24
Seivwright, Leah (Birmingham & West Mids)	20	26
Shaw, Natalie (Rotherham United)	19	22
Evans, Ashleigh (Radcliffe Olympic)	19	28

2016/17 WPL NORTHERN DIVISION ONE TOP GOALSCORERS

	Goals	Apps
Redgrave, Jodie (Brighouse Town)	39	31
Berko, Nikki (Blackpool Wren Rovers)	30	25
Danby, Sarah (Guiseley Vixens)	23	21
Proud, Charlotte (Brighouse Town)	20	31
Sarri, Veatriki (Leeds)	17	21
Thackray, Olivia (Guiseley Vixens)	17	27
Hockaday, Laura (Chester-le-Street Town)	16	23
Lee, Carla (Liverpool Marshall Feds)	16	25
Goundrey-Havery, Nichole (Chester-le-Street Town)	15	25
Beech, Rebecca (Hull City)	14	22
Johnson, Chloe (Chester-le-Street Town)	14	26
Thompson, Katie (Hull City)	14	28

CHAMPIONS LEAGUE
2016/17

England had two entrants in the 2016/17 Champions League – 2015 WSL1 Champions Chelsea, and runners-up Manchester City. They both entered the competition at the Round of 32 stage.

PRELIMINARY STAGE

In the preliminary stage, 36 teams were split into 9 groups of 4, of which each group has a host team. Most matches are played in the same stadium, where that isn't possible, they are played close by. The final group games kick-off at the same time and thus take place in different stadiums. Teams play the other teams in their group once. The nine group winners advance to the 'Round of 32' knock-out stage, where they are joined by 23 teams who qualified directly.

GROUP 1 - HOST TEAM: APOLLON LIMASSOL (CYPRUS)

	P	W	D	L	F	A	Pts	
1. Apollon Limassol (Cyprus)	**3**	**2**	**1**	**0**	**9**	**3**	**7**	**Q**
2. PAOK (Greece)	3	0	3	0	5	5	3	
3. Hajvalia (Kosovo)	3	0	2	1	2	3	2	
4. Ki Klaksvik (Faroes)	3	0	2	1	2	7	2	

23 Aug	Apollon Limassol	5-0	Ki Klaksvik	Paphos	150
23 Aug	PAOK	1-1	Hajvalia	Paphos	70
25 Aug	Ki Klaksvik	1-1	PAOK	Paphos	50
25 Aug	Apollon Limassol	1-0	Hajvalia	Paphos	175
28 Aug	PAOK	3-3	Apollon Limassol	Limassol	500
28 Aug	Hajvalia	1-1	Ki Klaksvik	Paphos	40

GROUP 2 - HOST TEAM: OSIJEK (CROATIA)

	P	W	D	L	F	A	Pts	
1. FC Minsk (Belarus)	**3**	**3**	**0**	**0**	**17**	**1**	**9**	**Q**
2. Standard Liege (Belgium)	3	1	1	1	13	4	4	
3. Osijek (Croatia)	3	1	1	1	15	7	4	
4. ZFK Dragon (Macedonia)	3	0	0	3	1	34	0	

23 Aug	Standard Liege	1-3	FC Minsk	Osijek	120
23 Aug	Osijek	14-1	ZFK Dragon	Osijek	400
25 Aug	Standard Liege	11-0	ZFK Dragon	Osijek	100
25 Aug	FC Minsk	5-0	Osijek	Osijek	400
28 Aug	Osijek	1-1	Standard Liege	Osijek	250
28 Aug	ZFK Dragon	0-9	FC Minsk	Vinkovci	50

GROUP 3 - HOST TEAM: CARDIFF MET. (WALES)

	P	W	D	L	F	A	Pts	
1. Breidablik (Iceland)	**3**	**2**	**1**	**0**	**14**	**1**	**7**	**Q**
2. Spartak Subotica (Serbia)	3	2	1	0	6	3	7	
3. Cardiff Met. (Wales)	3	1	0	2	6	11	3	
4. NSA Sofia (Bulgaria)	3	0	0	3	0	11	0	

23 Aug	NSA Sofia	0-4	Cardiff Met.	Cardiff	243
23 Aug	Spartak Subotica	1-1	Breidablik	Cardiff	58
25 Aug	Breidablik	5-0	NSA Sofia	Cardiff	65
25 Aug	Spartak Subotica	3-2	Cardiff Met.	Cardiff	357
28 Aug	NSA Sofia	0-2	Spartak Subotica	Barry	47
28 Aug	Cardiff Met.	0-8	Breidablik	Cardiff	374

GROUP 4 - HOST TEAM: MEDYK KONIN (POLAND)

	P	W	D	L	F	A	Pts	
1. Medyk Konin (Poland)	**3**	**3**	**0**	**0**	**13**	**1**	**9**	**Q**
2. Olimpia Cluj (Romania)	3	2	0	1	18	4	6	
3. Parnu JK (Estonia)	3	0	1	2	3	10	1	
4. Breznica (Montenegro)	3	0	1	2	2	21	1	

23 Aug	Olimpia Cluj	7-1	Parnu JK	Konin	50
23 Aug	Medyk Konin	9-0	Breznica	Konin	300
25 Aug	Olimpia Cluj	10-0	Breznica	Konin	50
25 Aug	Parnu JK	0-1	Medyk Konin	Konin	400
28 Aug	Medyk Konin	3-1	Olimpia Cluj	Konin	600
28 Aug	Breznica	2-2	Parnu JK	Wrzesnia	280

GROUP 5 - HOST TEAM: POMURJE (SLOVENIA)

	P	W	D	L	F	A	Pts	
1. Zurich (Switzerland)	**3**	**3**	**0**	**0**	**11**	**1**	**9**	**Q**
2. Pomurje (Slovenia)	3	2	0	1	10	8	6	
3. Slovan Bratislava (Slovakia)	3	1	0	2	5	8	3	
4. Vllaznia (Albania)	3	0	0	3	2	11	0	

23 Aug	Zurich	3-1	Slovan Bratislava	Beltinci	30
23 Aug	Pomurje	6-1	Vllaznia	Lendava	420
25 Aug	Zurich	3-0	Vllaznia	Beltinci	34
25 Aug	Slovan Bratislava	2-4	Pomurje	Lendava	380
28 Aug	Vllaznia	1-2	Slovan Bratislava	Lendava	30
28 Aug	Pomurje	0-5	Zurich	Beltinci	687

GROUP 6 - HOST TEAM: SFK 2000 (BOSNIA & HERZEGOVINA)

	P	W	D	L	F	A	Pts	
1. SFK 2000 (Bosnia & Herz.)	**3**	**2**	**1**	**0**	**6**	**2**	**7**	**Q**
2. Ramat HaSharon (Israel)	3	2	0	1	5	1	6	
3. Zhytlobud Kharkiv (Ukraine)	3	1	1	1	4	3	4	
4. Rigas FS (Latvia)	3	0	0	3	0	9	0	

23 Aug	SFK 2000	1-0	Ramat HaSharon	Sarajevo	200
23 Aug	Zhytlobud Kharkiv	2-0	Rigas FS	Sarajevo	30
25 Aug	Ramat HaSharon	1-0	Zhytlobud Kharkiv	Sarajevo	25
25 Aug	SFK 2000	3-0	Rigas FS	Sarajevo	250
28 Aug	Zhytlobud Kharkiv	2-2	SFK 2000	Sarajevo	250
28 Aug	Rigas FS	0-4	Ramat HaSharon	Sarajevo	50

GROUP 7 - HOST TEAM: WEXFORD YOUTHS (REPUBLIC OF IRELAND)

	P	W	D	L	F	A	Pts	
1. BIIK Kazygurt (Kazakhstan)	**3**	**3**	**0**	**0**	**9**	**1**	**9**	**Q**
2. Gintra Universitetas (Lithuania)	3	2	0	1	15	4	6	
3. Wexford Youths (Republic of Ireland)	3	0	1	2	2	5	1	
4. ARF Criuleni (Moldova)	3	0	1	2	0	16	1	

23 Aug	Gintra Uni.	13-0	ARF Criuleni	Waterford	20
23 Aug	BIIK Kazygurt	3-1	Wexford Youths	Wexford	613
25 Aug	BIIK Kazygurt	3-0	ARF Criuleni	Waterford	10
25 Aug	Wexford Youths	1-2	Gintra Uni.	Wexford	670
28 Aug	Gintra Uni.	0-3	BIIK Kazygurt	Waterford	65
28 Aug	ARF Criuleni	0-0	Wexford Youths	Wexford	560

GROUP 8 - HOST TEAM: PK-35 VANTAA (FINLAND)

	P	W	D	L	F	A	Pts	
1. Avaldsnes IL (Norway)	**3**	**3**	**0**	**0**	**19**	**1**	**9**	**Q**
2. CF Benfica (Portugal)	3	2	0	1	8	7	6	
3. PK-35 Vantaa (Finland)	3	1	0	2	3	4	3	
4. Newry City (Northern Ireland)	3	0	0	3	0	18	0	

23 Aug	Avaldsnes IL	11-0	Newry City	Vantaa	63
23 Aug	PK-35 Vantaa	1-2	CF Benfica	Vantaa	913
25 Aug	CF Benfica	1-6	Avaldsnes IL	Vantaa	53
25 Aug	PK-35 Vantaa	2-0	Newry City	Vantaa	302
28 Aug	Avaldsnes IL	2-0	PK-35 Vantaa	Vantaa	452
28 Aug	Newry City	0-5	CF Benfica	Helsinki	22

GROUP 9 - HOST TEAM: TWENTE (NETHERLANDS)

	P	W	D	L	F	A	Pts	
1. Twente (Netherlands)	**3**	**3**	**0**	**0**	**17**	**3**	**9**	**Q**
2. Ferencvaros (Hungary)	3	2	0	1	7	2	6	
3. Konak Belediyespor (Turkey)	3	1	0	2	7	8	3	
4. Hibernians (Malta)	3	0	0	3	0	18	0	

23 Aug	Twente	2-1	Ferencvaros	Geesteren	650
23 Aug	Konak B.	5-0	Hibernians	Oldenzaal	100
25 Aug	Twente	9-0	Hibernians	Geesteren	475
25 Aug	Ferencvaros	2-0	Konak B.	Oldenzaal	110
28 Aug	Konak B.	2-6	Twente	Oldenzaal	600
28 Aug	Hibernians	0-4	Ferencvaros	Geesteren	10

ROUND OF 32

The 9 group winners from the preliminary stage are joined by 23 teams who have qualified directly. They play over two legs with the winners advancing to the Round of 16.

5 Oct	Sturm Graz (Austria)	0-6	Zurich (Switzerland)	Graz	1,835
12 Oct	Zurich (Switzerland)	3-0	Sturm Graz (Austria)	Zurich	3,600
Agg:	**Zurich win 9-0**				

5 Oct	Breidablik (Iceland)	0-1	Rosengard (Sweden)	Kopavogur	232
12 Oct	Rosengard (Sweden)	0-0	Breidablik (Iceland)	Malmo	984
Agg:	**Rosengard win 1-0**				

6 Oct	Lillestrom SK (Norway)	3-1	Paris St-Germain (France)	Lillestrom	1,953
13 Oct	Paris St-Germain (France)	4-1	Lillestrom SK (Norway)	Paris	612
Agg:	**Paris St-Germain win 5-4**				

5 Oct	Avaldsnes IL (Norway)	2-5	Lyon (France)	Haugesund	4,619
12 Oct	Lyon (France)	5-0	Avaldsnes IL (Norway)	Decines	5,089
Agg:	**Lyon win 10-2**				

6 Oct	Eskilstuna Utd DFF (Sweden)	1-0	Glasgow City (Scotland)	Eskilstuna	3,987
13 Oct	Glasgow City (Scotland)	1-2	Eskilstuna Utd DFF (Sweden)	Airdrie	728
Agg:	**Eskilstuna Utd DFF win 3-1**				

5 Oct	SFK 2000 (Bosnia & Herz.)	0-0	Rossiyanka (Russia)	Sarajevo	570
13 Oct	Rossiyanka (Russia)	2-1	SFK 2000 (Bosnia & Herz.)	Khimki	300
Agg:	**Rossiyanka win 2-1**				

5 Oct	Chelsea (England)	0-3	Wolfsburg (Germany)	Stamford Bridge	3,783
12 Oct	Wolfsburg (Germany)	1-1	Chelsea (England)	AOK Stadion	1,945
Agg:	**Wolfsburg win 4-1**				

5 Oct	Twente (Netherlands)	2-0	Sparta Praha (Czech Republic)	De Grolsch Veste	2,365
12 Oct	Sparta Praha (Czech Republic)	1-3	Twente (Netherlands)	Generali Arena	876
Agg:	**Twente win 5-1**				

5 Oct	Apollon Limassol (Cyprus)	1-1	Slavia Praha (Czech Republic)	Pafiako Stadium	235
12 Oct	Slavia Praha (Czech Republic)	3-2	Apollon Limassol (Cyprus)	Eden Arena	1,078
Agg:	**Slavia Praha win 4-3**				

5 Oct	Athletic Club (Spain)	2-1	Fortuna Hjorring (Denmark)	San Mames Stadium	9,127
12 Oct	Fortuna Hjorring (Denmark)	3-1 (aet)	Athletic Club (Spain)	Hjorring Stadium	1,225
Agg:	**Fortuna Hjorring win 4-3**				

6 Oct	FC Minsk (Belarus)	0-3	FC Barcelona (Spain)	Minsk	2,300
12 Oct	FC Barcelona (Spain)	2-1	FC Minsk (Belarus)	Mini Estadi	1,201
Agg:	**FC Barcelona win 5-1**				

5 Oct	Medyk Konin (Poland)	4-3	Brescia (Italy)	Stadion im Zlotej Jedenastki	686
13 Oct	Brescia (Italy)	3-2	Medyk Konin (Poland)	Stadio Mario Rigamonti	1,200
Agg:	**6-6, Brescia on away goals**				

6 Oct	Manchester City (England)	2-0	Zvezda Perm (Russia)	Academy Stadium	1,101
12 Oct	Zvezda Perm (Russia)	0-4	Manchester City (England)	Zvezda Stadium	3,500
Agg:	**Manchester City win 6-0**				

5 Oct	BIIK Kazygurt (Kazakhstan)	3-1	AGSM Verona (Italy)	BIIK Stadium	1,300
12 Oct	AGSM Verona (Italy)	1-1	BIIK Kazygurt (Kazakhstan)	Stadio Marc'Antonio Bentegodi	1,900
Agg:	**BIIK Kazygurt win 4-2**				

5 Oct	Hibernian (Scotland)	0-6	Bayern Munich (Germany)	Easter Road	2,551
12 Oct	Bayern Munich (Germany)	4-1	Hibernian (Scotland)	Grunwalder Stadion	320
Agg:	**Bayern Munich win 10-1**				

5 Oct	St Polten-Spratzern (Austria)	0-2	Brondby (Denmark)	NV Arena	950
12 Oct	Brondby (Denmark)	2-2	St Polten-Spratzern (Austria)	Brondby Stadium	1,679
Agg:	**Brondby win 4-2**				

ROUND OF 16

10 Nov	BIIK Kazygurt (Kazakhstan)	0-3	Paris St-Germain (France)	BIIK Stadium	550
17 Nov	Paris St-Germain (France)	4-1	BIIK Kazygurt (Kazakhstan)	Stade Sebastien Charlety	1,645
Agg:	**Paris St-Germain win 7-1**				

9 Nov	FC Barcelona (Spain)	1-0	Twente (Netherlands)	Mini Estadi	1,051
16 Nov	Twente (Netherlands)	0-4	FC Barcelona (Spain)	De Grolsch Veste	7,035
Agg:	**FC Barcelona win 5-0**				

10 Nov	Slavia Praha (Czech Republic)	1-3	Rosengard (Sweden)	FK Viktoria Stadion	1,347
16 Nov	Rosengard (Sweden)	3-0	Slavia Praha (Czech Republic)	Malmo IP	532
Agg:	**Rosengard win 6-1**				

9 Nov	Manchester City (England)	1-0	Brondby (Denmark)	Academy Stadium	1,256
16 Nov	Brondby (Denmark)	1-1	Manchester City (England)	Brondby Stadium	2,513
Agg:	**Manchester City win 2-1**				

9 Nov	Brescia (Italy)	0-1	Fortuna Hjorring (Denmark)	Stadio Mario Rigamonti	1,107
16 Nov	Fortuna Hjorring (Denmark)	3-1	Brescia (Italy)	Hjorring Stadium	1,038
Agg:	**Fortuna Hjorring win 4-1**				

9 Nov	Lyon (France)	8-0	Zurich (Switzerland)	Parc Olympique Lyonnais	3,841
16 Nov	Zurich (Switzerland)	0-9	Lyon (France)	Letzigrund	4,022
Agg:	**Lyon win 17-0**				

10 Nov	Eskilstuna Utd DFF (Sweden)	1-5	Wolfsburg (Germany)	Tunavallen	3,784
17 Nov	Wolfsburg (Germany)	3-0	Eskilstuna Utd DFF (Sweden)	AOK Stadion	1,278
Agg:	**Wolfsburg win 8-1**				

9 Nov	Bayern Munich (Germany)	4-0	Rossiyanka (Russia)	Grunwalder Stadion	410
17 Nov	Rossiyanka (Russia)	0-4	Bayern Munich (Germany)	Rodina Stadium	500
Agg:	**Bayern Munich win 8-0**				

QUARTER-FINALS

23 Mar	Fortuna Hjorring (Denmark)	0-1	Manchester City (England)	Hjorring Stadium	2,036
30 Mar	Manchester City (England)	1-0	Fortuna Hjorring (Denmark)	Academy Stadium	2,148
Agg:	**Manchester City win 2-0**				

22 Mar	Rosengard (Sweden)	0-1	FC Barcelona (Spain)	Malmo IP	5,037
29 Mar	FC Barcelona (Spain)	2-0	Rosengard (Sweden)	Mini Estadi	7,350
Agg:	**FC Barcelona win 3-0**				

23 Mar	Wolfsburg (Germany)	0-2	Lyon (France)	AOK Stadion	3,705
29 Mar	Lyon (France)	0-1	Wolfsburg (Germany)	Parc Olympique Lyonnais	14,128
Agg:	**Lyon win 2-1**				

23 Mar	Bayern Munich (Germany)	1-0	Paris St-Germain (France)	Grunwalder Stadion	7,300
29 Mar	Paris St-Germain (France)	4-0	Bayern Munich (Germany)	Parc des Princes	12,000
Agg:	**Paris St-Germain win 4-1**				

SEMI-FINALS

22 Apr	Manchester City (England)	1-3	Lyon (France)	Academy Stadium	3,548
29 Apr	Lyon (France)	0-1	Manchester City (England)	Parque Olympique Lyonnais	19,214
Agg:	**Lyon win 3-2**				

22 Apr	FC Barcelona (Spain)	1-3	Paris St Germain (France)	Mini Estadi	10,352
29 Apr	Paris St Germain (France)	2-0	FC Barcelona (Spain)	Parc des Princes	19,192
Agg:	**Paris St Germain win 5-1**				

FINAL

Cardiff City Stadium, Wales. Attendance: 22,433

Lyon (France) 0-0 Paris St Germain (France)

Lyon win 7-6 on penalties after extra-time

Lyon (4-2-3-1): Sarah Bouhaddi; Griedge M'Bock Bathy, Kadeisha Buchanan, Wendie Renard, Amel Majri; Saki Kumagai, Camille Abily; Eugenie Le Sommer, Dzsenifer Marozsan, Alex Morgan (Elodie Thomis 23, Claire Lavogez 107); Ada Hegerberg (Pauline Bremer 60)

Paris St Germain (3-1-4-2): Katarzyna Kiedrzynek; Grace Geyoro, Sabrina Delannoy, Irene Paredes; Shirley Cruz Trana (Laura Georges 80); Eve Perisset (Perle Morroni 90+4), Aminata Diallo (Veronica Boquete 57), Formiga, Ashley Lawrence; Cristiane, Marie-Laure Delie

FA CUP *2016/17*

The FA accepted 254 entrants into the 2016/17 Women's FA Cup.

In the tables below the tier of football the team plays its League football at is given in parentheses, ie (5) = 5th tier.

(aet) denotes *after extra-time*
(4-2p) denotes *4-2 on penalties after extra-time*
hw/o denotes *home walkover*
aw/o denotes *away walkover*

FIRST QUALIFYING ROUND; 4 SEP 2016

South Shields (6)	2-0	Gateshead Leam Rangers (7)	25
Wigan Athletic (5)	1-0	MSB Woolton (5)	

SECOND QUALIFYING ROUND; 18 SEP 2016

158 teams entered at this stage and were joined by the two winners from the first qualifying round.

Wallsend Boys Club (5)	5-2	Boldon CA Villa (7)
South Shields (6)	1-1 (4-2p)	Cramlington United (6)
South Park Rangers (7)	hw/o	Kendal Town (6)
Penrith (6)	1-0 (aet)	Bishop Auckland (7)
RACA Tynedale (5)	hw/o	Rutherford (7)
Workington Reds (6)	2-1	Birtley Town (7)
Norton & Stockton Ancients (5)	7-0	Carlisle United (6)
Prudhoe Town (6)	0-9	Hartlepool United (6)
Boldon CA (5)	3-1	Blyth Town Lions (6)

Ossett Albion (6)	1-0	Malet Lambert (6)
Wakefield (5)	0-7	Farsley Celtic (6)
Bradford Park Avenue (7)	1-8	Sheffield United (5)
Sheffield Wednesday (6)	4-0	Brighouse Athletic (7)
Accrington (5)	11-2	Curzon Ashton (6)
FC United of Manchester (6)	2-1	Bolton Wanderers (5)
CMB (5)	0-4	Stockport County (5)
Burnley (7)	0-7	Wigan Athletic (5)
Merseyrail Bootle (6)	4-1	City of Manchester (5)
Chorltonians (6)	0-2	Warrington Wolverines (6)
Rise Park (5)	0-0 (3-4p)	Arnold Town (5)
Leicester City Women Development (6)	3-0	Winterton Rangers (6)
Dronfield Town (7)	4-4 (2-3p)	Lincoln Moorlands Railway (6)
Nettleham (5)	16-0	Teversal (6)
Market Warsop (7)	5-1	AFC Leicester (6)
Stourbridge (6)	2-1	Stockingford AA Pavilion (6)
Coundon Court (5)	9-0	Bilbrook (6)
Leamington Lions (5)	2-2 (5-4p)	Wolverhampton Sporting (5)
Bedworth United (5)	7-0	Stone Dominoes (6)
Coleshill Town (6)	0-3	Coventry Ladies Development (6)
Shrewsbury Town (6)	2-4	Wyrley (6)
Bradwell Belles (7)	1-5	Shrewsbury Juniors (6)
Knowle (5)	1-2	Leek Town (6)
Crusaders (5)	2-2 (3-4p)	Gornal (7)
Burton Albion (5)	3-1	Lye Town (5)
Rubery (6)	2-3 (aet)	Boldmere St Michaels (7)
Moulton (7)	2-5	Histon (5)
Riverside (6)	9-0	Woodford United (7)
Oadby & Wigston (6)	2-0	Roade (7)
Peterborough United (6)	0-1	Cambridge City (6)
Acle United (5)	2-0	Netherton United (7)
ICA Sports (7)	aw/o	Peterborough Northern Star (5)
Newmarket Town (7)	2-7	Wymondham Town (6)
Park (7)	0-14	Northampton Town (6)
Kettering Town (5)	4-0	Thrapston Town (7)
Colchester Town (5)	0-3	AFC Sudbury (5)
Brandon Town (7)	hw/o	Great Wakering Rovers (5)

Little Thurrock Dynamos (6)	1-2 (aet)	Brentwood Town (5)
Harlow Town (7)	2-3	Billericay Town (5)
Writtle (5)	0-3	Leyton Orient (5)
Haringey Borough (5)	12-0	Chelmsford City (7)
*Bishop's Stortford (7)	1-3	Bungay Town (7)
Hertford Town (6)	hw/o	Garston (7)
Houghton Athletic (7)	2-1	Sherrardswood (7)
AFC Dunstable (5)	8-0	Sandy (7)
Colney Heath (6)	1-3	Royston Town (5)
Hemel Hempstead Town (6)	2-1	Bedford (5)
QPR Development (6)	5-0	Wargrave (6)
Marlow (5)	2-4 (aet)	Oxford City (5)
Ascot United (6)	3-2	Milton Keynes City (5)
Newbury (5)	6-2	Chinnor (7)
Brentford (7)	0-8	Chesham United (5)
Carshalton Athletic (5)	1-3	Aylesford (5)
Meridian (6)	2-0	Eastbourne (6)
Haywards Heath & Wivelsfield (7)	1-5	Cowfold (7)
Burgess Hill Town (7)	0-4	Regents Park Rangers (6)
Long Lane (6)	2-3	Fulham Foundation (5)
Margate (7)	1-10	Bexhill United (6)
Herne Bay (5)	1-1 (3-1p)	Parkwood Rangers (6)
London Corinthians (5)	6-0	Victoire (7)
Abbey Rangers (6)	1-7	Crawley Wasps (5)
Worthing Town (7)	hw/o	Rottingdean Village (6)
Warsash Wasps (7)	1-2	Poole Town (5)
Fleet Town (6)	6-0	Team Solent (5)
New Milton Town (6)	1-0	AFC Bournemouth (7)
Bournemouth Sports (7)	0-12	Southampton (5)
Middlezoy Rovers (5)	2-2 (0-2p)	Ilminster Town (6)
AEK-Boco (6)	3-1 (aet)	Royal Wootton Bassett Town (7)
Buckland Athletic (6)	hw/o	Cheltenham Civil Service (6)
Downend Flyers (5)	7-1	Pen Mill (7)
Keynsham Town Development (5)	aw/o	Torquay United (5)

*played 17 September

THIRD QUALIFYING ROUND; 19 OCT 2016

This round consists of 64 ties. The 80 winners from the second qualifying round are joined by 48 teams from the WPL Division One level (the fourth tier of English football).

Wallsend Boys Club (5)	3-2	Wigan Athletic (5)
Norton & Stockton Ancients (5)	2-1	FC United of Manchester (6)
Leeds (4)	6-1	South Park Rangers (7)
Farsley Celtic (6)	2-4	Merseyrail Bootle (6)
Penrith (6)	4-2	Boldon CA (5)
Lincoln Moorlands Railway (6)	1-6	Warrington Wolverines (6)
Crewe Alexandra (4)	3-3 (4-2p)	Morecambe (4)
Steel City Wanderers (4)	1-4	Sheffield Wednesday (6)
Mossley Hill (4)	0-4	Liverpool Marshall Feds (4)
Guiseley Vixens (4)	7-2	Rotherham United (4)
Chester-le-Street Town (4)	0-1	Sheffield United (5)
Hartlepool United (6)	7-1	Ossett Albion (6)
Accrington (5)	3-0	Tranmere Rovers (4)
Stockport County (5)	1-2	Brighouse Town (4)
Blackpool Wren Rovers (4)	2-2 (5-3p)	Chorley (4)
Hull City (4)	4-2 (aet)	South Shields (6)
Workington Reds (6)	1-5	RACA Tynedale (5)
Wyrley (6)	1-6	Radcliffe Olympic (4)
Leamington Lions (5)	0-4	Burton Albion (5)
Sporting Khalsa (4)	7-0	Coundon Court (5)
Arnold Town (5)	3-3 (3-4p)	Coventry Ladies Development (6)
Bedworth United (5)	2-6	Leicester City Women Development (6)
Leicester City Ladies (4)	2-3	Birmingham & West Midlands (4)
Loughborough Foxes (4)	2-3	Wolverhampton Wanderers (4)
Shrewsbury Juniors (6)	2-6 (aet)	The New Saints (4)
Boldmere St Michaels (7)	2-8	Long Eaton United (4)
Stourbridge (6)	1-2	Gornal (7)
Oadby & Wigston (6)	0-6	Solihull (4)
Market Warsop (7)	3-4	Nettleham (5)
Loughborough Students (4)	1-3	Leek Town (6)
Norwich City (4)	10-0	Riverside (6)
Lowestoft Town (4)	2-0	Enfield Town (4)

Milton Keynes Dons (4)	4-0	Actonians (4)
Histon (5)	0-5	Peterborough Northern Star (5)
Northampton Town (6)	2-3	Cambridge City (6)
Denham United (4)	4-1	Ipswich Town (4)
Cambridge United (4)	3-0	Wymondham Town (6)
AFC Sudbury (5)	2-3	Luton Town (4)
Kettering Town (5)	6-0	Brandon Town (7)
Bungay Town (7)	3-6	Acle United (5)
Hemel Hempstead Town (6)	2-0	Herne Bay (5)
AFC Dunstable (5)	4-1	Meridian (6)
Houghton Athletic (7)	0-3	Brentwood Town (5)
Haringey Borough (5)	2-8	Chichester City (4)
Crawley Wasps (5)	0-2	Oxford City (5)
Newbury (5)	2-1	Hertford Town (6)
Leyton Orient (5)	16-0	Ascot United (6)
Billericay Town (5)	1-2	Basingstoke Town (4)
Fulham Foundation (5)	0-2	QPR Development (6)
Worthing Town (7)	0-15	Stevenage (4)
Cowfold (7)	1-2	Aylesford (5)
Chesham United (5)	2-1	London Corinthians (5)
Bexhill United (6)	0-6	AFC Wimbledon (4)
Royston Town (5)	2-3	Regents Park Rangers (6)
Gillingham (4)	4-0	Maidenhead United (4)
Southampton (5)	5-1	Fleet Town (6)
Shanklin (4)	3-2	St Nicholas (4)
Buckland Athletic (6)	2-3	Keynsham Town (4)
Torquay United (5)	2-4	Brislington (4)
Poole Town (5)	3-0	AEK-Boco (6)
Ilminster Town (6)	0-4	Plymouth Argyle (4)
Southampton Saints (4)	8-2	Downend Flyers (5)
Larkhall Athletic (4)	9-1	Cheltenham Town (4)
New Milton Town (6)	1-2	Exeter City (4)

FOURTH QUALIFYING ROUND; 13 NOV 2016

Sheffield United (5)	3-1	Merseyrail Bootle (6)
Penrith (6)	0-4	Norton & Stockton Ancients (5)
Guiseley Vixens (4)	7-1	Nettleham (5)
Liverpool Marshall Feds (4)	7-1	Warrington Wolverines (6)
RACA Tynedale (5)	2-1	Crewe Alexandra (4)
Brighouse Town (4)	5-0	Blackpool Wren Rovers (4)
Hartlepool United (6)	7-1	Accrington (5)
Hull City (4)	6-0	Leeds (4)
Wallsend Boys Club (5)	1-2	Sheffield Wednesday (6)
Sporting Khalsa (4)	2-4 (aet)	Wolverhampton Wanderers (4)
Solihull (4)	3-0	Burton Albion (5)
Radcliffe Olympic (4)	8-0	Gornal (7)
Leek Town (6)	1-2 (aet)	Leicester City Women Development (6)
The New Saints (4)	2-5	Birmingham & West Midlands (4)
Long Eaton United (4)	7-1	Coventry Ladies Development (6)
Acle United (5)	3-0	Brentwood Town (5)
Norwich City (4)	3-3 (4-3p)	Lowestoft Town (4)
Cambridge United (4)	3-0	Stevenage (4)
Kettering Town (5)	0-3	Peterborough Northern Star (5)
Leyton Orient (5)	3-1	Cambridge City (6)
Luton Town (4)	6-1	Oxford City (5)
Chesham United (5)	2-4	Regents Park Rangers (6)
Hemel Hempstead Town (6)	2-0	AFC Dunstable (5)
AFC Wimbledon (4)	4-2	Denham United (4)
Aylesford (5)	0-7	Gillingham (4)
QPR Development (6)	1-6	Milton Keynes Dons (4)
Brislington (4)	8-0	Poole Town (5)
Southampton Saints (4)	10-0	Exeter City (4)
Larkhall Athletic (4)	8-1	Newbury (5)
*Plymouth Argyle (4)	3-1	Basingstoke Town (4)
Shanklin (4)	0-3	Southampton (5)
*Chichester City (4)	1-2	Keynsham Town (4)

*played 20 Nov

FIRST ROUND; 4 DEC 2016

The teams from the third tier of English football (WPL North and South) entered at this stage.

Radcliffe Olympic (4)	6-0	Sheffield Wednesday (6)
Sheffield United (5)	2-0	Leicester City Women Development (6)
Bradford City (3)	0-1	Blackburn Rovers (3)
Stoke City (3)	1-1 (2-4p)	Liverpool Marshall Feds (4)
Guiseley Vixens (4)	0-1	Nottingham Forest (3)
Wolverhampton Wanderers (4)	4-0	Solihull (4)
Birmingham & West Midlands (4)	0-3	Leicester City Women (3)
Middlesbrough (3)	1-0	Hartlepool United (6)
West Bromwich Albion (3)	4-1	Fylde (3)
Huddersfield Town (3)	0-1	Derby County (3)
RACA Tynedale (5)	0-3	Newcastle United (3)
Norton & Stockton Ancients (5)	1-6	Hull City (4)
Long Eaton United (4)	hw/o	Nuneaton Town (3)
Brighouse Town (4)	3-2	Peterborough Northern Star (5)
Southampton Saints (4)	1-7	Gillingham (4)
Acle United (5)	0-2	C&K Basildon (3)
Cardiff City (3)	6-0	Larkhall Athletic (4)
Tottenham Hotspur (3)	1-0	Leyton Orient (5)
Cambridge United (4)	3-1	QPR (3)
Milton Keynes Dons (4)	3-1	Hemel Hempstead Town (6)
Plymouth Argyle (4)	hw/o	Forest Green Rovers (3)
Lewes (3)	5-0	Brislington (4)
West Ham United (3)	0-3	Coventry United (3)
Crystal Palace (3)	1-2	Charlton Athletic (3)
Luton Town (4)	1-4	Portsmouth (3)
Norwich City (4)	1-4	AFC Wimbledon (4)
*Southampton (5)	2-0	Swindon Town (3)
Regents Park Rangers (6)	1-6	Keynsham Town (4)

*played 11 Dec

SECOND ROUND; 8 JAN 2017

Long Eaton United (4)	3-4	Brighouse Town (4)
Derby County (3)	3-2 (aet)	Sheffield United (5)
West Bromwich Albion (3)	4-0	Radcliffe Olympic (4)
Nottingham Forest (3)	4-0	Wolverhampton Wanderers (4)
Middlesbrough (3)	1-2 (aet)	Leicester City Women (3)
Blackburn Rovers (3)	5-0	Hull City (4)
Liverpool Marshall Feds (4)	1-0	Newcastle United (3)
Coventry United (3)	4-0	Milton Keynes Dons (4)
C&K Basildon (3)	1-3	Keynsham Town (4)
Lewes (3)	2-0	Cardiff City (3)
Tottenham Hotspur (3)	3-0	Gillingham (4)
Plymouth Argyle (4)	0-3	AFC Wimbledon (4)
Cambridge United (4)	4-0	Southampton (5)
Charlton Athletic (3)	5-0	Portsmouth (3)

THIRD ROUND; 5 FEB 2017

The teams from WSL2 entered at this stage.

Blackburn Rovers (3)	1-2	Tottenham Hotspur (3)
Charlton Athletic (3)	0-2	Sheffield FC (2)
Aston Villa (2)	7-1	Cambridge United (4)
Millwall Lionesses (2)	1-0	London Bees (2)
Leicester City Women (3)	2-1	Liverpool Marshall Feds (4)
Keynsham Town (4)	0-7	Durham (2)
Coventry United (3)	2-0	Oxford United (2)
West Bromwich Albion (3)	3-1	Lewes (3)
Doncaster Rovers Belles (2)	hw/o	Watford (2)
Derby County (3)	0-1	Nottingham Forest (3)
Brighouse Town (4)	1-8	Everton (2)
AFC Wimbledon (4)	1-4	Brighton & Hove Albion (2)

FOURTH ROUND; 19 FEB 2017

Durham (2)	2-2 (3-4p)	Everton (2)
Coventry United (3)	0-1	Aston Villa (2)
Millwall Lionesses (2)	3-1	Nottingham Forest (3)
West Bromwich Albion (3)	2-1	Leicester City Women (3)
Tottenham Hotspur (3)	1-0	Brighton & Hove Albion (2)
Sheffield FC (2)	0-1	Doncaster Rovers Belles (2)

FIFTH ROUND; 19 MAR 2017

The teams from WSL1 entered at this stage.

Notts County (1)	3-2	Yeovil Town (1)
Liverpool (1)	2-1 (aet)	Everton (2)
Arsenal (1)	10-0	Tottenham Hotspur (3)
Sunderland (1)	3-2	Aston Villa (2)
Birmingham City (1)	2-0	West Bromwich Albion (3)
Bristol City (1)	5-0	Millwall Lionesses (2)
*Manchester City (1)	1-0	Reading (1)
Chelsea (1)	7-0	Doncaster Rovers Belles (2)

*played 11 Mar

SIXTH ROUND; 26 MAR 2017

Birmingham City (1)	1-0	Arsenal (1)
Chelsea (1)	5-1	Sunderland (1)
Bristol City (1)	1-2	Manchester City (1)
Liverpool (1)	2-0	Notts County (1)

SEMI-FINALS; 17 APR 2017

Birmingham City (1)	1-1 (4-2p)	Chelsea (1)
Manchester City (1)	1-0	Liverpool (1)

FINAL; 13 MAY 2017

Birmingham City (1)	1-4	Manchester City (1)
Wellings 73		*Bronze 18, Christiansen 25*
		Lloyd 32, Scott 80
Wembley Stadium: 35,271		

Birmingham City (3-4-1-2): Ann-Katrin Berger; Kerys Harrop, Aoife Mannion, Meaghan Sargeant; Paige Williams (Abbey-Leigh Stringer 88), Jess Carter, Andrine Hegerberg (Chloe Peplow 83), Sarah Mayling; Ellen White; Ellie Brazil, Freda Ayisi (Charlie Wellings 64)

Manchester City (4-3-3): Karen Bardsley; Lucy Bronze, Steph Houghton, Megan Campbell (Abbie McManus 78), Demi Stokes; Jill Scott, Keira Walsh, Izzy Christiansen; Nikita Parris (Georgia Stanway 71), Carli Lloyd, Melissa Lawley (Toni Duggan 56)

WSL CONTINENTAL CUP
2016

When the WSL was founded in 2011 the top-flight teams stopped competing in the WPL Cup and instead took part in their own League Cup, the WSL Cup. It has been sponsored by Continental since its outset. The final takes place on neutral territory, but the Academy Stadium had already been chosen as the 2016 venue prior to Manchester City qualifying for it. They effectively found themselves playing at home against Birmingham City in what Blues manager David Parker described as 'the most un-neutral final you'll see in football.'

PRELIMINARY ROUND: 8 MAY 2016

Sheffield FC	3-1	Durham
Oxford United	1-0	Millwall Lionesses
Watford	0-2	London Bees

FIRST ROUND: 2 JULY 2016

Aston Villa	0-8	Manchester City
Everton	0-1	Liverpool
Reading	1-3	Arsenal
London Bees	3-3 (4-2p)	Chelsea
Sheffield FC	2-0	Bristol City

FIRST ROUND: 3 JULY 2016

Doncaster Rovers Belles	2-1	Sunderland
Oxford United	0-2	Birmingham City
Yeovil Town	1-3	Notts County

SECOND ROUND: 5 AUGUST 2016

Arsenal	3-2	Notts County

SECOND ROUND: 7 AUGUST 2016

Birmingham City	1-0 (aet)	Liverpool
Manchester City	4-1	Doncaster Rovers Belles
Sheffield FC	0-2	London Bees

SEMI-FINAL: 3 SEPTEMBER 2016

London Bees	0-4	Birmingham City

SEMI-FINAL: 4 SEPTEMBER 2016

Manchester City	1-0	Arsenal

FINAL: 2 OCTOBER 2016

Played at Academy Stadium, Manchester

Birmingham City	0-1 (aet)	Manchester City
		Bronze 105

Birmingham City: Ann-Katrin Berger, Meaghan Sargeant, Jess Carter, Kerys Harrop, Freda Ayisi (Isabelle Linden 105), Kirsty Linnett (Charlie Wellings 75), Andrine Hegerberg (Chloe Peplow 90), Marisa Ewers, Melissa Lawley, Emily Westwood, Aoife Mannion

Manchester City: Marie Hourihan, Lucy Bronze, Steph Houghton, Jennifer Beattie, Demi Stokes, Keira Walsh, Jill Scott, Izzy Christiansen, Nikita Parris (Kosovare Asllani 65), Toni Duggan (Daphne Corboz 105), Jane Ross (Tessel Middag 84)

WPL CUP *2016/17*

All 72 WPL clubs (from the third and fourth tiers of English football) entered at the Determining Round. The winners continued in competition proper, losers entered the Premier League Plate. All matches go to extra-time if level after 90 minutes, and then penalties

(S) = WPL Southern Division; (N) = WPL Northern Division

(Both these divisions make up the third tier of English football.)

(SW1) = WPL South West Division One; (M1) = WPL Midlands Division One;
(SE1) = WPL South East Division One; (N1) = WPL Northern Division One

(These four divisions make up the fourth tier of English football.)

(aet) denotes *after extra-time*

(4-2p) denotes *4-2 on penalties after extra-time*

hw/o denotes *home walkover*

aw/o denotes *away walkover*

DETERMINING ROUND; 4 SEP 2016

AFC Wimbledon (SE1)	3-2	Plymouth Argyle (SW1)
Basingstoke (SW1)	3-0	Cheltenham Town (SW1)
Blackburn Rovers (N)	19-0	Rotherham United (M1)
Blackpool Wren Rovers (N1)	5-0	Crewe Alexandra (N1)
C&K Basildon (S)	8-0	St Nicholas (SW1)
Cambridge United (SE1)	3-3 (4-2p)	Lewes (S)
Charlton Athletic (S)	8-1	Shanklin (SW1)
Chichester City (SW1)	6-2	Actonians (SE1)
Coventry United (S)	9-0	Maidenhead United (SW1)
Denham United (SE1)	2-1 (aet)	Swindon Town (S)
Derby County (N)	7-0	Steel City Wanderers (M1)
Enfield Town (SE1)	3-1	Exeter City (SW1)
Huddersfield Town (N)	1-2	Fylde (N)
Hull City (N1)	3-0	Guiseley Vixens (N1)
Ipswich Town (SE1)	0-5	Cardiff City (S)
Keynsham Town (SW1)	1-2	Crystal Palace (S)
Long Eaton United (M1)	13-0	Loughborough Students (M1)
Loughborough Foxes (M1)	9-3	Leicester City Ladies (M1)
Luton Town (SE1)	1-3	Milton Keynes Dons (SE1)
Morecambe (N1)	0-3	Middlesbrough (N)
Mossley Hill (N1)	0-5	Brighouse Town (N1)
Newcastle United (N)	2-1	Leicester City Women (N)
Nottingham Forest (N)	3-1 (aet)	Chorley (N1)
Portsmouth (S)	8-2	Lowestoft Town (SE1)
QPR (S)	2-3	Norwich City (SE1)
Southampton Saints (SW1)	0-4	Gillingham (SE1)
Sporting Khalsa (M1)	2-4	Chester-le-Street Town (N1)
Stevenage (SE1)	0-3	Larkhall Athletic (SW1)
Stoke City (N)	13-0	Birmingham & West Mids
The New Saints (M1)	3-0	Solihull (M1)
Tranmere Rovers (N1)	0-5	Liverpool Marshall Feds (N1)
West Bromwich Albion (N)	2-1	Bradford City (N)
West Ham United (S)	0-10	Tottenham Hotspur (S)
Wolverhampton Wanderers (M1)	3-2	Radcliffe Olympic (M1)
Forest Green Rovers (S)	aw/o	Brislington (SW1)
Leeds (N1)	hw/o	Nuneaton Town (N)

FIRST ROUND; 25 SEP 2016

The 28 Determining Round winners were given byes to the Second Round. While eight Determining Round winners were drawn to play each other in the First Round, as follows:

Blackburn Rovers (N)	3-1	Nottingham Forest (N)
Denham United (SE1)	3-2	Brislington (SW1)
Gillingham (SE1)	8-2	Norwich City (SE1)
Long Eaton United (M1)	1-1 (3-4p)	Liverpool Marshall Feds (N1)

SECOND ROUND; 16 OCT 2016

Charlton Athletic (S)	3-2	C&K Basildon (S)
Hull City (N1)	3-1	Middlesbrough (N)
Leeds (N1)	1-4	Liverpool Marshall Feds (N1)
Loughborough Foxes (M1)	10-1	The New Saints (M1)
Stoke City (N)	1-2 (aet)	Derby County (N)
Wolverhampton Wanderers (M1)	2-2 (4-2p)	Brighouse Town (N1)
*AFC Wimbledon (SE1)	0-2	Crystal Palace (S)
*Chester-le-Street Town (N1)	3-0	Blackpool Wren Rovers (N1)
*Coventry United (S)	3-0	Denham United (SE1)
*Gillingham (SE1)	2-0	Milton Keynes Dons (SE1)
*Newcastle United (N)	0-1	Blackburn Rovers (N)
*Portsmouth (S)	3-2	Cambridge United (SE1)
*Tottenham Hotspur (S)	5-1	Enfield Town (SE1)
*West Bromwich Albion (N)	2-1 (aet)	Fylde (N)
+Basingstoke (SW1)	0-5	Chichester City (SW1)
Cardiff City (S)	hw/o Cardiff	Larkhall Athletic (SW1)

* played 23 October

+ played 30 October

THIRD ROUND; 6 NOV 2016

Blackburn Rovers (N)	5-0	Loughborough Foxes (M1)
Cardiff City (S)	7-1	Chichester City (SW1)
Charlton Athletic (S)	4-2	Portsmouth (S)
Chester-le-Street Town (N1)	2-1	Derby County (N)
Crystal Palace (S)	1-0	Coventry United (S)
Hull City (N1)	0-4	Liverpool Marshall Feds (N1)
West Bromwich Albion (N)	1-0 (aet)	Wolverhampton Wanderers (M1)
Tottenham Hotspur (S)	4-2	Gillingham (SE1)

QUARTER-FINALS; 11 DEC 2016

Liverpool Marshall Feds (N1)	0-2	Cardiff City (S)
Charlton Athletic (S)	1-1 (4-2p)	West Bromwich Albion (N)
Chester-le-Street Town (N1)	1-3	Blackburn Rovers (N)
Tottenham Hotspur (S)	4-1	Crystal Palace (S)

SEMI-FINALS; 5 MAR 2017

Tottenham Hotspur (S)	3-0	Cardiff City (S)
Charlton Athletic (S)	4-3 (aet)	Blackburn Rovers (N)

FINAL; 7 MAY 2017

			ATT
Charlton Athletic (S)	0-0 (3-4p)	Tottenham Hotspur (S)	544

Lamex Stadium, Stevenage

Tottenham Hotspur: Toni-Anne Wayne, Lucia Leon, Leah Rawle (Katie O'Leary 90), Sophie Mclean, Josie Green (Eartha Pond 100), Bianca Baptiste, Wendy Martin, Jenna Schillaci, Maya Vio, Renee Hector, Ronnell Humes (Nikita Whinnett 70)

Charlton Athletic: Alexandra Baker, Katie Flack, Kim Dixson, Rosey Sullivan, Grace Coombs, Charley Clifford, Avilla Bergin, Nicole Pepper (Charlotte Lee 66), Kit Graham, Daisy Monaghan (Stefanie Simmons 66), Ruby Southgate

WPL PLATE *2016/17*

The WPL Plate was first run in the 2014/15 season. The participating teams are decided by the Determining Round of the WPL Cup. All 72 WPL clubs are eligible to enter the WPL Cup. The WPL consists of two divisions at the third tier of English football (WPL Northern and WPL Southern) and four divisions at the fourth tier of English football (WPL Northern Division One, WPL Midlands Division One, WPL South East Division One, WPL South West Division One). The teams that win their WPL Cup Determining Round tie continue in the WPL Cup, but those who lose drop into the WPL Plate.

For the 2016/17 season two teams (Forest Green Rovers and Nuneaton Town) withdrew from the WPL Cup competition before playing a match meaning 36 teams progressed from the Determining Round to continue in the WPL Cup, and 34 dropped into the WPL Plate.

With just 34 teams in the WPL Plate, two first round ties were required to eliminate two teams ahead of the second round. As such, 30 teams entered at the second-round stage.

Key:

N (WPL Northern Division)

S (WPL Southern Division)

N1 (WPL Northern Division One)

M1 (WPL Midlands Division One)

SE1 (WPL South East Division One)

SW1 (WPL South West Division One)

aet = after extra time

(4-2p) = 4-2 on penalties after extra-time

hw/o = home walkover

aw/o = away walkover

Attendances are listed where known

FIRST ROUND; 25 SEP 2016

Sporting Khalsa (M1)	2-6	Huddersfield Town (N)
West Ham United (S)	2-2 (3-2p)	Swindon Town (S)

SECOND ROUND; 16 OCT 2016

Guiseley Vixens (N1)	4-4 (4-5p)	Huddersfield Town (N)
Leicester City Ladies (M1)	2-1	Steel City Wanderers (M1)
Leicester City Women (N)	6-1	Rotherham United (M1)
Mossley Hill (N1)	3-2	Loughborough Students (M1)
Plymouth Argyle (SW1)	2-4	Luton Town (SE1)
Solihull (M1)	0-2	Tranmere Rovers (N1)
St Nicholas (SW1)	7-2	Shanklin (SW1)
Crewe Alexandra (N1)	0-6	Bradford City (N)

SECOND ROUND CONTINUED; 23 OCT 2016

Actonians (SE1)	6-0	Ipswich Town (SE1)
Birmingham & West Mids (M1)	0-1	Radcliffe Olympic (M1)
Cheltenham Town (SW1)	1-2	West Ham United (S)
Exeter City (SW1)	0-4	Stevenage (SE1)
Lowestoft Town (SE1)	2-4	QPR (S)
Morecambe (N1)	0-5	Chorley (N1)
Southampton Saints (SW1)	2-3	Keynsham Town (SW1)
Lewes (S)	hw/o	Maidenhead United (SW1)

THIRD ROUND; 6 NOV 2016

Actonians (SE1)	2-1	QPR (S)
Bradford City (N)	2-2 (3-4p)	Huddersfield Town (N)
Chorley (N1)	3-5	Leicester City Women (N)
Leicester City Ladies (M1)	0-5	Radcliffe Olympic (M1)
Mossley Hill (N1)	1-2	Tranmere Rovers (N1)
Stevenage (SE1)	0-2	Luton Town (SE1)
West Ham United (S)	2-3	Keynsham Town (SW1)
Lewes (S)	hw/o	St Nicholas (SW1)

QUARTER-FINALS; 11 DEC 2016

Tranmere Rovers (N1)	0-7	Huddersfield Town (N)
Keynsham Town (SW1)	2-3 (aet)	Leicester City Women (N)
Actonians (SE1)	3-0	Radcliffe Olympic (M1)

QUARTER-FINALS CONTINUED; 18 DEC 2016

Luton Town (SE1)	0-6	Lewes (S)

SEMI-FINALS; 5 MAR 2017

Huddersfield Town (N)	6-1	Actonians (SE1)

SEMI-FINALS CONTINUED; 12 MAR 2017

Leicester City Women (N)	0-1	Lewes (S)

FINAL; 23 APR 2017

Huddersfield Town (N)	0-4	Lewes (S)	200
		Bridges 6, 78	
		Lane 59	
		Palmer 85	

Played at St James Park, Brackley Town FC

Huddersfield Town: Laura Carter, Millie Turner, Amy Battel, Kate Mallin, Vicky Abbott (Ella Harris 67), Hannah Spreckley, Katie Nutter, Charley Evans, Sarah Dobby, Emily Heckler (Isabel Thomas 78), Danielle Biglin (Beth Jennings 67)

Lewes: Lauren Dolbear, Claire Capon, Rebecca Thompson-Agbro, Katie McIntyre, Tammy Waine, Kelly Newton (Kellie Larkin 51), Sian Heather, Danielle Lane (Felicity Love 78), Rebecca Carter (Mia Hyland 87), Georgia Bridges, Rachel Palmer

WOMEN'S FOOTBALL PYRAMID *2017/18*

The women's football pyramid in England effectively extends to ten tiers. This next section of the book covers the teams who are competing in the top four tiers of the women's game in 2017/18, as well as those who were relegated out of the fourth tier at the end of 2016/17.

The Women's Super League (WSL) has been the top-flight in English football since 2011.

In 2014 it became WSL1 and a second tier – WSL2 – was introduced.

What is now the third tier of English football sees 12 clubs compete in the Women's Premier League (WPL) Southern division and 12 in the WPL Northern division. The winners of each division then meet in a play-off for the right to be promoted to WSL2, although they also have to fulfil off-field criteria to secure a WSL licence.

Level	League(s)/Division(s)							
1	FA WSL1 (10 clubs)							
2	FA WSL2 (10 clubs)							
3	FA Women's Premier League Northern Division WPL (12 clubs)				FA Women's Premier League Southern Division (12 clubs)			
4	WPL Northern Division 1 (12 clubs)		WPL Midlands Division 1 (12 clubs)		WPL South West Division 1 (11 clubs)		WPL South East Division 1 (12 clubs)	
5	North West Regional League Premier Div	North East Regional League Premier Div	West Midlands Regional League Premier Div	East Midlands Regional League Premier Div	Southern Region League Premier Div	South West Regional League Premier Div	Eastern Region League Premier Div	London & South East Regional League Premier Div

This is how to find specific team profiles over the next pages of the book.

2017/18 WSL1 teams: 10 teams, grouped in one section, listed alphabetically.

2017/18 WSL2 teams: 10 teams, grouped in one section, listed alphabetically.

2017/18 WPL teams: 77 teams, grouped in one section, listed alphabetically. This consists of the 71 teams competing in tiers three and four, the five teams who were relegated to tier five at the end of 2016/17, and Shanklin who withdrew.

WSL1

This section of the Yearbook details the 10 teams competing in WSL1 in 2017/18.

It lists their WSL results from the last full season (2016), and from the WSL Spring Series, as well as those from the 2015/16 and 2016/17 FA Cup competitions, the 2016 WSL Continental Cup, and where applicable the 2015/16 and 2016/17 Champions League seasons.

1 ARSENAL

2 BIRMINGHAM CITY

3 BRISTOL CITY

4 CHELSEA

5 EVERTON

6 LIVERPOOL

7 MANCHESTER CITY

8 READING

9 SUNDERLAND

10 YEOVIL TOWN

KEY:

RP = Preliminary Round

R1 = 1st Round

QF = Quarter-final

SF = Semi-final

F = Final

(aet) = after extra-time

(W 4-2p) = won 4-2 on penalties after extra-time

ARSENAL – WSL1

Founded: 1987	**Previous WSL Positions**
Stadium: Meadow Park, (Boreham Wood FC)	**2017 WSL1:** 3rd (Spring Series)
National Honours: FA Cup Winners: (14) 1993, 95, 98, 99, 2001, 04, 06, 07, 08, 09, 11, 13, 14, 16 **FA Cup Runners-up: (1)** 2010	**2016 WSL1:** 3rd **2015 WSL1:** 3rd **2014 WSL1:** 4th
WSL Champions: (2) 2011, 2012	**2013 WSL:** 3rd
WSL Continental Cup: (4) 2011, 12, 13, 15	**2012 WSL:** 1st
WSL Continental Cup Runners-up: (1) 2014	**2011 WSL:** 1st
UEFA Women's Cup Winners: 2007	**Nickname:** The Gunners
WPL (former top division) Champions: (12)	**Manager:** Pedro Martinez Losa (Aug 2014)
1993, 95, 97, 2001, 02, 04, 05, 06, 07, 08, 09, 10	
WPL Cup Winners: (10)	
1992, 93, 94, 98, 99, 00, 01, 05, 07, 09	
WPL Cup Runners-up: (3) 2003, 06, 08	

- Arsenal legend Kelly Smith is England Women's all-time record goalscorer, with 46 goals in 117 appearances for her country. Smith retired, aged 38, in January 2017.
- The Gunners have won the Women's FA Cup more times than any other club (14).
- Arsenal reached the first five finals of the WSL Continental Cup – introduced in 2011 – winning four of them.
- Manager Pedro Martinez Losa spent almost five years as head coach of Rayo Vallecano Femenino in Spain, leading them to their first ever major trophy, the Spanish Cup, in 2008.

SEASON 2016 RECORD

2016 WSL1:	3rd	P16	W10	D2	L4	F33	A14	GD+19	Pts32
2016 FA Cup:	Winners								
2016 Continental Cup:	Semi-finals								

SEASON 2017 RECORD

2017 WSL1 Spring Series:	3rd	P8	W5	D3	L0	F22	A9	GD+13	Pts18
2017 FA Cup:	Quarter-finals								

Alex Scott **Born:** 14.10.1984 London **Position:** Defender

Going into the 2017/18 season, Alex Scott still remains the only British player ever to have scored a goal in a Champions League final.

'It's a nice stat to have,' she says, 'but I'd sooner someone matches it and a British team wins it again – hopefully us. That would be nice. It is a great memory though. I'll never forget it.'

Scott's goal was a stunner. She was just 22 when she drilled home an injury-time winner from 25 yards as Arsenal beat Swedish side Umea 1-0 in the first leg of what was then known as the UEFA Cup final in the Gammliavallen Stadium. The second leg in Borehamwood finished goalless and Arsenal became the first – and so far only – British winners of the most prestigious prize in European club football.

'The 2006/07 season is the highlight of my career so far. To win the Quadruple (League, FA Cup, League Cup and Champions League) with Arsenal was amazing,' she says.

Scott's role models when she was growing up were in the men's game. 'I didn't even know there was women's football when I was a kid. I used to love Ian Wright at Arsenal because he played with such passion and always had a smile on his face. I used to play when I was six or seven in the East End with my brother and all the boys in the neighbourhood,' she says. 'We entered a local tournament in Tower Hamlets. The ref there knew someone down at Arsenal Ladies and told me that I should go along. I think it's great now that the current women's players are role models to boys and girls. I think it is so important that young boys and girls see football from an early age because then they just accept that it is normal for girls to play.'

Scott has six League titles, seven FA Cups and the Champions League to her name and has played in three World Cups for England. 'The reception we got after coming home from Canada having finished third in 2015 was just sensational,' she says.

'During the tournament our football did the talking. As we went deeper into the tournament we could just feel the public back home rooting for us. We are now playing in front of bigger crowds and that feels good. I remember coming home from the 2007 World Cup when we had reached the quarter-finals and played in front of big crowds in China, and then we were playing League games in front of two men and a dog. It's not like that any more, the public have really started to take an interest in women's football.

'My advice to any young player would be to always enjoy it and always believe in yourself. I had so many people tell me I wouldn't make it, but I kept faith in myself and my career has been an amazing adventure. I've loved every minute of it.'

Arsenal	2016 WSL1 Results		
23.03.16	Reading (h)	W 3-1	Janssen 33, 46, Carter 68
28.03.16	Manchester City (a)	L 0-2	*Rose sent off 13*
21.04.16	Chelsea (h)	L 0-2	
27.04.16	Reading (a)	W 2-1	Nobbs 30, Janssen 59
01.05.16	Birmingham City (h)	D 0-0	
25.06.16	Sunderland (h)	W 5-1	Pablos Sanchon 29, 39, Janssen 78, Bannon (og 2, og 20)
29.06.16	Birmingham City (a)	D 0-0	
10.07.16	Notts County (h)	W 2-0	Van de Donk 10, Nobbs 56
17.07.16	Chelsea (a)	W 2-1	Losada 44, Van de Donk 83
24.07.16	Sunderland (a)	W 4-0	Losada 10, Nobbs 24, Carter 47, Williams 53
31.07.16	Liverpool (h)	L 1-2	Williams 9
28.08.16	Notts County (a)	W 2-0	Oshoala 46, Van de Donk 69, Byrne sent off 62
11.09.16	Manchester City (h)	L 0-1	
06.10.16	Doncaster Rovers Belles (a)	W 5-0	Carter 13, 87, Pablos Sanchon 67, 84, Smith 90
30.10.16	Doncaster Rovers Belles (h)	W 2-0	Taylor 65, 72
06.11.16	Liverpool (a)	W 5-3	Carter 24, 27, Nobbs 57, Kelly 80, Oshoala 90+4

Arsenal	2016 FA Cup		
20.03.16 R5	Birmingham City (a)	D 1-1 (W 5-3p)	Carter 79
03.04.16 QF	Notts County (h)	D 2-2 (W 4-3p)	Smith 21, Pablos Sanchon 75
17.04.16 SF	Sunderland (h)	W 7-0	Van de Donk 39, 78, 85, Carter 55, 90+2, Williams 74, Nobbs 82, Mitchell sent off 33
14.05.16 F	Chelsea (at Wembley)	W 1-0	Carter 18

Arsenal	2016 Continental Cup		
02.07.16 R1	Reading (a)	W 3-1	Losada 47, Williams 48, 63
05.08.16 QF	Notts County (h)*	W 3-2	Stoney 9, Smith 82, Williams 90
04.09.16 SF	Manchester City (a)	L 0-1	

*Played at The Hive, Barnet men's

ARSENAL PLAYER APPEARANCES & GOALS 2016

				WSL1		FAC		CC		Total	
				A	G	A	G	A	G	A	G
Byrne, Emma	G	IRL	14.06.79	1	-	-	-	3	-	4	-
Carter, Danielle	F	ENG	18.05.93	13	6	3	3	2	-	18	9
Corredera, Marta	F	ESP	08.08.91	11	-	1	-	2	-	14	2
Dean, Rianna	M	ENG	21.10.98	-	-	-	-	-	-	-	-
Devlin, Charlotte	M	ENG	23.02.98	-	-	-	-	-	-	-	-
Henning, Josephine	D	GER	08.09.89	10	-	-	-	2	-	12	-
Hinds, Taylor	M	ENG	25.04.99	-	-	-	-	-	-	-	-
Janssen, Dominique	M	NED	17.01.95	15	4	3	-	3	-	21	4
Kelly, Chloe	F	ENG	05.01.98	4	1	-	-	-	-	4	1
Losada, Victoria	M	ESP	05.03.91	13	2	3	-	3	1	19	3
McCabe, Katie	F	IRL	01.09.95	10	-	2	-	1	-	13	-
Mitchell, Emma	D	SCO	19.09.92	13	-	2	-	2	-	17	-
Nobbs, Jordan	M	ENG	08.12.92	14	4	3	1	3	-	20	5
Oshoala, Asisat	F	NGA	09.10.94	13	2	1	-	2	-	16	2
Pablos Sanchon, Natalia	F	ESP	15.10.85	11	4	3	1	3	-	17	5
Rogers, Sian	G	ENG	28.06.98	-	-	-	-	-	-	-	-
Rose, Jemma	D	ENG	19.01.92	10	-	2	-	2	-	14	-
Sampson, Vyan	D	ENG	02.07.96	-	-	-	-	-	-	-	-
Scott, Alex	D	ENG	14.10.84	14	-	2	-	3	-	19	-
Smith, Kelly	F	ENG	29.10.78	4	1	3	1	3	1	10	3
Stoney, Casey	D	ENG	13.05.82	12	-	3	-	3	1	18	1
Taylor, Jodie	F	ENG	17.05.86	2	2	-	-	-	-	2	2
Van de Donk, Danielle	M	NED	05.08.91	15	3	2	3	3	-	20	6
Van Veenendaal, Sari	G	NED	03.04.90	16	-	3	-	-	-	19	-
Williams, Fara	M	ENG	25.01.84	15	2	3	1	2	3	20	6
Williamson, Leah	M	ENG	29.03.97	8	-	3	-	-	-	11	-
Wubben-Moy, Lotte	D	ENG	11.01.99	1	-	-	-	-	-	1	-

GOALSCORERS 2016

WSL1: Carter (6), Janssen (4), Nobbs (4), Pablos Sanchon (4), Van de Donk (3), Losada (2), Oshoala (2), Taylor (2), Williams (2), own goals (2), Kelly (1), Smith (1)

FAC: Van de Donk (3), Nobbs (1), Pablos Sanchon (1), Smith (1), Williams (1)

CC: Williams (3), Losada (1), Smith (1), Stoney (1)

Total: Carter (6), Van de Donk (6), Williams (6), Nobbs (5), Pablos Sanchon (5), Janssen (4), Losada (3), Smith (3), Taylor (1), Oshoala (2), own goals (2), Kelly (1), Stoney (1)

Arsenal	2017 WSL1 Spring Series		
30.04.17	Sunderland (a)	D 0-0	
04.05.17	Liverpool (h)	D 4-4	Kelly 36, Carter 54, 59, Nobbs 80
07.05.17	Yeovil Town (a)	W 5-1	Taylor (pen) 7, 24, Clark (og) 8, Carter 31, O'Reilly (pen) 53,
17.05.17	Chelsea (a)	D 2-2	Taylor 34, Nobbs 90+5
20.05.17	Birmingham City (h)	W 4-2	O'Reilly 43, Van de Donk 55, Quinn 78, 90
28.05.17	Manchester City (a)	W 1-0	Nobbs 75
31.05.17	Reading (h)	W 1-0	Carter 39
03.06.17	Bristol City (a)	W 5-0	Quinn 27, Nobbs 49, Kelly 73, Van de Donk 78, Mead 83

Arsenal	2017 FA Cup		
19.03.16 R5	Tottenham Hotspur (h)	W 10-0	Carter 22, 30, Janssen 29, Little 38, Van de Donk 43, 59, 84, Kelly 65, Mead 69, McCabe 77
26.03.16 QF	Birmingham City (a)	L 0-1	

ARSENAL PLAYER APPEARANCES & GOALS 2017

				WSL1 SS		FAC		Total	
				A	G	A	G	A	G
Carter, Danielle	F	ENG	18.05.93	7	4	2	2	9	6
Humphrey, Carla	M	ENG	15.12.96	2	-	-	-	2	-
Janssen, Dominique	M	NED	17.01.95	7	-	2	1	9	1
Kelly, Chloe	F	ENG	05.01.98	7	2	2	1	9	3
Little, Kim	F	SCO	29.06.90	-	-	2	1	2	1
McCabe, Katie	F	IRL	01.09.95	3	-	2	1	5	1
Mead, Beth	F	ENG	09.05.95	5	1	2	1	7	2
Moorhouse, Anna	G	ENG	30.03.95	1	-	-	-	1	-
Nobbs, Jordan	M	ENG	08.12.92	8	4	2	-	10	4
O'Reilly, Heather	M	USA	02.01.85	8	2	2	-	10	2
Patten, Anna	D	ENG	20.04.99	8	-	1	-	9	-
Quinn, Louise	D	IRL	17.06.90	5	3	-	-	5	3
Rose, Jemma	D	ENG	19.01.92	-	-	-	-	-	-
Scott, Alex	D	ENG	14.10.84	6	-	-	-	6	-
Taylor, Jodie	F	ENG	17.05.86	7	3	2	-	9	3
Van de Donk, Danielle	M	NED	05.08.91	8	2	2	3	10	5
Van Veenendaal, Sari	G	NED	03.04.90	7	-	2	-	9	-
Williams, Fara	M	ENG	25.01.84	7	-	2	-	9	-
Williamson, Leah	M	ENG	29.03.97	7	-	2	-	9	-
Wubben-Moy, Lotte	D	ENG	11.01.99	8	-	-	-	8	-

GOALSCORERS 2017

W**SL1 SS:** Carter (4), Nobbs (4), Quinn (3), Taylor (3), Kelly (2), O'Reilly (2), Van de Donk (2), Mead (1), own goals (1)

FAC: Van de Donk (3), Carter (2), Janssen (1), Kelly (1), Little (1), McCabe (1), Mead (1)

Total: Carter (6), Van de Donk (5), Nobbs (4) Kelly (3), Quinn (3), Taylor (3), Mead (2), O'Reilly (2), Janssen (1), Little (1), McCabe (1), own goals (1)

BIRMINGHAM CITY – WSL1

Founded: 1968	**Previous WSL Positions**
Stadium: Damson Park	**2017 WSL1:** 7th (Spring Series)
National Honours: FA Cup Runners-up: (1)	**2016 WSL1:** 4th
WSL Runners-up: (2) 2011, 12	**2015 WSL1:** 6th
WSL Continental Cup Runners-up: (3) 2011, 12, 16	**2014 WSL1:** 3rd
Nickname: The Blues	**2013 WSL:** 4th
Manager: Marc Skinner (since Dec 2016)	**2012 WSL:** 2nd
	2011 WSL: 2nd

- In 2016 Birmingham became only the second team (after Arsenal) to reach the Continental Cup final for a third time. Unfortunately for them, they have lost all three. They were beaten 1-0 after extra-time by Manchester City, to add to their 4-1 and 1-0 losses to the Gunners in 2011 and 2012 respectively.
- Defender Laura Bassett was the first player to come through the Birmingham City Academy to go on to play for England at senior level.
- Birmingham City have twice played in the Champions League. In 2012 they were knocked out at the first hurdle by Italian side Bardolino Verona, while two years later they made it all the way to the semi-finals where they fell to Swedish side Tyreso.
- Two years after their formation in 1968, Birmingham City joined the Heart of England League. They were Champions in 1971/72 and then won the League that replaced it – the West Midland Regional League – four times in 1974/75, 1976/77, 1987/88, and 1988/89. They were among the founding members of the WSL in 2011.

SEASON 2016 RECORD

2016 WSL1:	4th	P16	W7	D6	L3	F18	A13	GD+5	Pts27
2016 FA Cup:	5th Round								
2016 Continental Cup:	Runners-Up								

SEASON 2017 RECORD

2017 WSL1 Spring Series:	7th	P8	W1	D4	L3	F6	A10	GD-4	Pts7
2017 FA Cup:	Runners-Up								

Jess Carter **Born:** 27.10.1997 Warwick **Position:** Midfielder

'My friend saw that Birmingham had open trials on. We just thought we'd go for a kick-about. We didn't have footballs and we wanted a game. Neither of us thought it would be anything serious…'

Jess Carter may not have intended for a fun kick-about with a friend to lead to a flourishing professional football career, but it has. 'That was when I was about 15, playing at grassroots level back then,' Carter explains. 'Then, the next thing I knew, I'd got in! Thankfully, things grew from there.'

Carter would go on to make her senior debut for Birmingham City at the age of just 16, in the Champions League against Arsenal. Since then, she has become arguably the most consistent teenager in the WSL, playing with a maturity far beyond her 19 years, in the midfield anchor role.

Her displays earned her recognition from her peers across the country in 2017 when she was voted as the PFA Young Player of the Year. 'I didn't expect it so it came as a shock. It was so exciting,' Carter says of the prestigious award. 'I'd never been to the PFA awards before so it was the first time I'd been in that room surrounded by so many talented players. I think it came because I'm really enjoying my football at the moment, and the reason I've enjoyed it is because we've got a great team environment at Birmingham.'

That spirit showed in 2017 as the Blues enjoyed a fine FA Cup run, beating neighbours West Bromwich Albion, then stunning holders Arsenal, and then overcoming much-fancied Chelsea on penalties in the semi-finals to earn a place in the final at Wembley, where they lost to Manchester City. Despite a 4-1 defeat at football's spiritual home, Carter knows she and her teammates can benefit from the experience of playing under the famous arch.

'We have a lot of youngsters, so no one ever expected us to get there, and maybe we didn't either, but it was an incredible learning curve,' Carter adds. 'We've got good enough players to go again. I'd never even been to Wembley stadium before, let alone played there. Putting the Birmingham shirt on there, representing my club at the home of football, was amazing. We wanted a different result, but it's a day none of us will ever forget.'

Having been honoured with a first senior call-up to Mark Sampson's England squad, for two international friendlies in April 2017, Carter remains grateful to those who helped her at the beginning, at Warwick Juniors, aged seven. 'I played mixed football until I was around 12, when you couldn't play with boys anymore. Then my manager Dean Brandrick created a girls' team. We only had about eight players to start with. If he hadn't have done, I wouldn't be involved in football now. Dean noticed that I had a talent for football. If it wasn't for him, I would have just stopped playing football. I am so grateful to him.'

With Carter now tipped to shine at senior level for England in the future, Blues and Lionesses fans could have reason to be grateful to Brandrick too.

Birmingham City	2016 WSL1 Results		
23.03.16	Liverpool (a)	L 0-1	
24.04.16	Manchester City (h)	L 0-2	
27.04.16	Doncaster Rovers Belles (h)	W 2-1	Ayisi 15, Lawley 30
01.05.16	Arsenal (a)	D 0-0	
08.05.16	Notts County (a)	W 1-0	Westwood 69
19.05.16	Reading (h)	D 0-0	
22.05.16	Notts County (h)	W 1-0	Allen 51
29.06.16	Arsenal (h)	D 0-0	
10.07.16	Chelsea (a)	D 1-1	Ayisi 48
17.07.16	Sunderland (h)	W 1-0	Wellings 88
24.07.16	Reading (a)	D 1-1	Linden 74
30.07.16	Doncaster Rovers Belles (a)	W 1-0	Linnett 61
28.08.16	Chelsea (h)	L 0-4	
25.09.16	Liverpool (h)	W 2-1	Schroder 50, Harrop 70
30.10.16	Manchester City (a)	D 1-1	Mannion 6
06.11.16	Sunderland (a)	W 7-1	Harrop 35, Linnett 36, 50, 57, Wellings 45+2, Ayisi 69, Haines 77

Birmingham City	2016 FA Cup		
20.03.16 R5	Arsenal (h)	D 1-1 (L3-5p)	Ayisi 26

Birmingham City	2016 Continental Cup		
03.07.16 R1	Oxford United (a)	W 2-0	Hegerberg (pen) 35, Lawley 83
07.08.16 QF	Liverpool (h)	W 1-0 (aet)	Haines 120+1
03.09.16 SF	London Bees (a)	W 4-0	Linnett 26, Harrop 54, Wellings 83, Davies (og) 89
02.10.16 F	Manchester City (n)*	L 0-1 (aet)	

*Played at Academy Stadium, Manchester

BIRMINGHAM CITY PLAYER APPEARANCES & GOALS 2016

				WSL1		FAC		CC		Total	
				A	G	A	G	A	G	A	G
Allen, Remi	M	ENG	15.10.90	6	1	-	-	-	-	6	1
Ayisi, Freda	F	ENG	21.10.94	15	3	1	1	4	-	20	4
Baggaley, Sophie	G	ENG	29.11.96	10	-	1	-	1	-	12	-
Berger, Ann-Katrin	G	GER	09.10.90	6	-	-	-	3	-	9	-
Brazil, Ellie	F	ENG	10.01.99	3	-	-	-	1	-	4	-
Brown, Ashlee	D	ENG	04.08.96	-	-	-	-	-	-	-	-
Carter, Jessica	D	ENG	27.10.97	16	-	1	-	4	-	21	-
Davies, Keeley	F	ENG	01.07.99	1	-	-	-	-	-	1	-
Edwards, Cheryl	F	ENG	03.12.98	1	-	-	-	-	-	1	-
Ewers, Marisa	D	GER	24.02.89	4	-	-	-	1	-	5	-
Haines, Coral-Jade	M	ENG	21.06.96	3	1	1	-	3	1	7	2
Harrop, Kerys	D	ENG	03.12.90	16	2	1	-	4	1	21	3
Hegerberg, Andrine	M	NOR	06.06.93	8	-	-	-	4	1	12	1
Johnson, Sian	D	ENG	25.01.98	-	-	-	-	-	-	-	-
Lawley, Melissa	F	ENG	28.04.94	15	1	1	-	4	1	20	2
Linden, Anna Isabelle	M	GER	15.01.91	4	1	-	-	3	-	7	1
Linnett, Kirsty	F	ENG	24.09.93	6	4	1	-	3	1	10	5
Mannion, Aoife	D	ENG	24.09.95	14	1	1	-	4	-	19	1
Moore, Jade	M	ENG	22.10.90	6	-	-	-	-	-	6	-
Peplow, Chloe	M	ENG	03.12.98	14	-	1	-	3	-	18	-
Potter, Josanne	M	ENG	13.11.84	7	-	1	-	-	-	8	-
Sargeant, Meaghan	D	ENG	16.03.94	4	-	1	-	1	-	6	-
Scofield, Constance	M	ENG	26.05.99	2	-	-	-	1	-	3	-
Schroder, Corina	D	GER	15.08.86	2	1	-	-	-	-	2	1
Stringer, Abbey-Leigh	M	ENG	17.05.95	14	-	1	-	3	-	18	-
Wellings, Charlie	F	ENG	18.05.98	14	2	1	-	4	1	19	3
Westwood, Emily	M	ENG	05.04.84	12	1	-	-	4	-	16	1
Windell, Alexandra	M	ENG	18.09.90	8	-	1	-	1	-	10	-

GOALSCORERS 2016

WSL1: Linnett (4), Ayisi (3), Harrop (2), Wellings (2), Allen (1), Haines (1), Lawley (1), Linden (1), Mannion (1), Schroder (1), Westwood (1)

FAC: Ayisi (1)

CC: Haines (1), Harrop (1), Hegerberg (1), Lawley (1), Linnett (1), Wellings (1), own goals (1)

Total: Linnett (5), Ayisi (4), Harrop (3), Wellings (3), Haines (2), Lawley (2), Allen (1), Hegerberg (1), Linden (1) Mannion (1), Schroder (1), Westwood (1), own goals (1)

Birmingham City	2017 WSL1 Spring Series		
23.04.17	Sunderland (h)	D 0-0	
03.05.17	Manchester City (a)	D 1-1	Westwood 14
07.05.17	Liverpool (h)	L 0-2	
17.05.17	Bristol City (h)	W 2-0	White 39, 45
20.05.17	Arsenal (a)	L 2-4	R.Williams 1, 58
28.05.17	Reading (a)	D 1-1	Wellings 1
31.05.17	Yeovil Town (h)	D 0-0	
03.06.17	Chelsea (h)	L 0-2	

Birmingham City	2017 FA Cup		
19.03.17 R5	West Bromwich Albion (h)	W 2-0	Carter 43, White 60
26.03.17 QF	Arsenal (h)	W 1-0	Ewers 77
17.04.17 SF	Chelsea (h)	D 1-1 (W 4-2p)	Sargeant 64
13.05.17 F	Manchester City (n)*	L 1-4	Wellings 73

*Played at Wembley Stadium

BIRMINGHAM CITY PLAYER APPEARANCES & GOALS 2017

				WSL1		FAC		Total	
				A	G	A	G	A	G
Ayisi, Freda	F	ENG	21.10.94	6	-	4	1	10	1
Baggaley, Sophie	G	ENG	29.11.96	3	-	1	-	4	-
Berger, Ann-Katrin	G	GER	09.10.90	5	-	3	-	8	-
Brazil, Ellie	F	ENG	10.01.99	6	-	3	-	9	-
Carter, Jessica	D	ENG	27.10.97	7	-	4	1	11	1
Ewers, Marisa	D	GER	24.02.89	4	-	2	-	6	-
Haines, Coral-Jade	M	ENG	21.06.96	4	-	1	-	5	-
Hampton, Hannah	G	ENG	16.11.00	-	-	-	-	-	-
Harrop, Kerys	D	ENG	03.12.90	7	-	4	-	11	-
Hegerberg, Andrine	M	NOR	06.06.93	7	-	1	-	8	-
Johnson, Sian	D	ENG	25.01.98	-	-	-	-	-	-
Lawley, Melissa	F	ENG	28.04.94	-	-	1	-	1	-
Linnett, Kirsty	F	ENG	24.09.93	-	-	1	-	1	-
Mannion, Aoife	D	ENG	24.09.95	8	-	4	-	12	-
Mayling, Sarah	M	ENG	20.03.97	7	-	3	-	10	-
Peplow, Chloe	M	ENG	03.12.98	3	-	3	-	6	-
Potter, Josanne	M	ENG	13.11.84	-	-	1	-	1	-
Sargeant, Meaghan	D	ENG	16.03.94	7	-	4	1	11	1
Scofield, Constance	M	ENG	26.05.99	-	-	-	-	-	-
Stringer, Abbey-Leigh	M	ENG	17.05.95	7	-	4	-	11	-
Wellings, Charlie	F	ENG	18.05.98	7	1	3	1	10	2
Westwood, Emily	M	ENG	05.04.84	6	1	2	-	8	1
White, Ellen	F	ENG	09.05.89	4	2	3	1	7	3
Williams, Paige	D	ENG	10.03.95	8	-	3	-	11	-
Williams, Rachel	F	ENG	10.01.88	5	2	-	-	5	2
Windell, Alex	M	ENG	18.09.90	-	-	1	-	1	-

GOALSCORERS 2017

WSL1 SS: White (2), R.Williams (2), Wellings (1), Westwood (1)

FAC: Ayisi (1), Carter (1), Sargeant (1), Wellings (1), White (1)

Total: White (3), Wellings (2), R.Williams (2), Ayisi (1), Carter (1), Sargeant (1), Westwood (1)

BRISTOL CITY – WSL1

Founded: 1998 (as Bristol Rovers Women's)	**Previous WSL Positions**
Stadium: Stoke Gifford Stadium	**2017 WSL1:** 8th (Spring Series)
National Honours: FA Cup Runners-up: (2) 2011, 2013	**2016 WSL2:** 2nd (Promoted)
WSL Runners-up: (1) 2013	**2015 WSL1:** 8th (Relegated)
WSL2 Runners-up: (1) 2016	**2014 WSL1:** 7th
Nickname: The Vixens	**2013 WSL:** 2nd
Manager: Willie Kirk (since April 2015)	**2012 WSL:** 4th
	2011 WSL: 5th

- The club's all-time leading goalscorer is Spanish striker Natalia who hit 22 goals in 37 matches between 2011 and 2013. She left the club in 2016.
- Current England Women's boss Mark Sampson managed the club – then known as Bristol Academy – prior to taking the national team job in December 2013. He led the Vixens to two FA Cup finals and qualification for the 2011/12 and 2014/15 Champions League. In 2013 he achieved their highest League finish of second in the WSL.
- The Vixens beat Barcelona in the last 16 of the 2014/15 Champions League campaign before being knocked out by eventual tournament winners Frankfurt in the quarter-finals.
- The club are now affiliated with men's Championship outfit Bristol City. However, when they were founded in 1998, following a merger with Welsh side Cable-Tel, they were called Bristol Rovers Women's. In 2005/06 the name was changed to Bristol Academy, with the current name of Bristol City Women's being adopted for the 2016 season.

SEASON 2016 RECORD

2016 WSL2:	2nd (Promoted)	P18	W12	D3	L3	F37	A16	GD+21	Pts39
2016 FA Cup:	4th Round								
2016 Continental Cup:	1st Round								

SEASON 2017 RECORD

2017 WSL1 Spring Series:	8th	P8	W1	D1	L6	F5	A21	GD-16	Pts4
2017 FA Cup:	Quarter-final								

Jas Matthews **Born:** 24.03.1993 Truro **Position:** Defender or midfielder

A 0-0 draw away at Birmingham City on 29 April 2015 was not a match which many fans will have reason to remember, but it is one that is very hard for Bristol City's Jas Matthews to forget. That's because it was the night she suffered a ruptured Achilles.

'It was the last kick of the game and I simply went to clear the ball, but I just went down. I heard a loud smash and I thought someone had smacked me from behind. But no one had touched me,' she says. 'I went to A & E the next morning and it was my Achilles. I had to have two operations. It was horrendous. It was horrible.'

After more than two years of hard work and rehabilitation, versatile former England youth international defender Matthews is finally back to full fitness. 'At one point, I just wanted to give up football, it was so hard,' she admits. 'My teammates helped a lot, because they supported me, but it also didn't help, because on a game-day, they were all buzzing, getting ready to play, and I'd just be sat in my room, annoyed.'

The fateful moment had come in head coach Willie Kirk's first game in charge of the Vixens, one day on from his appointment, meaning that he did not see her play much football before the lengthy lay-off began. 'I've got to be thankful to Willie for sticking by me,' says Matthews. 'His support has meant a lot, because he had only just arrived.'

Now, while working hard on the training ground to try and revive her promising career as soon as possible, Matthews is also having to work part-time in a supermarket, a difficult reminder that – even in the top division – not every female player can rely solely on football to make a living. 'Training every day is a dream come true, but I also work 15 hours per week in Aldi,' she says. 'I've worked there for five years. I've managed to reduce my weekly hours there in the past two years, to do more football instead, so hopefully next year I can get to a stage when I can just train.'

Despite the unwelcome injury interruptions, Matthews has already enjoyed many highs in her fledgling career, including helping City knock Barcelona out of the Champions League in 2014/15. 'Beating Barcelona in a European tie is probably my career highlight so far,' she says. 'When we played them at home at Ashton Gate, the atmosphere was amazing.'

And while the Vixens may not currently be competing on the European stage, Matthews feels the club are on an upward curve following their promotion back to WSL1 ahead of 2017/18. 'Our new general manager – Kathryn Pacey – is putting things in place which are going to make the club a better environment for everybody. Willie wants to play enjoyable football and I think you can tell, because we are impressing a lot of clubs. When I first came to the club, we were only training on Tuesday and Thursday evenings, whereas now we do something every day, so things are going in the right direction.'

Bristol City	2016 WSL2 Results		
23.03.16	Yeovil Town (h)	W 3-2	Ayane 29, 52, Farrow 38
26.03.16	Sheffield FC (h)	D 0-0	
24.04.16	London Bees (a)	W 3-0	Arthur 66, Sawyer 71, Fergusson 75
28.04.16	Aston Villa (h)	W 2-0	Farrow 30, (pen) 48
01.05.16	Watford (a)	W 2-0	Ayane 7, Fergusson 30
19.05.16	Yeovil Town (a)	L 0-2	
22.05.16	Sheffield FC (a)	L 1-3	Ayane 34
25.06.16	Oxford United (h)	W 4-1	Farrow 17, 45, Emslie 28, 41
28.06.16	Aston Villa (a)	D 2-2	Brett 75, Estcourt 85
09.07.16	Millwall Lionesses (h)	W 2-1	Farrow 41, Emslie 58
17.07.16	Durham (a)	D 0-0	
23.07.16	London Bees (h)	W 3-0	Brett 6, Cooper (og) 11, Estcourt 78
30.07.16	Millwall Lionesses (a)	W 2-1	Emslie 10, 67
27.08.16	Everton (h)	L 0-1	
10.09.16	Watford (h)	W 4-1	Emslie 4, Arthur 22, Hemp 68, Ladd 90
24.09.16	Durham (h)	W 1-0	Fergusson 17
29.10.16	Everton (a)	W 3-2	Emslie 26, 69, Farrow 51
06.11.16	Oxford United (a)	W 5-0	Emslie 12, 31, E.Wilson 29, Farrow 45, 82

Bristol City	2016 FA Cup		
07.02.16 R3	QPR (h)	W 7-1	Farrow 1, 87, Yorston 3, Arthur 13, Brett 50, McCatty 81, Pinto 90
28.02.16 R4	Yeovil Town (h)	D 0-0 (L 2-3p)	

Bristol City	2016 Continental Cup		
02.07.16 R1	Sheffield FC (a)	L 0-2	

BRISTOL CITY PLAYER APPEARANCES & GOALS 2016

				WSL2		FAC		CC		Total	
				A	G	A	G	A	G	A	G
Alexander, Megan	D	ENG	11.11.93	16	-	2	-	1	-	19	-
Allen, Florence	D	ENG	13.08.99	11	-	-	-	1	-	12	-
Arthur, Chloe	M	SCO	21.01.95	18	2	1	1	1	-	20	3
Ayane, Rosella	F	ENG	16.03.96	7	4	1	-	-	-	8	4
Brett, Jodie	M	ENG	09.03.96	17	2	2	1	1	-	20	3
Brown, Frankie	D	SCO	08.10.87	6	-	2	-	1	-	9	-
Cleverly, Rhian	D	WAL	11.01.95	1	-	-	-	1	-	2	-
Dykes, Loren	D	WAL	05.02.88	11	-	2	-	-	-	13	-
Emslie, Claire	F	SCO	08.03.94	11	10	-	-	1	-	12	10
Estcourt, Charlie	M	WAL	27.05.98	9	2	-	-	1	-	10	2
Evans, Georgia	M	WAL	16.10.95	17	-	2	-	1	-	20	-
Farrow, Millie	F	ENG	03.06.96	13	9	2	2	1	-	16	11
Fergusson, Olivia	F	ENG	27.03.95	16	3	1	-	-	-	17	3
Hemp, Lauren	F	ENG	07.08.00	2	1	-	-	-	-	2	1
Jones, Katie	D	ENG	13.08.98	4	-	-	-	1	-	5	-
Ladd, Hayley	M	WAL	06.10.93	13	1	2	-	-	-	15	1
Leach, Caitlin	G	ENG	16.11.96	15	-	-	-	-	-	15	-
McCatty, Grace	D	ENG	28.09.89	15	-	2	1	-	-	17	1
Pinto, Tatiana Ferreira	M	POR	28.03.94	7	-	2	1	-	-	9	1
Randall, Estelle	G	ENG	20.08.97	-	-	-	-	-	-	-	-
Reid, Hannah	G	SCO	20.08.94	3	-	2	-	1	-	6	-
Sawyer, Paige	F	ENG	15.04.99	9	1	2	-	1	-	12	1
Syme, Emily	M	ENG	23.07.00	3	-	-	-	-	-	3	-
Tustin, Emma	M	ENG	29.03.98	-	-	-	-	-	-	-	-
Wilson, Eloise	D	ENG	11.05.97	12	1	1	-	-	-	13	1
Wilson, Poppy	M	ENG	06.08.99	4	-	-	-	1	-	5	-
Woodham, Lily	M	WAL	03.09.00	2	-	-	-	-	-	2	-
Yorston, Corinne	D	ENG	15.06.83	3	-	2	1	-	-	5	1

GOALSCORERS 2016

WSL2: Emslie (10), Farrow (9), Ayane (4), Fergusson (3), Arthur (2), Brett (2), Estcourt (2), Hemp (1), Ladd (1), Sawyer (1), E.Wilson (1), own goals (1)

FAC: Farrow (2), Arthur (1), Brett (1), McCatty (1), Pinto (1), Yorston (1)

CC: None

Total: Farrow (11), Emslie (10), Ayane (4), Arthur (3), Brett (3), Fergusson (3), Estcourt (2), Hemp (1), Ladd (1), McCatty (1), Pinto (1), Sawyer (1), E.Wilson (1), Yorston (1), own goals (1)

Bristol City	2017 WSL1 Spring Series		
22.04.17	Reading (h)	L 1-3	Hemp 73
03.05.17	Yeovil Town (a)	W 3-2	Emslie (pen) 5, Arthur 73, Cousins (og) 87
06.05.17	Sunderland (a)	L 0-1	
09.05.17	Manchester City (h)	L 0-3	
17.05.17	Birmingham City (a)	L 0-2	
20.05.17	Liverpool (h)	D 1-1	Agg 85
31.05.17	Chelsea (h)	L 0-4	
03.06.17	Arsenal (h)	L 0-5	

Bristol City	2017 FA Cup		
19.03.17 R5	Millwall Lionesses (h)	W 5-0	Turner 6, 19, Hemp 17, 69, Brett 75
26.03.17 QF	Manchester City (h)	L 1-2	Emslie 45

BRISTOL CITY PLAYER APPEARANCES & GOALS 2017

				WSL		FAC		Total	
				A	G	A	G	A	G
Agg, Lily	M	WAL	17.12.93	3	1	2	-	5	1
Alexander, Megan	D	ENG	11.11.93	6	-	2	-	8	-
Allen, Florence	D	ENG	13.08.99	5	-	-	-	5	-
Arthur, Chloe	M	SCO	21.01.95	8	1	2	-	10	1
Brett, Jodie	M	ENG	09.03.96	8	-	2	1	10	1
Brown, Frankie	D	SCO	08.10.87	5	-	2	-	7	-
Dykes, Loren	D	WAL	05.02.88	2	-	-	-	2	-
Emslie, Claire	F	SCO	08.03.94	8	1	2	1	10	2
Evans, Georgia	M	WAL	16.10.95	6	-	2	-	8	-
Farrow, Millie	F	ENG	03.06.96	-	-	2	-	2	-
Fergusson, Olivia	F	ENG	27.03.95	6	-	2	-	8	-
Hemp, Lauren	F	ENG	07.08.00	4	1	1	2	5	3
Jones, Katie	D	ENG	13.08.98	-	-	-	-	-	-
Ladd, Hayley	M	WAL	06.10.93	8	-	2	-	10	-
Leach, Caitlin	G	ENG	16.11.96	8	-	2	-	10	-
Matthews, Jasmine	M	ENG	24.03.93	4	-	2	-	6	-
Palmer, Aimee	M	ENG	25.07.00	3	-	-	-	3	-
Randall, Estelle	G	ENG	20.08.97	-	-	-	-	-	-
Sawyer, Paige	F	ENG	15.04.99	1	-	-	-	1	-
Syme, Emily	M	ENG	23.07.00	1	-	-	-	1	-
Turner, Millie	M	ENG	07.07.96	8	-	2	2	10	2
Watson, Aimee	M	WAL	04.08.00	-	-	-	-	-	-
Wilson, Eloise	D	ENG	11.05.97	8	-	-	-	8	-
Wilson, Poppy	M	ENG	06.08.99	3	-	-	-	3	-
Woodham, Lily	M	WAL	03.09.00	5	-	1	-	6	-

GOALSCORERS 2017

WSL1 SS: Agg (1), Arthur (1), Emslie (1), Hemp (1), own goals (1)

FAC: Hemp (2), Turner (2), Brett (1), Emslie (1)

Total: Hemp (3), Emslie (2), Turner (2), Agg (1), Arthur (1), own goals (1)

CHELSEA – WSL1

Founded: 1992	Previous WSL Positions
Stadium: Kingsmeadow (from winter 2017/18),	**2017 WSL1:** 1st (Spring Series)
(AFC Wimbledon)	**2016 WSL1:** 2nd
Honours: FA Cup Winners: (1) 2015	**2015 WSL1:** 1st
Runners-up: (2) 2012, 16	**2014 WSL1:** 2nd
WSL1 Champions: (1) 2015	**2013 WSL:** 7th
WSL1 Spring Series Champions: (1) 2017	**2012 WSL:** 6th
Nickname: The Blues	**2011 WSL:** 6th
Manager: Emma Hayes (since June 2012)	

- Former Chelsea and England men's captain John Terry, who made nearly 500 Premier League appearances for the Blues, is president of Chelsea Ladies and is credited with helping to save them from going out of business in 2009 through financial donations.
- Chelsea Ladies boss Emma Hayes received an MBE for services to football in 2016.
- Hayes was previously first-team assistant coach at Arsenal Ladies from 2006 to 2008 prior to a spell coaching Chicago Red Stars in the United States.
- Chelsea were the winners of the first Women's FA Cup final to be played at Wembley. They beat Notts County 1-0 in August 2015 with Ji So-Yun scoring the winner.
- The home matches listed below were played at Wheatsheaf Park, home of Staines Town FC. In May 2017 it was confirmed that the team would move to Kingsmeadow, home of men's team AFC Wimbledon, ahead of the 2017/18 season.

SEASON 2016 RECORD

2016 WSL1:	2nd	P16	W12	D1	L3	F42	A17	GD+25	Pts37
2015/16 Champs League:	Round of 16								
2016 FA Cup:	Runners-up								
2016 Continental Cup:	1st Round								

SEASON 2017 RECORD

2017 WSL1 Spring Series:	1st	P8	W6	D1	L1	F32	A3	GD+29	Pts19
2016/17 Champs League:	Round of 32								
2017 FA Cup:	Semi-finals								

Gilly Flaherty **Born:** 24.08.1991 Bermondsey **Position:** Central defender

Since joining Chelsea from Arsenal in 2014, England defender Gilly Flaherty has been at the heart of a Blues side that has won three major trophies in the finest era in the club's history so far.

As Chelsea's vice-captain, she has a deep-rooted relationship with manager Emma Hayes, someone she describes as being 'like a second mum' to her.

The pair previously worked together at Arsenal, when Hayes was an assistant coach to then-Gunners boss Vic Akers, but it was very nearly not so.

'It was meeting Emma as a teenager that saved my career at Arsenal,' says Flaherty.

'I'd had my heart set on going to the England academy at Loughborough since I was 14 but Emma personally showed me around the Arsenal academy and, by doing that, she changed my mind. She's continued to have a massive influence on my career. I'll be forever grateful to her and Chelsea for having the faith in me that I could be a professional, giving me my first pro contract.

'Emma has known me for so long now that she treats me like she's a second mum. She's very strict on me, she's very honest with me and she wants the best for me, but she knows how to get the maximum performance out of me as well. She knows how to wind me up, how to get a reaction. But I know she only does that because she cares. I respect that. She's an amazing woman, a great leader and a fantastic asset for Chelsea.'

Flaherty's displays for Hayes' side led to her senior England debut in 2015, against China. Passionate, vocal and – in her own words – sometimes hot-headed, Flaherty credits Hayes with improving her both mentally and emotionally, as well as technically.

'I've had to really learn over the years to try and bite my tongue and calm down sometimes, before I speak about stuff,' she added. I could be speaking about an incident on the pitch and I could get really teary-eyed, not because I was upset – it was because I have got so much passion for the game.

'Thankfully, Emma has taught me different ways to keep my head, whether it be to go to the toilet and just count to 10, or to just take some deep breaths, or sometimes just to sit there and let it chill. Emma knows when the right time is to put her arm around my shoulder, but then she also knows when to say "Gill, that's not good enough, I expect better from you".

'She is someone I can be very honest with. Her office door is always open and, with Emma having known me since I was so young, she knows a lot of stuff about my private life. Whether it be about your personal life or whether it be about football, she'll always be there to help. That's a fantastic thing for us to have in our manager at Chelsea.'

Chelsea	2016 WSL1		
24.03.16	Doncaster Rovers Belles (a)	W 4-1	Carney (pen) 12, England 23, Chapman 43, Aluko 84
21.04.16	Arsenal (a)	W 2-0	Kirby 17, 80
27.04.16	Liverpool (a)	W 2-1	Ji 15, Flaherty 64
08.05.16	Liverpool (h)	W 6-3	Carney 9, Kirby 30, 63, Spence 38, 67, Aluko 43
19.05.16	Manchester City (h)	L 0-2	
25.05.16	Sunderland (h)	W 2-1	Chapman 8, Kirby 21
29.06.16	Sunderland (a)	W 5-0	C.Rafferty 30, 41, Davison 43, Bright 72, Ji 77
10.07.16	Birmingham City (h)	D 1-1	Aluko 53, Chapman sent off 87
17.07.16	Arsenal (h)	L 1-2	Scott (og) 8
24.07.16	Doncaster Rovers Belles (h)	W 4-0	Aluko 13, 84, Ji 68, England 89
28.08.16	Birmingham City (a)	W 4-0	Aluko 3, Carney 6, Davison 23, Ji 27
01.09.16	Notts County (h)	W 2-1	Chapman 64, 76
11.09.16	Reading (a)	W 3-0	Chapman 53, Davison 90+1, Borges 90+4
25.09.16	Manchester City (a)	L 0-2	
30.10.16	Reading (h)	W 3-2	Aluko 19, 68, Borges 56
06.11.16	Notts County (a)	W 3-1	Aluko 9, Ji 58, England 59

Chelsea	2016 FA Cup		
20.03.16 R5	Doncaster Rovers Belles (a)	W 4-1	Hobbs (og) 12, Carney 59, Ji 70, Aluko 73
03.04.16 QF	Aston Villa (h)	W 6-0	Spence 42, Ji 62, 86, 90+2, Kirby 67, Aluko 90
17.04.16 SF	Manchester City (h)	W 2-1 (aet)	Ji 86, Kirby 120
14.05.16 F	Arsenal (at Wembley)	L 0-1	

Chelsea	2016 Continental Cup		
02.07.16 R1	London Bees (a)	D 3-3 (L 2-4p)	England 8, 95, Bright 90+2, Fahey sent off 75

Chelsea	2015/16 Champions League		
08.10.15 Rof32	Glasgow City (SCO) (h)	W 1-0	Kirby 39
14.10.15 Rof32	Glasgow City (SCO) (a)	W 3-0	Aluko 22, Kirby 57, Flaherty 61
		(W 4-0)	
11.11.15 Rof16	Wolfsburg (GER) (h)	L 1-2	Peter (og) 54
18.11.15 Rof16	Wolfsburg (GER) (a)	L 0-2	
		(L 1-4)	

CHELSEA PLAYER APPEARANCES & GOALS 2016

				WSL1		FAC		CC		CL		Total	
				A	G	A	G	A	G	A	G	A	G
Aluko, Eniola	F	ENG	21.02.87	16	9	4	2	1	-	4	1	25	12
Ayane, Rosella	F	ENG	16.03.96	-	-	-	-	-	-	1	-	1	-
Bailey, Jade	D	ENG	11.11.95	12	-	3	-	1	-	-	-	16	-
Blundell, Hannah	D	ENG	25.05.94	15	-	4	-	1	-	3	-	23	-
Borges, Ana Marques	M	POR	15.06.90	14	2	1	-	1	-	4	-	20	2
Bright, Millie	M	ENG	21.08.93	15	1	4	-	1	1	4	-	24	2
Carney, Karen	M	ENG	01.08.87	16	3	4	1	1	-	-	-	21	4
Chapman, Katie	M	ENG	15.06.82	13	5	4	-	-	-	3	-	20	5
Coombs, Laura	M	ENG	29.01.91	-	-	-	-	-	-	4	-	4	-
Cross, Zoe	M	ENG	06.02.98	-	-	-	-	-	-	-	-	-	-
Davison, Gemma	M	ENG	17.04.78	15	3	4	-	1	-	4	-	24	3
England, Bethany	M	ENG	03.06.94	13	3	4	-	1	2	-	-	18	5
Fahey, Niamh	D	IRL	13.10.87	12	-	3	-	1	-	4	-	20	-
Flaherty, Gilly	D	ENG	24.08.91	15	1	4	-	1	-	4	1	24	2
Ji, So-Yun	F	KOR	21.02.91	16	5	4	5	1	-	4	-	25	10
Joel, Lois	D	ENG	02.06.99	-	-	-	-	-	-	-	-	-	-
Kirby, Fran	F	ENG	29.06.93	7	5	3	2	-	-	4	2	14	9
Kitching, Frances	G	ENG	17.02.98	-	-	-	-	1	-	-	-	1	-
Legg, Jenna	M	ENG	23.06.97	-	-	1	-	-	-	-	-	1	-
Lindahl, Hedvig	G	SWE	29.04.83	11	-	3	-	-	-	4	-	18	-
Rafferty, Claire	D	ENG	11.01.89	12	2	1	-	-	-	3	-	16	2
Rafferty, Laura	M	NIR	29.04.96	1	-	-	-	-	-	-	-	1	-
Russo, Alessia	M	ENG	08.02.99	-	-	-	-	1	-	-	-	1	-
Spence, Drew	M	ENG	23.10.92	11	2	4	1	1	-	3	-	19	3
Spencer, Rebecca	G	ENG	22.02.91	6	-	1	-	-	-	-	-	7	-
Taylor, Miriael	M	ENG	02.02.00	2	-	-	-	-	-	-	-	2	-

GOALSCORERS 2016

WSL1: Aluko (9), Chapman (5), Ji (5), Kirby (5), Carney (3), Davison (3), England (3), Borges (2), C.Rafferty (2), Spence (2), Bright (1), Flaherty (1), own goals (1)

CL: Kirby (2), Aluko (1), Flaherty (1), own goals (1)

FAC: Ji (5) Aluko (2), Kirby (2), Carney (1), Spence (1), own goals (1)

CC: England (2), Bright (1)

Total: Aluko (12), Ji (10), Kirby (9), Chapman (5), England (5), Carney (4), Davison (3), Spence (3), own goals (3), Bright (2), Borges (2), Flaherty (2), C.Rafferty (1)

Chelsea	2017 WSL1 Spring Series		
30.04.17	Yeovil Town (h)	W 6-0	Ji 45, 45+1, Spence 54, Cuthbert 67, Dunn 73, Bachmann 75
03.05.17	Reading (a)	W 4-0	Carney 32, Spence 64, Ji 69, Blundell 81
17.05.17	Arsenal (h)	D 2-2	Bright 69, Spence 90+2
21.05.17	Sunderland (a)	W 7-0	Cuthbert 22, 45, Carney 31, Mjelde 35, Bachmann 41, Kirby 75, 86
25.05.17	Manchester City (a)	L 0-1	
28.05.17	Liverpool (h)	W 7-0	Flaherty 3, Kirby 43, Ji 45, Mjelde 49, Carney 66, Cuthbert 79, Spence 83
31.05.17	Bristol City (a)	W 4-0	Bright 30, Kirby 65, 73, Bachmann 80
03.06.17	Birmingham City (a)	W 2-0	Carney (pen) 22, Kirby 58

Chelsea	2017 FA Cup		
19.03.17 R5	Doncaster Rovers Belles (h)	W 7-0	Dunn 12, Ji 33, 37, Little (og) 41, Bachmann 45, Chapman 70, Spence 72
26.03.17 QF	Sunderland (h)	W 5-1	Bachmann 39, 44, Blundell 49, 58, Spence 90
17.04.17 SF	Birmingham City (a)	D 1-1 (L 2-4p)	Spence 88

Chelsea	2016/17 Champions League		
05.10.16 Rof32	Wolfsburg (GER) (h)*	L 0-3	
12.10.16 Rof32	Wolfsburg (GER) (a)	D 1-1	Aluko 43
		(L 1-4)	

*Played at Stamford Bridge

CHELSEA PLAYER APPEARANCES & GOALS 2017

				WSL1		FAC		CL		Total	
				A	G	A	G	A	G	A	G
Aluko, Eniola	F	ENG	21.02.87	2	-	1	-	2	1	5	1
Bachmann, Ramona	F	SUI	25.12.90	8	3	3	3	-	-	11	6
Bailey, Jade	D	ENG	11.11.95	-	-	2	-	-	-	2	-
Blundell, Hannah	D	ENG	25.05.94	5	1	3	2	2	-	10	3
Borges, Ana Marques	M	POR	15.06.90	-	-	-	-	2	-	2	-
Bright, Millie	M	ENG	21.08.93	7	2	3	-	2	-	12	2
Carney, Karen	M	ENG	01.08.87	7	4	3	-	2	-	12	4
Chapman, Katie	M	ENG	15.06.82	6	-	3	1	2	-	11	1
Cooper, Deanna	D	ENG	20.06.93	8	-	-	-	-	-	8	-
Cuthbert, Erin	M	SCO	19.07.98	5	4	2	-	-	-	7	4
Davison, Gemma	M	ENG	17.04.78	7	-	-	-	2	-	9	-
Dunn, Crystal	M	USA	03.07.92	8	1	3	1	-	-	11	2
England, Bethany	M	ENG	03.06.94	6	-	3	-	1	-	10	-
Fahey, Niamh	D	IRL	13.10.87	2	-	-	-	2	-	4	-
Flaherty, Gilly	D	ENG	24.08.91	6	1	1	-	2	-	9	1
Ji, So-Yun	F	KOR	21.02.91	7	4	3	2	2	-	12	6
Kirby, Fran	F	ENG	29.06.93	5	6	-	-	-	-	5	6
Kitching, Frances	G	ENG	17.02.98	1	-	1	-	-	-	2	-
Lindahl, Hedvig	G	SWE	29.04.83	-	-	2	-	2	-	4	-
Mjelde, Maren	M	NOR	06.11.89	8	2	3	-	-	-	11	2
Rafferty, Claire	D	ENG	11.01.89	-	-	3	-	2	-	5	-
Spence, Drew	M	ENG	23.10.92	7	4	3	3	1	-	11	7
Startup, Katie	G	ENG	28.01.99	-	-	-	-	-	-	-	-
Telford, Carly	G	ENG	07.07.87	7	-	-	-	-	-	7	-

GOALSCORERS 2017

WSL1 Spring Series: Kirby (6), Carney (4), Cuthbert (4), Ji (4), Spence (4), Bachmann (3), Bright (2), Mjelde (2), Blundell (1), Dunn (1), Flaherty (1)

CL: Aluko (1)

FAC: Bachmann (3), Spence (3), Blundell (2), Ji (2), Chapman (1), Dunn (1), own goals (1)

Total: Spence (7), Bachmann (6), Ji (6), Kirby (6), Carney (4), Cuthbert (4), Blundell (3), Bright (2), Dunn (2), Mjelde (2), Aluko (1), Chapman (1), Flaherty (1), own goals (1)

EVERTON – WSL1

Founded: 1983 (as Hoylake WFC)	**Previous WSL Positions**
Stadium: Select Security Stadium	**2017 WSL2:** 1st (Spring Series)
National Honours: FA Cup Winners: (2)	**2016 WSL2:** 3rd
1989 (as Leasowe Pacific), 2010	**2015 WSL2:** 3rd
FA Cup Runners-up: (3) 1988	**2014 WSL1:** 8th (Relegated)
(as Leasowe Pacific), 2005, 14	**2013 WSL:** 5th
National Premier League Champions: (1)	**2012 WSL:** 3rd
1998	**2011 WSL:** 3rd
National Premier League Runners-up: (5)	
2006, 07, 08, 09, 10	
WSL2 Spring Series Champions: (1) 2017	
WPL Cup Winners: (1) 2008	
WPL Cup Runners-up: (3) 1997, 99, 2010	
Nickname: The Toffees	
Manager: Andy Spence (since Nov 2012)	

- After starting life as Hoylake WFC the club became known as Leasowe Pacific following a merger with Dolphins FC. They went on to win the North West League in 1988 and also reached the FA Cup final that year where they lost to Doncaster Belles.
- A year later they secured their first national trophy as they again reached the FA Cup final, but this time beat Friends of Fulham 3-2 in a thrilling match at Old Trafford.
- The club changed its name to Everton Ladies in 1995 and three years later they were Champions of England when they won the old National Premier League.
- Everton were runners-up to Arsenal in each of the final five seasons of the old National Premier League (2005/06, 06/07, 07/08, 08/09, and 09/10) before the formation of the WSL of which they were founding members.

- The Toffees finished bottom of WSL1 in 2014 and were relegated to WSL2, but returned to the top-flight ahead of the 2017/18 season. They were 2017 WSL2 Spring Series winners and, although no promotions had been scheduled between the divisions, they were chosen to fill the vacant WSL1 spot left by Notts County who folded in April 2017.
- Former Everton and England captain Mo Marley served as manager between 2002 and 2012. The defender won the FA Cup with Everton (then Leasowe Pacific) in 1989 and again as manager in 2010. She was also a National Premier League Champion as an Everton player in 1998 and a WPL Cup winner as their manager in 2008.

SEASON 2016 RECORD

2016 WSL2:	3rd	P18	W10	D4	L4	F35	A18	GD+17	Pts34
2016 FA Cup:	5th Round								
2016 Continental Cup:	1st Round								

SEASON 2017 RECORD

2017 WSL2 Spring Series:	1st	P9	W7	D1	L1	F25	A7	GD+18	Pts22
2017 FA Cup:	5th Round								

Gabby George **Born:** 02.02.1997 **Position:** Defender

For young Everton defender Gabby George, 2017 could scarcely have gone better. At club level there was a WSL2 Spring Series title – with George playing a key role in helping keep five clean sheets from a possible nine – and promotion to the top-flight.

At international level there was an England Under-23 debut in a team which won the La Manga tournament and the annual Nordic Cup. Then, as her club took big strides behind the scenes, she became Everton Ladies' first ever full-time professional player. Several more full-time Everton players have since followed.

'Fans get to see some good football from us,' says George. We're a good attacking team and we're good defensively. At a club as big as Everton, we set our standards very high – anything but winning is not acceptable for us. So not getting promoted for two seasons on the run wasn't good enough for us.

'Before the Spring Series, we started training more, doing more day-time sessions and more gym sessions. That meant we all became closer as a team, because we were training more together. We lost a lot of experience when we got relegated to WSL2 in 2014. It's taken us a good few years to be able to get back to where we actually want to be.'

George – who has been with Everton since arriving just after her 17th birthday in 2014 – speaks highly of manager Andy Spence, who took charge in 2012 after eight years as assistant manager. 'Andy has helped me a lot, on and off the pitch, to become a better player and a better person. He's got a great personality. He is big on us having "big hearts" as well.

'We won the WSL2 Spring Series with a very young squad. We've got some extremely exciting prospects coming through the ranks now, so we are in a good place. At the moment, we have quite a young back line – I'm probably one of the most experienced ones and I'm only 20. As we mature as a group, we want to have that winning feeling more often.

'My strength has always been defending so, for the past couple of years, I've been trying to work to improve on the ball. That's something I've wanted to get better at, with the ball at my feet. Personally, I feel I'm improving a lot but there's never a stage when you can't improve any further.'

Everton	2016 WSL2		
24.03.16	Aston Villa (h)	W 2-1	Magill 43, Brougham 80
27.03.16	Millwall Lionesses (a)	D 2-2	Boye-Hlorkah 72, Magill 77
24.04.16	Watford (h)	W 3-0	Walker 26, D. Turner 46, Magill 52
01.05.16	London Bees (h)	W 5-1	K. Jones 44, D. Turner 54, 59, Hinnigan 56, Magill 90
17.05.16	Aston Villa (a)	W 2-0	Hinnigan 8, Stewart 53
22.05.16	Millwall Lionesses (h)	D 1-1	K. Jones 56
26.06.16	Watford (a)	L 1-2	Walker 16
10.07.16	Sheffield FC (a)	L 0-1	
17.07.16	Yeovil Town (h)	W 3-0	Kelly 10, (pen) 34, Ayane 17
24.07.16	Oxford United (a)	W 1-0	Hollinshead 77
30.07.16	Sheffield FC (h)	D 1-1	M. Turner 20
14.08.16	Durham (h)	D 1-1	Hinnigan 74
27.08.16	Bristol City (a)	W 1-0	Kelly (pen) 11
11.09.16	Oxford United (h)	W 3-0	Walker 28, 67, Hinnigan 62
25.09.16	Yeovil Town (a)	L 0-1	
09.10.16	Durham (a)	W 3-1	George 10, Walker 25, Davies 90+2
29.10.16	Bristol City (h)	L 2-3	Walker (pen) 30, D. Turner 85
06.11.16	London Bees (a)	W 4-3	Walker 67, D. Turner 74, Stewart 80, George 85

Everton	2016 FA Cup		
07.02.16 R3	Stoke City (h)	W 7-0	Magill 7, Hollinshead 11, 36, Hinnigan 56, Walker 68, K.Jones 75, Boye-Hlorkah 78
28.02.17 R4	Nottingham Forest (h)	W 5-0	K.Jones 41, Walker 43, Hinnigan 51, 76, Hollinshead 90+3
20.03.16 R5	Aston Villa (a)	L 0-1	

Everton	2016 Continental Cup		
02.07.16 R1	Liverpool (h)	L 0-1	

EVERTON PLAYER APPEARANCES & GOALS 2016

				WSL2		FAC		CC		Total	
				A	G	A	G	A	G	A	G
Ayane, Rosella	F	ENG	16.03.96	11	1	-	-	1	-	12	1
Boye-Hlorkah, Chantelle	F	ENG	08.09.95	4	1	3	1	-	-	7	2
Brooks, Alexandra	G	ENG	19.01.95	9	-	3	-	-	-	12	-
Brougham, Georgia	D	ENG	18.03.96	15	1	2	-	1	-	18	1
Bryson, Faye	D	ENG	04.07.97	2	-	1	-	-	-	3	-
Davies, Lauren	M	ENG	21.03.97	9	1	2	-	-	-	11	1
Dear, Jenna	M	ENG	29.05.96	8	-	1	-	1	-	10	-
Doyle, Emma	M	ENG	n/a	2	-	-	-	-	-	2	-
Finnigan, Megan	M	ENG	02.04.98	16	-	2	-	1	-	19	-
George, Gabrielle	D	ENG	02.02.97	17	2	3	-	1	-	21	2
Hinnigan, Michelle	M	ENG	12.06.90	18	4	3	3	1	-	22	7
Hollinshead, Emily	F	WAL	13.09.95	9	1	2	3	-	-	11	4
Johnston, Krystle	F	ENG	26.04.84	11	-	-	-	1	-	12	-
Johnson, Emma	M	ENG	n/a	1	-	1	-	-	-	2	-
Johnson, Lindsay	D	ENG	08.05.80	-	-	-	-	-	-	-	-
Jones, Kelly	M	ENG	24.04.88	18	2	3	2	1	-	22	4
Jones, Vicky	D	ENG	24.04.88	18	-	3	-	1	-	22	-
Kelly, Chloe	F	ENG	15.01.98	8	3	-	-	1	-	9	3
Kennerley, Eve	M	ENG	22.12.95	-	-	1	-	-	-	1	-
Levell, Kirstie	G	ENG	07.01.97	16	-	1	-	1	-	18	-
Magill, Simone	F	NIR	01.11.94	7	4	2	1	-	-	9	5
Morgan, Delyth	G	WAL	24.02.96	-	-	-	-	-	-	-	-
Myler, Jennifer	G	ENG	11.01.00	1	-	-	-	-	-	1	-
Rowe, Sasha	F	ENG	14.10.97	1	-	-	-	-	-	1	-
Stewart, Ellie	D	ENG	02.11.96	10	2	-	-	1	-	11	2
Turner, Danielle	D	ENG	10.09.91	18	5	3	-	1	-	22	5
Turner, Millie	M	ENG	07.07.96	16	1	3	-	-	-	19	1
Walker, Claudia	F	ENG	10.06.96	16	7	3	2	1	-	20	9

GOALSCORERS 2016

WSL2: Walker (7), D. Turner (5), Hinnigan (4), Magill (4), Kelly (3), George (2), K. Jones (2), Stewart (2), Ayane (1), Boye-Hlorkah (1), Brougham (1), Davies (1), Hollinshead (1), M. Turner (1)

FAC: Hinnigan (3), Hollinshead (3), K. Jones (2), Walker (2), Boye-Hlorkah (1), Magill (1)

CC: None

Total: Walker (9), Hinnigan (7), Magill (5), D. Turner (5), Hollinshead (4), K. Jones (4), Kelly (3), Boye-Hlorkah (2), George (2), Stewart (2), Ayane (1), Brougham (1), Bryson (1), Davies (1), M. Turner (1)

Everton	2017 WSL2 Spring Series		
12.02.17	Oxford United (a)	W 2-1	Magill 13, K. Jones 48
12.03.17	Sheffield FC (a)	W 2-1	Walker 67, Gilliatt (og) 80
02.04.17	Millwall Lionesses (a)	L 1-2	Walker (pen) 27
16.04.17	Aston Villa (h)	W 3-0	Magill 38, Walker 68, Bryson 76
23.04.17	Doncaster Rovers Belles (a)	D 3-3	Brougham 3, Walker 20, Chance 85
30.04.17	Brighton & Hove Albion (h)	W 5-0	Magill (pen) 11, D. Turner 16, 48, Walker 18, Brougham 83
06.05.17	Durham (h)	W 1-0	George 13
14.05.17	Watford (h)	W 4-0	Brougham 18, A. Whelan 48, Chance 81, Magill 90
20.05.17	London Bees (a)	W 4-0	Green 28, Hinnigan 34, Walker 70, 90

Everton	2017 FA Cup		
05.02.17 R3	Brighouse Town (a)	W 8-1	Magill 12, 33, Hinnigan 40, Walker 45, 81, 86 Chance 76, 89
19.02.17 R4	Durham (a)	D 2-2 (W 4-3p)	Hinnigan 50, Magill 78
19.03.17 R5	Liverpool (a)	L 1-2 (aet)	Magill 69

EVERTON PLAYER APPEARANCES & GOALS 2017

				WSL2		FAC		Total	
				A	G	A	G	A	G
Boye-Hlorkah, Chantelle	F	ENG	08.09.95	1	-	-	-	1	-
Brougham, Georgia	D	ENG	18.03.96	8	3	3	-	11	3
Bryson, Faye	D	ENG	04.07.97	8	1	1	-	9	1
Chance, Olivia	M	NZL	05.10.93	9	2	3	2	12	4
Davies, Lauren	M	ENG	21.03.97	3	-	-	-	3	-
Doyle, Emma	M	ENG	n/a	-	-	-	-	-	-
Finnigan, Megan	M	ENG	02.04.98	8	-	3	-	11	-
George, Gabrielle	D	ENG	02.02.97	9	1	2	-	11	1
Green, Mollie	F	ENG	04.08.97	7	1	-	-	7	1
Hinnigan, Michelle	M	ENG	12.06.90	9	1	3	2	12	3
Hollinshead, Emily	F	WAL	13.09.95	6	-	3	-	9	-
Jones, Kelly	M	ENG	24.04.88	9	1	3	-	12	1
Jones, Vicky	D	ENG	24.04.88	8	-	3	-	11	-
Levell, Kirstie	G	ENG	07.01.97	9	-	3	-	12	-
Magill, Simone	F	NIR	01.11.94	7	4	3	4	10	8
Myler, Jennifer	G	ENG	11.01.00	1	-	-	-	1	-
Stobbs, Amber	F	ENG	21.10.92	4	-	3	-	7	-
Turner, Danielle	D	ENG	10.09.91	9	2	3	-	12	2
Walker, Claudia	F	ENG	10.06.96	9	7	3	3	12	10
Whelan, Aileen	F	ENG	11.08.91	3	1	-	-	3	1
Whelan, Fern	D	ENG	05.12.88	1	-	-	-	1	-

GOALSCORERS 2017

WSL2 SS: Walker (7), Magill (4), Brougham (3), Chance (2), D. Turner (2), Bryson (1), George (1), Green (1), Hinnigan (1), K. Jones (1), A. Whelan (1), own goals (1)

FAC: Magill (4), Walker (3), Chance (2), Hinnigan (2)

Total: Walker (10), Magill (8), Chance (4), Brougham (3), Hinnigan (3), D. Turner (2), Bryson (1), George (1), Green (1), K. Jones (1), A. Whelan (1), own goals (1)

LIVERPOOL – WSL1

Founded: 1989 (as Newton Ladies)	**Previous WSL Positions**
Stadium: Select Security Stadium, Widnes	**2017 WSL1:** 4th (Spring Series)
WSL1 Champions: (2) 2013, 2014	**2016 WSL1:** 5th
Nickname: The Reds	**2015 WSL1:** 7th
Manager: Scott Rogers (since October 2015)	**2014 WSL1:** 1st
	2013 WSL: 1st
	2012 WSL: 8th
	2011 WSL: 8th

- Going into the 2017/18 campaign, Liverpool are one of only two teams – along with Arsenal – to have won the WSL title in a full season more than once. They were champions in 2013 and 2014, while the Gunners won it in 2011 and 2012. Chelsea won the full season title in 2015 and the Spring Series (in which teams played each other only once) in 2017.
- The Reds have never won the FA Cup, and lost three consecutive finals in the mid-90s. They were still known as Knowsley United when they were beaten by Doncaster Belles in 1994. In 1995 they lost to Arsenal before also being defeated by Croydon in 1996.
- Liverpool Ladies were founded as Newton Ladies in 1989 and became Knowsley United in 1991. They became fully integrated into men's professional club Liverpool FC in 2013.

SEASON 2016 RECORD

2016 WSL1:	5th	P16	W7	D4	L5	F27	A23	GD+4	Pts25
2015/16 Champions League:	Round of 32								
2016 FA Cup:	5th Round								
2016 Continental Cup:	2nd Round								

SEASON 2017 RECORD

2017 WSL1 Spring Series:	4th	P8	W4	D2	L2	F20	A18	GD+2	Pts14
2017 FA Cup:	Semi-finals								

Jess Clarke **Born:** 05.05.1989 Leeds **Position:** Forward

'No one played football in my family. I was brought up in a one-parent home, which was just me and my mum, with no siblings. One day at primary school, I just saw a football and asked my mum if I could have one. Then that football became like a sibling to me. As soon as I saw a ball, I fell in love with it.'

That's how Liverpool forward Jess Clarke describes the day when she first got into football, yet the spontaneous purchase started a journey that has so far led to more than 50 senior caps for England.

'From then onwards, all I wanted to do was play football and practice. I used to live in a block of flats and I was always kicking a ball up against a wall every night,' she says. 'Sometimes, I'd do it so much that I used to get told off by the neighbours. I aspired to be like Ruud van Nistelrooy – he was such a good finisher – and David Beckham, with his vision. I practised over and over. I don't think a single day went by when I didn't actually kick a football. I'd come home from school every night and I'd be on the field practising for hours and hours.'

Clarke's efforts were rewarded when she was signed by Leeds United – then led by Julie Chipchase – as a teenager. 'After all the hard work that I did, being brought into the first team at Leeds by Julie, was a great feeling,' Clarke said. 'You can't replicate those memories.'

Her performances for Leeds led to a move to Notts County in 2010 and – as part of Hope Powell's England team – to the 2011 Women's World Cup in Germany. And it was at that major international tournament that the young girl from a flat in Leeds would play a starring role for her country. After drawing their opening game of the group stage against Mexico, England were seemingly heading for another draw against relative-minnows New Zealand – a result which would have left their hopes of qualifying for the knock-out stages hanging by a thread – when substitute Clarke intervened in the final 10 minutes in Dresden.

She met Jill Scott's square pass first time and fired the ball high into the net from inside the penalty area, to give England a precious 2-1 win. 'Hope Powell looked at me from the bench and she said to me, "no pressure but I need you to go on and score a goal" and that's what I managed to do,' Clarke recalls. 'To do that, for your country, in front of a massive crowd, that was an overwhelming feeling. Everything felt so surreal and emotional that night, because it felt like I'd put all that hard work in for that exact moment.'

After reaching the FA Cup final with Notts County in 2015, Clarke is now part of a talented squad at Liverpool, helping them finish fourth in the 2017 WSL1 Spring Series. After scoring five goals in 15 League appearances in 2016 for Notts, she joined Liverpool on 11 April 2017, signing on the same day as fellow-England international Laura Coombs. 'Just training with the quality players in this team is unbelievable,' Clarke says. 'I'm so excited to see what this team brings, with so much strength in depth. I think we can be very successful.'

Liverpool	2016 WSL1		
23.03.16	Birmingham City (h)	W 1-0	Van de Sanden 8, *Van den Berg sent off 69*
23.04.16	Sunderland (h)	D 2-2	Weir 19, Coombs 21
27.04.16	Chelsea (h)	L 1-2	Weir 81
02.05.16	Notts County (a)	L 2-3	Zelem (pen) 80, 87
08.05.16	Chelsea (a)	L 3-6	Zelem 2, Weir 55, Lundh 56
18.05.16	Sunderland (a)	W 4-0	White 9, Greenwood (pen) 36, Bannon (og) 73, Zelem 90+1
25.05.16	Manchester City (h)	D 0-0	
26.06.16	Manchester City (a)	D 1-1	White 4
09.07.16	Reading (h)	W 2-0	Harding 17, Coombs 24
16.07.16	Notts County (h)	D 0-0	
31.07.16	Arsenal (a)	W 2-1	Van de Sanden 21, Weir 75
27.08.16	Doncaster Rovers Belles (h)	W 1-0	Harding 47
01.09.16	Reading (a)	W 1-0	Zelem 85
25.09.16	Birmingham City (a)	L 1-2	Zelem (pen) 63
09.10.16	Doncaster Rovers Belles (a)	W 3-1	Weir 37, 45, Harding 72
06.11.16	Arsenal (h)	L 3-5	Murray 18, Van de Sanden 60, Weir 90+5

Liverpool	2016 FA Cup		
19.03.16 R5	Manchester City (h)	L 0-2	

Liverpool	2016 Continental Cup		
02.07.16 R1	Everton (a)	W 1-0	Lundh 45+3
07.08.16 QF	Birmingham City (a)	L 0-1 (aet)	

Liverpool	2015/16 Champs League		
07.10.15 Rof32	Brescia (ITA) (a)	L 0-1	
14.10.15 Rof32	Brescia (ITA) (h)	L 0-1	
		(L 0-2 agg)	

LIVERPOOL PLAYER APPEARANCES & GOALS 2016

				WSL1		FAC		CC		CL		Total	
				A	G	A	G	A	G	A	G	A	G
Beckwith, Shannon	D	ENG	22.11.95	-	-	-	-	-	-	2	-	2	-
Bonner, Gemma	D	ENG	13.07.91	16	-	1	-	2	-	1	-	20	-
Chamberlain, Siobhan	G	ENG	15.08.83	16	-	1	-	2	-	-	-	19	-
Charles, Niamh	F	ENG	21.06.99	8	-	-	-	1	-	-	-	9	-
Coombs, Laura	M	ENG	29.01.91	13	2	1	-	1	-	-	-	15	2
Dale, Hannah	M	ENG	01.06.95	-	-	-	-	-	-	1	-	1	-
Dowie, Natasha	F	ENG	30.06.88	-	-	-	-	-	-	2	-	2	-
Gibbons, Danielle	G	ENG	31.07.92	-	-	-	-	-	-	1	-	1	-
Green, Mollie	F	ENG	04.08.97	1	-	-	-	-	-	-	-	1	-
Greenwood, Alex	D	ENG	07.09.93	8	-	1	-	1	-	-	-	10	-
Harding, Natasha	M	WAL	02.03.89	16	3	1	-	2	-	-	-	19	3
Harris, Martha	D	ENG	19.08.94	3	-	1	-	-	-	2	-	6	-
Hodson, Ashley	F	ENG	05.05.95	10	-	-	-	2	-	2	-	14	-
Ingle, Sophie	M	WAL	02.09.91	16	-	1	-	2	-	-	-	19	-
Longhurst, Kate	M	ENG	02.05.89	16	-	1	-	2	-	-	-	19	-
Lundh, Emma	F	SWE	26.06.89	12	1	1	-	2	1	-	-	15	2
Murray, Satara	D	USA	01.07.93	11	1	-	-	2	-	2	-	15	1
Omarsdottir, Katrin	M	ICE	27.06.87	-	-	-	-	-	-	2	-	2	-
Oshoala, Asisat	F	NGA	09.10.94	-	-	-	-	-	-	2	-	2	-
Ryland, Ingrid	D	NOR	29.05.89	-	-	-	-	-	-	2	-	2	-
Staniforth, Lucy	M	ENG	02.10.92	-	-	-	-	-	-	2	-	2	-
Stout, Libby	G	USA	16.06.90	-	-	-	-	-	-	-	1	-	1
Van de Sanden, Shanice	F	NED	02.10.92	16	3	1	-	2	-	-	-	19	3
Van den Berg, Mandy	D	NED	26.08.90	10	-	1	-	2	-	-	-	13	-
Weir, Caroline	M	SCO	20.06.95	16	7	1	-	2	-	-	-	19	7
White, Rosie	F	NZL	06.06.93	13	2	1	-	1	-	2	-	17	2
Williams, Fara	M	ENG	25.01.84	-	-	-	-	-	-	1	-	1	-
Zelem, Katie	M	ENG	20.01.96	15	4	1	-	2	-	2	-	20	4

GOALSCORERS 2016

WSL1: Weir (7), Zelem (4), Harding (3), Van de Sanden (3), Coombs (2), White (2), Lundh (1), Murray (1), own goals (1)

CL: None

FAC: None

CC: Lundh (1)

Total: Weir (7), Zelem (4), Harding (3), Van de Sanden (3), Coombs (2), Lundh (2), White (2), Murray (1), own goals (1)

Liverpool	2017 WSL1 Spring Series		
23.04.17	Yeovil Town (a)	W 4-1	Greenwood (pen) 23, Bonner 45, Zelem 65, 75
28.04.17	Reading (h)	W 4-2	Harding 2, 25, Weir 34, Coombs 50
04.05.17	Arsenal (a)	D 4-4	Greenwood 13, Harding 43, Weir 44, Bonner 83
07.05.17	Birmingham City (a)	W 2-0	Clarke 48, Bonner 81
17.05.17	Sunderland (h)	W 4-0	Weir 9, 58, Harding 22, Stoney 81
20.05.17	Bristol City (a)	D 1-1	Zelem 80
28.05.17	Chelsea (a)	L 0-7	
03.06.17	Manchester City (h)	L 1-3	Weir 90

Liverpool	2017 FA Cup		
19.03.17 R5	Everton (h)	W 2-1 (aet)	Harding 9, Van de Sanden 108
26.03.17 QF	Notts County (h)	W 2-0	Weir 3, Harding 19
17.04.17 SF	Manchester City (a)	L 0-1	

LIVERPOOL PLAYER APPEARANCES & GOALS 2017

				WSL1		FAC		Total	
				A	G	A	G	A	G
Bonner, Gemma	D	ENG	13.07.91	8	3	3	-	11	3
Chamberlain, Siobhan	G	ENG	15.08.83	8	-	3	-	11	-
Charles, Niamh	F	ENG	21.06.99	7	-	1	-	8	-
Clarke, Jessica	F	ENG	05.05.89	7	1	-	-	7	1
Coombs, Laura	M	ENG	29.01.91	8	1	-	-	8	1
Fletcher, Ellie	D	ENG	16.06.99	2	-	-	-	2	-
Gibbons, Danielle	G	ENG	31.07.92	-	-	-	-	-	-
Greenwood, Alex	D	ENG	07.09.93	6	2	3	-	9	2
Harding, Natasha	M	WAL	02.03.89	8	4	3	2	11	6
Hodson, Ashley	F	ENG	05.05.95	8	-	3	-	11	-
Ingle, Sophie	M	WAL	02.09.91	8	-	3	-	11	-
Johnson, Ali	M	ENG	24.12.98	-	-	3	-	3	-
Longhurst, Kate	M	ENG	02.05.89	7	-	3	-	10	-
Rodgers, Amy	D	ENG	04.05.00	2	-	-	-	2	-
Stoney, Casey	D	ENG	13.05.82	5	-	2	-	7	-
Van de Sanden, Shanice	F	NED	02.10.92	7	-	3	1	10	1
Weir, Caroline	M	SCO	20.06.95	8	5	3	1	11	6
Zelem, Katie	M	ENG	20.01.96	7	3	3	-	10	3

2017 GOALSCORERS

WSL1 Spring Series:

CL: Weir (5), Harding (4), Bonner (3), Zelem (3), Greenwood (2), Clarke (1), Coombs (1)

FAC: Harding (2), Van de Sanden (1), Weir (1)

Total: Harding (6), Weir (6), Bonner (3), Zelem (3), Greenwood (2), Clarke (1), Coombs (1), Van de Sanden (1)

MANCHESTER CITY – WSL1

Founded: 1988	**Previous WSL Positions**
Stadium: The Academy Stadium, Manchester	**2017 WSL1:** 2nd (Spring Series)
Honours: FA Cup Winners: (1) 2017	**2016 WSL1:** 1st
WSL1 Champions: (1) 2016	**2015 WSL1:** 2nd
WSL1 Runners-up: (1) 2015	**2014 WSL1:** 5th
WSL1 Spring Series Runners-up: (1) 2017	
WSL Continental Cup Winners: (2) 2014, 16	
Nickname: City, The Blues	
Manager: Nick Cushing (since Nov 2013)	

- Manchester City completed the entire 2016 League season unbeaten to finish as champions, a feat only previously achieved in WSL1 by Arsenal in 2012.
- City had the highest WSL attendance of the 2016 season as 4,096 fans watched them clinch the title at home to 2015 champions Chelsea.
- Manager Nick Cushing's wife Claire gave birth to their third child on the day of City's 2016 WSL Continental Cup final win over Birmingham. She went into labour several hours before kick-off but Cushing chose to stay on the sidelines for the match. His team won 1-0 after extra-time and he made it back in time for the birth of a baby girl later that day.
- The Academy Stadium was chosen as the neutral venue for that 2016 WSL Continental Cup final, but City reached it – and beat Birmingham – on their own patch.

SEASON 2016 RECORD

2016 WSL1:	1st	P16	W13	D3	L0	F36	A4	GD+32	Pts42
2016 FA Cup:	Semi-finals								
2016 Continental Cup:	Winners								

SEASON 2017 RECORD

2017 WSL1 Spring Series:	2nd	P8	W6	D1	L1	F17	A6	GD+11	Pts19
2017 FA Cup:	Winners								
2016/17 Champions League:	Semi-finals								

Georgia Stanway **Born:** 03.01.1999 Barrow-in-Furness **Position:** Forward

For most sixth-form students, your final A-level exams constitute a tense term of revision, such that there is very little room for anything else in either your busy schedule or your studious mind.

But one England youth international striker spent the final term of her studies doubling up her school exams with training sessions alongside the FIFA World Player of the Year, Carli Lloyd, and helping her club win their first ever FA Cup, reach the semi-finals of the Champions League and finish second in the WSL1 Spring Series.

Yes, Georgia Stanway is no ordinary Physical Education and Psychology A-level student. But how did she manage two A-levels alongside two full years as a Manchester City player? 'I've enjoyed it. It's been difficult at times but I'm willing to juggle both of them around and make sure I don't miss a training session,' the former Blackburn Rovers youngster explains.

'I make sure that, if I have to, I catch up on my work, because it's always good to have a backup. I've been committed to both my studies and football, because you never know what's going to happen in football. The new winter season is very exciting because, at that point, I'll be enjoying just being a professional footballer, and that's what I've always dreamed of.'

As well as learning in the classroom, Stanway has also been able to learn on the pitch from some of the world's best footballers, including Manchester City and England captain, Steph Houghton. 'To play and train with internationals from all around the world is unbelievable,' she says. 'I'm just being a sponge, trying to soak up everything that I can to learn from different experiences, to make me a better player when I'm their age. I look up to Steph Houghton as an example because she is always doing things right. Also, the way [England midfielder] Izzy Christiansen grafts in training, I admire her determination and effort.'

A former England Under-17 captain, Stanway has also been a key member of the national Under-19 squad and has her sights set on the Under-23 side and then the senior England team. She is already a regular member of City's first-team squad, playing at Wembley in the 2017 FA Cup final as well as in Europe, and featuring in five of their eight 2017 Spring Series games.

Able to play as a traditional 'number nine' as well as in deeper or wider roles, Stanway is a versatile forward and scored a hat-trick against Sunderland in the League in July 2016 aged just 17. Her goals-per-game record for England's youth outfits is particularly impressive, having netted 23 times in 27 games for the Under-17s and six times in seven appearances for the Under-19s. But her competitive spirit was instilled at an even earlier age, in a football-loving family. 'I started playing when I was three,' she reveals. 'I used to play with my older brother – he's four years older than me. We're a very competitive and sporty family. Everyone in our family wanted to win so I think I've got my spirit from there. I used to play in my older brother's under-sevens team and I've always had a love for the game. I always played with the boys, up until I was around 12, when you weren't allowed to anymore. I just have a sheer love for football.'

Manchester City	2016 WSL1 Results		
23.03.16	Notts County (h)	W 1-0	Houghton 90+1
28.03.16	Arsenal (h)	W 2-0	Ross 65, Duggan (pen) 78
24.04.16	Birmingham City (a)	W 2-0	Corboz 35, Ross 90+5
29.04.16	Sunderland (a)	W 2-0	Parris 40, Duggan 75
02.05.16	Doncaster Rovers Belles (h)	W 6-0	Bronze 7, Scott 10, Ross 40, Beattie 44, Asllani 45, Duggan 73
19.05.16	Chelsea (a)	W 2-0	Stokes 44, Beattie 48
25.05.16	Liverpool (a)	D 0-0	
26.06.16	Liverpool (h)	D 1-1	Ross 65
24.07.16	Notts County (a)	W 5-1	Ross 5, 41, Scott 25, Stanway 45+1, Christiansen 73
31.07.16	Sunderland (h)	W 3-0	Stanway 17, 55, 81
03.08.16	Reading (a)	W 2-1	Christiansen 38, Duggan 81
11.08.16	Doncaster Rovers Belles (a)	W 4-0	Ross 1, Christiansen 15, Bronze 62, Corboz 90
28.08.16	Reading (h)	W 2-0	Beattie 48, Houghton 87
11.09.16	Arsenal (a)	W 1-0	Ross 50
25.09.16	Chelsea (h)	W 2-0	Chapman (og) 34, Duggan (pen) 50
30.10.16	Birmingham City (h)	D 1-1	Stokes 54

Manchester City	2016 FA Cup		
19.03.16 R5	Liverpool (a)	W 2-0	Stanway 30, Parris 64
03.04.16 QF	Sporting Club Albion (h)	W 2-0	Parris 7, Ross 22
17.04.16 SF	Chelsea (a)	L 1-2 (aet)	Ross 72

Manchester City	2016 Continental Cup		
02.07.16 R1	Aston Villa (a)	W 8-0	Parris (pen) 3, 17, 59, Ross (pen) 16, 90+1, Middag 32, Corboz 79, Scott 90
07.08.16 QF	Doncaster Rovers Belles (h)	W 4-1	Christiansen 38, Stanway 76, Duggan 82, Ross 88
04.09.16 SF	Arsenal (h)	W 1-0	Beattie 79
02.10.16 F	Birmingham City (n)*	W 1-0 (aet)	Bronze 104

*Played at Academy Stadium, Manchester

MANCHESTER CITY PLAYER APPEARANCES & GOALS 2016

				WSL1		FAC		CC		Total	
				A	G	A	G	A	G	A	G
Asllani, Kosovare	F	SWE	29.07.89	11	1	3	-	3	-	17	1
Bardsley, Karen	G	ENG	14.10.84	16	-	2	-	-	-	18	-
Beattie, Jennifer	M	SCO	13.05.91	12	3	1	-	4	1	17	4
Bronze, Lucy	D	ENG	28.10.91	16	2	3	-	4	1	23	3
Campbell, Megan	D	IRE	28.06.93	3	-	-	-	1	-	4	-
Corboz, Daphne	M	USA	14.06.93	13	2	3	-	3	1	19	3
Christiansen, Izzy	M	ENG	20.09.91	9	3	1	-	3	1	13	4
Duggan, Toni	F	ENG	25.07.91	15	5	2	-	3	1	20	6
Holland, Ceri	D	WAL	12.12.97	-	-	-	-	-	-	-	-
Houghton, Stephanie	D	ENG	23.04.88	16	2	3	-	4	-	23	2
Hourihan, Marie	G	ENG	10.03.85	-	-	1	-	4	-	5	-
Kemp, Amelia	M	ENG	30.11.01	-	-	1	-	-	-	1	-
McManus, Abbie	D	ENG	14.01.93	9	-	3	-	-	-	12	-
Middag, Tessel	M	NED	23.12.92	8	-	-	-	3	1	11	1
Parris, Nikita	F	ENG	10.03.94	16	1	3	2	4	3	23	6
Paul, Alethea	M	ENG	27.08.98	-	-	1	-	-	-	1	-
Roebuck, Ellie	G	ENG	23.09.99	1	-	-	-	-	-	1	-
Ross, Jane	F	SCO	18.09.89	16	8	3	2	4	3	23	13
Scott, Jill	M	ENG	02.02.87	15	2	2	-	3	1	20	3
Stanway, Georgia	F	ENG	03.01.99	10	4	3	1	2	1	15	6
Stokes, Demi	D	ENG	12.12.91	16	2	3	-	4	-	23	2
Toone, Ella	F	ENG	02.09.99	-	-	-	-	1	-	1	-
Tynan, Zoe	M	ENG	20.05.98	-	-	1	-	-	-	1	-
Walsh, Kiera	M	ENG	08.04.97	8	-	-	-	4	-	12	-

GOALSCORERS 2016

WSL1: J. Ross (8), Duggan (5), Stanway (4), Beattie (3), Christiansen (3), Bronze (2), Corboz (2), Houghton (2), J. Scott (2), Stokes (2), Asllani (1), Parris (1), own goals (1)

FAC: Parris (2), J. Ross (2), Stanway (1)

CC: Parris (3), J. Ross (3), Beattie (1), Bronze (1), Corboz (1), Christiansen (1), Duggan (1), Middag (1), J. Scott (1), Stanway (1)

Total: J. Ross (13), Duggan (6), Parris (6), Stanway (6), Beattie (4), Christiansen (4), Bronze (3), Corboz (3), J.Scott (3), Houghton (2), Stokes (2), Asllani (1), Middag (1), own goals (1)

Manchester City	2017 WSL1 Spring Series		
03.05.17	Birmingham City (h)	D 1-1	Bronze 58
07.05.17	Reading (a)	W 3-2	Parris 6, 76, Scott 78
09.05.17	Bristol City (a)	W 3-0	Duggan 43, (pen) 51, 57
21.05.17	Yeovil Town (h)	W 5-1	Heatherson (og) 11, Scott 13, Ross 38, 62, Asllani 68, Lloyd sent off 89
25.05.17	Chelsea (h)	W 1-0	Duggan 28
28.05.17	Arsenal (h)	L 0-1	
31.05.17	Sunderland (a)	W 1-0	Stanway 90
03.06.17	Liverpool (a)	W 3-1	Scott 29, Lawley 45, Campbell 61

Manchester City	2017 FA Cup		
18.03.17 R5	Reading (h)	W 1-0	Bronze 82
26.03.17 QF	Bristol City (a)	W 2-1	Houghton 7, Parris 88
17.04.17 SF	Liverpool (h)	W 1-0	Lawley 58
13.05.17 F	Birmingham City (at Wembley)	W 4-1	Bronze 18, Christiansen 25, Lloyd 32, Scott 80

Manchester City	2016/17 CL		
06.10.16 Rof32	Zvezda-Perm (RUS) (h)	W 2-0	Scott 34, Bronze 90+3
12.10.16 Rof32	Zvezda-Perm (RUS) (a)	W 4-0 (W 6-0)	Beattie 23, 52, Bronze 32, Christiansen 74
09.11.16 Rof16	Brondby (DEN) (h)	W 1-0	Walsh 74
16.11.16 Rof16	Brondby (DEN) (a)	D 1-1 (W 2-1)	Duggan 65
23.03.17 QF	Fortuna Hjorring (DEN) (a)	W 1-0	Lloyd 36
30.03.17 QF	Fortuna Hjorring (DEN) (h)	W 1-0 (W 2-0)	Bronze 41
22.04.17 SF	Lyon (FRA) (h)	L 1-3	Asllani 10
29.04.17 SF	Lyon (FRA) (a)	W 1-0 (L 2-3)	Lloyd 57

MANCHESTER CITY PLAYER APPEARANCES & GOALS 2017

				WSL1		FAC		CL		Total	
				A	G	A	G	A	G	A	G
Asllani, Kosovare	F	SWE	29.07.89	4	1	1	-	8	1	13	2
Bardsley, Karen	G	ENG	14.10.84	2	-	3	-	8	-	13	-
Beattie, Jennifer	M	SCO	13.05.91	7	-	-	-	4	2	11	2
Bronze, Lucy	D	ENG	28.10.91	7	1	4	2	8	3	19	6
Campbell, Megan	D	IRE	28.06.93	7	1	1	-	-	-	8	1
Corboz, Daphne	M	USA	14.06.93	-	-	-	-	1	-	1	-
Christiansen, Izzy	M	ENG	20.09.91	7	-	3	1	6	1	16	2
Duggan, Toni	F	ENG	25.07.91	6	4	3	-	7	1	16	5
Houghton, Stephanie	D	ENG	23.04.88	8	-	4	1	8	-	20	1
Hourihan, Marie	G	ENG	10.03.85	3	-	1	-	-	-	4	-
Kemp, Amelia	M	ENG	30.11.01	-	-	-	-	-	-	-	-
Lawley, Melissa	F	ENG	28.04.94	5	1	4	1	3	-	12	2
Lloyd, Carli	M	USA	16.07.82	4	-	4	1	4	2	12	3
McManus, Abbie	D	ENG	14.01.93	3	-	4	-	4	-	11	-
Middag, Tessel	M	NED	23.12.92	2	-	1	-	6	-	9	-
Parris, Nikita	F	ENG	10.03.94	6	2	4	1	7	-	17	3
Paul, Alethea	M	ENG	27.08.98	-	-	-	-	-	-	-	-
Roebuck, Ellie	G	ENG	23.09.99	3	-	-	-	-	-	3	-
Ross, Jane	F	SCO	18.09.89	4	2	3	-	6	-	13	2
Scott, Jill	M	ENG	02.02.87	8	3	3	1	8	1	19	5
Stanway, Georgia	F	ENG	03.01.99	7	1	3	-	3	-	13	1
Stokes, Demi	D	ENG	12.12.91	7	-	4	-	8	-	19	-
Toone, Ella	F	ENG	02.09.99	2	-	-	-	-	-	2	-
Walsh, Kiera	M	ENG	08.04.97	8	-	4	-	8	1	20	1

GOALSCORERS 2017

WSL1 Spring Series: Duggan (4), J.Scott (3), Parris (2), J.Ross (2), Asllani (1), Bronze (1), Campbell (1), Lawley (1), Stanway (1), own goals (1)

CL: Bronze (3), Beattie (2), Lloyd (2), Asllani (1), Christiansen (1), Duggan (1), J.Scott (1), Walsh (1)

FAC: Bronze (2), Christiansen (1), Houghton (1), Lawley (1), Lloyd (1), Parris (1), J.Scott (1)

Total: Bronze (6), Duggan (5), J.Scott (5), Lloyd (3), Parris (3), Asllani (2), Beattie (2), Christiansen (2), Lawley (2), J.Ross (2), Campbell (1), Houghton (1), Stanway (1), Walsh (1), own goals (1)

READING – WSL1

Founded: 2006	Previous WSL Positions
Stadium: Adams Park, (Wycombe Wanderers FC)	**2017 WSL1:** 6th (Spring Series)
National Honours: WSL2 Title: (1) 2015	**2016 WSL1:** 8th
Nickname: The Royals	**2015 WSL2:** 1st (Promoted)
Manager: Kelly Chambers (since August 2012)	**2014 WSL2:** 3rd

- Reading's former manager Jayne Ludlow is the current boss of the Wales women's national team. As a player she won the Champions League (then known as the UEFA Cup) with Arsenal in 2006/07.
- Reading men's operated a Centre of Excellence for young female players prior to 2006 when they formed a partnership with Reading Girls FC and expanded to include the current senior team. The new Reading Women's team were WPL South Champions in 2012/13 and were then selected as one of the founding members of WSL2 in its opening season of 2014.
- In 2015 they were WSL2 champions, clinching promotion with two games to spare and securing the title away to Aston Villa on the final day of the season. They pipped Doncaster Rovers Belles (who were also promoted) to top spot on goal difference. An eighth goal in six games from Wales striker Helen Ward helped Kelly Chambers' side beat Villa 3-2.
- The Royals were the only team from the second tier of English football to have a player at the 2015 World Cup. Striker Fran Kirby helped Mark Sampson's Lionesses reach the semi-finals. After the tournament she signed for WSL1 side Chelsea.

SEASON 2016 RECORD

2016 WSL1:	8th	P16	W1	D6	L9	F15	A26	GD-11	Pts9
2016 FA Cup:	Quarter-finals								
2016 Continental Cup:	1st Round								

SEASON 2017 RECORD

2017 WSL1 Spring Series	6th	P8	W2	D2	L4	F10	A15	GD-5	Pts8
2017 FA Cup:	5th Round								

Jo Potter Born: 13.11.1984, Mansfield **Position:** Central / left midfield or left-back

Jo Potter has made a name for herself as something of a set-piece specialist over the years, as well as being a reliable, creative midfielder. But how did she develop one of the best left feet in the game? Practice, practice, practice. 'If you find something you love doing and you're good at it, you practice even more,' she says.

'It's something that I definitely worked hard at when I was younger, my accuracy and dead-ball specialisms. I practised a lot on my corners and free-kicks, and that linked into my field play, being able to shoot from distance and strike on goal. It's something you just have to keep practising.'

And practice has made perfect on many occasions for the former Birmingham City star, perhaps most evidently on 28 May 2013, when she scored one of the finest goals the Women's Super League has seen since it began in 2011. In a 2-1 win over Chelsea, she struck Birmingham's second goal from distance with unstoppable power past England keeper Carly Telford, and it's a strike Potter remembers fondly.

'The ball fell to my feet, about 40 yards out. I took a touch and I smashed one into the top corner. That goal always sticks out in my head, because of the distance on it really,' Potter recalls. But perhaps Potter's welcome habit of scoring long-range efforts and curling free-kicks is no surprise, when you consider which players she idolised as a youngster.

'My favourite player was Zinedine Zidane and – supporting Liverpool – Steven Gerrard was somebody who I always watched too,' she says. 'For the women's game, I always looked to Marieanne Spacey. I remember watching Marieanne in an FA Cup final and she picked the ball up on the left, floated in along the edge of the box and then powered it into the top corner. I remember thinking "wow" and I've never forgotten that goal.

'Also, as a young, left-footed player, I looked up to Sue Smith and Rachel Yankey. It was something that was later really nice for me, to be able to get to an international stage eventually where I could play with those players and actually become teammates with them.'

Potter, who made her England debut in 2004, has not only played alongside some of England's all-time greats, but has also witnessed the game's transition from an amateur level to professional – something which happened over the course of her playing career. 'Every single thing that could have improved within the women's game has improved,' she adds.

'Facilities, coaching, managers and the level of professionalism, sports science… Everything that needed to improve has done so, by at least 200 per cent. Reading want success. We want the best players. I feel that I'm at a club where we can go forward and still get better and still win things myself, so I'm definitely looking forward to the future.'

Reading	2016 WSL1		
23.03.16	Arsenal (a)	L 1-3	Boho-Sayo 58
26.03.16	Sunderland (a)	D 1-1	Roche 41
24.04.16	Notts County (a)	D 2-2	Ward 7, Bassett (og) 38
27.04.16	Arsenal (h)	L 1-2	Follis 78
02.05.16	Sunderland (h)	D 1-1	Ward (pen) 74
19.05.16	Birmingham City (a)	D 0-0	
09.07.16	Liverpool (a)	L 0-2	
24.07.16	Birmingham City (h)	D 1-1	Fletcher 47
31.07.16	Notts County (h)	D 1-1	Follis 65
03.08.16	Manchester City (h)	L 1-2	Bruton (pen) 89
28.08.16	Manchester City (a)	L 0-2	
01.09.16	Liverpool (h)	L 0-1	
11.09.16	Chelsea (h)	L 0-3	
24.09.16	Doncaster Rovers Belles (a)	W 4-1	Follis 9, 61, Jones 37, Rowe 84
30.10.16	Chelsea (a)	L 2-3	Bruton (pen) 65, Fletcher 90+3
06.11.16	Doncaster Rovers Belles (h)	L 0-1	

Reading	2016 FA Cup		
20.03.16 R5	Millwall Lionesses (h)	W 2-0	Boho-Sayo 61, Follis 72
26.03.16 QF	Sunderland (a)	L 0-3	

Reading	2016 Continental Cup		
02.07.16 R1	Arsenal (h)	L 1-3	Follis 66

READING PLAYER APPEARANCES & GOALS 2016

				WSL1		FAC		CC		Total	
				A	G	A	G	A	G	A	G
Allen, Remi	M	ENG	15.10.90	9	-	-	-	-	-	9	-
Bartrip, Molly	D	ENG	01.06.96	12	-	2	-	1	-	15	-
Boho-Sayo, Jade	F	EQG	30.08.86	8	1	1	1	1	-	10	2
Bruton, Lauren	M	ENG	22.11.92	16	2	2	-	1	-	19	2
Cox (Provan), Shelly	D	ENG	16.05.84	4	-	-	-	1	-	5	-
Cunningham, Zoe	M	ENG	10.12.94	2	-	-	-	-	-	2	-
Earps, Mary	G	ENG	07.03.93	12	-	1	-	1	-	14	-
Estcourt, Charlie	M	WAL	27.05.98	4	-	2	-	1		7	-
Davies, Kylie	D	WAL	25.09.87	7	-	-	-	-	-	7	-
Fletcher, Melissa	F	ENG	28.01.92	12	2	-	-	-	-	12	2
Follis, Emma	M	ENG	06.01.92	16	4	2	1	1	1	19	6
Hines, Kayleigh	M	ENG	27.02.91	15	-	2	-	1	-	18	-
Horwood, Bonnie	M	ENG	16.04.87	-	-	-	-	-	-	-	-
Jane, Rebecca	D	ENG	31.03.92	15	-	2	-	1	-	18	-
Jones, Nia	D	WAL	06.04.92	9	1	1	-	-	-	10	1
Knapton, Hannah	M	ENG	09.01.98	1	-	-	-	-	-	1	-
McGee, Kirsty	D	ENG	16.04.87	16	-	2	-	1	-	19	-
May-Walkley, Laura	M	WAL	19.05.91	6	-	1	-	-	-	7	-
Moloney, Grace	G	IRE	01.03.93	6	-	1	-	-	-	7	-
Perry, Sophie	D	IRE	11.11.86	4	-	-	-	-	-	4	-
Roche, Lois	M	IRE	18.06.93	5	1	2	-	1	-	8	1
Rowe, Rachel	M	WAL	13.09.92	16	1	2	-	1	-	19	1
Sansom, Chloe	G	ENG	17.10.96	-	-	-	-	-	-	-	-
Scott, Harriet	D	IRE	10.02.93	8	-	2	-	1	-	11	-
Stobbs, Amber	F	ENG	21.10.92	8	-	-	-	1	-	9	-
Ward, Helen	F	WAL	26.04.86	9	2	2	-	1	-	12	2

GOALSCORERS 2016

WSL1: Follis (4), Bruton (2), Fletcher (2), Ward (2), Boho-Sayo (1), Jones (1), Roche (1), Rowe (1)

FAC: Boho-Sayo (1), Follis (1)

CC: Follis (1)

Total: Follis (6), Boho-Sayo (2), Bruton (2), Fletcher (2), Ward (2), Jones (1), Roche (1), Rowe (1)

Reading	2017 WSL1 Spring Series		
22.04.17	Bristol City (a)	W 3-1	Furness 49, Rowe 59, Fletcher 61
28.04.17	Liverpool (a)	L 2-4	Chaplen 3, Fletcher 7
03.05.17	Chelsea (h)	L 0-4	
07.05.17	Manchester City (h)	L 2-3	Moore 59, Bruton (pen) 74
17.05.17	Yeovil Town (a)	W 1-0	Van den Berg 7
28.05.17	Birmingham City (h)	D 1-1	Bruton (pen) 64
31.05.17	Arsenal (a)	L 0-1	
03.06.17	Sunderland (a)	D 1-1	Fletcher 30

Reading	2017 FA Cup		
18.03.17 R5	Manchester City (a)	L 0-1	

READING PLAYER APPEARANCES & GOALS 2017

				WSL1		FAC		Total	
				A	G	A	G	A	G
Allen, Remi	M	ENG	15.10.90	8	-	1	-	9	-
Bartrip, Molly	D	ENG	01.06.96	2	-	1	-	3	-
Bruton, Lauren	M	ENG	22.11.92	7	2	1	-	8	2
Chaplen, Brooke	M	ENG	16.04.89	3	1	1	-	4	1
Earps, Mary	G	ENG	07.03.93	8	-	1	-	9	-
Estcourt, Charlie	M	WAL	27.05.98	4	-	1	-	5	-
Fletcher, Melissa	F	ENG	28.01.92	7	3	1	-	8	3
Furness, Rachel	M	NIR	19.06.88	7	1	1	-	8	1
Green, Anna	D	NZL	20.08.90	6	-	1	-	7	-
Hines, Kayleigh	M	ENG	27.02.91	3	-	-	-	3	-
Jane, Rebecca	D	ENG	31.03.92	7	-	1	-	8	-
Lahmari, Anissa	M	FRA	17.02.97	6	-	-	-	6	-
Linnett, Kirsty	F	ENG	24.09.93	6	-	-	-	6	-
McGee, Kirsty	D	ENG	16.04.87	8	-	-	-	8	-
Moloney, Grace	G	IRE	01.03.93	-	-	-	-	-	-
Moore, Jade	M	ENG	22.10.90	6	1	-	-	6	1
Potter, Jo	M	ENG	13.11.84	4	-	-	-	4	-
Rowe, Rachel	M	WAL	13.09.92	4	1	1	-	5	1
Scott, Harriet	D	IRE	10.02.93	8	-	1	-	9	-
Van den Berg, Mandy	D	NED	26.08.90	4	1	1	-	5	1

GOALSCORERS 2017

WSL1 SS: Fletcher (3), Bruton (2), Chaplen (1), Furness (1), Moore (1), Rowe (1), Van den Berg (1)

FAC: None

Total: Fletcher (3), Bruton (2), Chaplen (1), Furness (1), Moore (1), Rowe (1), Van den Berg (1)

SUNDERLAND – WSL1

Founded: 1989 (as The Kestrels)	Previous WSL Positions
Stadium: The Hetton Centre, Hettton-le-Hole	**2017 WSL1:** 5th (Spring Series)
National Honours: WSL2 Winners: (1) 2014	**2016 WSL1:** 7th
National Premier League Winners: (3)	**2015 WSL1:** 4th
2010/11, 2011/12, 2012/13	**2014 WSL2:** 1st (Promoted)
FA Cup Runners-up: (1) 2008/09	
WPL Cup Winners: (1) 2011/12	
Nickname: The Lady Black Cats	
Manager: Melanie Reay (since March 2017)	

- The club began life as a five-a-side team called Kestrels in 1989. Over the next decade, competing in full-scale football in the Northern Premier League, they were variously known as Cowgate Kestrels, RTM Kestrels and Blyth Spartans Kestrels. In 1999 they merged with Sunderland Ladies to become Sunderland Women's.
- They had a fleeting relationship with Sunderland men's at the start of the century, which ceased in 2004. In 2013 they came back under the Sunderland men's umbrella and changed their name from Sunderland Women to Sunderland Ladies.
- Current England and Manchester City captain Steph Houghton was born in Durham and began her career with Sunderland before leaving for Leeds in 2007.
- Sunderland's Republic of Ireland international forward Stephanie Roche is perhaps best known for a sensational goal she scored for former club Peamount against Wexford Youths in 2013. It became a YouTube hit and was nominated for the 2014 FIFA Puskas award for the best goal scored anywhere in the world. She finished second with 33% of the vote behind James Rodriguez who won for his volley for Colombia against Uruguay at the World Cup.

- Melanie Reay, who succeeded Carlton Fairweather as Sunderland head coach in March 2017, spent her playing career as a striker for the Black Cats and has been with them for 20 years.
- Before leaving for Arsenal in January 2017, Sunderland striker Beth Mead was WSL1 top scorer for the 2015 season with a remarkable return of 12 goals in 14 games.

SEASON 2016 RECORD

2016 WSL1:	7th	P16	W2	D4	L10	F17	A41	GD-24	Pts10
2016 FA Cup:	Semi-final								
2016 Continental Cup:	1st Round								

SEASON 2017 RECORD

2017 WSL1 Spring Series:	5th	P8	W2	D3	L3	F4	A14	GD-10	Pts9
2017 FA Cup:	Quarter-final								

Melanie Reay **Position:** Head coach **Appointed:** 16 March 2017

A long-serving, former Sunderland striker, Melanie Reay has been a stalwart for women's football in the North-East and received her first big break in top-level management when she was promoted from the role of assistant to replace Carlton Fairweather as the club's new head coach in 2017. After a winter which saw star striker Beth Mead signed by Arsenal, and less of the squad training full-time than in 2016, many outside the region were predicting Sunderland to struggle in the 2017 Spring Series – yet under new first-team boss Reay there was a rapid improvement. 'We finished an incredible fifth behind only the 'big four', so we're very happy overall,' Reay says. 'I'm pleased that the girls really bought into the way I wanted to go about things.'

An assistant to first Mick Mulhern and then to Fairweather at Sunderland, and having spent 15 years coaching at Gateshead College, Reay's apprenticeship had been a thorough one. 'I think I served my time as the assistant and then, to be offered the job as head coach, that was something I couldn't turn down,' she adds. 'My current employers, Gateshead College, offered me a sabbatical, keeping my role there at the College available until May 2018, to allow me to take this opportunity and see how it goes.'

Reay has been with Sunderland from the beginning, witnessing their evolution over the years. 'I've seen the club through the bad times and the good times. I've seen it when it wasn't professional at all and everyone was bag-packing in Asda to raise money for us,' she recalls.

'When I played for Sunderland, I didn't receive any payment whatsoever. I actually paid to play for them. We paid our subs annually to help keep the club ticking along. Now we're based at the Academy of Light and we're training on fantastic facilities. Some of the girls are full-time. Sometimes I remind them of just how lucky they are. I'm glad to be part of the club now when it's at its best.

'It was my Dad who spotted a club for me to go to in the first place, called Cowgate Kestrels, which developed over a 10-year period into Sunderland. It was the same cohort of ladies playing, but we moved around the North-East changing the club's name depending on who would back us.'

Prior to taking charge at Sunderland, Reay also worked as a coach within the England youth setup. So what sort of boss is Reay, on the training ground? 'I've got a mixture of different styles really. I can be very strict. I'm very friendly. I like to get to know the players and find out what makes the players tick,' she says. 'You've got to know how to press certain players' buttons, to get the best out of them. You can only do that by digging a little bit deeper and finding out who they actually are, away from football.'

Sunderland	2016 WSL1 Results		
26.03.16	Reading (h)	D 1-1	Mead 46
23.04.16	Liverpool (a)	D 2-2	Chaplen 30, 60
29.04.16	Manchester City (h)	L 0-2	
02.05.16	Reading (a)	D 1-1	Mead 8, *Beer sent off 77*
18.05.16	Liverpool (h)	L 0-4	
25.05.16	Chelsea (a)	L 1-2	Roche 5
25.06.16	Arsenal (a)	L 1-5	Mead 89
29.06.16	Chelsea (h)	L 0-5	
09.07.16	Doncaster Rovers Belles (h)	W 4-0	Mead 35, 45+3, Sharp 39, Chaplen 78
17.07.16	Birmingham City (a)	L 0-1	
24.07.16	Arsenal (h)	L 0-4	
31.07.16	Manchester City (a)	L 0-3	
01.09.16	Doncaster Rovers Belles (a)	W 4-1	Williams 34, Holmes 39, McDougall 69, Hill 80
25.09.16	Notts County (a)	L 1-2	Williams 45+1
29.10.16	Notts County (h)	D 1-1	Kelly 39
06.11.16	Birmingham City (h)	L 1-7	Mead 67

Sunderland	2016 FA Cup		
20.03.16 R5	Yeovil Town (a)	W 2-0	Chaplen 67, 80
03.04.16 QF	Reading (h)	W 3-0	Mead 35, Williams 41, Chaplen 90+2
17.04.16 SF	Arsenal (a)	L 0-7	

Sunderland	2016 Continental Cup		
03.07.16 R1	Doncaster Rovers Belles (a)	L 1-2	Ramshaw 62

SUNDERLAND PLAYER APPEARANCES & GOALS 2016

				WSL1		FAC		CC		Total	
				A	G	A	G	A	G	A	G
Bannon, Stephanie	D	ENG	22.03.89	16	-	3	-	-	-	19	-
Beer, Megan	D	ENG	22.03.93	6	-	-	-	-	-	6	-
Brown, Danielle	D	ENG	06.10.98	12	-	-	-	1	-	13	-
Chaplen, Brooke	M	ENG	16.04.89	12	3	3	3	1	-	16	6
Furness, Rachel	M	NIR	19.06.88	12	-	3	-	1	-	16	-
Galloway, Bridget	F	ENG	19.07.99	2	-	-	-	-	-	2	-
Gunn Olsen, Hilde	G	NOR	02.03.92	6	-	1	-	1	-	8	-
Hill, Madelaine	M	CAN/SCO	07.12.91	11	1	-	-	1	-	12	1
Holmes, Abby	D	ENG	26.05.91	14	1	3	-	1	-	18	1
Johnston, Krystle	F	ENG	26.04.84	3	-	3	-	-	-	6	-
Joice, Abbey	F	ENG	27.01.96	12	-	3	-	1	-	16	-
Kelly, Emma	M	ENG	26.01.97	6	1	1	-	-	-	7	1
Laws, Rachael	G	ENG	05.11.90	15	-	3	-	-	-	18	-
Leon, Beverly	M	USA	23.04.92	3	-	-	-	-	-	3	-
McDougall, Kelly	M	ENG	22.01.84	10	1	2	-	-	-	12	1
Mead, Beth	F	ENG	09.05.95	16	6	3	1	-	-	19	6
Potts, Charlotte	D	ENG	23.09.94	8	-	-	-	-	-	8	-
Pitman, Rachel	D	ENG	06.12.91	-	-	1	-	-	-	1	-
Ramshaw, Keira	M	ENG	12.01.94	13	-	3	-	1	1	17	1
Roche, Stephanie	F	IRE	13.06.89	11	1	2	-	1	-	14	1
Sharp, Hayley	D	ENG	12.11.90	14	1	1	-	1	-	16	1
Sjoman, Kylla	D	CAN	18.08.87	2	-	3	-	-	-	5	-
Staniforth, Lucy	M	ENG	02.10.92	12	-	3	-	1	-	16	-
Warren, Erika	D	ENG	05.05.99	1	-	-	-	-	-	1	-
Watt, Olivia	D	ENG	07.05.99	2	-	-	-	-	-	2	-
Williams, Victoria	D	ENG	05.04.90	14	2	3	1	1	-	18	3

GOALSCORERS 2016

WSL1: Mead (6), Chaplen (3), Williams (2), Hill (1), Holmes (1), Kelly (1), McDougall (1), Roche (1), Sharp (1)

FAC: Chaplen (3), Mead (1), Williams (1)

CC: Ramshaw (1)

Total: Mead (7), Chaplen (6), Williams (3), Hill (1), Holmes (1), Kelly (1), McDougall (1), Ramshaw (1), Roche (1), Sharp (1)

Sunderland	2017 WSL1 Spring Series		
23.04.17	Birmingham City (a)	D 0-0	
30.04.17	Arsenal (h)	D 0-0	
06.05.17	Bristol City (h)	W 1-0	Staniforth (pen) 76
17.05.17	Liverpool (a)	L 0-4	
21.05.17	Chelsea (h)	L 0-7	
28.05.17	Yeovil Town (a)	W 2-1	Lawrence (og) 2, Leon 77
31.05.17	Manchester City (h)	L 0-1	
03.06.17	Reading (h)	D 1-1	Leon 56

Sunderland	2017 FA Cup		
19.03.17 R5	Aston Villa (h)	W 3-2	Williams 13, Sharp 35, Staniforth (pen) 65
26.03.17 QF	Chelsea (a)	L 1-5	Staniforth 17

SUNDERLAND PLAYER APPEARANCES & GOALS 2017

				WSL1		FAC		Total	
				A	G	A	G	A	G
Bannon, Steph	D	ENG	22.03.89	8	-	2	-	10	-
Brown, Danielle	D	ENG	06.10.98	4	-	2	-	6	-
Bruinenberg, Dominique	M	NED	23.01.93	8	-	2	-	10	-
Galloway, Bridget	F	ENG	19.07.99	1	-	2	-	3	-
Gibson, Georgia	M	ENG	02.09.98	-	-	-	-	-	-
Gunn Olsen, Hilde	G	NOR	02.03.92	3	-	-	-	3	-
Hill, Madelaine	M	CAN/SCO	07.12.91	7	-	2	-	9	-
Holmes, Abby	D	ENG	26.05.91	8	-	2	-	10	-
Joice, Abbey	F	ENG	27.01.96	8	-	1	-	9	-
Lambert, Mollie	M	ENG	14.06.98	7	-	2	-	9	-
Leon, Beverly	M	USA	23.04.92	8	2	1	-	10	2
Pattinson, Poppy	D	ENG	30.04.00	2	-	-	-	2	-
Preuss, Anke	G	GER	22.09.92	6	-	2	-	8	-
Sharp, Hayley	D	ENG	12.11.90	7	-	2	1	9	1
Staniforth, Lucy	M	ENG	02.10.92	8	1	2	2	10	3
Ramshaw, Kiera	M	ENG	12.01.94	8	-	1	-	9	-
Roche, Stephanie	F	IRE	13.06.89	7	-	2	-	9	-
Stonehouse, Sophy	G	ENG	29.12.97	-	-	-	-	-	-
Watt, Olivia	D	ENG	07.05.99	2	-	1	-	3	-
Williams, Victoria	D	ENG	05.04.90	8	-	2	1	10	1

GOALSCORERS 2017

WSL1 SS: Staniforth (2), Leon (1), own goals (1)

FAC: Staniforth (2), Sharp (1), Williams (1)

Total: Staniforth (4), Leon (1), Sharp (1), Williams (1), own goals (1)

YEOVIL TOWN – WSL1

Founded: 1990 (as Yetminster)	**Previous WSL Positions**
Stadium: Huish Park, (Yeovil Town FC)	**2017 WSL1:** 9th (Spring Series)
National Honours: WSL2 Champions: (1)	**2016 WSL2:** 1st (Promoted)
2016	**2015 WSL2:** 4th
Nickname: The Lady Glovers	**2014 WSL2:** 5th
Manager: Jamie Sherwood (since Sep 2014)	

- The team was founded as Yetminster Ladies in 1990. They became Sherbourne Ladies in 1993 and Yeovil Town Ladies in 1999. They play at Yeovil Town men's Huish Park ground but used Taunton FC and Bridgwater FC's stadium's during the 2017 WSL1 Spring Series.
- They were founding members of WSL2 in 2014 and have improved in every season finishing fifth, then fourth and then going up to WSL1 as WSL2 2016 champions. Their first season among the elite was the 2017 Spring Series. They endured a tough campaign, picking up just one point and finishing bottom in ninth place.
- Yeovil Town forward Annie Heatherson won the 2005 FA Cup with Charlton before spells with teams including Stjarnan of Iceland and Buffalo Flash (now known as Western New York Flash) in the USA.
- Manager Jamie Sherwood previously led Cardiff City Ladies to the FA Women's Premier League Southern Division title in 2013/14.

SEASON 2016 RECORD

2016 WSL2:	1st (Promoted)	P18	W12	D3	L3	F41	A16	GD+25	Pts39
2016 FA Cup:	5th Round								
2016 Continental Cup:	1st Round								

SEASON 2017 RECORD

2017 WSL1 Spring Series:	9th	P8	W0	D1	L7	F6	A26	GD-20	Pts1
2017 FA Cup:	5th Round								

Annie Heatherson **Born:** 27.03.1984 Hackney, London **Position:** Forward

For few players is the expression 'been there and done that' more true than it is for Yeovil Town's Annie Heatherson. She's won trophies in the United States as well as in England, and even spent a season in Iceland. Now, after helping Yeovil reach the top-flight for the first time, the experienced forward aims to give something back to the next generation, helping with community coaching and ambassadorial roles.

'That's my motivation – being able to inspire kids to do what I've done,' Heatherson says. 'I was just an average kid who had an aggressive background, but needed something to do in my life. I was told I wasn't very good at football, but I had a heart for the game and I wanted to work hard. Back then, I never had support from players to inspire me with their own football stories. Yet, football – and sport in general – can do so much for people's lives, especially young people.

'Sometimes nowadays, an aggressive child – like I used to be – is just assumed to have problems and a "bad upbringing". People rarely say, "Let's see if they have got a sport that they're good at." I believe sport and coaching is key to kids growing up. I'm passionate about changing their lives. Football can help kids find a dream. It can get people back on their feet, so I want to inspire kids.'

So, has the ex-Charlton, Fulham and Chelsea player seen any future stars on the training ground? 'If I'm being honest, I'm kind of glad I'm coming towards the end of my career, because the talent coming through now at the ages of 16, 17 and 18 are starting to put me in my place!' she admits.

After a fairy-tale promotion in 2016, the Somerset club endured a tough 2017 Spring Series before earning their first ever point in WSL1, with a creditable 0-0 draw at FA Cup-finalists Birmingham. But what is it like to play for the team with the lowest budget in WSL1, while competing in a league that contains some of the best-known clubs in world football? 'The special part about Yeovil is, you aren't going to go to Yeovil if you want lots of money. With Yeovil, you go to play there because you're passionate, and you love the club,' she says. 'There are no egos. It's very welcoming. If you're going to go to Yeovil, you're going to be a fighter. Everyone is together, everyone is a team, a squad. The dedicated fans simply top it off. We get a fair amount of people that travel to our away games, committed to getting minibuses and trains all around the country. It's absolutely amazing.'

Training part-time alongside other jobs, many of Yeovil's squad and coaching staff travel long distances to attend sessions, showing a level of commitment that Heatherson really admires. 'When you play for Yeovil you can't help but give everything you've got to Yeovil,' she says.

Yeovil Town	2016 WSL2		
23.03.16	Bristol City (a)	L 2-3	Primus (pen) 54, Cousins 79
17.04.16	Watford (a)	W 2-1	Wiltshire 16, Lawrence 78
24.04.16	Millwall Lionesses (h)	D 1-1	Wiltshire 74
27.04.16	Oxford United (h)	W 2-0	Cousins 73, Heatherson 90
30.04.16	Millwall Lionesses (a)	W 4-0	Bleazard 44, Heatherson 70, 81, Wiltshire 87
19.05.16	Bristol City (h)	W 2-0	Wiltshire 1, Curson 30
22.05.16	Aston Villa (h)	W 4-2	Cousins 76, Wiltshire 47, 62, 89
26.06.16	Durham (a)	W 2-0	Primus 57, Wiltshire 73
30.06.16	Oxford United (a)	D 2-2	Short 25, Curson 58
10.07.16	Watford (h)*	W 5-0	Wiltshire 19, 63, Cousins 39, Primus 47, Bleazard 61
17.07.16	Everton (a)	L 0-3	
24.07.16	Durham (h)	W 4-0	Wiltshire 4, Bleazard 14, Heatherson 85, 87
31.07.16	Aston Villa (a)	W 2-0	Short 4, Heatherson 53
28.08.16	Sheffield FC (a)	D 1-1	Quinn 88
11.09.16	London Bees (h)	L 2-3	Quinn 20, 45
25.09.16	Everton (h)	W 1-0	Aldridge 23
30.10.16	London Bees (a)	W 2-0	Green 56, Lawrence 81
06.11.16	Sheffield FC (h)	W 3-0	Quinn 15, Heatherson 46, Cousins 78

Yeovil Town	2016 FA Cup		
07.02.16 R3	Bradford City (h)	W 2-0	Wiltshire 14, Knapman 90+4
28.02.16 R4	Bristol City (a)	D 0-0 (W 3-2p)	
20.03.16 R5	Sunderland (h)	L 0-2	

Yeovil Town	2016 Continental Cup		
03.07.16 R1	Notts County (h)*	L 1-3	Lawrence 75

*Played at Sherbourne Town FC

YEOVIL TOWN PLAYER APPEARANCES & GOALS 2016

				WSL2		FAC		CC		Total	
				A	G	A	G	A	G	A	G
Aldridge, Kelly	F	ENG	22.09.80	9	1	-	-	1	-	10	1
Bleazard, Helen	M	WAL	14.08.90	17	3	3	-	1	-	21	3
Burridge, Leah	M	ENG	03.01.97	2	-	1	-	1	-	4	-
Carlton, Danielle	M	ENG	30.07.91	9	-	-	-	-	-	9	-
Cousins, Nicola	D	WAL	22.10.88	18	5	3	-	1	-	22	5
Curson, Ellen	M	WAL	18.02.94	18	2	3	-	-	-	21	2
Donovan, Emily	M	ENG	06.02.97	8	-	3	-	1	-	12	-
Green, Kayleigh	D	WAL	23.03.98	16	1	-	-	-	-	16	1
Haynes, Charlotte	G	ENG	06.08.97	15	-	3	-	-	-	18	-
Heatherson, Annie	F	ENG	27.03.84	16	7	3	-	-	-	19	7
Hillman, Ellis	M	ENG	22.12.92	7	-	2	-	1	-	10	-
Howard, Bethany-May	G	ENG	06.05.95	3	-	-	-	1	-	4	-
Johnson, Charlotte	G	ENG	22.02.99	-	-	-	-	1	-	1	-
Jones, Jessie	M	ENG	12.05.99	7	-	-	-	1	-	8	-
Knapman, Natasha	F	ENG	22.08.91	11	-	2	1	1	-	14	1
Lawrence, Nadia	F	WAL	29.11.89	17	2	3	-	1	1	21	3
Primus, Atlanta	M	ENG	21.04.97	4	3	3	-	-	-	7	3
Quayle, Samantha	M	WAL	08.10.95	1	-	1	-	-	-	2	-
Quinn, Lucy	F	ENG	29.09.93	5	4	-	-	-	-	5	4
Short, Hannah	D	ENG	16.04.93	18	2	1	-	1	-	20	2
Snook, Kelly	D	ENG	22.02.99	15	-	2	-	-	-	17	-
Townsend, Lauren	D	WAL	10.11.90	8	-	1	-	1	-	10	-
Whitton, Kirsty	M	SCO	17.02.89	-	-	1	-	-	-	1	-
Williams, Stephanie	M	WAL	12.08.92	15	-	3	-	1	-	19	-
Wiltshire, Sarah	F	WAL	07.07.91	12	11	3	1	-	-	15	12

GOALSCORERS 2016

WSL2: Wiltshire (11), Heatherson (7), Cousins (5), Quinn (4), Bleazard (3), Primus (3), Curson (2), Lawrence (2), Short (2), Aldridge (1), Green (1)

FAC: Knapman (1), Wiltshire (1)

CC: Lawrence (1)

Total: Wiltshire (11), Heatherson (7), Cousins (5), Bleazard (3), Quinn (4), Knapman (2), Lawrence (3), Curson (2), Primus (2), Short (2), Aldridge (1), Green (1),

Yeovil Town	WSL1 Spring Series		
23.04.17	Liverpool (h)	L 1-4	Wiltshire (pen) 78
30.04.17	Chelsea (a)	L 0-6	
03.05.17	Bristol City (h)	L 2-3	Heatherson 27, Wiltshire 70
07.05.17	Arsenal (h)	L 1-5	Quinn 41
17.05.17	Reading (h)	L 0-1	
21.05.17	Manchester City (a)	L 1-5	Quinn 20
28.05.17	Sunderland (h)	L 1-2	James 76
31.05.17	Birmingham City (a)	D 0-0	

Yeovil Town	2017 FA Cup		
19.03.17 R5	Notts County (a)	L 2-3	Quinn (pen) 85, Snook 88

YEOVIL TOWN PLAYER APPEARANCES & GOALS 2017

				WSL		FAC		Total	
				A	G	A	G	A	G
Bleazard, Helen	M	WAL	14.08.90	8	-	1	-	9	-
Burridge, Leah	M	ENG	03.01.97	1	-	-	-	1	-
Clark, Molly	M	ENG	22.08.91	3	-	-	-	3	-
Cousins, Nicola	D	WAL	22.10.88	8	-	-	-	8	-
Curson, Ellen	M	WAL	18.02.94	8	-	1	-	9	-
Haigh, Natalie	D	ENG	08.02.89	6	-	1	-	7	-
Haynes, Charlotte	G	ENG	06.08.97	2	-	1	-	3	-
Heatherson, Annie	F	ENG	27.03.84	8	1	1	-	9	1
Howard, Bethany-May	G	ENG	06.05.95	-	-	-	-	-	-
Jackson, Bow	M	ENG	27.05.94	2	-	1	-	3	-
James, Angharad	M	WAL	01.06.94	4	1	-	-	4	1
Johnson, Charlotte	G	ENG	22.02.99	-	-	1	-	1	-
Jones, Jessie	M	ENG	12.05.99	6	-	-	-	6	-
Jones, Nia	M	WAL	06.04.92	8	-	1	-	9	-
Lawrence, Nadia	F	WAL	29.11.89	8	-	1	-	9	-
Pusey, Ella	F	ENG	10.03.00	5	-	1	-	6	-
Quinn, Lucy	F	ENG	29.09.93	8	2	1	1	9	3
Short, Hannah	D	ENG	16.04.93	8	-	1	-	9	-
Snook, Kelly	D	ENG	22.02.99	4	-	1	1	5	1
Walsh, Megan	G	ENG	12.11.94	6	-	-	-	6	-
Williams, Stephanie	M	WAL	12.08.92	2	-	1	-	3	-
Wiltshire, Sarah	F	WAL	07.07.91	6	2	-	-	6	2

GOALSCORERS 2017

WSL1 SS: Quinn (2), Wiltshire (2), Heatherson (1), James (1)

FAC: Quinn (1), Snook (1)

Total: Quinn (3), Wiltshire (2), Heatherson (1), James (1), Snook (1)

WSL2

This next section of the Yearbook details the 10 teams competing in WSL2 in 2017/18.

It lists their WSL results from the last full season (2016), and from the WSL 2017 Spring Series as well as their 2015/16 and 2016/17 FA Cup and 2016 WSL Continental Cup results.

For both Brighton and Tottenham, 2017/18 is their first full season in WSL2. Brighton won the 2015/16 WPL Southern title and the promotion play-off against Sporting Albion (now West Bromwich Albion), but had to wait until the 2017 Spring Series to make their WSL2 debut. Tottenham were 2016/17 WPL Southern champions, and beat Blackburn Rovers in the play-off final to claim their place in WSL2. Both clubs' WPL, FA Cup and WPL Cup results are also detailed here.

1 ASTON VILLA
2 BRIGHTON & HOVE ALBION
3 DONCASTER ROVERS BELLES
4 DURHAM
5 LONDON BEES
6 MILLWALL LIONESSES
7 OXFORD UNITED
8 SHEFFIELD FC
9 TOTTENHAM HOTSPUR
10 WATFORD

ASTON VILLA – WSL2

Founded: 1973 (as Solihull)	Previous WSL Positions
Stadium: The Lamb Ground (Tamworth FC)	2017 WSL2: 4th (Spring Series)
National Honours: WPL Cup: (1) 2013	2016 WSL2: 6th
WPL Cup Runners-up: (1) 1995 (as Villa Aztecs)	2015 WSL2: 5th
Nickname: The Lady Villans	2014 WSL2: 4th
Manager: Dave Stevens (since May 2017)	

- The club was founded as Solihull Ladies FC in 1973. In 1989, Aston Villa men's asked for help forming a ladies team. Solihull responded and changed their name to Villa Aztecs.
- Villa Aztecs reached the 1995 WPL Cup final where they were beaten 2-0 by Wimbledon.
- In 1996 they changed their name to Aston Villa Ladies and were officially recognised as the Premier League club's ladies team, but it wasn't until 2007 that they were fully integrated into the Aston Villa FC family.
- Promotion to the WPL Northern Division arrived in 1998. After 13 seasons at that level they won the 2011 WPL Northern Division and were promoted to the WPL National Division.
- Villa's first major trophy arrived in 2013 when they won the WPL Cup, beating Leeds 5-4 on penalties after a goalless draw. They were founding members of WSL2 in 2014.

SEASON 2016 RECORD

2016 WSL2:	6th	P18	W7	D3	L8	F26	A27	GD-1	Pts24
2016 FA Cup:	Quarter-finals								
2016 Continental Cup:	1st Round								

SEASON 2017 RECORD

2017 WSL2 Spring Series	4th	P9	W5	D2	L2	F19	A16	GD+3	Pts17
2017 FA Cup:	5th Round								

Aston Villa	2016 WSL 2		
24.03.16	Everton (a)	L 1-2	George 29
27.03.16	Oxford United (h)	W 2-1	Wilkinson 40, Merrick 70
23.04.16	Sheffield FC (a)	W 2-1	Wilkinson 25, 62
28.04.16	Bristol City (a)	L 0-2	
01.05.16	Durham (h)	W 2-0	Wilkinson 67, Rouse 82
17.05.16	Everton (h)	L 0-2	
22.05.16	Yeovil Town (a)	L 2-4	George 29, Wilkinson 45
26.06.16	London Bees (h)	D 1-1	Wilkinson 56
28.06.16	Bristol City (h)	D 2-2	Baptiste 84, Merrick 90+4
10.07.16	Durham (a)	L 0-3	
17.07.16	Millwall Lionesses (h)*	W 3-1	Merrick 29, 36, Smith 63
24.07.16	Watford (a)	W 2-0	Merrick 35, Baptiste 45
31.07.16	Yeovil Town (h)*	L 0-2	
28.08.16	London Bees (a)	L 1-2	Merrick 90+1
11.09.16	Sheffield FC (h)	L 1-2	Jones 25
25.09.16	Oxford United (a)	W 1-0	Welsh 55
30.10.16	Millwall Lionesses (a)	D 2-2	Merrick 56, George 89
06.11.16	Watford (h)+	W 4-0	Merrick 29, 85, Shepherd 48, Baptiste 51

*Played at Knights Lane (Stratford Town FC) +Played at Villa Park, (Aston Villa FC)

Aston Villa	2016 FA Cup		
07.02.16 R3	Portsmouth (h)	W 1-0	Wilkinson 65
28.02.16 R4	Tottenham Hotspur (a)	W 3-2 (aet)	Toussaint 29, Rouse 83, Wilkinson 109
20.03.16 R5	Everton (h)	W 1-0	George 57
03.04.16 QF	Chelsea (a)	L 0-6	

Aston Villa	2016 Continental Cup		
03.07.16 R1	Manchester City (h)	L 0-8	Jones sent off 16

ASTON VILLA PLAYER APPEARANCES & GOALS 2016

				WSL2		FAC		CC		Total	
				A	G	A	G	A	G	A	G
Baptiste, Natasha	F	ENG	29.07.91	13	3	-	-	-	-	13	3
Beattie, Chloe	G	ENG	24.04.98	2	-	-	-	-	-	2	-
Brown, Ashlee	D	ENG	04.08.96	1	-	1	-	-	-	2	-
Bryant, Leanne	D	ENG	02.10.96	1	-	2	-	-	-	3	-
Crackle, Hayley	D	NIR	13.05.95	9	-	4	-	1	-	14	-
Cusack, Maddy	M	ENG	28.10.95	17	-	3	-	1	-	21	-
George, Hannah	D	ENG	22.01.95	18	3	4	1	1	-	23	4
Harper, Chloe	M	ENG	16.09.96	-	-	1	-	-	-	1	-
Hinchcliffe, Alys	F	WAL	28.03.95	8	-	-	-	1	-	9	-
Jones, Chloe	M	ENG	01.07.88	10	1	-	-	1	-	11	1
Mayling, Sarah	M	ENG	20.03.97	18	-	1	-	1	-	20	-
Merrick, Bethany	F	ENG	12.10.95	18	9	4	-	1	-	23	9
Moloney, Grace	G	IRE	01.03.93	8	-	-	-	1	-	9	-
Moran, Katy	M	ENG	15.01.91	12	-	4	-	1	-	17	-
Myers, Jessica	G	ENG	03.02.95	9	-	4	-	-	-	13	-
N'Dow, Elisha	D	ENG	13.10.96	15	-	3	-	1	-	19	-
Porter, Lucy	M	ENG	27.09.98	3	-	-	-	1	-	4	-
Potts, Nicola	M	ENG	n/a	3	-	-	-	-	-	3	-
Richards, Jade	D	ENG	13.11.92	10	-	4	-	-	-	14	-
Robinson, Alicia	M	ENG	n/a	1	-	2	-	-	-	3	-
Rouse, Mollie	M	ENG	27.11.98	15	1	2	1	1	-	18	2
Shepherd, Lucy	F	ENG	14.11.98	4	1	-	-	-	-	4	1
Smith, Grace	D	ENG	20.01.99	4	1	-	-	-	-	4	1
Toussaint, Destiney	F	ENG	05.12.89	3	-	3	1	-	-	6	1
Welsh, Kerri	F	ENG	20.05.92	15	1	1	-	1	-	17	1
West, Amy	M	ENG	10.04.97	12	-	3	-	-	-	15	-
Wilkinson, Katie	F	ENG	05.11.94	10	6	4	2	1	-	15	8

GOALSCORERS 2016

WSL2: Merrick (9), Wilkinson (6), Baptiste (3), George (3), Jones (1), Rouse (1), Shepherd (1), Smith (1), Welsh (1)

FAC: Wilkinson (2), George (1), Rouse (1), Toussaint (1)

CC: None

Total: Merrick (9), Wilkinson (8), George (4), Baptiste (3), Rouse (2), Jones (1), Shepherd (1), Smith (1), Toussaint (1), Welsh (1)

Aston Villa	2017 WSL2 Spring Series		
12.02.17	Watford (h)	W 3-2	Baptiste 22, Merrick 38, Richards 48
05.03.17	Millwall (h)	D 1-1	N'Dow 1
12.03.17	Oxford United (a)	D 0-0	
02.04.17	Brighton & Hove Albion (h)	W 3-1	Welsh 33, Cusack 36, Baptiste 87
16.04.17	Everton (a)	L 0-3	
22.04.17	London Bees (h)	W 3-2	Welsh 17, Baptiste 27, Rouse 30
30.04.17	Sheffield FC (a)	W 3-1	Jones 7, Baptiste 58, Shepherd 87
13.05.17	Doncaster Rovers Belles (a)	L 1-2	Cusack 78
21.05.17	Durham (h)	W 5-4	Richards 6, 62, Shepherd 84, Cusack 89, Hinchcliffe 90+2

Aston Villa	2017 FA Cup		
05.02.17 R3	Cambridge United (h)	W 7-1	Jones 17, Merrick 26, Cusack 28, Rouse 57, 61, Hassall 68, Dale 70
19.02.17 R4	Coventry United (a)	W 1-0	Moran 15
19.03.17 R5	Sunderland (a)	L 2-3	

ASTON VILLA PLAYER APPEARANCES & GOALS 2017

				WSL2		FAC		Total	
				A	G	A	G	A	G
Baptiste, Natasha	F	ENG	29.07.91	9	4	3	2	12	6
Beattie, Chloe	G	ENG	24.04.98	7	-	3	-	10	-
Brown, Ashlee	D	ENG	04.08.96	1	-	-	-	1	-
Crackle, Hayley	D	NIR	13.05.95	1	-	-	-	1	-
Cusack, Maddy	M	ENG	28.10.95	8	3	2	1	10	4
Dale, Chloe	M	ENG	19.09.93	3	-	1	1	4	1
George, Hannah	D	ENG	22.01.95	6	-	1	-	7	-
Harper, Chloe	M	ENG	16.09.96	1	-	-	-	1	-
Hassall, Alice	D	ENG	08.02.97	8	-	3	1	11	1
Hinchcliffe, Alys	F	WAL	28.03.95	6	1	1	-	7	1
Hurley, Aoife	D	ENG	20.05.96	5	-	-	-	5	-
Jones, Chloe	M	ENG	01.07.88	6	1	1	1	7	2
Merrick, Bethany	F	ENG	12.10.95	6	1	3	2	9	3
Moran, Katy	M	ENG	15.01.91	2	-	2	-	4	-
N'Dow, Elisha	D	ENG	13.10.96	6	1	3	-	9	1
Porter, Lucy	D	ENG	27.09.98	8	-	3	-	11	-
Potts, Nicola	M	ENG	n/a	-	-	-	-	-	-
Richards, Jade	D	ENG	13.11.92	9	3	3	1	12	4
Rouse, Mollie	M	ENG	27.11.98	7	1	2	2	9	3
Shepherd, Lucy	F	ENG	14.11.98	8	2	2	1	10	3
Skinner, Claire	G	WAL	17.02.97	2	-	-	-	2	-
Smith, Grace	D	ENG	20.01.99	2	-	1	-	3	-
Welsh, Kerri	F	ENG	20.05.92	6	2	2	-	8	2
West, Amy	M	ENG	10.04.97	4	-	2	-	6	-

GOALSCORERS 2017

WSL2 SS: Baptiste (4), Cusack (3), Richards (3), Shepherd (2), Welsh (2), Hinchcliffe (1), Jones (1), Merrick (1), N'Dow (1), Rouse (1)

FAC: Baptiste (2), Merrick (2), Rouse (2), Cusack (1), Dale (1), Hassall (1), Jones (1), Richards (1), Shepherd (1)

Total: Baptiste (6), Cusack (4), Richards (4), Merrick (3), Rouse (3), Shepherd (3), Jones (2), Welsh (2), Dale (1), Hassall (1), Hinchcliffe (1), N'Dow (1)

BRIGHTON & HOVE ALBION – WSL2

Founded: 1991	**Previous WSL Positions:**
Stadium: Culver Road, (Lancing FC)	**2017 WSL2:** 6th (Spring Series)
Honours: WPL South title: (1) 2015/16	
WPL Play-off Winners: (1) 2016	
Nickname: The Seagulls	
Manager: Hope Powell (since July 2017)	

- Brighton were promoted to WSL2 after finishing the 2015/16 WPL Southern season as champions and then winning a play-off against WPL Northern champions Sporting Albion (now West Bromwich Albion) 4-2 at Adams Park.
- Their first ever WSL2 match was the opening game of the 2017 Spring Series away to London Bees. Alessia Russo had the honour of scoring their very first WSL goal when she put them ahead in the 14th minute, but the match at The Hive finished 1-1.
- In the summer of 2017, ahead of their first full WSL season, Brighton appointed former England boss Hope Powell as manager.
- During her reign as England manager between 1998 and 2013, Powell led England to runners-up position at Euro 2009 – where they lost the final to Germany – and also took charge of the Great Britain team at the London 2012 Olympics.

SEASON 2015/16 RECORD

2015/16 WPL Southern:	1st	P22	W17	D3	L2	F58	A18	GD+40	Pts54
2015/16 FA Cup:	5th Round								
2015/16 WPL Cup:	Quarter-finals								

SEASON 2017 RECORD

2017 WSL2 Spring Series:	6th	P9	W2	D4	L3	F8	A13	GD-5	Pts10
2016/17 FA Cup:	4th Round								

Brighton	2015/16 WPL Southern		
16.08.15	Forest Green Rovers (h)	W 4-0	Blackie 15, D. Cooper 27, Somes 72, Barton 82
23.08.15	Charlton Athletic (a)	D 0-0	
06.09.15	QPR (h)	W 2-0	Barton 7, D. Cooper 46
09.09.15	Lewes (h)	W 2-0	Gurr 3, Taylor 39
13.09.15	Plymouth Argyle (a)	W 4-0	D.Cooper 3, Gurr 10, 52, 59
20.09.15	C&K Basildon (h)	W 6-1	Gurr 15, Natkiel 18, Barton 31, Blackie 47, D. Cooper 50, Taylor 73
23.09.15	Lewes (a)	W 2-0	D.Cooper 7, Gurr 44
11.10.15	Coventry United (h)	W 2-1	Taylor 56, Young 90+4
18.10.15	Portsmouth (a)	W 3-2	Natkiel 7, Somes 57, Taylor 78
25.10.15	QPR (a)	L 1-2	Taylor 50
01.11.15	Cardiff City Ladies (h)	L 1-2	Perry 47
08.11.15	West Ham United (a)	D 2-2	Perry 3, Gurr 45
15.11.15	Cardiff City Ladies (a)	W 2-1	Taylor 15, Natkiel 69
22.11.15	West Ham United (h)	W 1-0	D.Cooper 73
06.12.15	Charlton Athletic (h)	W 2-0	Blackie 9, Gurr 45
13.12.15	Plymouth Argyle (h)	W 3-0	Gurr 42, Fulgence 90+1, 90+3
20.12.15	Tottenham Hotspur (h)	W 4-1	Gurr 20, 37, Blackie 68, Fulgence 90
24.01.16	Forest Green Rovers (a)	W 4-1	D.Cooper 40, Gurr 80, Somes 85, Fulgence 90
21.02.16	Coventry United (a)	D 2-2	Natkiel 27, Perry 90+2
27.03.16	C&K Basildon (a)	W 6-1	Gurr 1, Taylor 10, D. Cooper 26, 57, Blackie 63, Natkiel 89
03.04.16	Portsmouth (h)	W 3-1	Taylor 8, 19, Gurr 44
10.04.16	Tottenham Hotspur (a)	W 2-1	Taylor 45+2, 76

Brighton	2015/16 WPL Play-Off Final		
29.05.16	Sporting Club Albion (n)*	W 4-2	Natkiel 40, 67, Perry 72, Taylor 75

*Played at Adams Park, (Wycombe Wanderers FC)

Brighton	2015/16 FA Cup		
10.01.16 R2	Luton Town (h)	W 7-0	Blackie 29, Perry 37, Gurr 44, Barton 51, Fulgence 69, D. Cooper 73, Olding 90
07.02.16 R3	Oxford United (h)	W 10-0	Taylor 2, 53, Perry 10, Natkiel 27, 70, 72, Gurr 31, 85, 90, Fulgence 82
28.02.16 R4	Blackburn Rovers (h)	W 2-1+	Natkiel 3, Taylor 81
13.03.16 R4	Blackburn Rovers (h)	W 5-2+	Agg 4, Soames 7, Perry 16, Natkiel, Fulgence 90+1
20.03.16 R5	Sporting Club Albion (h)	L 3-4	Fulgence 40, Perry 55, Boswell 81

+Match originally played 28.02.16 with Brighton winning 2-1. They were forced to replay having named too many substitutes on the team sheet. Initial result expunged from records.

Brighton	2015/16 WPL Cup		
30.08.15 RD	Gillingham (h)	W 4-0	Barton 34, Stenning 54, Natkiel 66, Gurr 77
27.09.15 RP	Portsmouth (a)	W 3-1 (aet)	Natkiel 56, Gurr 95, 105
04.10.15 R1	QPR (a)	W 7-1	Taylor 14, 42, 82, Gurr 15, Natkiel 50, Russell 52, D. Cooper 88
29.11.15 R2	Chichester City (h)	W 6-0	Boswell 17, Gurr 33, 49, Natkiel 35, 90+2, Taylor 70
06.03.16 QF	Tottenham Hotspur (a)	L 0-1	

NB: RD = Determining Round

BRIGHTON & HOVE ALBION PLAYER APPEARANCES & GOALS 2015/2016

				WPL*		FAC		WPLC		Total	
				A	G	A	G	A	G	A	G
Agg, Lily	M	ENG	17.12.93	4	-	1	1	1	-	6	1
Ashton-Jones, Vicky	D	ENG	07.01.87	23	-	4	-	4	-	31	-
Baker, Emily	D	ENG	13.11.97	8	-	1	-	2	-	11	-
Baker, Faye	G	ENG	10.06.90	21	-	3	-	4	-	28	-
Baker-Carroll, Paige	F	ENG	23.08.96	2	-	-	-	-	-	2	-
Barton, Kirsty	M	ENG	29.05.92	23	3	4	1	4	1	31	5
Blackie, Jay	M	ENG	30.03.88	20	5	4	1	4	1	28	7
Boswell, Charley	D	ENG	26.11.90	16	-	4	1	4	1	24	2
Cooper, Catherine	D	ENG	08.04.96	14	-	1	-	3	-	18	-
Cooper, Deanna	D	ENG	20.06.93	21	9	3	1	4	1	28	11
Dorey, Ellie	M	ENG	04.12.95	4	-	1	-	2	-	7	-
Fox, Megan	M	ENG	17.08.96	4	-	-	-	-	-	4	-
Fulgence, Lisa	F	ENG	27.07.85	7	4	4	4	1	-	12	8
Gurr, Charlotte	M	ENG	16.08.89	21	14	4	4	4	5	29	23
Leitch, Phoebe	D	ENG	12.04.98	14	-	-	-	1	-	15	-
Markham, Charlotte	M	ENG	28.11.97	1	-	-	-	1	-	2	-
Natkiel, Kate	F	ENG	24.09.92	22	7	4	4	5	4	31	15
Olding, Hollie	M	ENG	03.01.99	4	-	1	1	1	-	6	1
Perry, Sophie	D	IRE	11.09.86	15	4	4	4	3	-	22	8
Pursey, Valentine	F	ENG	26.08.99	-	-	-	-	1	-	1	-
Ritchie, Amelia	D	WAL	09.05.99	4	-	3	-	-	-	7	-
Rolf, Annie	M	ENG	04.08.98	1	-	-	-	1	1	2	1
Rowe, Danielle	M	ENG	05.10.96	4	-	-	-	3	-	7	-
Russell, Ellie	D	ENG	09.10.97	-	-	-	-	1	1	1	1
Samain, Leah	G	ENG	20.12.96	-	-	-	-	1	-	1	-
Somes, Lucy	F	ENG	18.04.94	20	3	4	1	3	-	27	4
Stenning, Ellie	F	ENG	09.04.91	2	-	-	-	-	-	2	-
Stenning, Kim	F	ENG	20.04.88	5	-	-	-	1	-	6	-
Taylor, Amy	F	ENG	25.04.92	23	12	2	2	3	4	28	18
Thomas, Bronwen	M	WAL	10.02.00	-	-	2	-	1	-	3	-
Widdows, Jade	F	ENG	07.08.94	1	-	-	-	-	-	1	-
Wilson, Nina	G	ENG	10.06.99	1	-	1	-	-	-	2	-
Young, Charlotte	D	ENG	n/a	14	1	1	-	1	-	16	1

*Figures include WPL play-off

GOALSCORERS 2015/16

WPLS:* Gurr (14), A. Taylor (12), D. Cooper (9), Natkiel (7), Blackie (5), Fulgence (4), Perry (4), Barton (3), Somes (3), Young (1)

FAC: Fulgence (4), Gurr (4), Natkiel (4), Perry (4), A. Taylor (2), Agg (1), Barton (1), Blackie (1), Boswell (1), D. Cooper (1), Olding (1), Somes (1)

LC: Gurr (5), Natkiel (4), A. Taylor (4), Barton (1), Blackie (1), Boswell (1), D. Cooper (1), Rolf (1), Russell (1)

Total: Gurr (23), Taylor (18), Natkiel (15), D. Cooper (11), Fulgence (8), Perry (8), Blackie (6), Barton (5), Somes (4), Boswell (2), Agg (1), Olding (1), Rolf (1), Russell (1), Young (1)

*Figures include WPL play-off final

Brighton	2017 WSL2 Spring Series		
11.02.17	London Bees (a)	D 1-1	Russo 14
26.02.17	Oxford United (h)	D 1-1	Thomas 31
12.03.17	Millwall Lionesses (a)	D 0-0	
02.04.17	Aston Villa (a)	L 1-3	Thomas 68
16.04.17	Watford (h)	W 2-1	Russo 4, Thomas 33
23.04.17	Durham (a)	L 0-1	
30.04.17	Everton (a)	L 0-5	
06.05.17	Doncaster Rovers Belles (h)	D 0-0	
21.05.17	Sheffield FC (h)	W 3-1	Natkiel 23, Owen (og) 30, Russo 87,

Brighton	2016/17 FA Cup		
05.02.17 R3	AFC Wimbledon (a)	W 4-1	Dorey 29, A.Taylor 40, Perry (pen) 45, Somes 84
19.02.17 R4	Tottenham Hotspur (a)	L 0-1	

BRIGHTON & HOVE ALBION PLAYER APPEARANCES & GOALS 2017

				WSL2		FAC		Total	
				A	G	A	G	A	G
Ashton-Jones, Vicky	D	ENG	07.01.87	8	-	2	-	10	-
Baker, Faye	G	ENG	10.06.90	1	-	-	-	1	-
Barton, Kirsty	M	ENG	29.05.92	9	-	2	-	11	-
Boswell, Charley	D	ENG	26.11.90	1	-	-	-	1	-
Byrne, Emma	G	IRE	14.06.79	9	-	2	-	11	-
Dorey, Ellie	M	ENG	04.12.95	9	-	1	1	10	1
Legg, Jenna	M	ENG	23.06.97	3	-	2	-	5	-
Natkiel, Kate	F	ENG	24.09.92	9	1	2	-	11	1
Olding, Hollie	M	ENG	03.01.99	7	-	-	-	7	-
Perry, Sophie	D	IRE	11.09.86	9	-	2	1	11	1
Rafferty, Laura	D	ENG	29.04.96	9	-	2	-	11	-
Ritchie, Amelia	D	WAL	09.05.99	4	-	-	-	4	-
Russo, Alessia	F	ENG	08.02.99	7	3	2	-	9	3
Somes, Lucy	F	ENG	18.04.94	9	-	2	1	11	1
Taylor, Amy	F	ENG	25.04.92	8	-	2	1	10	1
Taylor, Natalie	M	ENG	10.10.99	1	-	1	-	2	-
Thomas, Bronwen	M	WAL	10.02.00	9	3	2	-	11	3
Young, Charlotte	D	ENG	n/a	7	-	2	-	9	-

GOALSCORERS 2017

WSL2 Spring Series: Russo (3), Thomas (3), Natkiel (1), own goals (1)

FAC: Dorey (1), Perry (1), Somes (1), A. Taylor (1)

Total: Russo (3), Thomas (3), Dorey (1), Natkiel (1), Perry (1), Somes (1), A. Taylor (1), own goals (1)

DONCASTER ROVERS BELLES – WSL2

Founded: 1969 (as Belle Vue Belles)	**Previous WSL Positions**
Stadium: Keepmoat Stadium (Doncaster Rovers FC)	**2017 WSL2:** 2nd (Spring Series)
National Honours: WPL Champions (ex top-	**2016 WSL1:** 9th (Relegated)
Flight: (2) 1991/92, 1993/94	**2015 WSL2:** 2nd (Promoted)
WPL Runners-up: (2) 1992/93, 2002/03	**2014 WSL2:** 2nd
FA Cup Winners: (6) 1983, 87, 88, 90, 92, 94	**2013 WSL:** 8th (Relegated)
FA Cup Runners-up: (7) 1984, 85, 86, 91, 93, 2000, 02	**2012 WSL:** 7th
WPL Cup Runners-up: (3) 1994, 1996, 2009	**2011 WSL:** 7th
Nickname: The Belles	
Manager: Emma Coates (since June 2016)	

- The club was formed as Belle Vue Belles in 1969, taking their name from the original home venue of Doncaster Rovers' men's team (Belle Vue) where the women who set up the club would sell half-time draw tickets on the terraces. In 1971 they changed their name to Doncaster Belles before going on to become one of the leading teams in English football.
- The Belles were founding members, and the first champions, of the new WPL National Division (the top-flight at the time) in 1991/92. They were champions again two years later.
- In their days as Doncaster Belles they won the FA Cup six times. Only Arsenal (14) and Southampton (eight) have won it more often. They have also been runners-up on seven occasions meaning only Arsenal (15) have appeared in more than their 13 finals.
- They changed their name to Doncaster Rovers Belles when they were taken under the umbrella of Doncaster Rovers men's professional outfit in 2003. They worked alongside Doncaster Rovers men's, Doncaster Lakers Rugby Club,

Doncaster Athletic Club and Doncaster Council to develop the 15,000-seat Keepmoat Stadium which opened in 2006, and which is where they now play.

SEASON 2016 RECORD

2016 WSL1:	9th (Relegated)	P16	W1	D0	L15	F8	A48	GD-40	Pts3
2016 FA Cup:	5th Round								
2016 Continental Cup:	Quarter-finals								

SEASON 2017 RECORD

2017 WSL2 Spring Series:	2nd	P9	W5	D3	L1	F19	A9	GD+10	Pts18
2017 FA Cup:	5th Round								

Doncaster R. B.	2016 WSL1		
24.03.16	Chelsea (h)	L 1-4	C.Rafferty (og) 6
27.04.16	Birmingham City (a)	L 1-2	Dowie 5
02.05.16	Manchester City (a)	L 0-6	
26.06.16	Notts County (a)	L 1-2	Sigsworth 23
09.07.16	Sunderland (a)	L 0-4	*Little sent off 23*
24.07.16	Chelsea (a)	L 0-4	
30.07.16	Birmingham City (h)	L 0-1	
11.08.16	Manchester City (h)	L 0-4	
27.08.16	Liverpool (a)	L 0-1	
01.09.16	Sunderland (h)	L 1-4	Pacheco 15
24.09.16	Reading (h)	L 1-4	Simpkins 46
06.10.16	Arsenal (h)	L 0-5	
09.10.16	Liverpool (h)	L 1-3	Roberts 20
16.10.16	Notts County (h)	L 1-2	Humphrey 7
30.10.16	Arsenal (a)	L 0-2	
06.11.16	Reading (a)	W 1-0	Omarsdottir 69

Doncaster R. B.	2016 FA Cup		
20.03.16 R5	Chelsea (h)	L 1-4	Sigsworth 5

Doncaster R. B.	2016 Continental Cup		
03.07.16 R1	Sunderland (h)	W 2-1	Little 21, Cresswell 82
07.08.16 QF	Manchester City (a)	L 1-4	Bakowska-Mathews 80

DONCASTER ROVERS BELLES PLAYER APPEARANCES & GOALS 2016

				WSL1		FAC		CC		Total	
				A	G	A	G	A	G	A	G
Bakowska-Mathews, Marta	M	ENG	26.06.93	9	-	-	-	1	1	10	1
Barker, Sophie	M	ENG	25.12.90	16	-	1	-	2	-	19	-
Cresswell, Lauren	D	ENG	10.01.90	7	-	-	-	2	1	9	1
Dowie, Natasha	F	ENG	30.06.88	3	1	1	-	-	-	4	1
Easton, Rebecca	D	ENG	16.04.74	3	-	1	-	-	-	4	-
Gummer, Alexandra	D	AUS	10.09.92	1	-	1	-	-	-	2	-
Hobbs, Nicola	G	ENG	10.05.87	12	-	1	-	2	-	15	-
Humphrey, Carla	M	ENG	15.12.96	15	1	-	-	2	-	17	1
Lipka, Kasia	M	ENG	26.05.93	16	-	1	-	2	-	19	-
Little, Leandra	D	ENG	08.11.84	15	-	1	-	2	1	18	1
Moorhouse, Anna	G	ENG	30.03.95	4	-	-	-	-	-	4	-
Mosby, Yasmin	M	ENG	15.11.98	1	-	1	-	1	-	3	-
Murray, Christie	M	SCO	03.05.90	11	-	-	-	1	-	12	-
Newborough, Rachel	D	NIR	19.11.96	6	-	-	-	1	-	7	-
O'Donnell, Bethany	M	ENG	03.07.00	2	-	2	-	-	-	4	-
Omarsdottir, Katrin	M	ICE	27.06.87	14	1	-	-	2	-	16	1
Pacheco, Mayumi	D	ENG	25.08.98	10	1	-	-	2	-	12	1
Rayner, Rebecca	M	ENG	n/a	7	-	-	-	-	-	7	-
Roberts, Rhiannon	D	ENG	30.08.90	16	1	1	-	2	-	19	1
Sigsworth, Jessica	F	ENG	13.10.94	7	1	1	1	1	-	9	2
Simpkins, Emily	M	ENG	25.05.90	16	1	1	-	1	-	18	1
Smith, Sue	F	ENG	24.11.79	2	-	-	-	1	-	3	-
Sweetman-Kirk, Courtney	F	ENG	16.11.90	3	-	1	-	-	-	4	-
Tierney, Samantha	D	ENG	08.10.98	16	-	1	-	2	-	19	-

GOALSCORERS 2016

WSL1: Dowie (1), Humphrey (1), Omarsdottir (1), Pacheco (1), Roberts (1), Simpkins (1), Sigsworth (1), own goals (1)

FAC: Sigsworth (1)

CC: Bakowska-Mathews (1), Cresswell (1), Little (1)

Total: Sigsworth (2), Bakowska-Mathews (1), Cresswell (1), Dowie (1), Humphrey (1), Little (1), Omarsdottir (1), Pacheco (1), Roberts (1), Simpkins (1), own goals (1)

Doncaster R. B.	2017 WSL2 Spring Series		
12.03.17	London Bees (h)	W 4-1	Sweetman-Kirk 6, 87, Murray 58, Simpkins 85
16.04.17	Durham (h)	W 2-1	Murray 20, Sweetman-Kirk 88
20.04.17	Watford (a)	D 1-1	Sweetman-Kirk 44
23.04.17	Everton (h)	D 3-3	Sweetman-Kirk 37, (pen) 47, Little 74
27.04.17	Sheffield FC (a)	W 2-0	Sweetman-Kirk 21, Hanson 70
30.04.17	Millwall Lionesses (a)	L 1-2	Sweetman-Kirk 9
06.05.17	Brighton & HA (a)	D 0-0	
13.05.17	Aston Villa (h)	W 2-1	Hanson 21, Sweetman-Kirk 40
21.05.17	Oxford United (a)	W 4-0	Murray 23, Hanson 45, Barker 50, Rayner 88

Doncaster R. B.	2017 FA Cup		
05.02.17 R3	Watford (h)	W w/o	
19.02.17 R4	Sheffield FC (a)	W 1-0	Sweetman-Kirk (pen)
19.03.17 R5	Chelsea (a)	L 0-7	

DONCASTER ROVERS BELLES PLAYER APPEARANCES & GOALS 2017

				WSL2		FAC		Total	
				A	G	A	G	A	G
Bakowska-Mathews, Marta	M	ENG	26.06.93	5	-	-	-	5	-
Barker, Sophie	M	ENG	25.12.90	8	1	2	-	10	1
Davies, Nicky	G	WAL	28.12.85	9	-	2	-	11	-
Hanson, Kirsty	F	SCO	17.04.98	9	3	2	-	11	3
Lipka, Kasia	M	ENG	26.05.93	6	-	2	-	8	-
Little, Leandra	D	ENG	08.11.84	9	1	2	-	11	1
Murray, Christie	M	SCO	03.05.90	9	3	2	-	11	3
Newborough, Rachel	D	NIR	19.11.96	5	-	2	-	7	-
Pacheco, Mayumi	D	ENG	25.08.98	9	-	2	-	11	-
Rayner, Rebecca	M	ENG	n/a	9	1	2	-	11	1
Simpkins, Emily	M	ENG	25.05.90	8	1	2	-	10	1
Sweetman-Kirk, Courtney	F	ENG	16.11.90	9	9	2	1	11	10
Tierney, Samantha	D	ENG	08.10.98	9	-	2	-	11	-
Walton, Sophie	M	ENG	07.11.89	8	-	-	-	8	-
Watson, Monique	M	ENG	n/a	1	-	-	-	1	-

GOALSCORERS 2017

WSL2 SS: Sweetman-Kirk (9), Hanson (3), Murray (3), Barker (1), Little (1), Rayner (1), Simpkins (1)

FAC: Sweetman-Kirk (1)

Total: Sweetman-Kirk (10), Hanson (3), Murray (3), Barker (1), Little (1), Rayner (1), Simpkins (1)

DURHAM – WSL2

Founded: 2013	**Previous WSL Positions**
Stadium: New Ferens Park	**2017 WSL2:** 5th (Spring Series)
National Honours: None	**2016 WSL2:** 4th
Nickname: The Wildcats	**2015 WSL2:** 7th
Manager: Andy Thorpe	**2014 WSL2:** 6th

- The club was formed in 2013 as a collaboration between South Durham & Cestria Girls and Durham University and was immediately awarded a licence to compete in the first WSL2 season of 2014.
- Their first competitive match as Durham was an FA Cup third round tie which ended in a 4-0 win over Chichester City on 14 February 2014.
- South Durham & Cestria Girls had themselves been founded in 2006 by Lee Sanders and quickly became one of the best teams in the region. They competed in international events in Portugal, Ghana and the USA and won a prestigious youth tournament, the World Peace Cup, in Oslo in 2010. In 2011 they were runners-up at the Gothia World Youth Cup.

SEASON 2016 RECORD

2016 WSL2:	4th	P18	W10	D3	L5	F30	A19	GD+11	Pts33
2016 FA Cup:	5th Round								
2016 Continental Cup:	Preliminary Rd								

SEASON 2017 RECORD

2017 WSL2 Spring Series:	5th	P9	W5	D1	L3	F14	A10	GD+4	Pts16
2017 FA Cup:	4th Round								

Durham	2016 WSL2		
23.03.16	Sheffield FC (a)	W 1-0	Atkinson 44
28.03.16	London Bees (h)	W 2-0	Atkinson 36, Hepple 72
24.04.16	Oxford United (a)	W 5-1	McFadden 2, Gears 8, Gutteridge 45+1, Hepple 64, 82
01.05.16	Aston Villa (a)	L 0-2	
19.05.16	Sheffield FC (h)	W 1-0	Gutteridge 83
22.05.16	London Bees (a)	D 2-2	Hepple (pen) 55, Darkoah 83
26.06.16	Yeovil Town (h)	L 0-2	
10.07.16	Aston Villa (h)	W 3-0	McFadden 39, Salicki 67, Eadon 72
17.07.16	Bristol City (h)	D 0-0	
24.07.16	Yeovil Town (a)	L 0-4	
31.07.16	Watford (h)	W 3-0	Hepple 17, 68, Roberts 65
14.08.16	Everton (a)	D 1-1	Roberts 15
28.08.16	Oxford United (h)	W 2-1	Hepple (pen) 20, Atkinson 30
11.09.16	Millwall Lionesses (a)	W 1-0	Hepple 29
24.09.16	Bristol City (a)	L 0-1	
09.10.16	Everton (h)	L 1-3	Hepple 35
30.10.16	Watford (a)	W 6-1	Gutteridge 40, Hepple 43, Roberts 44, Gibson 69, 71, Darkoah 72
06.11.16	Millwall Lionesses (h)	W 2-1	Gutteridge 32, Hepple 43

Durham	2016 FA Cup		
07.02.16 R3	London Bees (a)	W 9-0	Atkinson 8, 45, Hepple 10, 33, 53, Gutteridge 28, 89, Macek 80, White 90
28.02.16 R4	Charlton Athletic (h)	W 3-1	Hepple 20, Gutteridge 43, 87
20.03.16 R5	Notts County (a)	L 1-3	Hepple 76

Durham	2016 Continental Cup		
08.05.16 RP	Sheffield FC (a)	L 1-3	Lee 85

DURHAM PLAYER APPEARANCES & GOALS 2016

				WSL2		FAC		CC		Total	
				A	G	A	G	A	G	A	G
Alderson, Helen	G	ENG	05.07.89	17	-	3	-	1	-	21	-
Atkinson, Jordan	F	ENG	n/a	18	3	3	2	1	-	22	5
Banks, Gabrielle	D	ENG	n/a	-	-	1	-	-	-	1	-
Borthwick, Megan	G	ENG	n/a	2	-	-	-	-	-	2	-
Christon, Ellie	D	ENG	21.09.93	18	-	3	-	1	-	22	-
Corrie, Courtney	F	ENG	06.11.97	1	-	1	-	-	-	2	-
Darkoah, Mercy	F	GBR/GHA	n/a	7	2	1	-	1	-	9	2
Dodds, Tyler	F	ENG	n/a	13	-	-	-	-	-	13	-
Eadon, Sarah	M	ENG	09.10.91	14	1	2	-	1	-	17	1
Elliott, Megan	D	ENG	n/a	2	-	-	-	-	-	2	-
Gears, Nicki	F	ENG	n/a	4	1	3	-	-	-	7	1
Gibson, Nicola	M	ENG	n/a	10	2	1	-	-	-	11	2
Gutteridge, Natalie	M	ENG	26.09.88	17	4	3	4	1	-	21	8
Hepple, Beth	M	ENG	n/a	18	11	3	5	1	-	22	16
Jennings, Jennifer	D	ENG	n/a	4	-	-	-	-	-	4	-
Johnson, Annabel	D	ENG	n/a	6	-	-	-	-	-	6	-
Jordinson, Lauren	D	ENG	25.05.96	3	-	-	-	-	-	3	-
Lee, Rachel	M	ENG	n/a	13	-	3	-	1	1	17	1
Macek, Chloe	D	ENG	n/a	14	-	2	1	1	-	17	1
McFadden, Sarah	M	NIR	23.05.87	17	2	3	-	1	-	21	2
Pereira, Amelia	F	POR	n/a	2	-	3	-	-	-	5	-
Roberts, Emily	F	ENG	07.04.94	11	3	-	-	-	-	11	3
Salicki, Rebecca	D	ENG	30.07.92	18	1	2	-	1	-	21	1
White, Jessica	F	ENG	n/a	-	-	2	1	-	-	2	1
Wilson, Sarah	D	ENG	n/a	18	-	3	-	1	-	22	-

GOALSCORERS 2016

WSL2: Hepple (11), Gutteridge (4), Atkinson (3), Roberts (3), Darkoah (2), Gibson (2), McFadden (2), Eadon (1), Gears (1), Salicki (1)

FAC: Hepple (5), Gutteridge (4), Atkinson (2), Macek (1), White (1)

CC: Lee (1)

Total: Hepple (16), Gutteridge (8), Atkinson (5), Roberts (3), Darkoah (2), Gibson (2), McFadden (2), Eadon (1), Gears (1), Lee (1), Macek (1), Salicki (1), White (1)

Durham	2017 WSL2 Spring Series		
12.02.17	Millwall Lionesses (h)	W 1-0	McFadden 38
05.03.17	Sheffield FC (h)	W 1-0	Gutteridge 54
12.03.17	Watford (a)	D 1-1	Roberts 54
02.04.17	Oxford United (h)	W 2-1	Hepple 58, Ness 87
16.04.17	Doncaster Rovers Belles (a)	L 1-2	Salicki 62
23.04.17	Brighton & Hove Albion (h)	W 1-0	Wilson 18
30.04.17	London Bees (h)	W 3-0	Gears 5, Hepple 58, Ness 68
06.05.17	Everton (a)	L 0-1	
21.05.17	Aston Villa (a)	L 4-5	Ness 20, 36, 38, Hepple (pen) 52

Durham	2017 FA Cup		
05.02.17 R3	Keynsham Town (a)	W 7-0	Ness 19, 61, McFadden 21, 36, Gutteridge 51, Salicki 56, Roberts 81
19.02.17 R4	Everton (h)	D 2-2 (L 3-4p)	Hepple 34, Salicki 43

DURHAM PLAYER APPEARANCES & GOALS 2017

				WSL2		FAC		Total	
				A	G	A	G	A	G
Alderson, Helen	G	ENG	05.07.89	2	-	2	-	4	-
Atkinson, Jordan	F	ENG	n/a	6	-	2	-	8	-
Borthwick, Megan	G	ENG	n/a	1	-	1	-	2	-
Briggs, Lauren	M	ENG	n/a	7	-	-	-	7	-
Christon, Ellie	D	ENG	21.09.93	9	-	2	-	11	-
Dixon, Caroline	D	ENG	27.07.87	4	-	-	-	4	-
Dodds, Tyler	F	ENG	n/a	2	-	1	-	3	-
Gears, Nicki	F	ENG	n/a	6	1	-	-	6	1
Gibson, Nicola	M	ENG	n/a	6	-	-	-	6	-
Gutteridge, Natalie	M	ENG	26.09.88	4	1	2	1	6	2
Hepple, Beth	M	ENG	n/a	9	3	2	1	11	4
Jennings, Jennifer	D	ENG	n/a	6	-	2	-	8	-
Johnson, Annabel	D	ENG	n/a	8	-	2	-	10	-
Laws, Rachael	G	ENG	05.11.90	6	-	-	-	6	-
Lee, Rachel	M	ENG	n/a	8	-	2	-	10	-
McFadden, Sarah	M	NIR	23.05.87	1	1	2	2	3	3
Ness, Zoe	F	SCO	24.03.96	9	5	2	2	11	7
Roberts, Emily	F	ENG	07.04.94	9	1	2	1	11	2
Salicki, Rebecca	D	ENG	30.07.92	9	1	2	2	11	3
Wilson, Sarah	D	ENG	n/a	9	1	2	-	11	1

GOALSCORERS 2017

WSL2 SS: Ness (5), Hepple (3), Gears (1), Gutteridge (1), McFadden (1), Roberts (1), Salicki (1), Wilson (1)

FAC: McFadden (2), Ness (2), Salicki (2), Gutteridge (1), Hepple (1), Roberts (1)

Total: Ness (7), Hepple (4), McFadden (3), Salicki (3), Gutteridge (2), Roberts (2), Gears (1), Wilson (1)

LONDON BEES – WSL2

Founded: 1975 (as District Line Ladies)	Previous WSL Positions
Stadium: The Hive, (Barnet FC)	**2017 WSL2:** 7th (Spring Series)
National Honours: FA Cup Runners-up: (1)	**2016 WSL2:** 7th
1997 (as Wembley)	**2015 WSL2:** 8th
Nickname: The Bees	**2014 WSL2:** 10th
Manager: Luke Swindlehurst (since July 2017)	

- The club originated in 1975 as District Line Ladies, set up by a group of Transport for London employees who worked on that line. They started out playing in the Hounslow & District League but enjoyed a rapid rise and reached FA National League Southern Division level by the early 90s.
- As they continued to go from strength to strength they merged with Wembley. It was as Wembley Ladies FC that they reached the 1997 FA Cup final where they took on one of the strongest teams in the country at the time, Millwall Lionesses. A side containing England's 1995 World Cup goalkeeper Lesley Higgs was narrowly beaten 1-0 at Upton Park.
- They first formed an informal affiliation with Barnet men's club in 1998 at which point they changed their name to Barnet Ladies. In 2010 they were unsuccessful in their application to be one of the founding members of the WSL.
- In 2014 – the same year that they changed their name to London Bees – their application to join the first season of WSL2 was successful. They remain independent of Barnet men's but there is a close relationship, with both clubs training and playing at The Hive in Edgware.
- Their most notable result of the London Bees era came in the first round of the 2016 WSL Continental Cup when they beat Chelsea on penalties after a 3-3 draw. They then knocked out Sheffield FC in the quarter-finals before losing to Birmingham in the last four.

SEASON 2016 RECORD

2016 WSL2:	7th	P18	W6	D4	L8	F28	A39	GD-11	Pts22
2016 FA Cup:	3rd Round								
2016 Continental Cup:	Semi-final								

SEASON 2017 RECORD

2017 WSL2 Spring Series:	7th	P9	W3	D1	L5	F13	A21	GD-8	Pts10
2017 FA Cup:	3rd Round								

London Bees	2016 WSL2		
23.03.16	Watford (h)	D 2-2	Watts (pen) 18, Wilson 74
28.03.16	Durham (a)	L 0-2	
24.04.16	Bristol City (h)	L 0-3	
27.04.16	Millwall Lionesses (h)	W 2-1	Wilson 9, Watts (pen) 90
01.05.16	Everton (a)	L 1-5	Howells 90
16.05.16	Watford (a)	W 5-0	Wilson 13, 20, 24, Goddard 21, Howells 90+5
22.05.16	Durham (h)	D 2-2	S.Wilson (og) 43, J. Wilson 83
26.06.16	Aston Villa (a)	D 1-1	Popadinova 41
29.06.16	Millwall Lionesses (a)	D 1-1	Will 87
10.07.16	Oxford United (h)	W 3-1	Goddard 45, Cooper 90, Wilson 90+1
17.07.16	Sheffield FC (h)	L 0-5	
23.07.16	Bristol City (a)	L 0-3	
31.07.16	Oxford United (a)	L 2-4	Popadinova 36, 54
28.08.16	Aston Villa (h)	W 2-1	E.Clarke 32, Wilson 80
11.09.16	Yeovil Town (a)	W 3-2	E.Clarke 46, Wilson 56, Watts (pen) 71
25.09.16	Sheffield FC (a)	W 1-0	Wilson 19
30.10.16	Yeovil Town (h)	L 0-2	
06.11.16	Everton (h)	L 3-4	Wilson 61, 71, 73

London Bees	2016 FA Cup		
07.02.16 R3	Durham (h)	L 0-9	

London Bees	2016 Continental Cup		
08.05.16 RP	Watford (a)	W 2-0	Goddard 45, Watts 48
02.07.16 R1	Chelsea (h)	D 3-3 (W 4-2p)	Flaherty (og) 58, Wilson 81, Cooper 114
07.08.16 QF	Sheffield FC (a)	W 2-0	Goddard 63, E.Clarke 90
03.09.16 SF	Birmingham City (h)	L 0-4	

LONDON BEES PLAYER APPEARANCES & GOALS 2016

				WSL2		FAC		CC		Total	
				A	G	A	G	A	G	A	G
Anderson, Rebecca	M	ENG	04.04.95	16	-	-	-	4	-	20	-
Beckett, Emma	M	IRE	29.05.87	16	-	-	-	4	-	20	-
Bolger, Sarah	F	ENG	26.06.96	-	-	1	-	-	-	1	-
Clarke, Evie	F	ENG	17.10.97	7	2	-	-	2	1	9	3
Clarke, Zemeka	M	ENG	07.12.93	3	-	-	-	-	-	3	-
Clifford, Lucia	M	ENG	12.08.93	-	-	1	-	-	-	1	-
Cooper, Deanna	D	ENG	20.06.93	11	1	-	-	2	1	13	2
Davies, Bethan	G	ENG	17.09.97	3	-	-	-	3	-	6	-
Dempster, Jade	D	ENG	08.06.90	2	-	-	-	-	-	2	-
Fogarty, Sophie	D	ENG	25.08.93	16	-	-	-	3	-	19	-
Frith-Salem, Rosanna	M	ENG	14.03.97	-	-	1	-	-	-	1	-
Georgiou, Andria	M	ENG	15.04.96	3	-	-	-	1	-	4	-
Georgiou, Sofia	F	ENG	26.09.97	-	-	1	-	-	-	1	-
Goddard, Ashleigh	M	ENG	19.04.92	15	2	-	-	4	2	19	4
Greenwood, Holly	M	ENG	21.05.99	4	-	-	-	1	-	5	-
Gregoriou, Antonia	M	ENG	21.10.94	-	-	1	-	-	-	1	-
Harris, Sophie	G	ENG	25.08.94	12	-	-	-	-	-	12	-
Hinchcliffe, Sydney	M	WAL	28.03.95	9	-	-	-	2	-	11	-
Howells, Paula	M	ENG	22.03.97	18	2	-	-	-	-	18	2
Howes, Kara-May	D	ENG	28.11.96	-	-	1	-	4	-	5	-
Hurley, Aoife	D	ENG	20.05.96	10	-	-	-	3	-	13	-
Kinnane, Anya	D	ENG	09.12.98	-	-	1	-	-	-	1	-
Lalani, Hana	M	ENG	10.07.00	2	-	-	-	-	-	2	-
Lee, Vanna	D	ENG	09.01.96	-	-	1	-	-	-	1	-
Marcoci, Andra	M	ROM	16.10.94	-	-	1	-	-	-	1	-
Matthews, Charlotte	M	ENG	25.05.99	-	-	1	-	-	-	1	-
Miller, Samantha	D	ENG	22.09.93	-	-	1	-	-	-	1	-
Naprta, Manuela	D	ENG	03.02.97	10	-	-	-	2	-	12	-
Perkins, Ellie	D	ENG	06.04.00	1	-	-	-	-	-	1	-
Popadinova, Evdokia	F	BUL	26.10.96	13	3	-	-	3	-	16	3
Rabin, Rachel	F	ENG	07.05.98	-	-	1	-	-	-	1	-
Riches, Imogen	G	ENG	13.09.97	4	-	1	-	1	-	6	-
Scanlon, Danielle	M	ENG	18.03.93	8	-	-	-	2	-	10	-
Slater, Emma	D	ENG	16.02.97	-	-	-	-	1	-	1	-
Watts, Nicola	F	ENG	22.09.87	17	3	-	-	4	1	21	4
Whitter, Emma	F	ENG	20.07.80	1	-	-	-	-	-	1	-
Will, Merrick	M	ENG	21.12.96	15	1	-	-	3	-	18	1
Wilson, Jo	F	ENG	11.07.94	16	13	-	-	4	1	20	14

GOALSCORERS 2016

WSL2: Wilson (13)**,** Popadinova (3), Watts (3), E.Clarke (2), Goddard (2), Howells (2), Cooper (1), Will (1), own goals (1)

FAC: None

CC: Goddard (2), E. Clarke (1), Cooper (1), Watts (1), Wilson (1), own goals (1)

Total: Wilson (14)**,** Goddard (4), Watts (4), E.Clarke (3), Popadinova (3), Cooper (2), Howells (2), Will (1), own goals (2)

London Bees	2017 WSL2 Spring Series		
11.02.17	Brighton & Hove Albion (h)	D 1-1	Goddard 55
26.02.17	Watford (a)	W 3-2	Beckett 50, Goddard 76, Wilson 84
04.03.17	Oxford United (h)	W 3-1	Lalani 6, Beckett 16, Goddard 27
12.03.17	Doncaster Rovers Belles (a)	L 1-4	Beckett 90
01.04.17	Sheffield FC (h)	W 2-1	Wilson 82, 88
15.04.17	Millwall Lionesses (h)	L 1-2	Goddard 47
22.04.17	Aston Villa (a)	L 2-3	Loomes 29, Wilson 48
30.04.17	Durham (a)	L 0-3	
20.05.17	Everton (h)	L 0-4	

London Bees	2017 FA Cup	
05.02.17 R3	Millwall Lionesses (a)	L 0-1

LONDON BEES PLAYER APPEARANCES & GOALS 2017

				WSL		FAC		Total	
				A	G	A	G	A	G
Anderson, Rebecca	M	ENG	04.04.95	6	-	1	-	7	-
Beckett, Emma	M	IRE	29.05.87	9	3	1	-	10	3
Burgess, Mollie	D	ENG	23.10.96	1	-	-	-	1	-
Burgess, Shayla	G	ENG	21.08.97	1	-	-	-	1	-
Clarke, Evie	F	ENG	17.10.97	6	-	1	-	7	-
Fogarty, Sophie	D	ENG	25.08.93	9	-	1	-	10	-
Goddard, Ashleigh	M	ENG	19.04.92	9	4	1	-	10	4
Gould, Tricia	F	ENG	09.12.93	8	-	-	-	8	-
Greenwood, Holly	M	ENG	21.05.99	-	-	-	-	-	-
Harris, Sophie	G	ENG	25.08.94	8	-	1	-	9	-
Howells, Paula	M	ENG	22.03.97	9	-	1	-	10	-
Huggins, Katherine	M	ENG	28.01.96	1	-	-	-	1	-
Lalani, Hana	M	ENG	10.07.00	8	1	-	-	8	1
Littleboy, Jordan	M	ENG	29.06.98	2	-	1	-	3	-
Loomes, Lucy	F	ENG	18.05.97	9	1	1	-	10	1
May-Walkley, Laura	M	WAL	19.05.91	-	-	-	-	-	-
Meiwald, Anne	D	ENG	15.03.95	8	-	1	-	9	-
Perkins, Ellie	D	ENG	06.04.00	8	-	1	-	9	-
Rolandsen, Ocean	D	ENG	31.01.98	3	-	-	-	3	-
Stojko-Down, Alysha	M	ENG	30.09.97	1	-	-	-	1	-
Tullett. Amber	D	ENG	11.02.98	7	-	1	-	8	-
Will, Merrick	M	ENG	21.12.96	1	-	-	-	1	-
Wilson, Jo	F	ENG	11.07.94	9	4	1	-	10	4

GOALSCORERS 2017

WSL2 SS: Goddard (4), Wilson (4), Beckett (3), Lalani (1), Loomes (1)

FAC: None

Total: Goddard (4), Wilson (4), Beckett (3), Lalani (1), Loomes (1)

MILLWALL LIONESSES – WSL2

Founded: 1971	**Previous WSL Positions**
Stadium: The Den (Millwall FC) in 2016,	**2017 WSL2:** 3rd (Spring Series)
St Paul's Sports Ground (Fisher FC) from	**2016 WSL2:** 8th
February 2017	**2015 WSL2:** 9th
National Honours: FA Cup: (2) 1991, 97	**2014 WSL2:** 8th
WPL Cup Winners: (1) 1997	
WPL Cup Runners-up: (1) 1992	
Nickname: The Lionesses	
Manager: Lee Burch (since July 2016)	

- The Lionesses were founded in 1971 and became the first team to be officially affiliated with a professional men's outfit in the 1980s as Millwall FC strengthened their ties with the local community. They were also the first club to open a Girls Centre of Excellence.
- They were founder members of the Women's Premier League in 1991 and went on to become one of the leading teams of the 1990s. In 1991 they won their first major trophy, beating fellow heavweights Doncaster Belles 1-0 in the FA Cup final at Prenton Park. In 1992 they reached the first League Cup final but lost 1-0 to Arsenal.
- In 1997 the Lionesses won both the main cup competitions. They beat Wembley 1-0 at Upton Park in the FA Cup final and Everton 2-1 at Underhill in the League Cup final.
- At the turn of the century they dropped out of the top-flight but returned in 2009 a couple of years before the formation of the WSL. They were not among the WSL founding members, but their application to enter WSL2 for the opening season of 2014 was successful.

- Millwall Lionesses played their home matches in 2016 at The Den – home of Millwall men's. A fixture clash arose when Millwall men's reached the League One play-off semi-finals in 2016 and required use of the stadium. The Lionesses had to cancel their WSL2 match against Oxford and were unable to find a new date for the game, leading to Oxford being awarded the points. In February 2017 they announced St Paul's Sports Ground – home of men's non-League team Fisher – would be their new home.

SEASON 2016 RECORD

2016 WSL2:	8th	P18	W3	D7	L8	F24	A31	GD-7	Pts16
2016 FA Cup:	5th Round								
2016 Continental Cup:	Prelim Round								

SEASON 2017 RECORD

2017 WSL2 Spring Series:	3rd	P9	W5	D2	L2	F12	A8	GD+4	Pts17
2017 FA Cup:	5th Round								

Millwall	2016 WSL2		
24.03.16	Oxford United (a)	W 5-3	Hincks 11, 65, Loomes 42, 50, Babajide 82
27.03.16	Everton (h)	D 2-2	Robe 49, Hincks (pen) 54
24.04.16	Yeovil Town (a)	D 1-1	Gibbons 42
27.04.16	London Bees (a)	L 1-2	Cole 62
30.04.16	Yeovil Town (h)	L 0-4	
19.05.16	Oxford United (h)	L w/o*	
22.05.16	Everton (a)	D 1-1	Babajide 25
29.06.16	London Bees (h)	D 1-1	Babajide 35
09.07.16	Bristol City (a)	L 1-2	Hincks 44
17.07.16	Aston Villa (a)	L 1-3	Fisk 2
24.07.16	Sheffield FC (a)	D 2-2	Hincks (pen) 21, Gurr 75
30.07.16	Bristol City (h)	L 1-2	Babajide 62
28.08.16	Watford (a)	W 2-1	Hincks 2, Loomes 55
11.09.16	Durham (h)	L 0-1	
25.09.16	Watford (h)	W 2-1	Gaylor 22, Giddings 28
09.10.16	Sheffield FC (h)	D 1-1	Hincks 60
30.10.16	Aston Villa (h)	D 2-2	Gaylor 45, Wynne 65
06.11.16	Durham (a)	L 1-2	Gaylor 90

*Oxford awarded points after Millwall failed to find a new date for a fixture. Original fixture postponed when Millwall men's reached League One play-offs and required use of The Den.

Millwall	2016 FA Cup		
07.02.16 R3	Watford (a)	W 3-1 (aet)	Cole 57, Loomes 97, 119
28.02.17 R4	Loughborough Foxes (a)	W 2-1 (aet)	Cole 94, Carlton 102
20.03.16 R5	Reading (a)	L 0-2	

Millwall	2016 Continental Cup		
08.05.16 RP	Oxford United (a)	L 0-1	

MILLWALL LIONESSES PLAYER APPEARANCES & GOALS 2016

				WSL2		FAC		CC		Total	
				A	G	A	G	A	G	A	G
Babajide, Rinsola	F	ENG	17.06.98	14	4	2	-	1	-	17	4
Brooks, Billie	D	ENG	16.08.95	11	-	2	-	-	-	13	-
Burr, Chloe	F	ENG	03.04.93	1	-	-	-	-	-	1	-
Butler, Jordan	D	ENG	14.09.92	10	-	-	-	-	-	10	-
Carlton, Danielle	M	ENG	30.07.93	5	-	3	1	-	-	8	1
Cole, Naomi	D	ENG	30.03.92	5	1	3	2	1	-	9	3
Cowan, Leanne	D	ENG	01.02.96	15	-	2	-	1	-	18	-
Fisk, Grace	M	ENG	05.01.98	7	1	1	-	1	-	9	1
Fowle, Brionne	M	ENG	n/a	1	-	-	-	-	-	1	-
Gaylor, Amber	M	ENG	22.02.95	15	3	1	-	-	-	16	3
Gibbons, Felicity	M	ENG	09.07.94	5	1	3	-	1	-	9	1
Giddings, Georgina	M	ENG	30.06.90	7	1	-	-	-	-	7	1
Gurr, Charlotte	M	ENG	16.08.89	4	1	-	-	-	-	4	1
Harford, Bethany	F	ENG	16.09.99	2	-	-	-	-	-	2	-
Heaslip, Emily	M	ENG	29.09.93	7	-	2	-	1	-	10	-
Hincks, Ashlee	F	ENG	04.12.88	15	7	2	-	1	-	18	7
Horwood, Bonnie	M	ENG	16.04.87	9	-	-	-	-	-	9	-
Ivison, Lottie	G	ENG	n/a	1	-	-	-	-	-	1	-
Jones, Megan	D	MLT	04.11.98	1	-	-	-	-	-	1	-
Kanto, Sindi	G	ENG	01.02.00	1	-	-	-	-	-	1	-
Loomes, Lucy	F	ENG	18.05.97	14	3	2	2	1	-	17	5
Maple, Lilli	M	ENG	12.01.96	9	-	3	-	1	-	13	-
Mallett, Dawn	M	ENG	01.11.90	2	-	2	-	-	-	4	-
Nicol, Leigh	M	SCO	26.09.95	12	-	1	-	-	-	13	-
Quantrill, Sarah	G	ENG	21.07.90	16	-	3	-	1	-	20	-
Rolandsen, Ocean	D	ENG	31.01.98	3	-	-	-	-	-	3	-
Robe, Leighanne	D	ENG	26.12.93	16	1	3	-	1	-	20	1
Rutherford, Ella	M	ENG	28.04.00	9	-	-	-	1	-	10	-
Sherwood, Ciara	M	NIR	18.08.92	3	-	3	-	1	-	7	-
Strugnell, Francesca	D	ENG	n/a	5	-	2	-	-	-	7	-
Taylor, Grace	G	ENG	n/a	1	-	-	-	-	-	1	-
Wynne, Megan	M	WAL	21.01.93	17	1	2	-	1	-	20	1

GOALSCORERS 2016

WSL2: Hincks (7), Babajide (4), Gaylor (3), Loomes (3), Cole (1), Fisk (1), Gibbons (1), Giddings (1), Gurr (1), Robe (1), Wynne (1),

FAC: Cole (2), Loomes (2), Carlton (1)

CC: None

Total: Hincks (7), Loomes (5), Babajide (4), Cole (3), Gaylor (3), Carlton (1), Fisk (1), Gibbons (1), Giddings (1), Gurr (1), Robe (1), Wynne (1)

Millwall	2017 WSL2 Spring Series		
12.02.17	Durham (a)	L 0-1	
26.02.17	Sheffield FC (h)	L 1-2	Hincks 38
05.03.17	Aston Villa (a)	D 1-1	Mason 81
12.03.17	Brighton & Hove Albion (h)	D 0-0	
02.04.17	Everton (h)	W 2-1	Rutherford 21, Devlin 64
15.04.17	London Bees (a)	W 2-1	Rutherford 16, Devlin 24
22.04.17	Oxford United (h)	W 2-0	Rutherford 38, Horwood (pen) 82
30.04.17	Doncaster Rovers Belles (h)	W 2-1	Devlin 55, Brooks 75, *Giddings sent off 90*
20.05.17	Watford (a)	W 2-1	Brooks 65, Hincks 90+1

Millwall	2017 FA Cup		
05.02.17 R3	London Bees (h)	W 1-0	Wynne 12
19.02.17 R4	Nottingham Forest (h)	W 3-1	Hincks 18, 88, Cheatley 82
19.03.17 R5	Bristol City (a)	L 0-5	

MILLWALL LIONESSES PLAYER APPEARANCES & GOALS 2017

				WSL2		FAC		Total	
				A	G	A	G	A	G
Booker, Samine	M	ENG	12.12.99	1	-	-	-	1	-
Brooks, Billie	D	ENG	16.08.95	9	2	2	-	11	2
Butler, Jordan	D	ENG	14.09.92	6	-	2	-	8	-
Cheatley, Ashley	F	ENG	28.07.95	2	-	1	1	3	1
Cowan, Leanne	D	ENG	01.02.96	7	-	2	-	9	-
Devlin, Charlie	M	ENG	23.02.98	5	3	-	-	5	3
Fowle, Brionne	M	ENG	n/a	4	-	1	-	5	-
Gaylor, Amber	M	ENG	22.02.95	6	-	3	-	9	-
Giddings, Georgina	M	ENG	30.06.90	8	-	3	-	11	-
Glen, Freya	D	SCO	29.05.99	1	-	-	-	1	-
Harford, Bethany	F	ENG	16.09.99	2	-	-	-	2	-
Hincks, Ashlee	F	ENG	04.12.88	6	2	3	2	9	4
Horwood, Bonnie	M	ENG	16.04.87	9	1	3	-	12	1
Kempson, Sarah	M	ENG	n/a	8	-	-	-	8	-
Mason, Ellie	M	ENG	16.02.96	4	1	3	-	7	1
Nicol, Leigh	M	SCO	26.09.95	7	-	3	-	10	-
Quantrill, Sarah	G	ENG	21.07.90	9	-	3	-	12	-
Read, Phoebe	M	ENG	04.11.96	5	-	3	-	8	-
Robe, Leighanne	D	ENG	26.12.93	9	-	3	-	12	-
Rutherford, Ella	M	ENG	28.04.00	6	3	2	-	8	3
Wynne, Megan	M	WAL	21.01.93	9	-	3	1	12	1

GOALSCORERS 2017

WSL2 SS: Devlin (3), Rutherford (3), Brooks (2), Hincks (2), Horwood (1), Mason (1)

FAC: Hincks (2), Cheatley (1), Wynne (1)

Total: Hincks (4), Devlin (3), Rutherford (3), Brooks (2), Cheatley (1), Horwood (1), Mason (1), Wynne (1)

OXFORD UNITED – WSL2

Founded: Circa 1990	**Previous WSL Positions**
Stadium: The Northcourt, (Abingdon United FC)	**2017 WSL2:** 10th (Spring Series)
in 2016. Court Place Farm, (Oxford City FC) from	**2016 WSL2:** 9th
August 2017	**2015 WSL2:** 6th
Nickname: The U's	**2014 WSL2:** 9th
Manager: Andy Cook (since February 2017)	

- Founded in the early 1990s, they had a loose affiliation with Oxford United men's team until 2008. At that point the men's club founded a girls' Centre of Excellence and fully integrated the women's team into the Oxford United FC set-up.
- The U's have been part of WSL2 since its first season in 2014. They are yet to win any national honours, but have been hugely successful at regional level. They are three-time winners of the Oxfordshire FA Cup (2010/11, 2011/12, and 2012/13), were South Regional Premier League winners in 2011/12 and lifted the South Regional League Cup in 2010/11 and 2011/12. Other honours include the South West Counties League Cup in 2012/13 and runners-up position in the South Regional League Division One in 2008/09.
- Oxford's best FA Cup run to date came in 2012/13. Having beaten Keynsham Town in the second round they then caused a shock away to Charlton. For the fourth round tie at home to Newcastle they were granted use of Oxford United men's Kassam Stadium. A crowd of 700 saw them dispatch of Newcastle to reach the fifth round for the first time in the club's history. The reward was a home tie against top-flight Everton. Although the WSL1 outfit proved too strong, (winning 7-0), another impressive crowd of 945 came to the Kassam as Oxford's 'never-say-die' Cup spirit won them many new admirers.
- The Oxford home matches listed below were played at The Northcourt, which they shared with Abingdon United FC. In August 2017 it was announced they would move to Court Place Farm – home of Oxford City FC – for the next three seasons.

SEASON 2016 RECORD

2016 WSL2:	9th	P18	W4	D1	L13	F20	A42	GD-22	Pts13
2016 FA Cup:	3rd Round								
2016 Continental Cup:	1st Round								

SEASON 2017 RECORD

2017 WSL2 Spring Series:	10th	P9	W0	D2	L7	F7	A19	GD-12	Pts2
2017 FA Cup:	3rd Round								

Oxford United	2016 WSL2		
24.03.16	Millwall Lionesses (h)	L 3-5	Allison 18, Umotong 62, Nichol 70
27.03.16	Aston Villa (a)	L 1-2	Umotong 7
24.04.16	Durham (h)	L 1-5	Umotong 10
27.04.16	Yeovil Town (a)	L 0-2	
01.05.16	Sheffield FC (h)	W 1-0	Umotong 61
19.05.16	Millwall Lionesses (a)	W w/o*	
22.05.16	Watford (h)	W 2-0	Umotong 3, Nutman 30
25.06.16	Bristol City (a)	L 1-4	Umotong 25
30.06.16	Yeovil Town (h)	D 2-2	Umotong 3, 24
10.07.16	London Bees (a)	L 1-3	Umotong 82
17.07.16	Watford (a)	L 2-3	Franklin-Fraiture 14, Umotong 20
24.07.16	Everton (h)	L 0-1	
31.07.16	London Bees (h)	W 4-2	Umotong 30, 61, Allison 32, Noble 36
28.08.16	Durham (a)	L 1-2	Franklin-Fraiture 65
11.09.16	Everton (a)	L 0-3	
25.09.16	Aston Villa (h)	L 0-1	
30.10.16	Sheffield FC (a)	L 1-2	Umotong 90+2
06.11.16	Bristol City (h)	L 0-5	

*Oxford awarded win on 22.07.16 after Millwall failed to reschedule postponed match. Original match postponed after Millwall men's qualified for L1 play-off semi-finals and required use of venue.

Oxford United	2016 FA Cup		
07.02.16 R3	Brighton & Hove Albion (a)	L 0-10	

Oxford United	2016 Continental Cup		
08.05.16 RP	Millwall Lionesses (h)	W 1-0	Timms 78
03.07.16 R1	Birmingham City (h)	L 0-2	

OXFORD UNITED PLAYER APPEARANCES & GOALS 2016

				WSL2		FAC		CC		Total	
				A	G	A	G	A	G	A	G
Allison, Lauren	F	ENG	11.08.94	11	2	1	-	2	-	14	2
Baker, Sophie	M	ENG	14.12.96	10	-	1	-	-	-	11	-
Bruce, Chloe	D	ENG	n/a	1	-	1	-	-	-	2	-
Casley, Riva	D	ENG	27.01.99	13	-	-	-	1	-	14	-
Cox, Hannah	G	ENG	16.08.90	7	-	1	-	2	-	10	-
Deeley, Charlotte	D	ENG	28.11.97	7	-	-	-	2	-	9	-
Dyer, Mollie	M	ENG	n/a	2	-	1	-	-	-	3	-
Frampton, Jessica	D	ENG	14.06.91	17	-	-	-	2	-	19	-
Franklin-Fraiture, Ella	M	ENG	15.07.97	16	2	1	-	2	-	19	2
Hakala, Katja	D	FIN	19.02.96	10	-	-	-	1	-	11	-
Haynes, Lauren	M	ENG	15.09.95	13	-	1	-	2	-	16	-
Lambourne, Demi	G	ENG	30.04.96	10	-	1	-	1	-	12	-
Lane, Rosanna	D	ENG	14.06.94	16	-	1	-	1	-	18	-
Lee, Madison	D	ENG	18.06.93	12	-	1	-	1	-	14	-
Nichol, Laura	M	ENG	03.06.97	8	1	1	-	2	-	11	1
Noble, Ellie	M	ENG	12.09.99	8	1	-	-	1	-	9	1
Nutman, Katherine	M	ENG	09.10.92	11	1	1	-	-	-	12	1
Pickett, Holly	M	ENG	05.01.92	13	-	-	-	2	-	15	-
Rafferty, Laura	D	NIR	29.04.96	8	-	-	-	1	-	9	-
Timms, Georgia	M	ENG	24.04.98	12	-	-	-	2	1	14	1
Umotong, Ini-Abasi	F	NGA	15.05.94	17	13	-	-	2	-	19	13
Weston, Stephanie Anne	M	ENG	07.04.99	4	-	1	-	-	-	5	-

GOALSCORERS 2016

WSL2: Umotong (13), Allison (2), Franklin-Fraiture (2), Nichol (1), Noble (1), Nutman (1)

FAC: None

CC: Timms (1)

Total: Umotong (13), Allison (2), Franklin-Fraiture (2), Nichol (1), Noble (1), Nutman (1), Timms (1)

Oxford United	2017 WSL2 Spring Series		
12.02.17	Everton (h)	L 1-2	Umotong 88
26.02.17	Brighton & Hove Albion (a)	D 1-1	Gane 66
04.03.17	London Bees (a)	L 1-3	Umotong 88
12.03.17	Aston Villa (h)	D 0-0	
02.04.17	Durham (a)	L 1-2	Noble 47
15.04.17	Sheffield FC (a)	L 2-3	Umotong (pen) 17, 76, *Umotong sent off 77*
22.04.17	Millwall Lionesses (a)	L 0-2	
30.04.17	Watford (h)	L 1-2	Noble 7
21.05.17	Doncaster Rovers Belles (h)	L 0-4	

Oxford United	2017 FA Cup	
05.02.17 R3	Coventry United (a)	L 0-2

OXFORD UNITED PLAYER APPEARANCES & GOALS 2017

				WSL		FAC		Total	
				A	G	A	G	A	G
Allison, Lauren	F	ENG	11.08.94	2	-	1	-	3	-
Baker, Sophie	M	ENG	14.12.96	7	-	-	-	7	-
Casley, Riva	D	ENG	27.01.99	9	-	1	-	10	-
Deeley, Charlotte	D	ENG	28.11.97	7	-	1	-	8	-
Donovan, Emily	F	ENG	16.02.97	9	-	1	-	10	-
Frampton, Jessica	D	ENG	14.06.91	8	-	1	-	9	-
Franklin-Fraiture, Ella	M	ENG	15.07.97	8	-	1	-	9	-
Gane, Evie	D	WAL	10.12.99	7	1	-	-	7	1
Graham, Jess	M	ENG	n/a	1	-	-	-	1	-
Haynes, Lauren	M	ENG	15.09.95	7	-	1	-	8	-
Kemp, Caitlin	M	ENG	n/a	1	-	-	-	1	-
Lambourne, Demi	G	ENG	30.04.96	7	-	1	-	8	-
Lane, Rosanna	D	ENG	14.06.94	9	-	1	-	10	-
Lee, Madison	D	ENG	18.06.93	1	-	1	-	2	-
Noble, Ellie	M	ENG	12.09.99	9	2	1	-	10	2
Oliver, Taome	M	ENG	11.05.96	6	-	-	-	6	-
Pickett, Holly	M	ENG	05.01.92	7	-	1	-	8	-
Roberts, Amber	D	WAL	26.04.99	4	-	-	-	4	-
Thomas, Lucy	G	ENG	21.03.00	3	-	-	-	3	-
Timms, Georgia	M	ENG	24.04.98	2	-	1	-	3	-
Umotong, Ini-Abasi	F	NGA	15.05.94	7	4	1	-	8	4

GOALSCORERS 2017

WSL2 SS: Umotong (4), Noble (2), Gane (1)

FAC: None

Total: Umotong (4), Noble (2), Gane (1)

SHEFFIELD FC – WSL2

Founded: 2003	**Previous WSL Positions**
Stadium: Home of Football Ground, (Sheffield FC men's)	**2017 WSL2:** 9th (Spring Series) **2016 WSL2:** 5th
National Honours: WPL Play-Off Winners: (1) 2015	
WPL Cup Winners: (1) 2014	
WPL Cup Runners-up: (1) 2015	
Nickname: The Club	
Manager: Zoe Johnson (since January 2016)	

- Sheffield FC are officially affiliated with the oldest football club in the world, Sheffield FC men's, who were founded on 24 October 1857.
- Sheffield FC Ladies were formed in 2003 when Norton Ladies were taken under the umbrella of Sheffield FC men's. They began life in Division One East of the Yorkshire & Humberside League which was the bottom level of the women's football pyramid at the time.
- They rapidly rose to reach the elite ranks by 2016. They were the first club to be promoted to WSL2 via a play-off, doing so thanks to Lisa Giampalma's stop-page-time winner against Portsmouth in 2015.
- Their best FA Cup run to date came in 2014/15 when they reached the fifth round before losing 2-0 to Aston Villa.

SEASON 2016 RECORD

2016 WSL2:	5th	P18	W7	D5	L6	F25	A18	GD+7	Pts26
2016 FA Cup:	4th Round								
2016 Continental Cup:	Quarter-finals								

SEASON 2017 RECORD

2017 WSL2 Spring Series:	9th	P9	W2	D0	L7	F9	A18	GD-9	Pts6
2017 FA Cup:	4th Round								

Sheffield FC	2016 WSL2 Results		
23.03.16	Durham (h)	L 0-1	
26.03.16	Bristol City (a)	D 0-0	
23.04.16	Aston Villa (h)	L 1-2	Cain 53
01.05.16	Oxford United (a)	L 0-1	
19.05.16	Durham (a)	L 0-1	
22.05.16	Bristol City (h)	W 3-1	Flanagan 4, Michalska 43, Dale 74
10.07.16	Everton (h)	W 1-0	Michalska 24
17.07.16	London Bees (a)	W 5-0	Johnson 8, Michalska 55, Flanagan 71, 84, Gilliatt 82
24.07.16	Millwall Lionesses (h)	D 2-2	Lipman 44, 70
30.07.16	Everton (a)	D 1-1	Dale 48
14.08.16	Watford (h)	W 3-0	Michalska 2, Dale 26, Cain 46
28.08.16	Yeovil Town (h)	D 1-1	Michalska 69
11.09.16	Aston Villa (a)	W 2-1	Michalska 35, McCue 68
25.09.16	London Bees (h)	L 0-1	
09.10.16	Millwall Lionesses (a)	D 1-1	Johnson 33
16.10.16	Watford (a)	W 3-1	Ward 2, Michalska 72, Jones 80, *McCue sent off 90+2*
30.10.16	Oxford United (h)	W 2-1	Ward 56, Lord-Mears 58
06.11.16	Yeovil Town (a)	L 0-3	

Sheffield FC	2016 FA Cup		
07.02.16 R3	Leicester City Women (h)	W 5-1	Michalska 46, 49, 51, Gilliatt 68, 77
28.02.16 R4	Sporting Club Albion (h)	L 1-3	Ward 32

Sheffield FC	2016 Continental Cup		
08.05.16 RP	Durham (h)	W 3-1	Johnson 29, Flanagan 85, Dale 88
02.07.16 R1	Bristol City (h)	W 2-0	Michalska 58, Flanagan 81
07.08.17 QF	London Bees (h)	L 0-2	

SHEFFIELD FC PLAYER APPEARANCES & GOALS 2016

				WSL2		FAC		CC		Total	
				A	G	A	G	A	G	A	G
Anderson, Katie	F	ENG	n/a	1	-	-	-	-	-	1	-
Cain, Hannah	F	ENG	11.02.99	8	2	1	-	1	-	10	2
Cox, Danielle	D	ENG	16.09	11	-	-	-	2	-	13	-
Dale, Hannah	M	ENG	01.06.95	18	3	2	-	3	1	23	4
Dixon, Chloe	M	ENG	12.07.96	9	-	1	-	2	-	12	-
Draycott, Juliana	G	ENG	15.07.92	13	-	-	-	3	-	16	-
Flanagan, Chelsea	F	ENG	24.03.95	9	3	-	-	2	2	11	5
Gilliatt, Ellie	D	ENG	25.08.88	17	1	2	2	3	-	22	3
Goodman, Lynn	D	ENG	n/a	3	-	1	-	1	-	5	-
Hanson, Kirsty	F	SCO	17.04.98	8	-	-	-	2	-	10	-
Hartley, Ella	M	ENG	23.08.97	-	-	1	-	-	-	1	-
Jackson, Sarah	D	ENG	29.05.96	7	-	-	-	1	-	8	-
Johnson, Emma	M	ENG	12.10.91	16	2	2	-	3	1	21	3
Jones, Sophie	F	ENG	03.01	8	1	-	-	1	-	9	1
Knight, Hope	F	ENG	14.02.96	2	-	-	-	1	-	3	-
Lea, Danielle	D	ENG	10.08.94	2	-	-	-	1	-	3	-
Lord-Mears, Rhema	F	ENG	05.08.95	15	1	2	-	1	-	18	1
Lipman, Emma	D	ENG	23.02.89	15	2	2	-	2	-	19	2
McCue, Sherry	M	ENG	16.09.94	15	1	1	-	2	-	18	1
Michalska, Jodie	F	ENG	02.09.86	18	7	2	3	3	1	23	11
Murphy, Billie	D	ENG	27.01.93	18	-	2	-	3	-	23	-
Owen, Emily	F	ENG	n/a	3	-	2	-	1	-	6	-
Owen, Kenedy	M	ENG	22.12.98	8	-	2	-	1	-	11	-
Parkin, Kerry	F	ENG	n/a	1	-	2	-	-	-	3	-
Roberts, Emily	F	ENG	07.04.94	1	-	1	-	-	-	2	-
Wallhead, Claire	G	ENG	22.03	5	-	2	-	-	-	7	-
Ward, Carla	M	ENG	21.12.83	14	2	2	1	3	-	19	3
Wild, Olivia	D	ENG	21.06.96	1	-	-	-	-	-	1	-

GOALSCORERS 2016

WSL2: Michalska (7), Dale (3), Flanagan (3), Cain (2), Johnson (2), Lipman (2), Ward (2), Gilliatt (1), Jones (1), Lord-Mears (1), McCue (1)

FAC: Michalska (3), Gilliatt (2), Ward (1)

CC: Flanagan (2), Dale (1), Johnson (1), Michalska (1)

Total: Michalska (11), Flanagan (5), Dale (4), Gilliatt (3), Johnson (3), Ward (3), Cain (2), Lipman (2), Jones (1), Lord-Mears (1), McCue (1)

Sheffield FC	2017 WSL2 Spring Series		
26.02.17	Millwall Lionesses (a)	W 2-1	Cain 9, Jones 36
05.03.17	Durham (a)	L 0-1	
12.03.17	Everton (h)	L 1-2	McCue 78
01.04.17	London Bees (a)	L 1-2	Gilliatt 90
15.04.17	Oxford United (h)	W 3-2	Dear 52, Johnson 58, Gilliatt 65
23.04.17	Watford (a)	L 0-2	
27.04.17	Doncaster Rovers Belles (h)	L 0-2	
30.04.17	Aston Villa (h)	L 1-3	Dale 19
21.05.17	Brighton & Hove Albion (a)	L 1-3	Ward (pen) 90+1

Sheffield FC	2017 FA Cup		
05.02.17 R3	Charlton Athletic (a)	W 2-0	Jones 48, Flint 76
19.02.17 R4	Doncaster Rovers Belles (h)	L 0-1	

SHEFFIELD FC PLAYER APPEARANCES & GOALS 2017

				WSL2		FAC		Total	
				A	G	A	G	A	G
Anderson, Katie	F	ENG	n/a	2	-	-	-	2	-
Cain, Hannah	F	ENG	11.02.99	9	1	2	-	11	1
Cox, Danielle	D	ENG	16.09.na	5	-	-	-	5	-
Dale, Hannah	M	ENG	01.06.95	9	1	2	-	11	1
Davies, Suzanne	F	ENG	30.06.na	4	-	-	-	4	-
Dear, Jenna	M	ENG	29.05.96	4	1	-	-	4	1
Dixon, Chloe	M	ENG	12.07.96	5	-	1	-	6	-
Draycott, Juliana	G	ENG	15.07.92	9	-	2	-	11	-
Flanagan, Chelsea	F	ENG	24.03.95	-	-	-	-	-	-
Flint, Natasha	F	ENG	02.08.96	5	-	2	1	7	1
Gilliatt, Ellie	D	ENG	25.08.88	8	2	1	-	9	2
Hartley, Ella	M	ENG	23.08.97	-	-	-	-	-	-
Housley, Holly	D	ENG	n/a	2	-	1	-	3	-
Jackson, Sarah	D	ENG	29.05.96	8	-	2	-	10	-
Johnson, Emma	M	ENG	12.10.91	6	1	2	-	8	1
Jones, Sophie	F	ENG	03.01.na	6	1	2	1	8	2
Lord-Mears, Rhema	F	ENG	05.08.95	8	-	2	-	10	-
Lipman, Emma	D	ENG	23.02.89	4	-	1	-	5	-
Makin, Lagan	F	ENG	10.05.91	7	-	1	-	8	-
McCue, Sherry	M	ENG	16.09.94	7	1	1	-	8	1
Michalska, Jodie	F	ENG	02.09.86	-	-	-	-	-	-
Murphy, Billie	D	ENG	27.01.na	4	-	2	-	6	-
Owen, Kenedy	M	ENG	22.12.98	4	-	1	-	5	-
Ward, Carla	M	ENG	21.12.na	9	1	2	-	11	1

GOALSCORERS 2017

WSL2 SS: Gilliatt (2), Cain (1), Dale (1), Dear (1), Johnson (1), Jones (1), McCue (1), Ward (1)

FAC: Jones (1), Flint (1)

Total: Jones (2), Gilliatt (2), Cain (1), Dale (1), Dear (1), Flint (1), Johnson (1), McCue (1), Ward (1)

TOTTENHAM HOTSPUR – WSL2

Founded: 1985 (as Broxbourne Ladies)	**Previous WSL Positions:**
Stadium: Theobalds Lane, (Cheshunt FC)	None
Significant Honours:	
WPL Southern Champions: (1) 2016/17	
WPL Play-off Winners: (1) 2017	
WPL Cup Winners: (2) 2016 & 2017	
Nickname: Spurs / Lilywhites	
Manager: Karen Hills (since August 2009)	

- On 19 April 2017 Tottenham Ladies played their first competitive match at White Hart Lane, just a month before demolition started on Spurs' famous home stadium. It proved to be a particularly special night as they beat West Ham 4-0 to clinch the WPL Southern title with three matches still to play. A crowd of 2,140 was present.
- As WPL Southern champions, Tottenham faced a play-off for promotion with WPL Northern champions Blackburn. The match took place at The Valley on 28 May 2017 with Spurs winning 3-0 to seal promotion to the WSL for the first time.
- The team was founded as Broxbourne Ladies in 1985 but was granted permission to use the Tottenham Hotspur name from 1991/92. The club now trains at Tottenham Hotspur men's world class facility, Hotspur Way in Enfield.
- Tottenham's first-choice goalkeeper Toni-Anne Wayne found herself playing up front during the WPL Cup 2nd round tie against Enfield on 23 October 2016 – and she scored her first goal for the club. With Megen Lynch having been given a start in goal, Wayne was on the bench. But she was called into action with five minutes remaining to replace Wendy Martin in attack and she scored to make it 5-1.
- The first of Nikita Whinnett's two goals in the 4-1 WPL Cup quarter-final win over Crystal Palace on 11 December 2016 was scored after just 14 seconds.

SEASON 2016/17 RECORD

2016/17 WPL Southern:	1st	P20	W17	D1	L2	F58	A13	GD+45	Pts52
2016/17 FA Cup:	5th Round								
2016/17 WPL Cup:	Winners								

Tottenham	2016/17 WPL Southern		
28.08.16	Swindon Town (h)	W 4-1	Baptiste 32, Martin 80, 90, Whinnett 82
11.09.16	Crystal Palace (a)	W 1-0	Baptiste 8
14.09.16	QPR (a)	W 4-0	Whinnett 44, 56, Blanchflower 66, Green 85
18.09.16	Lewes (a)	W 6-1	Blanchflower 4, Whinnett 6, Baptiste 22, 45, 70, Martin 43
02.10.16	C&K Basildon (h)	D 1-1	Soobadoo 63
05.10.16	QPR (h)	W 3-0	Baptiste 79, Pond 90, 90+2
30.10.16	C&K Basildon (a)	W 4-0	Humes 30, Martin 39, Baptiste 63, Williams 78
13.11.16	Coventry United (a)	W 1-0	Hector 44
27.11.16	Swindon Town (a)	W 4-0	Baptiste 56, Hector 58, 61, Blanchflower 74
18.12.16	Portsmouth (h)	W 4-0	Leon 6, Blanchflower 12, 15, Baptiste 24
12.02.17	Lewes (h)	W 2-0	Martin 34, 85
12.03.17	Charlton Athletic (a)	W 1-0	Martin 32
26.03.17	Crystal Palace (h)	W 2-1	Baptiste 44, Martin 78
02.04.17	Coventry United (h)	W 2-0	Whinnett 68, Baptiste 81
09.04.17	Portsmouth (a)	W 4-1	Martin 13, Blanchflower 31, Baptiste 41, Leon 58
16.04.17	Cardiff City (h)	W 2-1	Whinnett 84, Martin 90+6
19.04.17	West Ham United (h)*	W 4-0	Green 20, Martin 51, Whinnett 70, Baptiste 83
23.04.17	Charlton Athletic (h)	L 2-3	Coombs (og) 38, Georgiou 78
30.04.17	Cardiff City (a)	L 0-4	
14.05.17	West Ham United (a)	W 7-0	O'Leary 36, Martin 45, 52, Soobadoo 61, Baptiste 66, 74, Leon 67

*Played at White Hart Lane, (Tottenham Hotspur FC)

Tottenham	2016/17 WPL Play-off		
28.05.17	Blackburn Rovers (n)	W 3-0	Baptiste 35, 66, Martin 90+3

Played at The Valley, (Charlton Athletic FC)

Tottenham	2016/17 FA Cup		
04.12.16 R1	Leyton Orient (h)	W 1-0	Martin 76
08.01.17 R2	Gillingham (h)	W 3-0	Vio 75, Baptiste 77, 87
05.02.17 R3	Blackburn Rovers (a)	W 2-1	Whinnett 19, Baptiste 90+3
19.02.17 R4	Brighton & Hove Albion (h)	W 1-0	Baptiste 57
19.03.17 R5	Arsenal (a)	L 0-10	

Tottenham	2016/17 WPL Cup		
04.09.16 DR	West Ham United (a)	W 10-0	Leon 5, Pond (pen) 8, Baptiste 10, Whinnett 23, 36, Martin (pen) 35, Hector 54, Blanchflower 56, 71, Schillaci 72
R1	Bye		
23.10.16 R2	Enfield Town (h)	W 5-1	Martin 39, 59, 61, Leon 75, Wayne 90
06.11.16 R3	Gillingham (h)	W 4-2	Leon 10, Blackie (og) 12, Vio 48, Martin 90
11.12.16 QF	Crystal Palace (h)	W 4-1	Whinnett 1, 7, Martin 41, Baptiste 68
05.03.17 SF	Cardiff City (h)	W 3-0	Martin 31, Rawle 53, Whinnett 82
07.05.17 F	Charlton Athletic (n)*	D 0-0 (W 4-3p)	

*Played at Lamex Stadium, Stevenage FC

TOTTENHAM HOTSPUR PLAYER APPEARANCES & GOALS 2016/17

				WPL*		FAC		WPLC		Total	
				A	G	A	G	A	G	A	G
Baptiste, Bianca	F	ENG	15.01.92	21	17	5	4	4	2	30	23
Bensted, Abbie	M	ENG	16.06.98	1	-	-	-	1	-	2	-
Blanchflower, Kelley	F	ENG	12.04.93	19	6	4	-	4	2	27	8
Carlton, Dan	M	ENG	30.07.92	2	-	-	-	-	-	2	-
Georgiou, Andrea	M	GRE	15.04.96	1	1	-	-	-	-	1	1
Green, Josie	M	WAL	25.04.93	18	2	4	-	6		28	2
Hector, Renee	D	ENG	21.06.95	19	3	5	-	6	1	30	4
Humes, Ronnell	F	ENG	10.06.99	3	1	-	-	1	-	4	1
Keown, Alex	D	ENG	12.05.92	3	-	-	-	-	-	3	-
Leon, Lucia	D	ESP	01.02.98	19	3	5	-	6	3	30	6
Lynch, Megen	G	ENG	03.09.91	6	-	1	-	4	-	11	-
Martin, Wendy	F	ENG	25.08.82	19	14	4	1	6	7	29	22
Mclean, Sophie	M	ENG	11.02.96	20	-	5	-	5	-	30	-
Moloney, Shannon	D	IRE	24.11.88	7	-	-	-	3	-	10	-
O'Leary, Katie	F	ENG	24.04.90	4	1	-	-	1	-	5	1
Pond, Eartha	D	ENG	04.09.83	15	2	4	-	4	1	23	3
Rawle, Leah	D	ENG	22.01.90	13	-	5	-	4	1	22	1
Schillaci, Jenna	D	ENG	21.03.84	19	-	5	-	5	1	29	1
Soobadoo, Riana	M	MRI	12.05.92	20	2	5	-	5	-	30	2
Vio, Maya	M	ENG	24.03.97	15	-	4	1	6	1	25	2
Wayne, Toni-Anne	G	ENG	08.05.83	17	-	4	-	4	1	25	1
Whinnett, Nikita	F	ENG	17.03.91	18	7	5	1	6	5	29	13
Williams, Cheryl	F	ENG	20.10.86	8	1	1	-	2	-	11	1

*Figures include WPL play-off

GOALSCORERS 2016/17

WPLS*: Baptiste (17), Martin (14), Whinnett (7), Blanchflower (6), Hector (3), Leon (3), Green (2), Pond (2), Soobadoo (2), Georgiou (1), Humes (1), O'Leary (1), Williams (1), own goals (1)

FAC: Baptiste (4), Martin (1), Vio (1), Whinnett (1)

WPLC: Martin (7), Whinnett (5), Leon (3), Baptiste (2), Blanchflower (2), Hector (1), Pond (1), Rawle (1), Schillaci (1), Vio (1), Wayne (1), own goals (1)

Total: Baptiste (23), Martin (22), Whinnett (13), Blanchflower (8), Leon (6), Hector (4), Pond (3), Green (2), Soobadoo (2), Vio (2), own goals (2), Georgiou (1), Humes (1), O'Leary (1), Rawle (1), Schillaci (1), Wayne (1), Williams (1)

*Figures include WPL Play-off

WATFORD – WSL2

Founded: 1970 (as Watford Supporters' Ladies Club)	**Previous WSL Positions**
	2017 WSL2: 8th (Spring Series)
Stadium: Gaywood Park, (Kings Langley FC)	**2016 WSL2:** 10th
National Honours: WPL Runners-up: (1) 2012/13	**2015 WSL2:** 10th
	2014 WSL2: 7th
Nickname: The Lady Hornets / Golden Girls	
Manager: Keith Boanas (since February 2017)	

- Female fans of Watford men's formed their own team in 1970 under the name the Supporters' Ladies Club. For a while the name was changed to the "Willy Walker Wonders" in homage to manager Doug Hewish and coaches John Williams and Mike Walker.
- In 1997 they merged with Watford Town Girls, and then came their first link-up with Watford men's club via the men's Community, Sports and Education Trust. It wasn't until early 2016 that Watford Ladies were formally brought under the Watford FC umbrella.
- Watford were Women's Premier League runners-up (behind champions Sunderland) in 2012/13. At that point the WPL was the second tier of English football. It was the final season that the division operated as a national division prior to the introduction of WSL2 in 2014. From then on the WPL became the third tier and was split in to WPL Southern and WPL Northern divisions.

SEASON 2016 RECORD

2016 WSL2:	10th	P18	W2	D1	L15	F13	A53	GD-40	Pts7
2016 FA Cup:	3rd Round								
2016 Continental Cup:	Preliminary Rd								

SEASON 2017 RECORD

2017 WSL2 Spring Series:	8th	P9	W2	D2	L5	F12	A17	GD-5	Pts8
2017 FA Cup:	3rd Round								

Watford	2016 WSL2		
23.03.16	London Bees (a)	D 2-2	Kerr 88, Burgess 90+3
17.04.16	Yeovil Town (h)	L 1-2	Stanley 90+2
24.04.16	Everton (a)	L 0-3	
01.05.16	Bristol City (h)	L 0-2	
16.05.16	London Bees (h)	L 0-5	
22.05.16	Oxford United (a)	L 0-2	
26.06.16	Everton (h)	W 2-1	Mason (pen) 19, Kerr 74
10.07.16	Yeovil Town (a)	L 0-5	
17.07.16	Oxford United (h)	W 3-2	Davy 45, 56, Ferrandi 48
24.07.16	Aston Villa (h)	L 0-2	
31.07.16	Durham (a)	L 0-3	
14.08.16	Sheffield FC (a)	L 0-3	
28.08.16	Millwall Lionesses (h)	L 1-2	Davy 53
10.09.16	Bristol City (a)	L 1-4	Kerr 74
25.09.16	Millwall Lionesses (a)	L 1-2	Mason 47
16.10.16	Sheffield FC (h)	L 1-3	Read 54
30.10.16	Durham (h)	L 1-6	Mason (pen) 10
06.11.16	Aston Villa (a)	L 0-4	

Watford	2016 FA Cup		
07.02.16 R3	Millwall Lionesses (a)	L 1-3 (aet)	Nuttall 70

Watford	2016 Continental Cup		
08.05.16 RP	London Bees (h)	L 0-2	

WATFORD PLAYER APPEARANCES & GOALS 2016

				WSL2		FAC		CC		Total	
				A	G	A	G	A	G	A	G
Bassett, Chloe	D	ENG	13.09.90	2	-	-	-	-	-	2	-
Baxter, Ruby	D	ENG	04.11.95	8	-	-	-	-	-	8	-
Burgess, Mollie	D	ENG	23.10.96	9	1	1	-	-	-	10	1
Charles, Otesha	F	GUY	14.04.93	6	-	-	-	-	-	6	-
Cheadle, Sophie	G	ENG	10.07.93	4	-	-	-	-	-	4	-
Davy, Anne-Laure	F	FRA	30.01.92	14	3	-	-	-	-	14	3
Deacon, Ashleigh	M	ENG	n/a	-	-	1	-	-	-	1	-
Donnelly, Stacie	M	IRE	07.06.93	9	-	1	-	1	-	11	-
Farrow, Kim	F			5	-	-	-	-	-	5	-
Fatuga-Dada, Adekite	M	ENG	05.09.96	7	-	-	-	-	-	7	-
Ferrandi, Giulia	M	ITA	30.09.92	6	1	-	-	-	-	6	1
Gillett, Lucy	G	ENG/USA	23.10.93	15	-	-	-	1	-	16	-
Gunn, Chloe	D	ENG	n/a	2	-	-	-	1	-	3	-
Jordinson, Lauren	D	ENG	25.05.96	6	-	-	-	-	-	6	-
Kerr, Charlotte	M	ENG	26.11.94	17	3	1	-	1	-	19	3
Kingshott, Katie	M	ENG	n/a	1	-	-	-	-	-	1	-
Lawrence, Chontele	D	ENG	04.07.95	3	-	-	-	1	-	4	-
Littleboy, Jordan	M	ENG	29.06.98	17	-	1	-	1	-	19	-
Mason, Ellie	M	ENG	16.02.96	13	3	1	-	-	-	14	3
Miller, Georgia	M	ENG	11.08.96	1	-	-	-	-	-	1	-
Nuttall, Anneka	D	ENG	26.02.91	18	-	1	1	1	-	20	1
Osborne-Ricketts, Sahara	D	ENG	20.03.91	8	-	-	-	1	-	9	-
Pepper, Nicole	D	ENG	29.07.95	14	-	1	-	1	-	16	-
Read, Phoebe	M	ENG	04.11.96	17	1	1	-	1	-	19	1
Richardson, Natalie	M	ENG	n/a	6	-	-	-	1	-	7	-
Samuels, Hannah	D	ENG	05.08.97	3	-	-	-	-	-	3	-
Stanley, Katie	M	ENG	n/a	12	1	-	-	1	-	13	1
Tullett, Amber	D	ENG	11.02.98	14	-	1	-	1	-	16	-
Walklett, Kerry	M	ENG	05.08.95	1	-	-	-	-	-	1	-
Ward-Chambers, Courtnay	F	ENG	09.10.97	-	-	1	-	-	-	1	-
Witney, Trippoli	G	ENG	n/a	-	-	1	-	-	-	1	-
Wotton, Victoria	D	ENG	01.11.90	3	-	1	-	1	-	5	-

GOALSCORERS 2016

WSL2: Davy (3), Kerr (3), Mason (3), M. Burgess (1), Ferrandi (1), Read (1), Stanley (1)

FAC: Nuttall (1)

CC: None

Total: Davy (3), Kerr (3), Mason (3), M. Burgess (1), Ferrandi (1), Nuttall (1), Read (1), Stanley (1)

Watford	2017 WSL2 Spring Series		
12.02.17	Aston Villa (a)	L 2-3	Nuttall 68, Kerr 89
26.02.17	London Bees (h)	L 2-3	Babajide (pen) 27, Neal 49
12.03.17	Durham (h)	D 1-1	Babajide 58
16.04.17	Brighton & Hove Albion (a)	L 1-2	Will 51
20.04.17	Doncaster Rovers Belles (h)	D 1-1	Cudone 54
23.04.17	Sheffield FC (h)	W 2-0	Will 3, Babajide 90+10
30.04.17	Oxford United (a)	W 2-1	Kerr 19, 76
14.05.17	Everton (a)	L 0-4	
20.05.17	Millwall Lionesses (h)	L 1-2	Will 76, *Puddefoot sent off 68*

Watford	2017 FA Cup	
05.02.17 R3	Doncaster Rovers Belles (a)	L w/o*

*Watford unable to fulfil fixture due to shortage of players

WATFORD PLAYER APPEARANCES & GOALS 2017

				WSL		FAC		Total	
				A	G	A	G	A	G
Albert, Cherrelle	F	ENG	24.02.88	6	-	-	-	6	-
Babajide, Rinsola	F	ENG	17.06.98	9	3	-	-	9	3
Bassett, Chloe	D	ENG	13.09.90	2	-	-	-	2	-
Baxter, Ruby	D	ENG	04.11.95	3	-	-	-	3	-
Charles, Natalie	M	ENG	n/a	1	-	-	-	1	-
Charles, Otesha	F	GUY	14.04.93	5	-	-	-	5	-
Cudone, Leah	F	ENG	17.09.94	9	1	-	-	9	1
Fatuga-Dada, Adekite	M	ENG	05.09.96	7	-	-	-	7	-
Fletcher, Josephine	G	ENG	31.12.80	4	-	-	-	4	-
Gillett, Lucy	G	ENG/USA	23.10.93	5	-	-	-	5	-
Jordinson, Lauren	D	ENG	25.05.96	7	-	-	-	7	-
Kerr, Charlotte	M	ENG	26.11.94	9	3	-	-	9	3
Maple, Lilli	M	ENG	12.01.96	7	-	-	-	7	-
McKeag, Meghan	D	ENG	12.08.89	5	-	-	-	5	-
Neal, Vicky	D	ENG	18.01.90	8	1	-	-	8	1
Nuttall, Anneka	D	ENG	26.02.91	9	1	-	-	9	1
Petkova, Simona	M	BUL	03.09.93	6	-	-	-	6	-
Poole, Tyra	D	ENG	28.05.97	4	-	-	-	4	-
Puddefoot, Danielle	M	ENG	24.06.92	7	-	-	-	7	-
Walklett, Kerry	M	ENG	05.08.95	1	-	-	-	1	-
Will, Merrick	M	ENG	21.12.96	7	3	-	-	7	3
Wotton, Victoria	D	ENG	01.11.90	1	-	-	-	1	-

GOALSCORERS 2017

WSL2 SS: Babajide (3), Kerr (3), Will (3), Cudone (1), Neal (1), Nuttall (1)

FAC: None

Total: Babajide (3), Kerr (3), Will (3), Cudone (1), Neal (1), Nuttall (1)

WOMEN'S PREMIER LEAGUE (WPL)

This next section of the Yearbook details the 71 teams competing in tiers three and four of English football in 2017/18 as well as five who were relegated to tier five at the end of 2016/17 and Shanklin who withdrew from the WPL South West Division One.

For ease of locating the teams within this book they have all been grouped alphabetically, regardless of which division they are in.

Tier three of English football consists of the 12 teams in WPL Southern and the 12 teams in WPL Northern. At the end of the season the champions of those divisions meet in a play-off to determine who wins the right to be promoted to WSL2, although they also have to satisfy off-field criteria to obtain a WSL licence.

Tier four of English football consists of four divisions. Two of them – WPL South West Division One and WPL South East Division One – feed to WPL Southern. The other two – WPL Northern Division One and WPL Midland Division One – feed to WPL Northern.

The key to this section of the book is as follows:

ACTONIANS:	Team name
WPL SE DIV ONE (Tier 4):	Level the team is competing at in 2017/18
SEASON 2016/17:	
WPL South East Div One: 6th:	Division and final League position in 2016/17
FA Cup: RQ3:	FA Cup round reached in 2016/17
WPL Cup: DR:	WPL Cup round reached in 2016/17
WPL Plate: SF:	WPL Plate round reached in 2016/17 (where applicable)

For reasons of space we have only included League results and those from national Cup competitions: the FA Cup, WPL Cup, and – where applicable – the WPL Plate. We have not been able to include results from regional Cup competitions.

The WPL Cup (the main League Cup for WPL sides) starts with a Determining Round (denoted as DR within these pages). Teams that win at this stage continue in the WPL Cup, while those who lose drop into the WPL Plate.

Other abbreviations used in this section:

RQ3 = Third qualifying round

R3 = Third round

QF = Quarter-final

SF = Semi-final

F = Final

(aet) = after extra-time

(L 2-4p) = lost 2-4 on penalties after extra-time

DR = Determining Round

ACTONIANS

WPL SE DIVISION ONE (TIER 4)

Founded: 1998 (as Chiswick United)
Nickname: None
Ground: Berkeley Fields, (North Greenford United FC)

SEASON 2016/17

WPL South East Division One: 6th
WPL Cup: DR **WPL Plate: SF**
FA Cup: RQ3

2016/17 WPL SE DIVISION ONE RESULTS

21.08	Cambridge United (a)	W 2-1
28.08	Luton Town (h)	L 0-1
11.09	Stevenage (a)	D 3-3
18.09	Denham United (h)	W 1-0
25.09	Milton Keynes Dons (a)	L 1-4
28.09	Enfield Town (a)	D 2-2
02.10	Norwich City (h)	W 5-4
05.10	Enfield Town (h)	W 3-1
30.10	Lowestoft Town (h)	W 3-0
27.11	Milton Keynes Dons (h)	D 1-1
04.12	Denham United (a)	L 2-4
18.12	Lowestoft Town (a)	W 7-0
08.01	Ipswich Town (a)	W 1-0
05.02	Gillingham (h)	L 0-4
19.03	AFC Wimbledon (h)	W 2-0
26.03	Cambridge United (h)	D 1-1
02.04	AFC Wimbledon (a)	D 1-1
09.04	Luton Town (a)	W 3-1
23.04	Gillingham (a)	L 1-7
30.04	Stevenage (h)	D 0-0
07.05	Ipswich Town (h)*	L 1-2
14.05	Norwich City (a)	W 11-0

*Played at Middlesex Stadium, (Hillingdon Borough FC)

2016/17 WPL CUP RESULTS

04.09	DR	Chichester City (a)	L 2-6

2016/17 WPL PLATE RESULTS

23.10	R2	Ipswich Town (h)	W 6-0
06.11	R3	QPR (h)+	W 2-1
11.12	QF	Radcliffe Olympic (h)	W 3-0
05.03	SF	Huddersfield Town (a)	L 1-6

+Played at Honeycroft, (Uxbridge FC)

2016/17 FA CUP RESULTS

09.10	RQ3	Milton Keynes Dons (a)	L 0-4

2016/17 WPL SE DIVISION ONE

	GD	Pts
1. Gillingham	90	57 (P)
2. Milton Keynes Dons	42	49
3. AFC Wimbledon	29	44
4. Cambridge United	20	41
5. Luton Town	5	37
6. Actonians	**14**	**36**
7. Enfield Town	-20	25
8. Denham United	-21	25
9. Ipswich Town	-22	25
10. Norwich City	-50	16
11. Stevenage	-26	15
12. Lowestoft Town	-61	6 (R)

Chiswick United Ladies was the club's first name. They were founded by Everoy Johnson in 1998, entering the Greater London League in Division Three West in their first season.

In the summer of 2003 they moved to Acton and became Acton Sports Club. When they found themselves without a home in the summer of 2008 they were taken under the wing of existing club Actonians.

Actonians won the London & South East Regional League and League Cup Double in 2014/15. It was their title success that season, which saw them promoted to WPL South East Division One.

AFC WIMBLEDON

WPL SE DIVISION ONE (TIER 4)

Founded: 1973 (as Friends of Fulham)
Nickname: The Dons
Ground: Gander Green Lane, (Sutton United FC)

SEASON 2016/17

WPL South East Division One: 3rd
WPL Cup: R2
FA Cup: R3

2016/17 WPL SE DIVISION ONE RESULTS

21.08	Ipswich Town (h)	W 4-3
11.09	Milton Keynes Dons (a)	W 2-0
18.09	Norwich City (h)	W 3-0
22.09	Denham United (h)	W 2-0
25.09	Lowestoft Town (a)	W 4-3
02.10	Stevenage (h)	W 4-0
05.10	Denham United (a)	L 1-4
16.10	Gillingham (a)	D 1-1
30.10	Cambridge United (h)	L 0-1
20.11	Luton Town (h)	L 2-4
27.11	Enfield Town (a)	W 3-2
11.12	Norwich City (a)	D 1-1
18.12	Ipswich Town (a)	W 4-1
26.02	Cambridge United (a)	D 1-1
05.03	Stevenage (a)	W 5-1
12.03	Milton Keynes Dons (h)	W 1-0
19.03	Actonians (a)	L 0-2
26.03	Luton Town (a)	D 1-1
02.04	Actonians (h)	D 1-1
09.04	Enfield Town (h)	W 4-0
30.04	Lowestoft Town (h)	W 10-0
14.05	Gillingham (h)	W 3-2

2016/17 WPL CUP RESULTS

04.09	DR	Plymouth Argyle (h)	W 3-2
	R1	Bye	
23.10	R2	Crystal Palace (h)	L 0-2

2016/17 FA CUP RESULTS

09.10	RQ3	Bexhill United (a)	W 6-0
13.11	RQ4	Denham United (h)	W 4-2

2016/17 FA Cup Results cont.

04.12	R1	Norwich City (a)	W 4-1
08.01	R2	Plymouth Argyle (a)	W 3-0
05.02	R3	Brighton & Hove Albion (h)	L 1-4

2016/17 WPL SE DIVISION ONE

	GD	Pts
1. Gillingham	90	57 (P)
2. Milton Keynes Dons	42	49
3. AFC Wimbledon	**29**	**44**
4. Cambridge United	20	41
5. Luton Town	5	37
6. Actonians	14	36
7. Enfield Town	-20	25
8. Denham United	-21	25
9. Ipswich Town	-22	25
10. Norwich City	-50	16
11. Stevenage	-26	15
12. Lowestoft Town	-61	6 (R)

Female fans of professional side Fulham formed a women's team in 1973 and called it Friends of Fulham. They started out in the Hounslow & District League before progressing to the Greater London League and later into the Women's National Premier League.

They enjoyed their most successful year in 1984 when they won the Treble of FA Cup (beating Doncaster Belles in the final at Craven Cottage), the Home Counties League and the League Cup.

They were also FA Cup runners-up in 1989 (losing to Leasowe Pacific, who later became Everton) and 1990 (when they were beaten by Doncaster Belles).

In 1986 they teamed up with professional men's outfit Wimbledon FC and became Wimbledon Ladies. In 1993 a 3-2 win at Plough Lane saw them become the first team to beat Doncaster Belles in a League game for 15 years.

When the original men's Wimbledon football club relocated to Milton Keynes, the Ladies team opted against moving and instead teamed up with fans' phoenix club AFC Wimbledon in 2003.

BARNSLEY

WPL NORTHERN DIVISION ONE (TIER 4)

Founded: 1986
Nickname: None
Ground: Oakwell Under-21 pitch

SEASON 2016/17

NE Regional League Premier: 1st (P)
FA Cup: Did not enter

2016/17 NE REGIONAL LEAGUE PREMIER RESULTS

04.09	Norton & Stockton Ancients (h)	L 1-2
11.09	Wallsend BC (a)	W 2-1
18.09	Castleford White Rose (h)	W 4-2
25.09	East Yorkshire Carnegie (a)	W 11-2
02.10	York City (h)	W 6-0
09.10	York City (a)	L 2-3
16.10	Tynedale (a)	W 8-3
23.10	Wakefield (h)	W 7-0
30.10	Boldon (a)	W 9-0
06.11	Oughtibridge WM (h)	W 3-0
04.12	Wallsend BC (h)	L 1-2
11.12	Castleford White Rose (a)	W 5-2
08.01	Scunthorpe & Bottesford (h)	W 10-0
22.01	Tynedale (h)	W 4-1
05.02	Boldon (h)	W w/o
26.02	Scunthorpe & Bottesford (a)	W 1-0
26.03	Wakefield (a)	W 6-1
02.04	Norton & Stockton Ancients (a)	W 4-1
09.04	East Yorkshire Carnegie (h)	W 13-0
30.04	Oughtibridge WM (a)	W 3-0

2016/17 NE REGIONAL PREMIER

	GD	Pts
1. Barnsley	**80**	**51 (P)**
2. Norton & Stockton Ancients	47	51
3. Wallsend BC	27	42
4. Castleford White Rose	23	42
5. Tynedale	22	42
6. York City	-9	25*
7. Scunthorpe & Bottesford	-40	18
8. Oughtibridge WM	-4	15*
9. Wakefield	-49	12
10. East Yorkshire Carnegie	-56	8*
11. Boldon	-41	-7*

*York docked 3 points (no-show)

*Oughtibridge WM docked 3 points (no-show)

*East Yorkshire Carnegie docked 6 points (multiple no-shows)

*Boldon docked 15 points (multiple no-shows)

The 2016/17 season was the most successful in Barnsley's history. As well as claiming the North East Regional Premier League title, they also won the North East League Cup final beating Wallsend BC 3-2.

In 2016 Barnsley won the Sheffield & Hallamshire FA Challenge Cup for the first time in their history thanks to a 4-2 victory against Huddersfield. Netherwood schoolgirl Brittany Sanderson, aged 16, scored a hat-trick in the final.

Barnsley Ladies were founded in 1986. Ahead of the 2016/17 season they signed a contract with the professional men's club Barnsley for the use of their pitch, but there is no formal affiliation between the clubs.

BASINGSTOKE TOWN

WPL SW DIVISION ONE (TIER 4)

Founded: 1992
Nickname: Town
Ground: Ark Cancer Charity Stadium, (Basingstoke Town FC) in 2016/17, Winklebury Football Complex in 2017/18

SEASON 2016/17

WPL South West Division One: 9th
WPL Cup: R2
FA Cup: RQ4

2016/17 WPL SW DIVISION ONE RESULTS

28.08	Southampton Saints (h)	L 2-4
11.09	Cheltenham Town (h)	W 1-0
14.09	Maidenhead United (a)	L 1-2
02.10	*Shanklin (h)*	W 7-2 (ex)
05.10	Maidenhead United (h)+	D 2-2
23.10	Brislington (h)	L 0-2
08.01	Cheltenham Town (a)	L 1-2
12.02	Keynsham Town (h)	L 2-6
19.02	*Shanklin (a)*	*W 2-0 (ex)*
26.02	Chichester City (h)	L 0-5
19.03	Larkhall Athletic (h)	D 1-1
26.03	Plymouth Argyle (a)	L 1-4
02.04	Larkhall Athletic (a)	L 0-1
13.04	Southampton Saints (a)	L 1-3
16.04	St Nicholas (a)	D 4-4
20.04	Chichester City (a)	L 0-4
23.04	Basingstoke Town (h)	D 3-3
30.04	Keynsham Town (a)	L 1-6
07.05	St Nicholas (h)*	W 2-0
11.05	Exeter City (h)	W 5-0
14.05	Brislington (a)	D 2-2
21.05	Plymouth Argyle (h)	L 0-6

(ex) Shanklin withdrew from League: results expunged

*Played at Everest Community Academy 4G

+Played at Wrinklebury, Hants FA

2016/17 WPL CUP RESULTS

04.09	DR	Cheltenham Town (h)	W 3-1
	R1	Bye	
30.10	R2	Chichester City (h)	L 0-5

2016/17 FA CUP RESULTS

09.10	RQ3	Billericay Town (a)	W 2-1
13.11	RQ4	Plymouth Argyle (a)	L 1-3

2016/17 WPL SW DIVISION ONE

	GD	Pts
1. Chichester City	92	58 (P)
2. Plymouth Argyle	85	54
3. Southampton Saints	20	41
4. Keynsham Town	39	38
5. Larkhall Athletic	3	36
6. Brislington	-19	22
7. Maidenhead United	-28	16*
8. St Nicholas	-43	15
9. Basingstoke Town	**-28**	**14**
10. Cheltenham Town	-49	13
11. Exeter City	-72	4 (R)

*Maidenhead docked 1 point

NB: Shanklin withdrew from League, all results expunged

Basingstoke Town Ladies won promotion to WPL South West Division One for the 2016/17 season. With their existing facilities not eligible to host football at that level, Basingstoke Town men's FC agreed they could groundshare at the Ark Cancer Charity Stadium, (previously known as The Camrose).

The team was formed in 1992 but almost went out of business in 1999. The efforts of, then chairman, Ian Walkom and secretary Clare Hodder ensured the club survived.

Helen Ogle was the club's top scorer for 2016/17 with 13 goals in 24 appearances in all competitions.

BIRMINGHAM & WEST MIDLANDS

WPL MIDS DIVISION ONE (TIER 4)

Founded: 2001 (as Birmingham University)
Nickname: None
Ground: Shenley Lane, (Northfield Town FC) in 2016/17, The Vale Stadium (Castle Vale FC) in 2017/18

SEASON 2016/17

WPL Midlands Division One: 5th
WPL Cup: DR **WPL Plate: R2**
FA Cup: R1

2016/17 WPL MIDS DIVISION ONE RESULTS

21.08	Rotherham United (a)	L 1-5
28.08	Long Eaton United (a)	W 2-1
14.09	Wolverhampton Wanderers (h)*	L 1-3
18.09	Leicester City Ladies (h)	L 0-2
02.10	Radcliffe Olympic (a)	L 1-2
05.10	Wolverhampton Wanderers (a)	L 2-5
30.10	Steel City Wanderers (a)	W 4-3
06.11	The New Saints (h)	W 4-2
27.11	The New Saints (a)	W 2-0
11.12	Rotherham United (h)	W 5-1
18.12	Solihull (a)	W 4-0
08.01	Loughborough Students (h)	W 5-0
05.02	Sporting Khalsa (h)+	W 4-1
19.02	Leicester City Ladies (a)	W 5-3
26.02	Solihull (h)**	W 4-2
12.03	Sporting Khalsa (a)	L 1-5
19.03	Loughborough Foxes (h)	L 0-4
26.03	Steel City Wanderers (h)	W 1-0
02.04	Loughborough Foxes (a)	L 0-1
23.04	Loughborough Students (a)	W 8-2
07.05	Radcliffe Olympic (h)	D 1-1
14.05	Long Eaton United (h)	W 4-2

*Played at Vale Stadium, (Castle Vale FC)

**Played at The Lamb, (Tamworth FC)

+Played at Central Ground, (Sutton Coldfield FC)

2016/17 WPL CUP RESULTS

04.09	DR	Stoke City (a)	L 0-13

2016/17 WPL PLATE RESULTS

23.10	R2	Radcliffe Olympic (h)	L 0-1

2016/17 FA CUP RESULTS

09.10	RQ3	Leicester City Ladies (a)	W 3-2
13.11	RQ4	The New Saints (a)	W 5-2
04.12	R1	Leicester City Women (a)	L 0-3

2016/17 WPL MIDS DIVISION ONE

	GD	Pts
1. Wolverhampton Wanderers	39	56
2. Loughborough Foxes	80	54
3. Sporting Khalsa	24	41
4. Radcliffe Olympic	22	40
5. Birmingham & WM	**14**	**40**
6. The New Saints	21	39
7. Long Eaton United	9	30
8. Steel City Wanderers	-16	28
9. Solihull	-14	23
10. Leicester City Ladies	-61	17
11. Rotherham United	-25	16
12. Loughborough Students	-93	-1* (R)

*Loughborough Students docked 2 points

Founded in 2001 as Birmingham University they then became Birmingham Athletic and subsequently West Midlands Police before settling on the current name of Birmingham & West Midlands in 2014.

Birmingham & West Midlands were promoted to the WPL Midlands Division One as 2014/15 West Midlands Regional League Premier Division champions. That season they also won the West Midlands Regional League Cup.

Leah Seivwright was the club's top scorer in 2016/17 with 20 goals over 26 games in all competitions.

BLACKBURN ROVERS

WPL NORTHERN DIVISION (TIER 3)

Founded: 1991
Nickname: Rovers
Ground: Sir Tom Finney Stadium, (Bamber Bridge FC)

SEASON 2016/17

WPL Northern Division: 1st
WPL Cup: SF
FA Cup: R3

2016/17 WPL NORTHERN DIVISION

21.08	Stoke City (a)	W 2-0
28.08	Huddersfield Town (a)	D 3-3
11.09	West Bromwich Albion (h)	W 5-1
18.09	Bradford City (a)	W 4-0
02.10	Newcastle United (a)	W 1-0
05.10	Fylde (a)	W 2-1
09.10	Nottingham Forest (h)	W 4-1
30.10	Bradford City (h)	W 4-2
20.11	Middlesbrough (a)	W 2-1
15.01	Leicester City Women (a)	W 4-0
29.01	Nottingham Forest (a)	W 2-1
12.02	Middlesbrough (h)	W 5-1
16.02	Fylde (h)	W 1-0
19.02	Newcastle United (h)	W 3-0
12.03	West Bromwich Albion (a)	W 3-2
26.03	Derby County (h)	W 3-2
02.04	Leicester City Women (h)	D 2-2
09.04	Derby County (a)	W 4-0
08.05	Huddersfield Town (h)*	W 3-1
14.05	Stoke City (h)*	D 2-2

*played at Ewood Park

2016/17 WPL PLAY-OFF RESULT

28.05	Tottenham Hotspur (n)*	L 0-3

*The Valley, Charlton Athletic FC

2016/17 WPL CUP RESULTS

04.09	DR	Rotherham United (h)	W 19-0
25.09	R1	Nottingham Forest (h)	W 3-1
23.10	R2	Newcastle United (a)	W 1-0

2016/17 WPL Cup Results cont.

06.11	R3	Loughborough Foxes (h)	W 5-0
11.12	QF	Chester-le-Street Town (a)	W 3-1
05.03	SF	Charlton Athletic (a)	L 3-4 (aet)

2016/17 FA CUP RESULTS

04.12	R1	Bradford City (a)	W 1-0
08.01	R2	Hull City (h)	W 5-0
05.02	R3	Tottenham Hotspur (h)	L 1-2

2016/17 WPL NORTHERN DIVISION

	GD	Pts
1. Blackburn Rovers	**39**	**54**
2. Middlesbrough	29	43
3. Leicester City Women	7	34
4. Stoke City	6	30
5. Derby County	4	29
6. West Bromwich Albion	-4	27
7. Fylde	6	26*
8. Bradford City	0	22
9. Huddersfield Town	-16	20
10. Nottingham Forest	-22	18
11. Newcastle United	-49	7 (R)

*Fylde docked 3 points (ineligible player)

Rovers were WPL Northern champions in 2016/17 but missed out on promotion to the WSL by losing a play-off 3-0 to WPL Southern champions Tottenham Hotspur at The Valley on 28 May.

Rovers went through the entire 2003/04 Northern Combination campaign without dropping a single point – they won every match to take the title and also lifted the Lancashire County Cup that season.

They almost repeated the feat in the 2005/06 Women's Premier League Northern Division campaign. They claimed the title without losing a single game, winning 20 and drawing two of their 22 matches.

On the back of that 2005/06 title success, manager Andy McNally became the first manager from outside the top-flight to win the FA Manager of the Year award.

BOLTON WANDERERS

WPL NORTHERN DIVISION ONE (TIER 4)

Founded: 1989
Nickname: None
Ground: Eddie Davies Academy in 2016/17, moving to Kensite Stadium (Atherton Collieries FC) for 2017/18

SEASON 2016/17

NW Regional Premier: 1st (P)
FA Cup: RQ2

2016/17 NW REG PREMIER RESULTS

04.09	Stockport County (a)	W 4-1
07.09	CMB (a)	D 0-0
11.09	Wigan Athletic (h)	W 4-0
02.10	Blackburn Community (a)	W 3-0
09.10	Blackpool FC (h)	W 5-1
16.10	Accrington (a)	W 8-1
30.10	Manchester Stingers (h)	W 8-0
06.11	CMB (h)	W 4-0
13.11	MSB Woolton (h)	D 3-3
20.11	Accrington (h)	W 2-0
27.11	Stockport County (h)	D 3-3
04.12	Wigan Athletic (a)	W 2-0
11.12	City of Manchester (h)	W 7-1
18.12	Burnley FC (a)	W 4-1
08.01	Blackburn Community (h)	W 6-1
05.02	Manchester Stingers (a)	W 5-2
26.02	MSB Woolton (a)	W 3-1
05.03	Burnley FC (h)	D 2-2
19.03	Birkenhead (h)	W 7-0
26.03	Birkenhead (a)	W 3-1
02.04	Blackpool FC (a)	W 3-0
23.04	City of Manchester (a)	L 1-3

2016/17 FA CUP RESULTS

18.09	RQ2	FC United of Manchester (a)	L 1-2

2016/17 NW REGIONAL PREMIER

	GD	Pts
1. Bolton Wanderers	**66**	**55 (P)**
2. Wigan Athletic	45	50
3. Burnley FC	40	49
4. Blackpool FC	17	41
5. Stockport County	2	34
6. MSB Woolton	12	29
7. Blackburn Comm.	-11	27
8. CMB	-1	25
9. Manchester Stingers	-21	23
10. Accrington	-24	21
11. City of Manchester	-50	18*
12. Birkenhead	-75	6

*City of Manchester docked 1 point (no-show)

Bolton Wanderers Ladies were founded in 1989 and officially joined the Bolton Wanderers Football Club family in 2010.

Bolton Wanderers won their first League title in 2016/17 and with it promotion to the WPL Northern Division One. They secured the NW Regional Premier League title with one game to spare thanks to a 3-0 win away to Blackpool FC when they needed only a point.

The Eddie Davies Academy – home of professional men's team Bolton Wanderers' academy side – was the site at which Bolton Wanderers Ladies played most of their home games in 2016/17.

In June 2017 they announced they would spend 2017/18 at the 2,500 capacity Kensite Stadium, home of men's non-League side Atherton Collieries FC.

BRADFORD CITY

WPL NORTHERN DIVISION (TIER 3)

Founded: 1988
Nickname: The Bantams
Ground: Kingsway, (Eccleshill United FC)

SEASON 2016/17

WPL Northern Division: 8th
WPL Cup: DR **WPL Plate: R3**
FA Cup: R1

2016/17 WPL NORTHERN DIVISION

21.08	Derby County (h)	L 0-2
28.08	Middlesbrough (h)	L 0-2
11.09	Fylde (a)	L 2-3
14.09	Huddersfield Town (h)	W 1-0
18.09	Blackburn Rovers (h)	L 0-4
25.09	Stoke City (h)	W 5-1
02.10	Derby County (a)	L 1-3
05.10	Huddersfield Town (a)	L 1-2
09.10	Leicester City Women (h)	W 4-1
23.10	Nottingham Forest (h)	W 6-0
30.10	Blackburn Rovers (a)	L 2-4
27.11	Stoke City (a)	W 3-1
11.12	Newcastle United (h)	D 0-0
15.01	Newcastle United (a)	W 5-1
19.02	Middlesbrough (a)	L 1-2
19.03	Nottingham Forest (a)	L 1-2
02.04	Fylde (h)	L 1-2
09.04	West Bromwich Albion (h)	W 2-1
23.04	West Bromwich Albion (a)	L 1-4
07.05	Leicester City Women (a)	L 4-5

2016/17 WPL CUP RESULTS

04.09	DR	West Bromwich Albion (a)	L 1-2

2016/17 WPL PLATE RESULTS

16.10	R2	Crewe Alex. (a)	W 6-0
06.11	R3	Huddersfield Town (h)	D 2-2 (L 3-4p)

2016/17 FA CUP RESULTS

04.12	R1	Blackburn Rovers (h)	L 0-1

2016/17 WPL NORTHERN DIVISION

	GD	Pts
1. Blackburn Rovers	39	54
2. Middlesbrough	29	43
3. Leicester City Women	7	34
4. Stoke City	6	30
5. Derby County	4	29
6. West Bromwich Albion	-4	27
7. Fylde	6	26*
8. Bradford City	**0**	**22**
9. Huddersfield Town	-16	20
10. Nottingham Forest	-22	18
11. Newcastle United	-49	7 (R)

*Fylde docked 3 points (ineligible player)

In 1989 – a year after their formation – Bradford City were founding members of the Yorkshire and Humberside League.

In 1997 the Bantams won promotion to the WPL for the first time after winning the Northern Division.

Their best run in the WPL League Cup came in 1997/98 when they made it to the semi-finals before being knocked out on penalties by eventual winners Arsenal after a 2-2 draw.

BRIGHOUSE TOWN

WPL NORTHERN DIVISION ONE (TIER 4)

Founded: 2013
Nickname: Town
Ground: Dual Seal Stadium, (Brighouse Town FC)

SEASON 2016/17

WPL Northern Division One: 6th
WPL Cup: R1
FA Cup: R3

2016/17 WPL NORTHERN DIVISION ONE

21.08	Morecambe (h)	L 0-3
28.08	Liverpool Feds (h)	D 3-3
11.09	Hull City (a)	L 0-1
18.09	Tranmere Rovers (a)	W 6-0
27.09	Guiseley Vixens (a)	L 1-3
02.10	Chester-le-Street Town (h)	D 2-2
05.10	Guiseley Vixens (h)	L 0-4
30.10	Leeds United (h)	L 1-3
06.11	Morecambe (a)	D 1-1
27.11	Mossley Hill Athletic (a)	W 2-1
11.12	Hull City (h)	L 1-2
29.01	Chester-le-Street Town (a)	L 0-2
19.02	Mossley Hill Athletic (h)	W 4-0
26.02	Chorley (h)	W 3-2
05.03	Liverpool Feds (a)	W 1-0
12.03	Crewe Alexandra (a)	W 4-0
26.03	Blackpool Wren Rovers (h)	W 4-0
09.04	Tranmere Rovers (h)	W 1-0
23.04	Chorley (a)	W 6-2
30.04	Crewe Alexandra (h)	D 2-2
04.05	Leeds United (a)	W 4-2
14.05	Blackpool Wren Rovers (a)	W 4-1

2016/17 WPL CUP RESULTS

04.09	DR	Mossley Hill Athletic (a)	W 5-0
16.10	R1	Wolverhampton Wanderers (a)	D 2-2 (L 2-4p)

2016/17 FA CUP RESULTS

09.10	R3Q	Stockport County (a)	W 2-1
13.11	R4Q	Blackpool Wren Rovers (h)	W 5-0
04.12	R1	Peterborough N. S. (h)	W 3-2
08.01	R2	Long Eaton United (a)	W 4-3
05.02	R3	Everton (h)	L 1-8

2016/17 WPL NORTHERN DIVISION ONE

	GD	Pts
1. Guiseley Vixens	52	59 (P)
2. Liverpool Feds	37	44
3. Hull City	16	43
4. Chester-le-Street Town	16	41
5. Chorley	7	38
6. Brighouse Town	**16**	**37**
7. Morecambe	1	29*
8. Leeds United	-8	23
9. Mossley Hill Athletic	-27	19
10. Crewe Alexandra	-28	18
11. Blackpool Wren Rovers	-31	18 (R)
12. Tranmere Rovers	-51	7 (R)

*Morecambe docked 3 points (unregistered player)

Brighouse Town have enjoyed a rapid rise since they were formed in 2013, going from the sixth tier to the fourth tier in three years.

They were crowned North East Regional League South champions in 2013/14 and then North East Regional League Premier Division champions in 2015/16, an achievement which saw them promoted to the WPL Northern Division One.

The team was established when non-League men's team Brighouse was given the go-ahead to formalise their women's team. They merged with Kirklees Ladies to create Brighouse Town Ladies.

BRISLINGTON

WPL SW DIVISION ONE (TIER 4)

Founded: 2011
Nickname: None
Ground: Ironmould Lane, (Brislington FC)

SEASON 2016/17

WPL South West Division One: 6th
WPL Cup: R1
FA Cup: R1

2016/17 WPL SW DIVISION ONE RESULTS

21.08	Southampton Saints (h)	D 2-2
28.08	*Shanklin (h)*	*W 1-0 (ex)*
11.09	Maidenhead United (h)	W 5-2
18.09	Chichester City (a)	L 1-7
02.10	Plymouth Argyle (a)	L 1-5
06.10	Keynsham Town (h)	L 1-4
16.10	Southampton Saints (a)	L 3-5
23.10	Basingstoke Town (a)	W 2-0
30.10	*Shanklin (a)*	*W 3-1 (ex)*
10.11	Keynsham Town (a)	L 0-4
27.11	Chichester City (h)	L 0-4
18.12	Larkhall Athletic (a)	L 2-3
05.02	Cheltenham Town (a)	W 3-1
12.02	Exeter City (h)	W 6-0
19.02	Larkhall Athletic (h)	L 3-4
23.03	St Nicholas (a)	L 2-5
26.03	Exeter City (a)	D 2-2
30.03	Cheltenham Town (h)	W 4-1
02.04	St Nicholas (h)	D 0-0
23.04	Plymouth Argyle (h)	L 0-8
07.05	Maidenhead United (a)	W 5-4
14.05	Basingstoke Town (h)	D 2-2

(ex) Shanklin withdrew from League: results expunged

2016/17 WPL CUP RESULTS

04.09	DR	Forest Green Rovers (a)	W w/o
25.09	R1	Denham United (a)	L 2-3

2016/17 FA CUP RESULTS

09.10	RQ3	Torquay United (a)	W 4-2
13.11	RQ4	Poole Town (h)	W 8-0
04.12	R1	Lewes (a)	L 0-5

2016/17 WPL SW DIVISION ONE

	GD	Pts
1. Chichester City	92	58 (P)
2. Plymouth Argyle	85	54
3. Southampton Saints	20	41
4. Keynsham Town	39	38
5. Larkhall Athletic	3	36
6. Brislington	**-19**	**22**
7. Maidenhead United	-28	16*
8. St Nicholas	-43	15
9. Basingstoke Town	-28	14
10. Cheltenham Town	-49	13
11. Exeter City	-72	4 (R)

*Maidenhead docked 1 point

NB: Shanklin withdrew from League, all results expunged

The team ground shares Brislington Stadium at Ironmould Lane with the non-League men's club of the same name.

Kim Maggs and Polly Wardle were the club's joint top scorers in 2016/17. Sports lecturer Wardle, who plays as a striker or on the right-wing, hit 14 goals in 20 appearances. Attacking midfielder/striker Maggs, who is a pharmacy dispenser by trade, scored 14 from 23 appearances.

Brislington won the South West Regional Premier Division in 2015/16 to gain promotion to WPL South West Division One for 2016/17. During their first season at that level they enjoyed a comfortable mid-table finish.

In 2011/12 – their first season after formation – Brislington competed in the Somerset County League Division Two. Despite most of their players being just 16 or 17 years old they won the title without dropping a point and with a goal difference of +186.

BURTON ALBION

WPL MIDLANDS DIVISION ONE (TIER 4)

Founded: 2000
Nickname: Brewers
Ground: St George's Park for 2016/17 moving to Marston Road (Stafford Rangers FC) for 2017/18

SEASON 2016/17

WM Regional Premier League: **1st (P)**
FA Cup: RQ4

2016/17 WM REGIONAL PREMIER

21.08	Crusaders (a)	W 4-1
04.09	Kingshurst Sporting Club (h)	W 4-3
11.09	Knowle (a)	W 3-0
25.09	Leafield Athletic (h)	W 6-1
02.10	Leamington Lions (a)	L 1-2
23.10	Wolverhampton Sporting (a)	W 1-0
30.10	Wrockwardine Wood (h)	W 3-1
06.11	Leafield Athletic (a)	W 6-0
18.12	Knowle (h)	W 2-0
29.01	Wolverhampton Sporting (h)	W 4-1
05.02	Wrockwardine Wood (a)	W 2-1
12.02	Coundon Court (h)	D 0-0
26.02	Lye Town (h)	D 2-2
19.03	Leamington Lions (h)	W 1-0
09.04	Lye Town (a)	W 4-1
16.04	Kingshurst Sporting Club (a)	W 2-1
23.04	Coundon Court (a)	W 1-0
07.05	Crusaders (h)	W 7-0

2016/17 FA CUP RESULTS

18.09	RQ2	Lye Tow (h)	W 3-1
09.10	RQ3	Leamington Lions (a)	W 4-0
13.11	RQ4	Solihull (a)	L 0-3

2016/17 WM REGIONAL PREMIER

	GD	Pts
1. Burton Albion	**39**	**47 (P)**
2. Crusaders	1	31
3. Lye Town	3	30
4. Leafield Athletic	-4	27
5. Kingshurst Sporting Club	-12	27
6. Coundon Court	2	24
7. Wrockwardine Wood	-3	22
8. Wolverhampton Sporting	-2	21
9. Knowle	-10	14
10. Leamington Lions	-14	12

Burton Albion won the West Midlands Regional Premier League 2016/17 which saw them promoted to the WPL Midlands Division One.

They completed the 2016/17 Double by winning their region's League Cup. They beat Coundon Court 2-1 in the final.

The club has enjoyed a rapid rise to prominence having won four League titles in a row, including League and Cup Doubles in 2014/15, 2015/16 and 2016/17.

They played their home matches in 2016/17 at St George's Park, but in the summer of 2017 they moved to the home ground of men's non-League team Stafford Rangers.

C&K BASILDON

WPL SOUTHERN DIVISION (TIER 3)

Founded: 2004 (as Basildon Town Ladies)
Nickname: None
Ground: Frost Financial Stadium, (Canvey Island FC)

SEASON 2016/17

WPL Southern Division: 6th
WPL Cup: R2
FA Cup: R2

2016/17 WPL SOUTHERN DIVISION

21.08	Portsmouth (h)	W 2-0
28.08	Charlton Athletic (a)	L 0-6
11.09	QPR (h)	W 4-0
14.09	West Ham United (a)	D 0-0
25.09	Cardiff City (a)	L 1-2
02.10	Tottenham Hotspur (a)	D 1-1
05.10	West Ham United (h)	L 0-1
09.10	Portsmouth (a)	W 3-1
23.10	Swindon Town (h)	W 2-0
30.10	Tottenham Hotspur (h)	L 0-4
11.12	Coventry United (h)	L 0-3
18.12	Coventry United (a)	L 0-6
12.03	Cardiff City (h)	W 3-2
19.03	Crystal Palace (h)	D 2-2
26.03	Lewes (a)	L 0-3
09.04	Crystal Palace (a)	L 0-5
23.04	Swindon Town (a)	W 3-0
30.04	QPR (a)	W 4-1
07.05	Lewes (h)+	L 0-2
14.05	Charlton Athletic (h)*	W 4-3

+Played at Ship Lane, (Thurrock FC)

*Played at Barrows Farm, (Harlow Town FC)

2016/17 WPL CUP RESULTS

04.09	DR	St Nicholas (h)	W 8-0
	R1	Bye	
16.10	R2	Charlton Athletic (a)	L 2-3

2016/17 FA CUP RESULTS

04.12	R1	Acle United (a)	W 2-0
08.01	R2	Keynsham Town (h)	L 1-3

2016/17 WPL SOUTHERN DIVISION

	GD	Pts
1. Tottenham Hotspur	45	52 (P)
2. Coventry United	40	48
3. Cardiff City	53	44
4. Charlton Athletic	30	42
5. Crystal Palace	25	33
6. C&K Basildon	**-13**	**27**
7. Lewes	-5	25
8. Portsmouth	-35	17
9. West Ham United	-47	9
10. Swindon Town	-40	8
11. QPR	-53	8

The team started out as part of Basildon Town men's club before founder and former manager Peter King changed the name to C&K Basildon after his insurance company CKRe.

In 2008 they were promoted out of the Essex County League. Five League titles in seven seasons took them into the WPL Southern for the 2015/16 season.

C&K Basildon won their first trophy in 2008/09 when they produced an upset in the Essex County League Cup final to beat League Champions Hannikins 2-1. C&K Basildon also finished as League runners-up that season.

In the 2010/11 season, Tina Lindsay and Claire Lacey became the first former England players to play for C&K Basildon.

In 2015 Steve Tilson – former manager of men's teams Southend United, Lincoln City and Canvey Island – took over as C&K Basildon Ladies manager.

CAMBRIDGE UNITED

WPL SE DIVISION ONE (TIER 4)

Founded: 2009 (as Cambridge Women)
Nickname: The U's
Ground: Recreation Way, (Mildenhall Town FC)

SEASON 2016/17

WPL South East Division One: 4th
WPL Cup: R2
FA Cup: R3

2016/17 WPL SE DIVISION ONE RESULTS

21.08	Actonians (h)	L 1-2
28.08	Lowestoft Town (h)	W 2-0
11.09	Norwich City (a)	W 3-1
14.09	Stevenage (h)	W 3-2
18.09	Luton Town (h)	W 3-1
02.10	Denham United (a)	W 5-1
05.10	Stevenage (a)	W 3-1
30.10	AFC Wimbledon (a)	W 1-0
06.11	Enfield Town (h)	W 3-2
27.11	Gillingham (a)	L 1-4
11.12	Ipswich Town (a)	W 5-0
26.02	AFC Wimbledon (h)	D 1-1
12.03	Enfield Town (a)	L 1-2
26.03	Actonians (a)	D 1-1
02.04	Ipswich Town (h)*	W 4-1
09.04	Lowestoft Town (a)	W 2-0
16.04	Norwich City (h)	W 5-4
23.04	Denham United (h)	W 7-0
30.04	Luton Town (a)	L 2-4
07.05	Gillingham (h)	L 1-2
09.05	Milton Keynes Dons (a)	L 1-4
14.05	Milton Keynes Dons (h)	L 0-2

*Played at the Cambs Glass Stadium, (Cambridge United FC)

2016/17 WPL CUP RESULTS

04.09	DR	Lewes (h)	D 3-3 (W 4-2 pens)
	R1	Bye	
23.10	R2	Portsmouth (a)	L 2-3

2016/17 FA CUP RESULTS

09.10	RQ3	Wymondham Town (h)	W 3-0
13.11	RQ4	Stevenage (h)	W 3-0
04.12	R1	QPR (h)	W 3-1
08.01	R2	Southampton (h)	W 4-0
05.02	R3	Aston Villa (a)	L 1-7

2016/17 WPL SE DIVISION ONE

	GD	Pts
1. Gillingham	90	57 (P)
2. Milton Keynes Dons	42	49
3. AFC Wimbledon	29	44
4. Cambridge United	**20**	**41**
5. Luton Town	5	37
6. Actonians	14	36
7. Enfield Town	-20	25
8. Denham United	-21	25
9. Ipswich Town	-22	25
10. Norwich City	-50	16
11. Stevenage	-26	15
12. Lowestoft Town	-61	6 (R)

Cambridge Women's FC merged with the Cambridge United men's professional outfit in May 2015 and changed their name to the same.

Cambridge Women had themselves been formed when two clubs – Cambridge City and Cambridge United (who weren't affiliated to the men's club) joined forces in 2009.

In 2016/17 the club played one of their matches at the Abbey Stadium (officially known as the Cambs Glass Stadium for sponsorship reasons), which is the home of Cambridge United men's. The game ended in a 4-1 win over Ipswich.

CARDIFF CITY LADIES

WPL SOUTHERN DIVISION (TIER 3)

Founded: 1975 (as Llanedeyrn)
Nickname: The Bluebirds
Ground: CCB Centre for Sporting Excellence

SEASON 2016/17

WPL Southern Division: 3rd
WPL Cup: SF
FA Cup: R2

2016/17 WPL SOUTHERN DIVISION

28.08	Lewes (a)	D 1-1
11.09	Lewes (h)	W 6-0
25.09	C&K Basildon (h)	W 2-1
02.10	QPR (a)	W 4-1
06.10	Swindon Town (a)	W 4-0
09.10	West Ham United (h)	W 3-0
30.10	Crystal Palace (h)	W 3-2
13.11	West Ham United (a)	W 4-0
18.12	Charlton Athletic (a)	W 4-1
05.02	Portsmouth (h)	W 5-0
12.02	Charlton Athletic (h)	L 0-2
19.02	Swindon Town (h)	W 8-0
12.03	C&K Basildon (a)	L 2-3
26.03	Portsmouth (a)	W 5-1
09.04	Coventry United (a)	D 2-2
16.04	Tottenham Hotspur (a)	L 1-2
23.04	QPR (h)	W 12-1
30.04	Tottenham Hotspur (h)	W 4-0
07.05	Coventry United (h)	L 1-2
14.05	Crystal Palace (a)	W 1-0

2016/17 WPL CUP RESULTS

Date	Round	Opponent	Result
04.09	DR	Ipswich Town (a)	W 5-0
	R1	Bye	
23.10	R2	Larkhall Athletic (h)	W w/o
06.11	R3	Chichester City (h)	W 7-1
11.12	QF	Liverpool Feds (a)	W 2-0
05.03	SF	Tottenham Hotspur (a)	L 0-3

2016/17 FA CUP RESULTS

Date	Round	Opponent	Result
04.12	R1	Larkhall Athletic (h)	W 6-0
08.01	R2	Lewes (a)	L 0-2

2016/17 WPL SOUTHERN DIVISION

	GD	Pts
1. Tottenham Hotspur	45	52 (P)
2. Coventry United	40	48
3. Cardiff City	**53**	**44**
4. Charlton Athletic	30	42
5. Crystal Palace	25	33
6. C&K Basildon	-13	27
7. Lewes	-5	25
8. Portsmouth	-35	17
9. West Ham United	-47	9
10. Swindon Town	-40	8
11. QPR	-53	8

Cardiff City Ladies are not to be confused with Cardiff City Women who play in the Welsh Premier League. Formed as Llanedeyrn in 1975, Cardiff City Ladies are the oldest women's club in Wales.

Cardiff City Ladies were formerly affiliated to the men's professional Cardiff City between 2001 and 2003. It is now Cardiff City Women who are affiliated to Cardiff City men's club.

Cardiff City Ladies were champions of the WPL Southern Division in 2005/06 and were promoted to the WPL National Division for the first time. The WPL National Division was scrapped when WSL2 was introduced ahead of 2014/15.

CHARLTON ATHLETIC

WPL SOUTHERN DIVISION (TIER 3)

Founded: 2000 (from Croydon FC)
Nickname: The Addicks
Ground: Sporting Club Thamesmead, Bayliss Avenue

SEASON 2016/17

WPL Southern Division: 4th
WPL Cup: Runners-up
FA Cup: R3

2016/17 WPL SOUTHERN DIVISION

21.08	Swindon Town (h)	W 4-0
28.08	C&K Basildon (h)	W 6-0
14.09	Crystal Palace (a)	D 3-3
18.09	Swindon Town (a)	W 3-0
25.09	Coventry United (h)	L 1-5
02.10	West Ham United (a)	W 2-0
06.10	Crystal Palace (h)	D 2-2
09.10	Lewes (h)	W 2-1
13.11	QPR (h)	W 2-0
27.11	Portsmouth (h)	W 4-2
18.12	Cardiff City (h)	L 1-4
29.01	West Ham United (h)	W 5-0
12.02	Cardiff City (a)	W 2-0
26.02	QPR (a)	W 6-0
12.03	Tottenham Hotspur (h)	L 0-1
26.03	Coventry United (a)	D 1-1
02.04	Portsmouth (a)	W 3-0
09.04	Lewes (a)	W 2-0
23.04	Tottenham Hotspur (a)	W 3-2
14.05	C&K Basildon (a)	L 3-4

2016/17 WPL CUP RESULTS

04.09	DR	Shanklin (h)	W 8-1
	R1	Bye	
16.10	R2	C&K Basildon (h)	W 3-2
06.11	R3	Portsmouth (h)	W 4-2
11.12	QF	West Bromwich Albion (h)	D 1-1 (W 4-2 p)
05.03	SF	Blackburn Rovers (h)	W 4-3 (aet)
07.05	F	Tottenham Hotspur (n)*	D 0-0 (L 3-4p)

*played at Lamex Stadium, Stevenage FC

2016/17 FA CUP RESULTS

04.12	R1	Crystal Palace (a)	W 2-1
08.01	R2	Portsmouth (h)	W 5-0
05.02	R3	Sheffield FC (h)	L 0-2

2016/17 WPL SOUTHERN DIVISION

	GD	Pts
1. Tottenham Hotspur	45	52 (P)
2. Coventry United	40	48
3. Cardiff City	53	44
4. Charlton Athletic	**30**	**42**
5. Crystal Palace	25	33
6. C&K Basildon	-13	27
7. Lewes	-5	25
8. Portsmouth	-35	17
9. West Ham United	-47	9
10. Swindon Town	-40	8
11. QPR	-53	8

Charlton Athletic was controversially born when the club took over two-time FA Women's Cup winners Croydon in 2000.

The Addicks were one of the most successful women's teams of the noughties. They won the FA Cup in 2005 and were runners-up on three other occasions. They also finished as runners-up to Arsenal in the top-flight in both 2003/04 and 2004/05.

When Charlton Athletic men's team was relegated from the Premier League in 2007, the women's team was disbanded for financial reasons. A sponsorship announced in August ensured the team was able to continue, but in the interim many of the players had joined other clubs.

The club's all-time leading goalscorer is Kit Graham who notched 151 goals in 172 games in all competitions by the end of 2016/17 season. She hit 37 goals in 32 games during the 2016/17 campaign.

Charlton reached the WPL Cup final in 2016/17 but were beaten on penalties by Tottenham after a goalless draw.

CHELTENHAM TOWN

WPL SW DIVISION ONE (TIER 4)

Founded: Circa 1997
Nickname: Robins
Ground: Petersfield Park, (Cheltenham Saracens FC)

SEASON 2016/17

WPL South West Division One: 10th
WPL Cup: DR **WPL Plate: R2**
FA Cup: RQ3

2016/17 WPL SW DIVISION ONE RESULTS

21.08	Chichester City (a)	L 0-4
28.08	Keynsham Town (h)	L 0-3
11.09	Basingstoke Town (a)	L 0-1
18.09	Plymouth Argyle (h)	L 2-5
25.09	Larkhall Athletic (h)	L 1-3
02.10	Maidenhead United (a)	L 1-2
30.10	St Nicholas (h)	W 2-1
13.11	Maidenhead United (h)	W 3-2
04.12	St Nicholas (a)	L 2-5
08.01	Basingstoke Town (h)	W 2-1
22.01	*Shanklin (h)*	*W 4-1 (ex)*
05.02	Brislington (h)	L 1-3
12.02	Southampton Saints (a)	L 2-3
16.02	Exeter City (h)	W 4-1
05.03	Keynsham Town (a)	L 0-7
19.03	*Shanklin (a)*	*W 4-0 (ex)*
30.03	Brislington (a)	L 1-4
09.04	Exeter City (a)	D 2-2
23.04	Chichester City (h)	L 0-4
02.05	Larkhall Athletic (a)	L 2-3
07.05	Southampton Saints (h)	L 0-3
09.05	Plymouth Argyle (a)	L 0-17

(ex) Shanklin withdrew from League: results expunged

2016/17 WPL CUP RESULTS

Date	Round	Opponent	Result
04.09	DR	Basingstoke Town (a)	L 1-3

2016/17 WPL PLATE RESULTS

Date	Round	Opponent	Result
23.10	R2	West Ham United (h)	L 1-2

2016/17 FA CUP RESULTS

Date	Round	Opponent	Result
09.10	RQ3	Larkhall Athletic (a)	L 1-9

2016/17 WPL SW DIVISION ONE

	GD	Pts
1. Chichester City	92	58 (P)
2. Plymouth Argyle	85	54
3. Southampton Saints	20	41
4. Keynsham Town	39	38
5. Larkhall Athletic	3	36
6. Brislington	-19	22
7. Maidenhead United	-28	16*
8. St Nicholas	-43	15
9. Basingstoke Town	-28	14
10. Cheltenham Town	**-49**	**13**
11. Exeter City	-72	4 (R)

*Maidenhead docked 1 point

NB: Shanklin withdrew from League, all results expunged

Cheltenham Ladies groundshare with men's non-League team Cheltenham Saracens who play in the Hellenic League.

Top scorer for 2016/17 was striker Ella Hitchcox who was signed from Forest Green. She hit 8 goals in 22 appearances in all competitions.

CHESTER-LE-STREET TOWN

WPL NORTHERN DIVISION ONE (TIER 4)

Founded: 2009
Nickname: Town
Ground: Moor Park, (Chester-le-Street Town FC)

SEASON 2016/17

WPL Northern Division One: 4th
WPL Cup: QF
FA Cup: RQ3

2016/17 WPL NORTHERN DIVISION ONE

21.08	Blackpool Wren Rovers (h)	W 4-1
28.08	Chorley (h)	L 1-2
11.09	Crewe Alexandra (a)	W 2-0
25.09	Blackpool Wren Rovers (a)	L 2-4
02.10	Brighouse Town (a)	D 2-2
16.10	Chorley (a)	L 1-3
30.10	Hull City (h)	W 4-2
13.11	Mossley Hill Athletic (h)	W 4-2
27.11	Crewe Alexandra (h)	D 2-2
04.12	Morecambe (a)	L 1-5
22.01	Tranmere Rovers (h)	W 5-0
29.01	Brighouse Town (h)	W 2-0
05.02	Leeds United (h)	W 3-0
26.02	Tranmere Rovers (a)	W 2-0
12.03	Leeds United (a)	W 5-3
19.03	Mossley Hill Athletic (a)	W 2-1
26.03	Liverpool Feds (h)	L 1-4
02.04	Hull City (a)	W 5-3
09.04	Guiseley Vixens (a)	L 0-1
16.04	Guiseley Vixens (h)	L 1-3
07.05	Liverpool Feds (a)	W 3-2
14.05	Morecambe (h)	W 6-2

2016/17 WPL CUP RESULTS

04.09	DR	Sporting Khalsa (a)	W 4-2
	R1	Bye	
23.10	R2	Blackpool Wren Rovers (h)	W 3-0
06.11	R3	Derby County (h)	W 2-1
11.12	QF	Blackburn Rovers (h)	L 1-3

2016/17 FA CUP RESULTS

09.10	RQ3	Sheffield United (h)	L 0-1

2016/17 WPL NORTHERN DIVISION ONE

	GD	Pts
1. Guiseley Vixens	52	59 (P)
2. Liverpool Feds	37	44
3. Hull City	16	43
4. Chester-le-Street Town	**16**	**41**
5. Chorley	7	38
6. Brighouse Town	16	37
7. Morecambe	1	29*
8. Leeds United	-8	23
9. Mossley Hill Athletic	-27	19
10. Crewe Alexandra	-28	18
11. Blackpool Wren Rovers	-31	18 (R)
12. Tranmere Rovers	-51	7 (R)

*Morecambe docked 3 points (unregistered player)

Three successive promotions carried Chester-le-Street Town into the FA WPL Northern Division One ahead of the 2013/14 season. They have played at that level ever since.

Laura Hockaday was the club's top scorer for 2016/17 with 16 goals in 23 appearances in all competitions.

The team plays its home games at the same ground as Chester-le-Street Town men's – Moor Park.

CHICHESTER CITY

WPL SOUTHERN DIVISION (TIER 3)

Founded: 1991
Nickname: Lilywhites / Green Army
Ground: Oaklands Park, (Chichester City FC)

SEASON 2016/17

WPL South West Division One: 1st (P)
WPL Cup: R3
FA Cup: RQ4

2016/17 WPL SW DIVISION ONE RESULTS

21.08	Cheltenham Town (h)	W 4-0
28.08	Maidenhead United (a)	W 4-1
11.09	Larkhall Athletic (a)	W 2-0
15.09	Southampton Saints (a)	D 1-1
18.09	Brislington (h)	W 7-1
02.10	St Nicholas (a)	W 9-0
23.10	Plymouth Argyle (a)	W 5-4
27.11	Brislington (a)	W 4-0
18.12	Keynsham Town (h)	W 5-0
08.01	*Shanklin (h)*	*W 14-0 (ex)*
29.01	Shanklin (a)	*W 6-0 (ex)*
09.02	Southampton Saints (h)	W 8-0
12.02	Maidenhead United (h)	W 3-0
26.02	Basingstoke Town (a)	W 5-0
12.03	Larkhall Athletic (h)	W 2-1
19.03	Exeter City (h)	W 5-0
09.04	Plymouth Argyle (h)	W 3-0
20.04	Basingstoke Town (h)	W 4-0
23.04	Cheltenham Town (a)	W 4-0
30.04	Exeter City (a)	W 13-0
04.05	St Nicholas (h)	W 10-0
14.05	Keynsham Town (a)	W 2-0

(ex) Results expunged: Shanklin withdrew from League

2016/17 WPL CUP RESULTS

04.09	DR	Actonians (h)	W 6-2
	R1	Bye	
30.10	R2	Basingstoke Town (a)	W 5-0
06.11	R3	Cardiff City (a)	L 1-7

2016/17 FA CUP RESULTS

09.10	RQ3	Haringey Borough (a)	W 8-2
20.11	RQ4	Keynsham Town (h)	L 1-2

2016/17 WPL SW DIVISION ONE

	GD	Pts
1. Chichester City	**92**	**58 (P)**
2. Plymouth Argyle	85	54
3. Southampton Saints	20	41
4. Keynsham Town	39	38
5. Larkhall Athletic	3	36
6. Brislington	-19	22
7. Maidenhead United	-28	16*
8. St Nicholas	-43	15
9. Basingstoke Town	-28	14
10. Cheltenham Town	-49	13
11. Exeter City	-72	4 (R)

*Maidenhead docked 1 point

NB: Shanklin withdrew from League, all results expunged

Chichester City won the 2016/17 WPL South West Division One title with a game to spare thanks to a 10-0 victory against St Nicholas in front of their own fans at Oaklands Park. The result meant they had racked up 23 goals in two games, having won 13-0 away at Exeter the previous Sunday.

In their final 13 League matches of 2016/17, Chichester scored 68 goals and conceded just one. That record would have been even better but for the fact that 14-0 and 6-0 victories against Shanklin were expunged from the records when the Isle of Wight-based club withdrew from the League.

CHORLEY

WPL NORTHERN DIVISION ONE (TIER 4)

Founded: 1983
Nickname: None
Ground: Jim Fowler Memorial Ground, (Euxton Villa FC)

SEASON 2016/17

WPL Northern Division One: 5th
WPL Cup: DR **WPL Plate: R3**
FA Cup: RQ3

2016/17 WPL NORTHERN DIVISION ONE

21.08	Crewe Alexandra (a)	W 4-0
28.08	Chester-le-Street Town (a)	W 2-1
11.09	Tranmere Rovers (h)	W 5-1
13.09	Blackpool Wren Rovers (h)*	W 3-1
02.10	Guiseley Vixens (h)	L 1-4
06.10	Blackpool Wren Rovers (a)	W 3-2
16.10	Chester-le-Street Town (h)	W 3-1
30.10	Morecambe (h)	W 2-1
13.11	Tranmere Rovers (a)	D 1-1
04.12	Leeds United (a)	W 1-0
11.12	Mossley Hill Athletic (a)	W 6-4
18.12	Liverpool Feds (a)	L 0-1
08.01	Crewe Alexandra (h)	W 4-1
22.01	Morecambe (a)	D 1-1
12.02	Mossley Hill Athletic (h)	L 1-2
19.02	Hull City (a)	L 2-4
26.02	Brighouse Town (a)	L 2-3
12.03	Liverpool Feds (h)	L 1-6
19.03	Guiseley Vixens (a)	L 0-2
26.03	Hull City (h)	W 2-1
23.04	Brighouse Town (h)	L 2-6
30.04	Leeds United (h)	W 5-1

*Played at UCLan Sports Arena

2016/17 WPL CUP RESULTS

04.09	DR	Nottingham Forest (a)	L 1-3 (aet)

2016/17 WPL PLATE RESULTS

23.10	R2	Morecambe (a)	W 5-0
06.11	R3	Leicester Women (h)	L 3-5

2016/17 FA CUP RESULTS

09.10	RQ3	Blackpool W. R. (a)	D 2-2 (L 2-4p)

2016/17 WPL NORTHERN DIVISION ONE

	GD	Pts
1. Guiseley Vixens	52	59 (P)
2. Liverpool Feds	37	44
3. Hull City	16	43
4. Chester-le-Street Town	16	41
5. Chorley	**7**	**38**
6. Brighouse Town	16	37
7. Morecambe	1	29*
8. Leeds United	-8	23
9. Mossley Hill Athletic	-27	19
10. Crewe Alexandra	-28	18
11. Blackpool Wren Rovers	-31	18 (R)
12. Tranmere Rovers	-51	7 (R)

*Morecambe docked 3 points (unregistered player)

Chorley Ladies teamed up with non-League men's club Euxton Villa in May 2015. The partnership enables young boys and girls to train at the same site, and for Chorley Ladies to play at the Jim Fowler Memorial Ground.

In 2016/17 Dani Toward, who joined the club as a 14-year-old, made her 550th appearance for the first team.

Chorley Ladies, founded in 1983, are the only women's club in the North West of England, (apart from relative newcomers Manchester City), to have kept their original name since formation.

COVENTRY UNITED

WPL SOUTHERN DIVISION (TIER 3)

Founded: 1991
Nicknames: The Red & Greens / United / Cov
Ground: Pack Meadow, (Coleshill Town FC) moving to Butts Park Arena for 2017/18

SEASON 2016/17

WPL Southern Division: 2nd
WPL Cup: R3
FA Cup: R4

2016/17 WPL SOUTHERN DIVISION

21.08	Crystal Palace (a)	D 2-2
11.09	West Ham United (h)	W 1-0
18.09	Portsmouth (h)	W 8-1
25.09	Charlton Athletic (a)	W 5-1
02.10	Swindon Town (h)	W 2-1
09.10	QPR (h)	W 5-0
30.10	West Ham United (a)	W 5-0
13.11	Tottenham Hotspur (h)	L 0-1
11.12	C&K Basildon (a)	W 3-0
18.12	C&K Basildon (h)	W 6-0
12.02	QPR (a)	W 2-0
26.02	Lewes (h)	W 3-1
26.03	Charlton Athletic (h)	D 1-1
02.04	Tottenham Hotspur (a)	L 0-2
09.04	Cardiff City (h)	D 2-2
23.04	Crystal Palace (h)+	W 1-0
26.04	Swindon Town (a)	W 3-1
30.04	Lewes (a)	W 1-0
07.05	Cardiff City (a)	W 2-1
14.05	Portsmouth (a)	W 3-1

+played at Knights Lane, Stratford Town FC

2016/17 WPL CUP RESULTS

04.09	DR	Maidenhead United (h)	W 9-0
	R1	Bye	
23.10	R2	Denham United (h)	W 3-0
06.11	R3	Crystal Palace (a)	L 0-1

2016/17 FA CUP RESULTS

04.12	R1	West Ham United (a)	W 3-0
08.01	R2	Milton Keynes D. (h)	W 4-0
05.02	R3	Oxford United (h)	W 2-0
19.02	R4	Aston Villa (h)	L 0-1

2016/17 WPL SOUTHERN DIVISION

	GD	Pts
1. Tottenham Hotspur	45	52 (P)
2. Coventry United	**40**	**48**
3. Cardiff City	53	44
4. Charlton Athletic	30	42
5. Crystal Palace	25	33
6. C&K Basildon	-13	27
7. Lewes	-5	25
8. Portsmouth	-35	17
9. West Ham United	-47	9
10. Swindon Town	-40	8
11. QPR	-53	8

A previous incarnation of the club was founded in 1921, but in 1991 they reformed and affiliated with Coventry City, who were then in the top-flight of the men's game.

In July 2015, they broke away from Coventry City and affiliated with men's non-League team Coventry United, changing their name to the same.

They recently achieved back-to-back promotions, winning the Midland Combination League in 2010 and the WPL Northern Division in 2011.

That latter promotion took them into the FA National Premier League for the first time, before the restructuring of the women's game saw them placed into the WPL Southern Division. In 2013/14 they were WPL Southern Division champions.

Coventry United men's and women's teams moved into Butts Park Arena – also home of Coventry Rugby Union Football Club and Coventry Bears Rugby League Club – ahead of the 2017/18 season.

CREWE ALEXANDRA

WPL NORTHERN DIVISION ONE (TIER 4)

Founded: 2000 (as Crewe Vagrants)
Nickname: The Alex
Ground: Cumberland Arena

SEASON 2016/17

WPL Northern Division One: 10th
WPL Cup: DR WPL Plate: R2
FA Cup: RQ4

2016/17 WPL NORTHERN DIVISION ONE

21.08	Chorley (h)	L 0-4
28.08	Morecambe (a)	L 1-5
11.09	Chester-le-Street Town (h)	L 0-2
14.09	Tranmere Rovers (a)	L 1-4
18.09	Liverpool Feds (h)	D 3-3
02.10	Mossley Hill Athletic (a)	W 5-4
05.10	Tranmere Rovers (h)	D 1-1
23.10	Leeds United a)	L 1-2
30.10	Liverpool Feds (a)	L 0-5
06.11	Blackpool Wren Rovers (h)	D 3-3
27.11	Chester-le-Street Town (a)	D 2-2
04.12	Blackpool Wren Rovers (a)	L 0-2
11.12	Leeds United (h)	W 3-2
18.12	Mossley Hill Athletic (h)	D 1-1
08.01	Chorley (a)	L 1-4
12.02	Morecambe (h)	W 3-0
26.02	Hull City (h)	L 0-1
05.03	Hull City (a)	L 0-3
12.03	Brighouse Town (h)	L 0-4
26.03	Guiseley Vixens (h)	W 4-2
30.04	Brighouse Town (a)	D 2-2
14.05	Guiseley Vixens (a)	L 0-3

2016/17 WPL CUP RESULTS

04.09	DR	Blackpool Wren Rovers (a)	L 0-5

2016/17 WPL PLATE RESULTS

16.10	R2	Bradford (h)	L 0-6

2016/17 FA CUP RESULTS

09.10	RQ3	Morecambe (h)	D 3-3 (W 4-2p)
13.11	RQ4	RACA Tynedale (a)	L 1-2

2016/17 WPL NORTHERN DIVISION ONE

	GD	Pts
1. Guiseley Vixens	52	59 (P)
2. Liverpool Feds	37	44
3. Hull City	16	43
4. Chester-le-Street Town	16	41
5. Chorley	7	38
6. Brighouse Town	16	37
7. Morecambe	1	29*
8. Leeds United	-8	23
9. Mossley Hill Athletic	-27	19
10. Crewe Alexandra	**-28**	**18**
11. Blackpool Wren Rovers	-31	18 (R)
12. Tranmere Rovers	-51	7 (R)

*Morecambe docked 3 points (unregistered player)

The original Crewe Ladies club joined the North West Regional League in 1985 but folded before the end of the 1992/93 season.

A new club was formed, called Crewe Alexandra, which was elected into the North West Regional League in 1999/00. They also folded in August 2001.

A rival club named Crewe Vagrants, which had been set up in 2000/01, won the West Midlands Regional League Premier Division in 2002/03. In 2005/06 they became the Crewe Alexandra which exists today and also won the Midlands Combination title that season.

The Alex's greatest ever player is striker Kerry Davis who scored 44 goals in 82 games for England. She was her country's top scorer until Kelly Smith broke her record in 2012.

CRYSTAL PALACE

WPL SOUTHERN DIVISION (TIER 3)

Founded: 1992
Nickname: The Eagles
Ground: Hayes Lane, (Bromley FC)

SEASON 2016/17

WPL Southern Division: 5th
WPL Cup: QF
FA Cup: R1

2016/17 WPL SOUTHERN DIVISION

21.08	Coventry United (h)	D 2-2
28.08	QPR (a)	W 1-0
11.09	Tottenham Hotspur (h)	L 0-1
14.09	Charlton Athletic (h)	D 3-3
18.09	West Ham United (a)	W 4-0
06.10	Charlton Athletic (a)	D 2-2
09.10	Swindon Town (a)	W 1-0
30.10	Cardiff City (a)	L 2-3
13.11	Lewes (a)	D 2-2
18.12	Swindon Town (h)	W 3-0
08.01	West Ham United (h)	W 6-1
29.01	QPR (h)	W 1-0
19.03	C&K Basildon (a)	D 2-2
26.03	Tottenham Hotspur (a)	L 1-2
02.04	Lewes (h)	D 1-1
09.04	C&K Basildon (h)*	W 5-0
16.04	Portsmouth (a)	W 5-2
23.04	Coventry United (a)	L 0-1
30.04	Portsmouth (h)*	W 7-0
14.05	Cardiff City (h)*	L 0-1

*played at Eden Park Avenue, (Beckenham Town FC)

2016/17 WPL CUP RESULTS

04.09	DR	Keynsham Town (a)	W 2-1
	R1	Bye	
23.10	R2	AFC Wimbledon (a)	W 2-0
06.11	R3	Coventry United (h)	W 1-0
11.12	QF	Tottenham Hotspur (a)	L 1-4

2016/17 FA CUP RESULTS

04.12	R1	Charlton Athletic (h)	L 1-2

2016/17 WPL SOUTHERN DIVISION

	GD	Pts
1. Tottenham Hotspur	45	52 (P)
2. Coventry United	40	48
3. Cardiff City	53	44
4. Charlton Athletic	30	42
5. Crystal Palace	**25**	**33**
6. C&K Basildon	-13	27
7. Lewes	-5	25
8. Portsmouth	-35	17
9. West Ham United	-47	9
10. Swindon Town	-40	8
11. QPR	-53	8

Crystal Palace have a partnership with men's club Bromley and play their home matches at the National League side's Hayes Lane stadium.

With work required on Bromley's pitch, Palace's final three home games of 2016/17 against C&K Basildon, Portsmouth and Cardiff were played at the home ground of nearby men's club Beckenham Town FC.

As well as their partnership with Bromley, Palace have a relationship with men's Premier League club Crystal Palace which includes the sharing of resources and commercial contacts.

DENHAM UNITED

WPL SE DIVISION ONE (TIER 4)

Founded: 1987
Nickname: None
Ground: The Den

SEASON 2016/17

WPL South East Division One: 8th
WPL Cup: R2
FA Cup: RQ4

2016/17 WPL SE DIVISION ONE RESULTS

21.08	Milton Keynes Dons (h)*	L 0-3
28.08	Stevenage (h)*	W 5-0
11.09	Enfield Town (h)	W 3-1
18.09	Actonians (a)	L 0-1
22.09	AFC Wimbledon (a)	L 0-2
02.10	Cambridge United (h)	L 1-5
05.10	AFC Wimbledon (h)*	W 4-1
30.10	Luton Town (h)	W 1-0
06.11	Milton Keynes Dons (a)	L 0-7
27.11	Ipswich Town (h)	L 1-2
04.12	Actonians (h)	W 4-2
11.12	Gillingham (h)	L 0-9
08.01	Luton Town (a)	L 2-3
29.01	Lowestoft Town (a)	W 5-2
12.02	Enfield Town (a)	L 0-2
26.02	Gillingham (a)	L 0-2
19.03	Lowestoft Town (h)	W 5-0
26.03	Stevenage (a)	L 1-4
02.04	Norwich City (a)	W 2-0
23.04	Cambridge United (a)	L 0-7
07.05	Norwich City (h)	L 2-4
14.05	Ipswich Town (a)	D 2-2

2016/17 WPL CUP RESULTS

04.09	DR	Swindon Town (h)*	W 2-1 (aet)
25.09	R1	Brislington (h)	W 3-2
23.10	R2	Coventry United (a)	L 0-3

2016/17 FA CUP RESULTS

09.10	RQ3	Ipswich Town (h)	W 4-1
13.11	RQ4	AFC Wimbledon (a)	L 2-4

*Played at Middlesex Stadium, (Hillingdon Borough FC)

2016/17 WPL SOUTH EAST DIVISION ONE

	GD	Pts
1. Gillingham	90	57 (P)
2. Milton Keynes Dons	42	49
3. AFC Wimbledon	29	44
4. Cambridge United	20	41
5. Luton Town	5	37
6. Actonians	14	36
7. Enfield Town	-20	25
8. Denham United	**-21**	**25**
9. Ipswich Town	-22	25
10. Norwich City	-50	16
11. Stevenage	-26	15
12. Lowestoft Town	-61	6 (R)

Based in Uxbridge, in North West London, Denham United are recognised as the largest all-female football club in the South East of England.

Alissa Down finished as the club's top goalscorer in 2016/17 with 8 goals in 28 appearances in all competitions.

Denham's Under-15s team had a successful 2016/17 season, winning the League Cup final courtesy of a 2-0 victory over Carshalton.

DERBY COUNTY

WPL NORTHERN DIVISION (TIER 3)

Founded: 1989
Nickname: Ewe Rams
Ground: Don Amott LG Arena, (Mickleover Sports FC)

SEASON 2016/17

WPL Northern Division: 5th
WPL Cup: R3
FA Cup: R3

2016/17 WPL NORTHERN DIVISION

21.08	Bradford City (a)	W 2-0
28.08	Nottingham Forest (a)	W 2-0
11.09	Huddersfield Town (h)	W 3-1
25.09	West Bromwich Albion (h)	L 0-2
02.10	Bradford City (h)	W 3-1
09.10	Huddersfield Town (a)	L 1-4
23.10	Middlesbrough (a)	L 2-3
27.11	Middlesbrough (h)	L 2-3
11.12	Fylde (a)	D 0-0
12.02	Stoke City (a)	L 1-2
26.02	Leicester City Women (a)	L 1-2
05.03	Newcastle United (h)	W 2-0
12.03	Stoke City (h)	W 4-3
19.03	Fylde (h)	W 5-0
26.03	Blackburn Rovers (a)	L 2-3
09.04	Blackburn Rovers (h)	L 0-4
23.04	Newcastle United (a)	W 4-1
30.04	Leicester City Women (h)*	L 1-3
09.05	West Bromwich Albion (a)	D 2-2
14.05	Nottingham Forest (h)	W 2-1

*played at Steve Bloomer ATP

2016/17 WPL CUP RESULTS

04.09	DR	Steel City Wanderers (h)	W 7-0
	R1	Bye	
16.10	R2	Stoke City (a)	W 2-1 (aet)
06.11	R3	Chester-le-Street Town (a)	L 1-2

2016/17 FA CUP RESULTS

04.12	R1	Huddersfield Town (a)	W 1-0
08.01	R2	Sheffield United (h)	W 3-2 (aet)
05.02	R3	Nottingham Forest (h)	L 0-1

2016/17 WPL NORTHERN DIVISION

	GD	Pts
1. Blackburn Rovers	39	54
2. Middlesbrough	29	43
3. Leicester City Women	7	34
4. Stoke City	6	30
5. Derby County	**4**	**29**
6. West Bromwich Albion	-4	27
7. Fylde	6	26*
8. Bradford City	0	22
9. Huddersfield Town	-16	20
10. Nottingham Forest	-22	18
11. Newcastle United	-49	7 (R)

*Fylde docked 3 points (ineligible player)

Derby County's breakthrough season came in 2008/09 when they won the Midland Combination League for the first time in their history.

The Ewe Rams sealed the title that season, and with it promotion to the WPL, in the final game of the season when they beat Crewe 4-2 in a match that was played at Pride Park.

In 2013/14 a home friendly against an Arsenal team containing England internationals Rachel Yankey, Kelly Smith and Casey Stoney was watched by a then club record crowd of 600. The Gunners won 5-0. That record has twice been beaten, first when 700 attended a prestige friendly against WSL champions Liverpool in 2015 and then when more than 800 came to watch the FA Cup tie against Nottingham Forest in February 2017.

The club was named Premier League Club of the Year at the annual FA Awards at Wembley in 2015 and was runner-up in the same award category in both 2014 and 2016.

ENFIELD TOWN

WPL SE DIVISION ONE (TIER 4)

Founded: 1985 (as Merryhill Midgets)
Nickname: None
Ground: Queen Elizabeth II Stadium, (Enfield Town FC)

SEASON 2016/17

WPL South East Division One: 7th
WPL Cup: R2
FA Cup: RQ3

2016/17 WPL SE DIVISION ONE RESULTS

21.08	Stevenage (a)	W 2-1
28.08	Ipswich Town (a)	D 1-1
11.09	Denham United (a)	L 1-3
18.09	Lowestoft Town (a)	L 0-3
28.09	Actonians (h)	D 2-2
02.10	Luton Town (h)	L 0-5
05.10	Actonians (a)	L 1-3
30.10	Norwich City (h)	W 2-1
06.11	Cambridge United (a)	L 2-3
13.11	Ipswich Town (h)	W 4-1
27.11	AFC Wimbledon (h)	L 2-3
04.12	Stevenage (h)	D 0-0
18.12	Norwich City (a)	D 2-2
29.01	Luton Town (a)	W 2-1
12.02	Denham United (h)	W 2-0
26.02	Milton Keynes Dons (a)	L 0-1
05.03	Gillingham (a)	L 0-6
12.03	Cambridge United (h)	W 2-1
19.03	Gillingham (h)	L 0-7
09.04	AFC Wimbledon (a)	L 0-4
07.05	Milton Keynes Dons (h)	L 1-2
14.05	Lowestoft Town (h)	W 5-1

2016/17 WPL CUP RESULTS

04.09	DR	Exeter City (h)	W 3-1 (aet)
	R1	Bye	
23.10	R2	Tottenham Hotspur (a)	L 1-5

2016/17 FA CUP RESULTS

09.10	RQ3	Lowestoft Town (a)	L 0-2

2016/17 WPL SE DIVISION ONE

	GD	Pts
1. Gillingham	90	57 (P)
2. Milton Keynes Dons	42	49
3. AFC Wimbledon	29	44
4. Cambridge United	20	41
5. Luton Town	5	37
6. Actonians	14	36
7. Enfield Town	**-20**	**25**
8. Denham United	-21	25
9. Ipswich Town	-22	25
10. Norwich City	-50	16
11. Stevenage	-26	15
12. Lowestoft Town	-61	6 (R)

The club was formed in 1985 under the name Merryhill Midgets. They then formed an association with Enfield men's club and changed their name to the same. In 2001, when Enfield men's club split into Enfield and the supporter-led Enfield Town, the ladies aligned with the latter.

In 2015/16 they reached their first ever national Cup final when they made it to the WPL Plate final under manager Kyri Neocleous. They took on Coventry United at Keys Park in Hednesford but were beaten 5-1.

Enfield Town have twice won the Middlesex FA Community Club of the Year award, most recently in 2016/17.

EXETER CITY

SW REGIONAL LEAGUE PREMIER (TIER 5)

Founded: 2006
Nickname: The Grecians
Ground: Minster Park (St Martins FC)

SEASON 2016/17

WPL South West Division One: 11th (R)
WPL Cup: DR **WPL Plate: R2**
FA Cup: RQ4

2016/17 WPL SW DIVISION ONE RESULTS

18.09	Southampton Saints (h)	L 0-1
22.09	Plymouth Argyle (a)	L 1-4
25.09	Keynsham (a)	L 0-13
02.10	Larkhall Athletic (a)	L 1-2
05.10	Plymouth Argyle (h)*	L 0-6
11.12	St Nicholas (a)	D 2-2
05.02	Southampton Saints (a)	L 0-2
12.02	Brislington (a)	L 0-6
16.02	Cheltenham Town (a)	L 1-4
26.02	St Nicholas (h)	L 2-5
12.03	*Shanklin (a)*	*L 2-3 (ex)*
19.03	Chichester City (h)	L 0-5
26.03	Brislington (h)	D 2-2
02.04	Keynsham Town (h)	L 0-5
09.04	Cheltenham Town (h)	D 2-2
23.04	Basingstoke Town (h)	D 3-3
30.04	Chichester City (h)	L 0-13
11.05	Basingstoke Town (a)	L 0-5
14.05	Maidenhead United (h)	L 0-1
18.05	Larkhall Athletic (h)	L 2-7
21.05	Maidenhead United (a)	P-P

(ex) Shanklin withdrew from League: result expunged

*Played at Speeds Meadow, (Cullompton FC)

2016/17 WPL CUP RESULTS

04.09	DR	Enfield Town (a)	L 1-3 (aet)

2016/17 WPL PLATE RESULTS

23.10	R2	Stevenage (h)	L 0-4

2016/17 FA CUP RESULTS

09.10	RQ3	New Milton Town (a)	W 2-1 (aet)
13.11	RQ4	Southampton Saints (a)	L 0-10

2016/17 WPL SW DIVISION ONE

	GD	Pts
1. Chichester City	92	58 (P)
2. Plymouth Argyle	85	54
3. Southampton Saints	20	41
4. Keynsham Town	39	38
5. Larkhall Athletic	3	36
6. Brislington	-19	22
7. Maidenhead United	-28	16*
8. St Nicholas	-43	15
9. Basingstoke Town	-28	14
10. Cheltenham Town	-49	13
11. Exeter City	**-72**	**4 (R)**

*Maidenhead docked 1 point

NB: Shanklin withdrew from League, all results expunged

The original Exeter City Ladies was founded in 1997 as Elmore Eagles. In 2001 they came under the umbrella of men's team Exeter City and changed their name to the same. In 2006 Exeter City Ladies were taken over by Newton Abbot Ladies to form a new club called Cullompton Rangers Ladies. So Exeter City men's club set up a new Exeter City Ladies which is the one that exists today.

Exeter were promoted to the WPL South West Division One for the 2016/17 season but found it tough to acclimatise to that level and experienced immediate relegation. They put up a number of spirited displays but were unable to win any of their League matches.

FLEETWOOD TOWN WRENS

WPL NW REGIONAL PREMIER (TIER 5)

Founded: 1989 (as Blackpool)
Nickname: Wrens
Ground: Brews Park, (Blackpool Wren Rovers FC) in 2016/17. Poolfoot Farm for 2017/18

SEASON 2016/17

WPL Northern Division One: 11th (R)
WPL Cup: R2
FA Cup: RQ4

2016/17 WPL NORTHERN DIVISION ONE

21.08	Chester-le-Street Town (a)	L 1-4
28.08	Tranmere Rovers (h)	D 0-0
11.09	Liverpool Feds (a)	W 3-2
13.09	Chorley (a)	L 1-3
25.09	Chester-le-Street Town (h)	W 4-2
02.10	Hull City (h)	L 2-3
06.10	Chorley (h)	L 2-3
30.10	Tranmere Rovers (a)	W 4-0
06.11	Crewe Alexandra (a)	D 3-3
04.12	Crewe Alexandra (h)	W 2-0
11.12	Morecambe (h)	W 3-2
15.01	Leeds United (h)	L 1-5
29.01	Hull City (a)	L 0-7
12.02	Leeds United (a)	L 1-5
19.02	Liverpool Feds (h)	D 2-2
26.02	Morecambe (a)	L 0-3
05.03	Guiseley Vixens (a)	L 0-4
12.03	Mossley Hill Athletic (a)	L 3-5
26.03	Brighouse Town (a)	L 0-4
23.04	Guiseley Vixens (h)	L 2-3
30.04	Mossley Hill Athletic (h)	L 2-4
14.05	Brighouse Town (h)	L 1-4

2016/17 WPL CUP RESULTS

04.09	DR	Crewe Alexandra (h)	W 5-0
	R1	Bye	
23.10	R2	Chester-le-Street Town (a)	L 0-3

2016/17 FA CUP RESULTS

09.10	RQ3	Chorley (h)	D 2-2 (W 4-2 pens)
13.11	RQ4	Brighouse Town (a)	L 0-5

2016/17 WPL NORTHERN DIVISION ONE

	GD	Pts
1. Guiseley Vixens	52	59 (P)
2. Liverpool Feds	37	44
3. Hull City	16	43
4. Chester-le-Street Town	16	41
5. Chorley	7	38
6. Brighouse Town	16	37
7. Morecambe	1	29*
8. Leeds United	-8	23
9. Mossley Hill Athletic	-27	19
10. Crewe Alexandra	-28	18
11. Blackpool Wren Rovers	**-31**	**18 (R)**
12. Tranmere Rovers	-51	7 (R)

*Morecambe docked 3 points (fielding unregistered player)

In the summer of 2017, Blackpool Wren Rovers were formally adopted by men's professional outfit Fleetwood Town and changed their name to Fleetwood Town Wrens.

They started life as Blackpool Ladies in 1989, before becoming part of the men's non-League club Blackpool Wren Rovers in 1996, changing their name to the same.

In 2012/13 they enjoyed their most successful season, winning the Treble of North West Women's Regional Football League, North West Women's Regional Football League Cup & Lancashire Cup.

The Lancashire Cup final triumph in 2013 was particularly notable as the club caused a huge shock against WPL Northern side Blackburn Rovers. It was only the second time in 10 years that Blackburn had failed to win the trophy. Blackpool Wren Rovers won 3-1 on penalties after a 2-2 draw.

They finished second from bottom of the WPL Northern Division One in 2016/17 and, having spent two seasons at that level, were relegated back into the North West Regional Premier.

FYLDE

WPL NORTHERN DIVISION (TIER 3)

Founded: 1971 (as Duke of York)
Nickname: The Coasters
Ground: Mill Farm, (AFC Fylde)

SEASON 2016/17

WPL Northern Division: 7th
WPL Cup: R2
FA Cup: R1

2016/17 WPL NORTHERN DIVISION

21.08	Leicester City Women (h)	W 4-0
28.08	West Bromwich Albion (a)	W 2-0
11.09	Bradford City (h)	W 3-2
25.09	Newcastle United (a)	W 5-1
02.10	Stoke City (a)	D 3-3
05.10	Blackburn Rovers (h)	L 1-2
09.10	West Bromwich Albion (h)	D 2-2
30.10	Stoke City (h)	L 0-2
06.11	Middlesbrough (a)	L 1-3
13.11	Leicester City Women (a)	D 1-1
11.12	Derby County (h)	D 0-0
08.01	Huddersfield Town (h)	W 6-1
16.02	Blackburn Rovers (a)	L 0-1
19.02	Huddersfield Town (a)	D 2-2
12.03	Nottingham Forest (h)	W 1-0
19.03	Derby County (a)	L 0-5
26.03	Newcastle United (h)*	W 3-0
02.04	Bradford City (a)	W 2-1
23.04	Nottingham Forest (a)	L 0-1
14.05	Middlesbrough (h)	L 0-3

*played at Kellamergh Park

2016/17 WPL CUP RESULTS

04.09	DR	Hudderfield Town (a)	W 2-1
	R1	Bye	
23.10	R2	West Bromwich Albion (a)	L 1-2 (aet)

2016/17 FA CUP RESULTS

04.12	R1 West Bromwich Albion (a)	L 1-4

2016/17 WPL NORTHERN DIVISION

	GD	Pts
1. Blackburn Rovers	39	54
2. Middlesbrough	29	43
3. Leicester City Women	7	34
4. Stoke City	6	30
5. Derby County	4	29
6. West Bromwich Albion	-4	27
7. Fylde	**6**	**26***
8. Bradford City	0	22
9. Huddersfield Town	-16	20
10. Nottingham Forest	-22	18
11. Newcastle United	-49	7 (R)

*Fylde docked 3 points (ineligible player)

Fylde were called Duke of York when they were founded in 1971. They became Preston Rangers in 1977 and then Preston North End in 1997. In May 2016, they switched their association from Preston North End to AFC Fylde who offered them the chance to play at Mill Farm and made funds available.

As Preston Rangers they reached the semi-finals of the FA Women's Cup in 1982/83 and 1989/90.

In 2005/06 they were promoted to the FA Women's Premier League Northern Division for the first time having won the Northern Combination Football League in their days as Preston North End.

The club won the 2014/15 WPL Plate, beating League rivals Huddersfield Town 3-0 in the final.

In January 2017 they appointed 24-year-old Conrad Prendergast as manager. He joined from Manchester City women's coaching staff.

GILLINGHAM

WPL SOUTHERN DIVISION (TIER 3)

Founded: 1995
Nickname: The Gills
Ground: K Sports, Aylesford (K Sports FC) in 2016/17, Maidstone Road (Chatham FC) in 2017/18

SEASON 2016/17

WPL South East Division One: 1st (P)
WPL Cup: R3
FA Cup: R2

2016/17 WPL SOUTH EAST DIVISION ONE

21.08	Luton Town (a)	D 1-1
28.08	Milton Keynes D. (h)*	W 3-1
11.09	Ipswich Town (h)*	D 1-1
02.10	Lowestoft Town (h)*	W 5-1
16.10	AFC Wimbledon (h)*	D 1-1
30.10	Ipswich Town (a)	W 6-0
27.11	Cambridge United (h)*	W 4-1
11.12	Denham United (a)	W 9-0
05.02	Actonians (a)	W 4-0
12.02	Luton Town (h)*	W 10-1
19.02	Norwich City (a)	W 9-0
26.02	Denham United (h)*	W 2-0
05.03	Enfield Town (h)*	W 6-0
12.03	Lowestoft Town (a)	W 4-0
19.03	Enfield Town (a)	W 7-0
02.04	Stevenage (h)	W 5-1
09.04	Milton Keynes D. (a)	W 2-1
16.04	Stevenage (a)	W 1-0
23.04	Actonians (h)	W 7-1
30.04	Norwich City (h)	W 13-0
07.05	Cambridge United (a)	W 2-1
14.05	AFC Wimbledon (a)	L 2-3

2016/17 WPL CUP RESULTS

04.09	DR	Southampton Saints (a)	W 4-0
25.09	R1	Norwich City (h)+	W 8-2
23.10	R2	Milton Keynes Dons (h)+	W 2-0
06.11	R3	Tottenham Hotspur (a)	L 2-4

2016/17 FA CUP RESULTS

09.10	RQ3	Maidenhead United (h)*	W 4-0
13.11	RQ4	Aylesford (a)	W 7-0
04.12	R1	Southampton Saints (a)	W 7-1
08.01	R2	Tottenham Hotspur (a)	L 0-3

*Played at Corinthian Sports Club

+Played at Chatham Town FC

2016/17 WPL SOUTH EAST DIVISION ONE

	GD	Pts
1. Gillingham	**90**	**57 (P)**
2. Milton Keynes Dons	42	49
3. AFC Wimbledon	29	44
4. Cambridge United	20	41
5. Luton Town	5	37
6. Actonians	14	36
7. Enfield Town	-20	25
8. Denham United	-21	25
9. Ipswich Town	-22	25
10. Norwich City	-50	16
11. Stevenage	-26	15
12. Lowestoft Town	-61	6 (R)

Gillingham were promoted to WPL Southern Division in style at the end of 2016/17. They were runaway champions of the WPL South East Division One and would have completed the entire League season unbeaten but for a final day defeat away to AFC Wimbledon.

Gillingham Ladies come under the umbrella of Gillingham men's professional outfit. It is the third link-up with Gillingham men's in their history. The first came in 1995 when Gillingham men's chairman Paul Scally co-opted a local team called Borstal 88.

After a period of independence they were brought back into the Gillingham fold in 2008 and then, after another break, again in 2014.

GUISELEY VIXENS

WPL NORTHERN DIVISION (TIER 3)

Founded: 1993 (as Meanwood Vixens)
Nickname: Vixens
Ground: Nethermoor Park, (Guiseley AFC)

SEASON 2016/17:

WPL Northern Division One: 1st (P)
WPL Cup: DR **WPL Plate: R2**
FA Cup: R1

2016/17 WPL NORTHERN DIVISION ONE

21.08	Liverpool Feds (a)	W 3-1
28.08	Hull City (a)	W 2-0
11.09	Morecambe (h)	W 7-0
18.09	Leeds United (h)	D 1-1
27.09	Brighouse Town (h)	W 3-1
02.10	Chorley (a)	W 4-1
05.10	Brighouse Town (a)	W 4-0
30.10	Mossley Hill Athletic (h)	W 3-2
06.11	Leeds United (a)	W 5-1
27.11	Tranmere Rovers (a)	W 4-1
19.02	Morecambe (a)	W 5-2
05.03	Blackpool Wren Rovers (h)	W 4-0
12.03	Tranmere Rovers (h)	W 4-0
19.03	Chorley (h)	W 2-0
26.03	Crewe Alexandra (a)	L 2-4
02.04	Mossley Hill Athletic (a)	W 2-0
09.04	Chester-le-Street Town (h)	W 1-0
16.04	Chester-le-Street Town (a)	W 3-1
23.04	Blackpool Wren Rovers (a)	W 3-2
30.04	Liverpool Feds (h)	D 1-1
07.05	Hull City (h)*	W 6-2
14.05	Crewe Alexandra (h)*	W 3-0

*played at Bradford Academy 3G

2016/17 WPL CUP RESULTS

04.09	DR	Hull City (a)	L 0-3

2016/17 WPL PLATE RESULTS

16.10	R2	Huddersfield Town (h)	D 4-4
			(L 4-5 p)

2016/17 FA CUP RESULTS

09.10	RQ3	Rotherham United (h)	W 7-2
13.11	RQ4	Nettleham (h)	W 7-1
04.12	R1	Nottingham Forest (h)	L 0-1

2016/17 WPL NORTHERN DIVISION ONE

	GD	Pts
1. Guiseley Vixens	**52**	**59 (P)**
2. Liverpool Feds	37	44
3. Hull City	16	43
4. Chester-le-Street Town	16	41
5. Chorley	7	38
6. Brighouse Town	16	37
7. Morecambe	1	29*
8. Leeds United	-8	23
9. Mossley Hill Athletic	-27	19
10. Crewe Alexandra	-28	18
11. Blackpool Wren Rovers	-31	18
12. Tranmere Rovers	-51	7 (R)

*Morecambe docked 3 points (unregistered player)

The club that was founded as Meanwood Vixens in 1993 quickly grew in stature and soon changed its name to Leeds City Vixens.

They have been affiliated with men's non-League team Guiseley AFC since 2005 and changed their name to the same at that point.

The Vixens wrapped up the 2016/17 WPL Northern Division One title when they won 3-2 at Blackpool Wren Rovers on 23 April. It was the second time they had won the division in three seasons. The success saw them promoted to the WPL Northern Division for the 2017/18 season.

HARINGEY BOROUGH

WPL SE DIVISION ONE (TIER 4)

Founded: 1999
Nickname: Borough
Ground: Coles Park, (Haringey Borough FC)

SEASON 2016/17

Eastern Regional Premier: 1st (P)
FA Cup: RQ3

2016/17 EASTERN REGIONAL PREMIER

21.08	Billericay Town (a)	W 4-1
28.08	Brentwood Town (h)	W 5-1
04.09	Colchester Town (a)	W 3-2
25.09	Histon (a)	W 6-0
02.10	Royston Town (h)	L 0-1
23.10	AFC Sudbury (a)	W 1-0
30.10	Bedford (h)	W 5-2
06.11	Royston Town (a)	W 3-1
13.11	Billericay Town (h)	L 2-3
20.11	AFC Dunstable (h)	W 2-1
27.11	Colchester Town (h)	W 10-1
22.01	AFC Sudbury (h)	D 2-2
05.02	Writtle (a)	W 5-1
19.02	Acle United (a)	L 0-1
05.03	Brentwood Town (a)	D 2-2
12.03	Writtle (h)	D 5-5
19.03	AFC Dunstable (a)	W 3-1
26.03	Bedford (a)	D 0-0
16.04	Histon (h)	W 8-0
23.04	Acle United (h)	W 4-1

2016/17 FA CUP RESULTS

18.09	RQ2	Chelmsford City (h)	W 12-0
09.10	RQ3	Chichester City (h)	L 2-8

2016/17 EASTERN REGIONAL PREMIER

	GD	Pts
1. Haringey Borough	**44**	**43 (P)**
2. Acle United	15	41
3. Bedford	19	40
4. AFC Dunstable	10	36
5. AFC Sudbury	6	31
6. Billericay Town	3	29
7. Writtle	6	28
8. Brentwood Town	-8	25
9. Royston Town	-12	24
10. Colchester Town	-29	11
11. Histon	-54	7

Haringey Borough Women's club was set up ahead of the 1999/00 season but played only occasional friendlies that year.

In 2000 they merged with Mill Hill United who had been accepted into the Eastern Region League, Division Two. The new club continued with the Haringey Borough name and groundshared Coles Park with the men's team as they still do today.

Coles Park is a stone's throw from Tottenham Hotspur football club and is actually situated *on* the road called White Hart Lane, which Spurs' now demolished stadium of the same name never was.

The 2016/17 Eastern Regional Premier Division title brought with it promotion to the WPL South East Division One meaning the chance to play in the fourth tier of English football for the first time. They completed the 2016/17 Double by winning their regional League Cup final.

HUDDERSFIELD TOWN

WPL NORTHERN DIVISION (TIER 3)

Founded: 1988 (as Huddersfield Ladies)
Nickname: Town
Ground: The Stafflex Arena, (Shelley FC)

SEASON 2016/17

WPL Northern Division: 9th
WPL Cup: DR **WPL Plate: RU**
FA Cup: R1

2016/17 WPL NORTHERN DIVISION

28.08	Blackburn Rovers (h)	D 3-3
11.09	Derby County (a)	L 1-3
14.09	Bradford City (a)	L 0-1
18.09	Newcastle United (a)	L 2-6
02.10	Nottingham Forest (a)	W 5-2
05.10	Bradford City (h)	W 2-1
09.10	Derby County (h)	W 4-1
30.10	Middlesbrough (h)	L 1-2
13.11	Nottingham Forest (h)	D 3-3
27.11	Leicester City Women (h)	L 1-6
08.01	Fylde (a)	L 1-6
12.02	Newcastle United (h)	W 2-0
19.02	Fylde (h)	D 2-2
26.02	Stoke City (h)	D 2-2
19.03	Leicester City Women (a)	D 2-2
26.03	Stoke City (a)	L 0-2
02.04	West Bromwich Albion (a)	L 1-3
09.04	Middlesbrough (a)	L 2-4
08.05	Blackburn Rovers (a)	L 1-3
14.05	West Bromwich Albion (h)	W 2-1

2016/17 WPL CUP RESULTS

04.09	DR	Fylde (h)	L 1-2

2016/17 WPL PLATE RESULTS

25.09	R1	Sporting Khasla (a)	W 6-2
16.10	R2	Guiseley Vixens (a)	D 4-4 (W 5-4 p)
06.11	R3	Bradford City (a)	D 2-2 (W 4-3p)
11.12	QF	Tranmere Rovers (a)	W 7-0
05.03	SF	Actonians (h)	W 6-1
23.04	F	Lewes (n)*	L 0-4

*played at St James Park, Brackley

2016/17 FA CUP RESULTS

04.12	R1	Derby County (h)	L 0-1

2016/17 WPL NORTHERN DIVISION

	GD	Pts
1. Blackburn Rovers	39	54
2. Middlesbrough	29	43
3. Leicester City Women	7	34
4. Stoke City	6	30
5. Derby County	4	29
6. West Bromwich Albion	-4	27
7. Fylde	6	26*
8. Bradford City	0	22
9. Huddersfield Town	**-16**	**20**
10. Nottingham Forest	-22	18
11. Newcastle United	-49	7 (R)

*Fylde docked 3 points (ineligible player)

The club's longest-serving manager was Mickey Booth who was in charge for 14 years before standing down at the end of the 2012/13 season.

Huddersfield Ladies became Huddersfield Town Ladies ahead of the 1993/94 season and went on to win the Treble of North East Regional Division One, League Cup and Yorkshire Cup in their first season under that name.

The following year they claimed the League title again, winning all 16 of their games and scoring 101 goals.

HULL CITY

WPL NORTHERN DIVISION ONE (TIER 4)

Founded: 2001
Nickname: City / Tigresses
Ground: Hull University Sports Ground

SEASON 2016/17

WPL Northern Division One: 3rd
WPL Cup: R3
FA Cup: R2

2016/17 WPL NORTHERN DIVISION ONE

28.08	Guiseley Vixens (h)	L 0-2
11.09	Brighouse Town (h)	W 1-0
14.09	Leeds United (a)	W 2-0
25.09	Mossley Hill Athletic (a)	W 5-1
02.10	Blackpool Wren Rovers (a)	W 3-2
05.10	Leeds United (h)*	W 2-0
23.10	Tranmere Rovers (h)	W 5-1
30.10	Chester-le-Street Town (a)	L 2-4
11.12	Brighouse Town (a)	W 2-1
18.12	Tranmere Rovers (a)	W 3-2
22.01	Liverpool Feds (a)	L 2-3
29.01	Blackpool Wren Rovers (h)	W 7-0
12.02	Liverpool Feds (h)	D 2-2
19.02	Chorley (h)	W 4-2
26.02	Crewe Alexandra (a)	W 1-0
05.03	Crewe Alexandra (h)	W 3-0
12.03	Morecambe (a)	W 2-1
26.03	Chorley (a)	L 1-2
02.04	Chester-le-Street Town (h)	L 3-5
23.04	Morecambe (h)	W 2-1
07.05	Guiseley Vixens (a)	L 2-6
14.05	Mossley Hill Athletics (h)	L 0-3

*Played at Henry Thirsk Amenity Centre

2016/17 WPL CUP RESULTS

04.09	DR	Guiseley Vixens (h)	W 3-0
	R1	Bye	
16.10	R2	Middlesbrough (h)	W 3-1
06.11	R3	Liverpool Feds (h)	L 0-4

2016/17 FA CUP RESULTS

09.10	RQ3	South Shields (h)	W 4-2 (aet)
13.11	RQ4	Leeds United (h)	W 6-0
04.12	R1	Norton & S. A. (a)	W 6-1
08.01	R2	Blackburn Rovers (a)	L 0-5

2016/17 WPL NORTHERN DIVISION ONE

	GD	Pts
1. Guiseley Vixens	52	59 (P)
2. Liverpool Feds	37	44
3. Hull City	**16**	**43**
4. Chester-le-Street Town	16	41
5. Chorley	7	38
6. Brighouse Town	16	37
7. Morecambe	1	29*
8. Leeds United	-8	23
9. Mossley Hill Athletic	-27	19
10. Crewe Alexandra	-28	18
11. Blackpool Wren Rovers	-31	18 (R)
12. Tranmere Rovers	-51	7 (R)

*Morecambe docked 3 points (unregistered player)

The club is not affiliated with the men's professional outfit Hull City.

The furthest that Hull have ever progressed in the FA Cup is the Second Round proper. They did so for the first time in 2014/15 before exiting to Radcliffe Olympic, and repeated the feat in 2016/17 only to be knocked out by WPL Northern side Blackburn Rovers.

Hull City's recent progress, and promotion to the WPL Northern Division One in 2014/15, is in part thanks to their merger with Beverley Town Ladies in 2011/12.

IPSWICH TOWN

WPL SOUTH EAST DIVISION ONE (TIER 4)

Founded: Unknown
Nickname: Town
Ground: Goldstar Ground, (Felixstowe & Walton United FC)

SEASON 2016/17:

WPL South East Division One: 9th
WPL Cup: DR **WPL Plate: R2**
FA Cup: RQ3

2016/17 WPL SOUTH EAST DIVISION ONE

21.08	AFC Wimbledon (a)	L 3-4
28.08	Enfield Town (h)	D 1-1
11.09	Gillingham (a)	D 1-1
14.09	Lowestoft Town (a)	W 3-2
18.09	Stevenage (h)	W 2-1
02.10	Milton Keynes Dons (a)	L 3-5
05.10	Lowestoft Town (h)	W 3-2
30.10	Gillingham (h)	L 0-6
13.11	Enfield Town (a)	L 1-4
27.11	Denham United (a)	W 2-1
11.12	Cambridge United (h)	L 0-5
18.12	AFC Wimbledon (h)	L 1-4
08.01	Actonians (h)	L 0-1
05.02	Milton Keynes Dons (h)	L 1-4
12.03	Luton Town (h)	L 0-1
19.03	Stevenage (a)	W 3-2
26.03	Norwich City (a)	D 1-1
02.04	Cambridge United (a)	L 1-4
23.04	Luton Town (a)	L 1-5
02.05	Norwich City (h)	W 5-1
07.05	Actonians (a)	W 2-1
14.05	Denham United (h)*	D 2-2

*Played at Ipswich Town FC training ground

2016/17 WPL CUP RESULTS

04.09	DR	Cardiff City (h)	L 0-5

2016/17 WPL PLATE RESULTS

23.10	R2	Actonians (a)	L 0-6

2016/17 FA CUP RESULTS

09.10	RQ3	Denham United (a)	L 1-4

2016/17 WPL SOUTH EAST DIVISION ONE

	GD	Pts
1. Gillingham	90	57 (P)
2. Milton Keynes Dons	42	49
3. AFC Wimbledon	29	44
4. Cambridge United	20	41
5. Luton Town	5	37
6. Actonians	14	36
7. Enfield Town	-20	25
8. Denham United	-21	25
9. Ipswich Town	**-22**	**25**
10. Norwich City	-50	16
11. Stevenage	-26	15
12. Lowestoft Town	-61	6 (R)

Ipswich Town's formal association with the men's professional club of the same name was announced in February 2012.

Natasha Thomas and Hollie Clement were joint top goalscorers for Ipswich in 2016/17. They both hit eight goals, with Thomas doing so from 23 appearances and Clement from 25.

Ipswich have won the last three Suffolk FA Women's Cups beating AFC Sudbury 2-0 in the 2015 final, Kirkley & Pakefield 8-0 in 2016 and Lowestoft Town 5-0 in 2017. They have won the competition a record seven times.

KEYNSHAM TOWN

WPL SW DIVISION ONE (TIER 4)

Founded: 1993 (as Super Strikers Girls)
Nickname: The Ks
Ground: AJN Stadium, (Keynsham Town FC)

SEASON 2016/17

WPL South West Division One: 4th
WPL Cup: DR **WPL Plate: QF**
FA Cup: R3

2016/17 WPL SOUTH WEST DIVISION ONE

21.08	Larkhall Athletic (h)	L 1-5
28.08	Cheltenham Town (a)	W 3-0
11.09	Southampton Saints (a)	L 2-3
18.09	Maidenhead United (h)	W 2-1
25.09	Exeter City (h)	W 13-0
06.10	Brislington (a)	W 4-1
30.10	Southampton Saints (h)	D 0-0
10.11	Brislington (h)	W 4-0
18.12	Chichester City (a)	L 0-5
22.01	St Nicholas (a)	W 7-0
12.02	Basingstoke Town (a)	W 6-2
19.02	Plymouth Argyle (a)	L 2-5
26.02	*Shanklin (a)*	*W 7-0 (ex)*
05.03	Cheltenham Town (h)	W 7-0
12.03	St Nicholas (h)	W 5-2
02.04	Exeter City (a)	W 5-0
09.04	Larkhall Athletic (a)	D 1-1
16.04	*Shanklin (h)*	*W 7-0 (ex)*
23.04	Maidenhead United (a)	W 2-1
30.04	Basingstoke Town (h)	W 6-1
07.05	Plymouth Argyle (h)	L 1-3
14.05	Chichester City (h)	L 0-2

(ex) Shanklin withdrew from League: results expunged

2016/17 WPL CUP RESULTS

04.09	DR	Crystal Palace (h)	L 1-2

2016/17 WPL PLATE RESULTS

23.10	R2	Southampton Saints (a)	W 3-2
06.11	R3	West Ham United (a)	W 3-2
11.12	QF	Leicester City Women (h)	L 2-3 (aet)

2016/17 FA CUP RESULTS

09.10	RQ3	Buckland Athletic (a)	W 3-2
20.11	RQ4	Chichester City (a)	W 2-1
04.12	R1	Regents Park Rangers (a)	W 6-1
08.01	R2	C&K Basildon (a)	W 3-1
05.02	R3	Durham (h)	L 0-7

2016/17 WPL SOUTH WEST DIVISION ONE

	GD	Pts
1. Chichester City	92	58 (P)
2. Plymouth Argyle	85	54
3. Southampton Saints	20	41
4. Keynsham Town	**39**	**38**
5. Larkhall Athletic	3	36
6. Brislington	-19	22
7. Maidenhead United	-28	16*
8. St Nicholas	-43	15
9. Basingstoke Town	-28	14
10. Cheltenham Town	-49	13
11. Exeter City	-72	4 (R)

*Maidenhead docked 1 point

NB: Shanklin withdrew from League, all results expunged

The club was initially formed as an Under-11s six-a-side team in 1993 by pupils of Chandag Junior School in Keynsham, Bristol under the name Super Strikers Girls.

The name was later changed to Protel Super Strikers following sponsorship by a local telecoms company. At this point the club also adopted Celtic's green and white colours.

In 1998/99 the club became closely affiliated with Keynsham Town men's team and was granted use of their facilities. They changed their name to the same.

Their tremendous FA Cup run in 2016/17 included away wins over eventual WPL South West Division One champions Chichester City and WPL Southern side C&K Basildon. They finally fell to WSL2 side Durham in the third round.

LARKHALL ATHLETIC

WPL SW DIVISION ONE (TIER 4)

Founded: 2008
Nickname: The Larks
Ground: Plain Ham, (Larkhall Athletic FC)

SEASON 2016/17

WPL South West Division One: 5th
WPL Cup: R2
FA Cup: R1

2016/17 WPL SOUTH WEST DIVISION ONE

21.08	Keynsham Town (a)	W 5-1
11.09	Chichester City (h)	L 0-2
14.09	St Nicholas (h)	W 3-1
25.09	Cheltenham Town (a)	W 3-1
02.10	Exeter City (h)	W 2-1
05.10	St Nicholas (a)	L 0-3
06.11	Maidenhead United (h)	W 5-1
18.12	Brislington (h)	W 3-2
08.01	Southampton Saints (a)	L 2-6
12.02	Plymouth Argyle (h)	L 0-4
19.02	Brislington (a)	W 4-3
26.02	Maidenhead United (a)	W 1-0
12.03	Chichester City (a)	L 1-2
19.03	Basingstoke Town (a)	D 1-1
26.03	Southampton Saints (h)	D 2-2
02.04	Basingstoke Town (h)	W 1-0
09.04	Keynsham Town (h)	D 1-1
30.04	Plymouth Argyle (a)	L 1-7
02.05	Cheltenham Town (h)	W 3-2
18.05	Exeter City (a)	W 7-2

2016/17 WPL CUP RESULTS

04.09	DR	Stevenage (a)	W 3-0
	R1	Bye	
23.10	R2	Cardiff City (a)	L w/o

2016/17 FA CUP RESULTS

09.10	RQ3	Cheltenham Town (h)	W 9-1
13.11	RQ4	Newbury (h)	W 8-1
04.12	R1	Cardiff City (a)	L 0-6

2016/17 WPL SOUTH WEST DIVISION ONE

	GD	Pts
1. Chichester City	92	58 (P)
2. Plymouth Argyle	85	54
3. Southampton Saints	20	41
4. Keynsham Town	39	38
5. Larkhall Athletic	**3**	**36**
6. Brislington	-19	22
7. Maidenhead United	-28	16*
8. St Nicholas	-43	15
9. Basingstoke Town	-28	14
10. Cheltenham Town	-49	13
11. Exeter City	-72	4 (R)

*Maidenhead docked 1 point

NB: Shanklin withdrew from League, all results expunged

Larkhall Athletic Ladies were formed in 2008 following their move across from Bath City Ladies.

The Larks groundshare with Larkhall Athletic's men's team at the Plain Ham Stadium on Charlcombe Lane.

Kate German was the club's top goalscorer in 2016/17 with an impressive 18 goals in 22 games in all competitions.

LEEDS UNITED

WPL NORTHERN DIVISION ONE (TIER 4)

Founded: 1989
Nickname: The Phoenix
Ground: Wheatley Park, (Garforth Town FC)

SEASON 2016/17

WPL Northern Division One: 8th
WPL Cup: R2
FA Cup: RQ4

2016/17 WPL NORTHERN DIVISION ONE

21.08	Tranmere Rovers (a)	W 5-3
11.09	Mossley Hill Athletic (h)	W 7-1
14.09	Hull City (h)	L 0-2
18.09	Guiseley Vixens (a)	D 1-1
02.10	Tranmere Rovers (h)	D 1-1
05.10	Hull City (a)	L 0-2
23.10	Crewe Alexandra (h)	W 2-1
30.10	Brighouse Town (a)	W 3-1
06.11	Guiseley Vixens (h)	L 1-5
04.12	Chorley (h)	L 0-1
11.12	Crewe Alexandra (a)	L 2-3
08.01	Mossley Hill Athletic (a)	W 5-2
15.01	Blackpool Wren Rovers (a)	W 5-1
05.02	Chester-le-Street Town (a)	L 0-3
12.02	Blackpool Wren Rovers (h)	W 5-1
05.03	Morecambe (a)	L 4-7
12.03	Chester-le-Street Town (h)	L 3-5
19.03	Liverpool Feds (a)	L 0-4
30.04	Chorley (a)	L 1-5
04.05	Brighouse Town (h)	L 2-4
07.05	Morecambe (h)	L 1-2
14.05	Liverpool Feds (h)	L 3-4

2016/17 WPL CUP RESULTS

04.09	DR	Nuneaton Town (h)	W w/o
	R1	Bye	
16.10	R2	Liverpool Feds (h)	L 1-4

2016/17 FA CUP RESULTS

09.10	RQ3	South Park Rangers (h)	W 6-1
13.11	RQ4	Hull City (a)	L 0-6

2016/17 WPL NORTHERN DIVISION ONE

	GD	Pts
1. Guiseley Vixens	52	59 (P)
2. Liverpool Feds	37	44
3. Hull City	16	43
4. Chester-le-Street Town	16	41
5. Chorley	7	38
6. Brighouse Town	16	37
7. Morecambe	1	29*
8. Leeds	**-8**	**23**
9. Mossley Hill Athletic	-27	19
10. Crewe Alexandra	-28	18
11. Blackpool Wren Rovers	-31	18 (R)
12. Tranmere Rovers	-51	7 (R)

*Morecambe docked 3 points

In June 2017 Leeds Ladies re-established their association with Leeds United men's team. The agreement saw them again take on the name of Leeds United Ladies, return to the same Thorp Arch training ground and adopt the same playing kit.

The club was initially formed as Leeds United Ladies in 1989 and has had intermittent funding and support from the men throughout its lifetime. In 2013/14 that support was withdrawn, and the club was known as Leeds Ladies until the summer of 2017.

Leeds have twice reached the FA Women's Cup final (2006 & 2008) only to lose both times to overwhelming favourites Arsenal.

Former England international Sue Smith is the best-known player ever to have represented the club.

LEICESTER CITY LADIES

WPL MIDLANDS DIVISION ONE (TIER 4)

Founded: 1966
Nickname: Foxes / Blues / City
Ground: Linwood Playing Fields

SEASON 2016/17

WPL Midlands Division One: 10th
WPL Cup: DR **WPL Plate: R3**
FA Cup: RQ3

2016/17 WPL MIDLANDS DIVISION ONE

28.08	Steel City Wanderers (h)	L 1-3
11.09	Long Eaton United (a)	D 1-1
18.09	Birmingham & WM (a)	W 2-0
25.09	Wolverhampton Wanderers (a)	L 0-5
02.10	Sporting Khalsa (h)	L 0-2
23.10	Rotherham United (a)	L 0-6
30.10	Radcliffe Olympic (a)	L 0-13
13.11	Loughborough Foxes (h)	L 0-4
27.11	Sporting Khalsa (a)	L 0-8
08.01	The New Saints (a)	L 2-8
15.01	Rotherham United (h)	L 1-6
29.01	Loughborough Students (h)	W 4-1
05.02	Long Eaton United (h)	W 4-1
19.02	Birmingham & WM (h)	L 3-5
26.02	Radcliffe Olympic (h)	L 1-3
05.03	Loughborough Foxes (a)	L 0-9
12.03	Loughborough Students (a)	W 4-2
19.03	The New Saints (h)	L 0-5
09.04	Steel City Wanderers (a)	L 2-4
23.04	Solihull (a)	D 0-0
07.05	Solihull (h)	W 2-1
14.05	Wolverhampton Wanderers (h)	L 0-1

2016/17 WPL CUP RESULTS

04.09	DR	Loughborough Foxes (a)	L 3-9

2016/17 WPL PLATE RESULTS

16.10	R2	Steel City Wanderers (h)	W 2-1
06.11	R3	Radcliffe Olympic (h)	L 0-5

2016/17 FA CUP RESULTS

09.10	RQ3	Birmingham & WM (h)	L 2-3

2016/17 WPL MIDLANDS DIVISION ONE

	GD	Pts
1. Wolverhampton Wanderers	39	56 (P)
2. Loughborough Foxes	80	54
3. Sporting Khalsa	24	41
4. Radcliffe Olympic	22	40
5. Birmingham & WM	14	40
6. The New Saints	21	39
7. Long Eaton United	9	30
8. Steel City Wanderers	-16	28
9. Solihull	-14	23
10. Leicester City Ladies	**-61**	**17**
11. Rotherham United	-25	16
12. Loughborough Students	-93	-1* (R)

*Loughborough Students docked 2 points

Formed in 1966, the club is believed to be the oldest women's club in the country still in action under its original guise today.

Leicester City Ladies is a grassroots club and a separate entity to Leicester City Women which is affiliated to the men's Premier League side Leicester City.

In 1992, well before the creation of Leicester City Women, Leicester City Ladies did have a close relationship with the men's Leicester City club.

In 1996 Leicester City Ladies played Crystal Palace Ladies at Wembley before their male counterparts faced each other in the Championship play-off final.

LEICESTER CITY WOMEN

WPL NORTHERN DIVISION (TIER 3)

Founded: 2004
Nickname: The Foxes
Ground: Riverside Stadium in 2016/17, Farley Way, (Quorn FC) in 2017/18

SEASON 2016/17

WPL Northern Division: 3rd
WPL Cup: DR **WPL Plate: SF**
FA Cup: R4

2016/17 WPL NORTHERN DIVISION

21.08	Fylde (a)	L 0-4
28.08	Stoke City (h)	W 5-3
11.09	Middlesbrough (a)	W 3-0
18.09	West Bromwich Albion (h)	W 2-1
09.10	Bradford City (a)	L 1-4
23.10	Stoke City (a)	W 2-1
30.10	Newcastle United (a)	L 0-1
13.11	Fylde (h)	D 1-1
27.11	Huddersfield Town (a)	W 6-1
15.01	Blackburn Rovers (h)	L 0-4
12.02	Nottingham Forest (a)	D 2-2
26.02	Derby County (h)	W 2-1
19.03	Huddersfield Town (h)	D 2-2
26.03	Middlesbrough (h)	L 0-3
02.04	Blackburn Rovers (a)	D 2-2
09.04	Nottingham Forest (h)	W 2-1
16.04	West Bromwich Albion (a)	L 0-1
30.04	Derby County (a)	W 3-1
07.05	Bradford City (h)	W 5-4
14.05	Newcastle United (h)	W 6-0

2016/17 WPL CUP RESULTS

04.09	DR	Newcastle United (a)	L 1-2 (aet)

2016/17 WPL PLATE RESULTS

16.10	R2	Rotherham United (h)	W 6-1
06.11	R3	Chorley (a)	W 5-3
11.12	QF	Keynsham Town (a)	W 3-2 (aet)
12.03	SF	Lewes (h)	L 0-1

2016/17 FA CUP RESULTS

04.12	R1	Birmingham & WM (a)	W 3-0
08.01	R2	Middlesbrough (a)	W 2-1 (aet)
05.02	R3	Liverpool Feds (h)	W 2-1
19.02	R4	West Bromwich Albion	L 1-2

2016/17 WPL NORTHERN DIVISION

	GD	Pts
1. Blackburn Rovers	39	54
2. Middlesbrough	29	43
3. Leicester City Women	**7**	**34**
4. Stoke City	6	30
5. Derby County	4	29
6. West Bromwich Albion	-4	27
7. Fylde	6	26*
8. Bradford City	0	22
9. Huddersfield Town	-16	20
10. Nottingham Forest	-22	18
11. Newcastle United	-49	7 (R)

*Fylde docked 3 points (ineligible player)

Leicester City Women are officially affiliated to Leicester City FC – the men's Premier League champions of 2016 – and are not to be confused with grassroots club Leicester City Ladies.

They were among the clubs who applied to join the WSL in the inaugural season of 2011, but their application was turned down.

In 2015/16 they secured the WPL Northern Division One title by winning all 22 of their League games and were promoted to WPL Northern.

Former captain Remi Allen won more than 20 caps for England at youth level before leaving for Notts County in 2011.

LEWES

WPL SOUTHERN DIVISION (TIER 3)

Founded: 2002
Nickname: The Rookettes
Ground: The Dripping Pan, (Lewes FC)

SEASON 2016/17

WPL Southern Division: 7th
WPL Cup: DR **WPL Plate: Winners**
FA Cup: R3

2016/17 WPL SOUTHERN DIVISION

21.08	West Ham United (h)	W 7-2
28.08	Cardiff City (h)	D 1-1
11.09	Cardiff City (a)	L 0-6
14.09	Portsmouth (a)	L 3-4
18.09	Tottenham Hotspur (h)	L 1-6
05.10	Portsmouth (h)	L 1-2
09.10	Charlton Athletic (a)	L 1-2
30.10	Swindon Town (a)	W 2-1
13.11	Crystal Palace (h)	D 2-2
29.01	Swindon Town (h)	W 3-1
12.02	Tottenham Hotspur (a)	L 0-2
19.02	QPR (a)	W 2-0
26.02	Coventry United (a)	L 1-3
19.03	QPR (h)	W 1-0
26.03	C&K Basildon (h)	W 3-0
02.04	Crystal Palace (a)	D 1-1
09.04	Charlton Athletic (h)	L 0-2
16.04	West Ham United (a)	D 0-0
30.04	Coventry United (h)	L 0-1
07.05	C&K Basildon (a)	W 2-0

2016/17 WPL CUP RESULTS

04.09	DR	Cambridge United (a)	D 3-3 (L 2-4p)

2016/17 WPL PLATE RESULTS

16.10	R2	Maidenhead United (h)	W w/o
06.11	R3	St Nicholas (h)	W w/o
18.12	QF	Luton Town (a)	W 6-0
12.03	SF	Leicester City Women (a)	W 1-0
23.04	F	Huddersfield Town (n)*	W 4-0

*played at St James Park, Brackley

2016/17 FA CUP RESULTS

04.12	R1	Brislington (h)	W 5-0
08.01	R2	Cardiff City (h)	W 2-0
05.02	R3	West Bromwich Albion (a)	L 1-3

2016/17 WPL SOUTHERN DIVISION

	GD	Pts
1. Tottenham Hotspur	45	52 (P)
2. Coventry United	40	48
3. Cardiff City	53	44
4. Charlton Athletic	30	42
5. Crystal Palace	25	33
6. C&K Basildon	-13	27
7. Lewes	**-5**	**25**
8. Portsmouth	-35	17
9. West Ham United	-47	9
10. Swindon Town	-40	8
11. QPR	-53	8

The 2017 WPL Plate final against Huddersfield was Lewes' first ever national Cup final. They won 4-0.

The match also represented their first Cup final at any level since 2013 when they reached the Sussex Women's Challenge Cup final.

Lewes were awarded walkovers in both the third and fourth rounds of the 2017 WPL Plate with respective opponents Maidenhead United and St Nicholas both unable to fulfil the fixtures.

LEYTON ORIENT

WPL SE DIVISION ONE (TIER 4)

Founded: 2004 (as KIKK United)
Nickname: Os
Ground: Mile End Stadium in 2016/17, Matchroom Stadium (Leyton Orient FC) in 2017/18

SEASON 2016/17

London & SE Regional Premier: 1st (P)
FA Cup: R1

2016/17 LONDON & SE REGIONAL PREMIER

21.08	Aylesford (h)	W 4-0
28.08	Watford Development (a)	W 7-0
04.09	Herne Bay (h)	W 8-0
11.09	Carshalton Athletic (h)	W 8-0
25.09	Camden Town (a)	W 5-0
23.10	Camden Town (h)	W 7-0
30.10	Crawley Wasps (a)	W 4-1
27.11	Eastbourne Town (h)	W 4-0
08.01	Eastbourne Town (a)	W 4-0
29.01	Crawley Wasps (h)	D 3-3
05.02	London Corinthians (a)	L 2-5
12.02	Watford Development (h)	W 7-0
19.02	London Corinthians (h)	W 4-0
12.03	Fulham FC Foundation (a)	W 5-0
19.03	Aylesford (a)	W 2-0
23.04	Herne Bay (a)	W 1-0
30.04	Carshalton Athletic (a)	W 4-0
07.05	Fulham FC Foundation (h)*	W 8-0

*played at Brisbane Road, (Leyton Orient FC)

2016/17 FA CUP RESULTS

18.09	RQ2	Writtle (a)	W 3-0
09.10	RQ3	Ascot United (h)	W16-0
13.11	RQ4	Cambridge City (h)	W 3-1
04.12	R1	Tottenham Hotspur (a)	L 0-1

2016/17 LONDON & SE PREMIER

	GD	Pts
1. Leyton Orient	**78**	**49 (P)**
2. London Corinthians	39	41
3. Crawley Wasps	38	39
4. Watford Development	4	34
5. Carshalton Athletic	12	30
6. Aylesford	-21	18
7. Camden Town	-31	16
8. Fulham Foundation	-39	12*
9. Eastbourne Town	-36	11
10. Herne Bay	-44	6*

*Fulham Foundation docked 2 points

*Herne Bay docked 1 point

The club began life as KIKK United in 2004. It was set up by a group of Swedish women and took its name from the Swedish expression *Kick In Kulan I Krysset*, which means 'scoring in the top corner'.

KIKK United became officially affiliated with the men's professional outfit Leyton Orient in the summer of 2015. They took the same name, and played their first League match as Leyton Orient Women on 23 August that year, beating Fulham 1-0.

The Os played their final League match of 2016/17 at Brisbane Road, the home of the men's club. A crowd of 300 watched on as they beat Fulham Foundation 8-0. They were crowned London & South East Regional Premier champions and promoted to WPL SE1.

The following week they completed the Double with a 3-1 win over Crawley Wasps in the London & South East Regional League Cup final.

LIVERPOOL MARSHALL FEDS

WPL NORTHERN DIVISION ONE (TIER 4)

Founded: 1991
Nickname: Feds
Ground: IM Marsh Campus

SEASON 2016/17

WPL Northern Division One: 2nd
WPL Cup: QF
FA Cup: R3

2016/17 WPL NORTHERN DIVISION ONE

21.08	Guiseley Vixens (h)	L 1-3
28.08	Brighouse Town (a)	D 3-3
11.09	Blackpool Wren Rovers (h)	L 2-3
14.09	Mossley Hill Athletic (a)	W 6-0
18.09	Crewe Alexandra (a)	D 3-3
02.10	Morecambe (h)	W 3-0
04.10	Mossley Hill Athletic (h)*	W 1-0
30.10	Crewe Alexandra (h)	W 5-0
18.12	Chorley (h)	W 1-0
22.01	Hull City (h)	W 3-2
12.02	Hull City (a)	D 2-2
19.02	Blackpool Wren Rovers (a)	D 2-2
05.03	Brighouse Town (h)	L 0-1
12.03	Chorley (a)	W 6-1
19.03	Leeds United (h)	W 4-0
26.03	Chester-le-Street Town (a)	W 4-1
02.04	Tranmere Rovers (h)	W 3-0
09.04	Morecambe (a)	W 4-0
26.04	Tranmere Rovers (a)	W 6-1
30.04	Guiseley Vixens (a)	D 1-1
07.05	Chester-le-Street Town (h)	L 2-3
14.05	Leeds United (a)	W 4-3

*Played at JMO Sports Park

2016/17 WPL CUP RESULTS

04.09	DR	Tranmere Rovers (a)	W 5-0
25.09	R1	Long Eaton United (a)	D 1-1 (W 4-3p)
16.10	R2	Leeds United (a)	W 4-1
06.11	R3	Hull City (a)	W 4-0
11.12	QF	Cardiff City Ladies (h)	L 0-2

2016/17 FA CUP RESULTS

09.10	RQ3	Mossley Hill Athletic (a)	W 4-0
13.11	RQ4	Warrington Wolverines (h)	W 7-1
04.12	R1	Stoke City (a)	D 1-1 (W 4-2p)
08.01	R2	Newcastle United (h)	W 1-0
05.02	R3	Leicester City Women (a)	L 1-2

2016/17 WPL NORTHERN DIVISION ONE

	GD	Pts
1. Guiseley Vixens	52	59 (P)
2. Liverpool Feds	**37**	**44**
3. Hull City	16	43
4. Chester-le-Street Town	16	41
5. Chorley	7	38
6. Brighouse Town	16	37
7. Morecambe	1	29*
8. Leeds United	-8	23
9. Mossley Hill Athletic	-27	19
10. Crewe Alexandra	-28	18
11. Blackpool Wren Rovers	-31	18 (R)
12. Tranmere Rovers	-51	7 (R)

*Morecambe docked 3 points (unregistered player)

The team was formed at the Liverpool Institute of Higher Education (now known as Liverpool Hope University).

The 'Feds' part of the club's name came about because sports teams at the Institute of Higher Education competed as a Federation of the St Katherine's and Christ Notre Dame Colleges.

Carla Lee was Feds' top goalscorer for 2016/17, notching 16 goals in 25 appearances in all competitions.

LONG EATON UNITED

WPL MIDLANDS DIVISION ONE (TIER 4)

Founded: Circa 1996
Nickname: Blues
Ground: Grange Park, (Long Eaton United FC)

SEASON 2016/17

WPL Midlands Division One: 7th
WPL Cup: R1
FA Cup: R2

2016/17 WPL MIDLANDS DIVISION ONE

21.08	The New Saints (a)	L 2-5
28.08	Birmingham & West Midlands (h)	L 1-2
11.09	Leicester City Ladies (h)	D 1-1
14.09	Radcliffe Olympic (a)	W 2-1
18.09	Loughborough Students (h)	W 13-1
05.10	Radcliffe Olympic (h)	L 1-4
16.10	Sporting Khalsa (a)	L 1-4
23.10	Loughborough Foxes (a)	L 3-4
06.11	Solihull (h)	W 2-1
27.11	Loughborough Students (a)	W 4-1
04.12	Rotherham United (h)	D 3-3
11.12	Sporting Khalsa (h)	W 3-0
18.12	The New Saints (h)	D 2-2
15.01	Loughborough Foxes (h)	W 5-1
05.02	Leicester City Ladies (a)	L 1-4
26.02	Rotherham United (a)	W 2-0
05.03	Steel City Wanderers (a)	L 2-3
12.03	Steel City Wanderers (h)	W 3-1
26.03	Solihull (a)	L 0-2
09.04	Wolverhampton Wanderers (a)	L 0-1
16.04	Wolverhampton Wanderers (h)	W 1-0
14.05	Birmingham & West Midlands (a)	L 2-4

2016/17 WPL CUP RESULTS

04.09	DR	Loughborough Students (h)	W 13-0
25.09	R1	Liverpool Feds (h)	D 1-1 (L 3-4p)

2016/17 FA CUP RESULTS

09.10	RQ3	Boldmere St Michaels (a)	W 8-2
13.11	RQ4	Coventry Ladies Dev. (h)	W 7-1
04.12	R1	Nuneaton Town (h)	Ww/o
08.01	R2	Brighouse Town (h)	L 3-4

2016/17 WPL MIDLANDS DIVISION ONE

	GD	Pts
1. Wolverhampton Wanderers	39	56 (P)
2. Loughborough Foxes	80	54
3. Sporting Khalsa	24	41
4. Radcliffe Olympic	22	40
5. Birmingham & West Midlands	14	40
6. The New Saints	21	39
7. Long Eaton United	**9**	**30**
8. Steel City Wanderers	-16	28
9. Solihull	-14	23
10. Leicester City Ladies	-61	17
11. Rotherham United	-25	16
12. Loughborough Students	-93	-1* (R)

*Loughborough Students docked 2 points

In 2015/16 Long Eaton United reached the FA Cup First Round proper for the first time in their history. As a fifth tier team they beat fourth tier Wolverhampton Wanderers 3-2 and were knocked out in the Second Round by third tier Sporting Albion.

Long Eaton United secured promotion to the WPL Midlands Division One for the first time in their history when they were crowned East Midlands Regional League champions in 2015/16 with three games to spare. They also won their regional League Cup that season.

They groundshare with non-League men's team Long Eaton United at Grange Park.

Cara Newton scored 38 goals in 25 games in all competitions in 2016/17 and was the WPL Northern Division One's overall top goalscorer.

LOUGHBOROUGH FOXES

WPL MIDLANDS DIVISION ONE (TIER 4)

Founded: 2006
Nickname: Foxes
Ground: The Stadium Pitch, Loughborough University

SEASON 2016/17

WPL Midlands Division One: 2nd
WPL Cup: R3
FA Cup: RQ3

2016/17 WPL MIDLANDS DIVISION ONE

21.08	Sporting Khalsa (h)	W 5-1
28.08	Solihull (a)	W 7-1
11.09	The New Saints (h)	W 4-0
15.09	Loughborough Students (h)	W 5-0
18.09	Steel City Wanderers (h)	W 6-1
06.10	Loughborough Students (a)	W 12-0
23.10	Long Eaton United (h)	W 4-3
30.10	Wolverhampton Wanderers (h)	L 1-2
13.11	Leicester City Ladies (a)	W 4-0
27.11	Rotherham United (h)	W 7-1
11.12	Solihull (h)	W 9-0
08.01	Steel City Wanderers (a)	W 10-4
15.01	Long Eaton United (a)	L 1-5
05.03	Leicester City Ladies (h)	W 9-0
19.03	Birmingham & West Midlands (a)	W 4-0
02.04	Birmingham & West Midlands (h)	W 1-0
09.04	Rotherham United (a)	W 9-1
23.04	Radcliffe Olympic (h)	W 3-2
26.04	Wolverhampton Wanderers (a)	L 2-3
04.05	Radcliffe Olympic (a)	L 1-3
07.05	The New Saints (a)	W 5-3
14.05	Sporting Khalsa (a)	W 2-1

2016/17 WPL CUP RESULTS

04.09	DR	Leicester City Ladies (h)*	W 9-3
	R1	Bye	
16.10	R2	The New Saints (h)	W 10-1
06.11	R3	Blackburn Rovers (a)	L 0-5

*Played at Saffron Lane, (Aylestone Park FC)

2016/17 FA CUP RESULTS

09.10	RQ3	Wolverhampton Wanderers (h)	L 2-3

2016/17 WPL MIDLANDS DIVISION ONE

	GD	Pts
1. Wolverhampton Wanderers	39	56 (P)
2. Loughborough Foxes	**80**	**54**
3. Sporting Khalsa	24	41
4. Radcliffe Olympic	22	40
5. Birmingham & West Midlands	14	40
6. The New Saints	21	39
7. Long Eaton United	9	30
8. Steel City Wanderers	-16	28
9. Solihull	-14	23
10. Leicester City Ladies	-61	17
11. Rotherham United	-25	16
12. Loughborough Students	-93	-1(R)

*Loughborough S docked 2 points

The club started out in Shepshed but was reformed and renamed as Loughborough Foxes in 1999 in memory of player Rachael Fox who died that year.

At that time the club only had a junior team but a ladies first team was added in 2006. They have been promoted five times in their 11-year history.

Foxes won the Leicestershire & Rutland County Cup in 2015/16 and again in 2016/17.

The club has an additional senior team which is nicknamed the Vixens to distinguish it from the first team.

LOUGHBOROUGH STUDENTS

EAST MIDS REGIONAL PREMIER (TIER 5)

Founded: Unknown
Nickname: The Scholars
Ground: Holywell Park, Loughborough University

SEASON 2016/17

WPL Midlands Division One: 12th (R)
WPL Cup: DR **WPL Plate: R2**
FA Cup: RQ3

2016/17 WPL MIDLANDS DIVISION ONE

15.09	Loughborough Foxes (a)	L 0-5
18.09	Long Eaton United (a)	L 1-13
25.09	Rotherham United (h)	L 3-4
06.10	Loughborough Foxes (h)	L 0-12
23.10	Solihull (a)	L 0-6
30.10	The New Saints (h)	L 0-6
06.11	Sporting Khalsa (h)	L 0-2
13.11	Rotherham United (a)	L 1-6
27.11	Long Eaton United (h)	L 1-4
04.12	The New Saints (a)	L 1-3
11.12	Steel City Wanderers (a)	L 1-6
08.01	Birmingham & WM (a)	L 0-5
29.01	Leicester City Ladies (a)	L 1-4
05.02	Radcliffe Olympic (a)	L 3-5
12.03	Leicester City Ladies (h)	L 2-4
19.03	Sporting Khalsa (a)	L 0-4
26.03	Wolverhampton Wanderers (a)	D 1-1
23.04	Birmingham & WM (h)	L 2-8
30.04	Solihull (h)	L 1-4
09.05	Radcliffe Olympic (h)	L 0-5
11.05	Wolverhampton Wanderers (h)	L 0-3
14.05	Steel City Wanderers (h)	L 1-2

2016/17 WPL CUP RESULTS

04.09	DR	Long Eaton United (a)	L 0-13

2016/17 WPL PLATE RESULTS

16.10	R2	Mossley Hill Athletic (a)	L 2-3

2016/17 FA CUP RESULTS

09.10	RQ3	Leek Town (h)*	L 1-3

*played at Loughborough University football stadium

2016/17 WPL MIDLANDS DIVISION ONE

	GD	Pts
1. Wolverhampton Wanderers	39	56
2. Loughborough Foxes	80	54
3. Sporting Khalsa	24	41
4. Radcliffe Olympic	22	40
5. Birmingham & West Midlands	14	40
6. The New Saints	21	39
7. Long Eaton United	9	30
8. Steel City Wanderers	-16	28
9. Solihull	-14	23
10. Leicester City Ladies	-61	17
11. Rotherham United	-25	16
12. Loughborough Students	**-93**	**-1* (R)**

*Loughborough Students docked 2 points

Loughborough Students' highest ever League finish came in 2014/15 when they were fifth in the WPL Midlands Division One, the fourth tier of English football.

The first team also competes in the BUCS Premier North, the highest level of University football.

England manager Mark Sampson named Loughborough alumni Siobhan Chamberlain, Jill Scott, Karen Carney, Jade Moore, Toni Duggan, Ellen White and Steph Houghton in his Euro 2017 squad.

LOWESTOFT TOWN

EASTERN REGION PREMIER (TIER 5)

Founded: 2011
Nickname: The Trawler Girls
Ground: Crown Meadow, (Lowestoft Town men's)

SEASON 2016/17

WPL South East Division One: 12th (R)
WPL Cup: DR **WPL Plate: R2**
FA Cup: RQ4

2016/17 WPL SOUTH EAST DIVISION ONE

21.08	Norwich City (h)	L 1-5
28.08	Cambridge United (a)	L 0-2
11.09	Luton Town (a)	L 1-4
14.09	Ipswich Town (h)	L 2-3
18.09	Enfield Town (h)	W 3-0
25.09	AFC Wimbledon (h)	L 3-4
02.10	Gillingham (a)	L 1-5
05.10	Ipswich Town (a)	L 2-3
30.10	Actonians (a)	L 0-3
11.12	Milton Keynes Dons (h)	L 2-6
18.12	Actonians (h)	L 0-7
29.01	Denham United (h)	L 2-5
12.02	Stevenage (a)	W 1-0
26.02	Stevenage (h)	L 0-1
12.03	Gillingham (h)	L 0-4
19.03	Denham United (a)	L 0-5
26.03	Milton Keynes Dons (a)	L 0-1
09.04	Cambridge United (h)	L 0-2
30.04	AFC Wimbledon (a)	L 0-10
07.05	Luton Town (h)	L 0-3
14.05	Enfield Town (a)	L 1-5
17.05	Norwich City (a)	L 2-4

2016/17 WPL CUP RESULTS

04.09	DR	Portsmouth (a)	L 2-8

2016/17 WPL PLATE RESULTS

23.10	R2	QPR (h)	L 2-4

2016/17 FA CUP RESULTS

09.10	RQ3	Enfield Town (h)	W 2-0
20.11	RQ4	Norwich City (a)	D 3-3 (L 3-4p)

2016/17 WPL SE DIVISION ONE

	GD	Pts
1. Gillingham	90	57 (P)
2. Milton Keynes Dons	42	49
3. AFC Wimbledon	29	44
4. Cambridge United	20	41
5. Luton Town	5	37
6. Actonians	14	36
7. Enfield Town	-20	25
8. Denham United	-21	25
9. Ipswich Town	-22	25
10. Norwich City	-50	16
11. Stevenage	-26	15
12. Lowestoft Town	**-61**	**6 (R)**

The original Lowestoft Town Ladies club was founded in the 1960s and won the 1982 FA Cup, beating Cleveland Spartans 2-0 in the final at Loftus Road. They folded shortly after that and the current club was formed in 2011.

Hannah Waters was the club's top scorer in 2016/17 with 10 goals in 21 appearances in all competitions.

Lowestoft endured a difficult 2016/17 campaign in the WPL South East Division One. They won just two of their matches, beating Enfield 3-0 at home in September and Stevenage 1-0 away in February. Their other 20 games resulted in defeats as they finished bottom of the table and were relegated.

Lowestoft reached the Suffolk FA Women's Cup final in 2017 but were beaten 5-0 by Ipswich at Colchester United FC, Weston Homes Community Stadium. It was the second time they had reached the final of the competition, losing 6-1 to Ipswich in 2013.

LUTON TOWN

WPL SOUTH EAST DIVISION ONE (TIER 4)

Founded: 1997
Nickname: Lady Hatters
Ground: Stockwood Park Athletics Centre

SEASON 2016/17

WPL South East Division One: 5th
WPL Cup: DR WPL Plate: QF
FA Cup: R1

2016/17 WPL SOUTH EAST DIVISION ONE

21.08	Gillingham (h)	D 1-1
28.08	Actonians (a)	W 1-0
11.09	Lowestoft Town (h)	W 4-1
18.09	Cambridge United (a)	L 1-3
28.09	Milton Keynes Dons (h) *	W 2-1
02.10	Enfield Town (a)	W 5-0
05.10	Milton Keynes Dons (a)	L 1-5
30.10	Denham United (a)	L 0-1
20.11	AFC Wimbledon (a)	W 4-2
27.11	Stevenage (a)	D 1-1
08.01	Denham United (h)	W 3-2
29.01	Enfield Town (h)	L 1-2
12.02	Gillingham (a)	L 1-10
26.02	Norwich City (h)	W 3-1
12.03	Ipswich Town (a)	W 1-0
26.03	AFC Wimbledon (h)	D 1-1
09.04	Actonians (h)	L 1-3
23.04	Ipswich Town (h)	W 5-1
30.04	Cambridge United (h)	W 4-2
07.05	Lowestoft Town (a)	W 3-0
14.05	Stevenage (h)	D 0-0
21.05	Norwich City (a)	L 1-2

*Played at Kenilworth Road, (Luton Town FC)

2016/17 WPL CUP RESULTS

04.09	DR	Milton Keynes Dons (h)	L 1-3

2016/17 WPL PLATE RESULTS

16.10	R2	Plymouth Argyle (a)	W 4-2
06.11	R3	Stevenage (a)	W 2-0
18.12	QF	Lewes (h)	L 0-6

2016/17 FA CUP RESULTS

09.10	RQ3	AFC Sudbury (a)	W 3-2
13.11	RQ4	Oxford City (h)	W 6-1
04.12	R1	Portsmouth (h)	L 1-4

2016/17 WPL SOUTH EAST DIVISION ONE

	GD	Pts
1. Gillingham	90	57 (P)
2. Milton Keynes Dons	42	49
3. AFC Wimbledon	29	44
4. Cambridge United	20	41
5. Luton Town	**5**	**37**
6. Actonians	14	36
7. Enfield Town	-20	25
8. Denham United	-21	25
9. Ipswich Town	-22	25
10. Norwich City	-50	16
11. Stevenage	-26	15
12. Lowestoft Town	-61	6 (R)

Luton Town Ladies formed a partnership with Luton Town men's in 2000.

Joanne Rutherford was Luton's top scorer in 2016/17 with 11 goals in 26 appearances in all competitions.

In the past, Luton have played at The Carlsberg Stadium, home of Biggleswade Town. In 2016/17 their home matches were played at Stockwood Park Athletics Centre with the exception of the home League match against Milton Keynes Dons which took place at Kenilworth Road and ended in a 2-1 win.

MAIDENHEAD UNITED

WPL SW DIVISION ONE (TIER 4)

Founded: 2013
Nickname: The Magpies
Ground: York Road, (Maidenhead United FC)

SEASON 2016/17

WPL South West Division One: 7th
WPL Cup: DR **WPL Plate: R2**
FA Cup: RQ3

2016/17 WPL SOUTH WEST DIVISION ONE

28.08	Chichester City (h)	L 1-4
11.09	Brislington (a)	L 2-5
14.09	Basingstoke Town (h)	W 2-1
18.09	Keynsham Town (a)	L 1-2
02.10	Cheltenham Town (h)	W 2-1
05.10	Basingstoke Town (a)	D 2-2
30.10	Plymouth Argyle (h)	L 0-8
06.11	Larkhall Athletic (a)	L 1-5
13.11	Cheltenham Town (a)	L 2-3
12.02	Chichester City (a)	L 0-3
26.02	Larkhall Athletic (h)	L 0-1
12.03	Southampton Saints (a)	L 2-4
19.03	Plymouth Argyle (a)	L 0-6
26.03	*Shanklin (h)*	*W 1-0 (ex)*
02.04	Southampton Saints (h)	D 1-1
09.04	St Nicholas (a)	W 2-1
23.04	Keynsham Town (h)	L 1-2
07.05	Brislington (h)	L 4-5
10.05	St Nicholas (h)	W 2-0
14.05	Exeter City (a)	W 1-0
21.05	Exeter City (h)	P-P

(ex) Shanklin withdrew from League: result expunged

2016/17 WPL CUP RESULTS

04.09	DR	Coventry United (a)	L 0-9

2016/17 WPL PLATE RESULTS

16.10	R2	Lewes (a)	L w/o

2016/17 FA CUP RESULTS

09.10	RQ3	Gillingham (a)	L 0-4

2016/17 WPL SOUTH WEST DIVISION ONE

	GD	Pts
1. Chichester City	92	58 (P)
2. Plymouth Argyle	85	54
3. Southampton Saints	20	41
4. Keynsham Town	39	38
5. Larkhall Athletic	3	36
6. Brislington	-19	22
7. Maidenhead United	**-28**	**16***
8. St Nicholas	-43	15
9. Basingstoke Town	-28	14
10. Cheltenham Town	-49	13
11. Exeter City	-72	4 (R)

*Maidenhead docked 1 point

NB: Shanklin withdrew from League, all results expunged

Maidenhead United Ladies play at the home ground of Maidenhead United men's team – York Road. The stadium is the oldest continuously used football ground in the country.

Their first ever match was a friendly against Reading Women. Around 100 fans attended the fixture at York Road in the summer of 2013.

Rachel Panting was the club's top scorer in 2016/17, hitting 10 goals in 22 appearances in all competitions.

MIDDLESBROUGH

WPL NORTHERN DIVISION (TIER 3)

Founded: 1976 (as Cleveland Spartans)
Nickname: Boro
Ground: Teesdale Park, (Thornaby FC)

SEASON 2016/17

WPL Northern Division: 2nd
WPL Cup: R2
FA Cup: R2

2016/17 WPL NORTHERN DIVISION

21.08	West Bromwich Albion (h)	W 6-0
28.08	Bradford City (a)	W 2-0
11.09	Leicester City Women (h)	L 0-3
13.09	Newcastle United (h)	W 7-1
18.09	Nottingham Forest (h)	L 0-1
04.10	Newcastle United (a)	W 6-1
09.10	Stoke City (h)	D 1-1
23.10	Derby County (h)	W 3-2
30.10	Huddersfield Town (a)	W 2-1
06.11	Fylde (h)	W 3-1
20.11	Blackburn Rovers (h)	L 1-2
27.11	Derby County (a)	W 3-2
11.12	Nottingham Forest (a)	W 8-3
18.12	Stoke City (a)	L 1-5
12.02	Blackburn Rovers (a)	L 1-5
19.02	Bradford City (h)	W 2-1
26.02	West Bromwich Albion (a)	W 4-0
26.03	Leicester City Women (a)	W 3-0
09.04	Huddersfield Town (h)	W 4-2
14.05	Fylde (a)	W 3-0

2016/17 WPL CUP RESULTS

04.09	DR	Morecambe (a)	W 3-0
	R1	Bye	
16.10	R2	Hull City (a)	L 1-3

2016/17 FA CUP RESULTS

04.12	R1	Hartlepool United (h)	W 1-0
08.01	R2	Leicester City Women (h)	L 1-2 (aet)

2016/17 WPL NORTHERN DIVISION

	GD	Pts
1. Blackburn Rovers	39	54
2. Middlesbrough	**29**	**43**
3. Leicester City Women	7	34
4. Stoke City	6	30
5. Derby County	4	29
6. West Bromwich Albion	-4	27*
7. Fylde	6	26
8. Bradford City	0	22
9. Huddersfield Town	-16	20
10. Nottingham Forest	-22	18
11. Newcastle United	-49	7 (R)

*Fylde docked 3 points (ineligible player)

In their early days as Cleveland Spartans the team was coached by Middlesbrough men's players Mark Proctor and David Hodgson.

Middlesbrough's longest-serving manager was former central midfielder Marrie Wieczorek who remained in charge for 20 years.

In autumn 2015, Middlesbrough forward Bianca Owens twice achieved the feat of scoring 8 goals in one game, doing so in an 11-0 win against Lowick United in the FA Cup third qualifying round on 11 October and again in the 10-2 League victory against Stockport County on 15 November.

MILTON KEYNES DONS

WPL SOUTH EAST DIVISION ONE (TIER 4)

Founded: 2009
Nickname: The Dons
Ground: Willen Road, (Newport Pagnell Town FC)

SEASON 2016/17

WPL South East Division One: 2nd
WPL Cup: R2
FA Cup: R2

2016/17 WPL SOUTH EAST DIVISION ONE

21.08	Denham United (a)	W 3-0
28.08	Gillingham (a)	L 1-3
11.09	AFC Wimbledon (h)	L 0-2
25.09	Actonians (h)	W 4-1
28.09	Luton Town (a)	L 1-2
02.10	Ipswich Town (h)	W 5-3
05.10	Luton Town (h)	W 5-1
30.10	Stevenage (a)	W 4-0
06.11	Denham United (h)	W 7-0
27.11	Actonians (a)	D 1-1
11.12	Lowestoft Town (a)	W 6-2
18.12	Stevenage (h)	W 2-0
29.01	Norwich City (h)	W 7-0
05.02	Ipswich Town (a)	W 4-1
26.02	Enfield Town (h)	W 1-0
12.03	AFC Wimbledon (a)	L 0-1
26.03	Lowestoft Town (h)	W 1-0
09.04	Gillingham (h)	L 1-2
23.04	Norwich City (a)	W 2-0
07.05	Enfield Town (a)	W 2-1
09.05	Cambridge United (h)*	W 4-1
14.05	Cambridge United (a)	W 2-0

*Played at Stadium MK, (Milton Keynes Dons FC)

2016/17 WPL CUP RESULTS

04.09	DR	Luton Town (a)	W 3-1
	R1	Bye	
23.10	R2	Gillingham (a)	L 0-2

2016/17 FA CUP RESULTS

09.10	RQ3	Actonians (h)	W 4-0
13.11	RQ4	QPR Development (a)	W 6-1
04.12	R1	Hemel Hempstead Town (h)	W 3-1
08.01	R2	Coventry United (a)	L 0-4

2016/17 WPL SOUTH EAST DIVISION ONE

	GD	Pts
1. Gillingham	90	57 (P)
2. Milton Keynes Dons	**42**	**49**
3. AFC Wimbledon	29	44
4. Cambridge United	20	41
5. Luton Town	5	37
6. Actonians	14	36
7. Enfield Town	-20	25
8. Denham United	-21	25
9. Ipswich Town	-22	25
10. Norwich City	-50	16
11. Stevenage	-26	15
12. Lowestoft Town	-61	6 (R)

Milton Keynes Dons had an erratic start to the 2016/17 League campaign, winning just two of their opening five fixtures. A 5-3 victory at home to Ipswich then kick-started a 10-game run in which they dropped just two points and catapulted them on their way towards runners-up position in the WPL South East One.

They lost just two home games in the League all season, going down 2-0 to AFC Wimbledon in September and 2-1 to eventual champions Gillingham in April.

Heather McDonnell and Hannah Barrett were joint top scorers for the club in 2016/17 with 19 goals apiece.

MORECAMBE

WPL NORTHERN DIVISION ONE (TIER 4)

Founded: 2005
Nickname: The Seagals
Ground: Lancaster & Morecambe College

SEASON 2016/17

WPL Northern Division One: 7th
WPL Cup: DR **WPL Plate: R2**
FA Cup: R3Q

2016/17 WPL NORTHERN DIVISION ONE

21.08	Brighouse Town (a)	W 3-0
28.08	Crewe Alexandra (h)	W 5-1
11.09	Guiseley Vixens (a)	L 0-7
18.09	Mossley Hill Athletic (h)	W 6-1
02.10	Liverpool Feds (a)	L 0-3
30.10	Chorley (a)	L 1-2
06.11	Brighouse Town (h)	D 1-1
04.12	Chester-le-Street Town (h)	W 5-1
11.12	Blackpool Wren Rovers (a)	L 2-3
08.01	Tranmere Rovers (a)	W 1-0
22.01	Chorley (h)	D 1-1
29.01	Tranmere Rovers (h)	W 3-1
05.02	Mossley Hill Athletic (a)	W 5-2
12.02	Crewe Alexandra (a)	L 0-3
19.02	Guiseley Vixens (h)	L 2-5
26.02	Blackpool Wren Rovers (h)	W 3-0
05.03	Leeds United (h)	W 7-4
12.03	Hull City (h)	L 1-2
09.04	Liverpool Feds (h)	L 0-4
23.04	Hull City (a)	L 1-2
07.05	Leeds United (a)	W 2-1
14.05	Chester-le-Street Town (a)	L 2-6

2016/17 WPL CUP RESULTS

04.09	DR	Middlesbrough (h)	L 0-3

2016/17 WPL PLATE RESULTS

23.10	R2	Chorley (h)	L 0-5

2016/17 FA CUP RESULTS

09.10	R3Q	Crewe Alexandra (a)	D 3-3 (L 2-4p)

2016/17 WPL NORTHERN DIVISION ONE

	GD	Pts
1. Guiseley Vixens	52	59 (P)
2. Liverpool Feds	37	44
3. Hull City	16	43
4. Chester-le-Street Town	16	41
5. Chorley	7	38
6. Brighouse Town	16	37
7. Morecambe	**1**	**29***
8. Leeds United	-8	23
9. Mossley Hill Athletic	-27	19
10. Crewe Alexandra	-28	18
11. Blackpool Wren Rovers	-31	18 (R)
12. Tranmere Rovers	-51	7 (R)

*Morecambe docked 3 points (unregistered player)

Morecambe were promoted from the North West Regional League Premier Division as champions in time for the first season of the WPL Northern Division One in 2014/15 and have been at that level (tier 4) ever since.

Their pitch at Lancaster & Morecambe College is of FA-approved 3G quality.

Morecambe have had two cup successes over the years, winning the North West Regional League Cup in 2013/14 and the Lancashire County Cup in 2009/10.

Morecambe were docked three points in the 2016/17 League campaign when an administrative error led to them technically fielding an ineligible player for the final five minutes of their 5-1 home win over Crewe on 28 August.

MOSSLEY HILL ATHLETIC

WPL NORTHERN DIVISION ONE (TIER 4)

Founded: 2005
Nickname: Maroons
Ground: Mossley Hill Athletic Club

SEASON 2016/17

WPL Northern Division One: 9th
WPL Cup: DR **WPL Plate: R3**
FA Cup: RQ3

2016/17 WPL NORTHERN DIVISION ONE

11.09	Leeds United (a)	L 1-7
14.09	Liverpool Feds (h)*	L 0-6
18.09	Morecambe (a)	L 1-6
25.09	Hull City (h)	L 1-5
02.10	Crewe Alexandra (h)	L 4-5
04.10	Liverpool Feds (a)	L 0-1
30.10	Guiseley Vixens (a)	L 2-3
13.11	Chester-le-Street Town (a)	L 2-4
27.11	Brighouse Town (h)	L 1-2
04.12	Tranmere Rovers (h)	W 5-2
11.12	Chorley (h)	L 4-6
18.12	Crewe Alexandra (a)	D 1-1
08.01	Leeds United (h)	L 2-5
15.01	Tranmere Rovers (a)	W 4-0
05.02	Morecambe (h)	L 2-5
12.02	Chorley (a)	W 2-1
19.02	Brighouse Town (a)	L 0-4
12.03	Blackpool Wren Rovers (h)	W 5-3
19.03	Chester-le-Street Town (h)	L 1-2
02.04	Guiseley Vixens (h)	L 0-2
30.04	Blackpool Wren Rovers (a)	W 4-2
14.05	Hull City (a)	W 3-0

*Played at JMO Sports Club

2016/17 WPL CUP RESULTS

Date	Round	Opponent	Result
04.09	DR	Brighouse Town (h)	L 0-5

2016/17 WPL PLATE RESULTS

Date	Round	Opponent	Result
16.10	R2	Loughborough Students (h)	W 3-2
06.11	R3	Tranmere Rovers (h)	L 1-2

2016/17 FA CUP RESULTS

Date	Round	Opponent	Result
09.10	RQ3	Liverpool Feds (h)	L 0-4

2016/17 WPL NORTHERN DIVISION ONE

	GD	Pts
1. Guiseley Vixens	52	59 (P)
2. Liverpool Feds	37	44
3. Hull City	16	43
4. Chester-le-Street Town	16	41
5. Chorley	7	38
6. Brighouse Town	16	37
7. Morecambe	1	29*
8. Leeds United	-8	23
9. Mossley Hill Athletic	**-27**	**19**
10. Crewe Alexandra	-28	18
11. Blackpool Wren Rovers	-31	18 (R)
12. Tranmere Rovers	-51	7 (R)

*Morecambe docked 3 points (unregistered player)

The most famous player to come through the youth ranks at Mossley Hill Athletic is Barcelona and England winger Toni Duggan.

Mossley Hill Athletics club was formed in 1924 with men's football among its sports section. Girls' football was introduced in the late 1990s and then a ladies team was created ahead of the 2005/06 season.

The furthest Mossley Hill Athletic have progressed in the FA Cup is the last 16.

In 2016/17 Mossley Hill Athletic won the Liverpool County FA Senior Cup for the fifth time. They were Lancashire County FA First Division Champions in 2005/06, North West League Division 1 North Champions in 2006/07 and North West Premier Division Champions in 2009/10.

NEWCASTLE UNITED

WPL NORTHERN DIVISION ONE (TIER 4)

Founded: 1989
Nickname: The Lady Magpies
Ground: Newcastle United Sport Ground 3G in 2016/17, Newcastle University in 2017/18

SEASON 2016/17

WPL Northern Division: 11th (R)
WPL Cup: R2
FA Cup: R2

2016/17 WPL NORTHERN DIVISION

21.08	Nottingham Forest (h)+	L 0-1
11.09	Stoke City (a)	L 1-2
13.09	Middlesbrough (a)	L 1-7
18.09	Huddersfield Town (h)+	W 6-2
25.09	Fylde (h)	L 1-5
02.10	Blackburn Rovers (h)	L 0-1
04.10	Middlesbrough (h)	L 1-6+
30.10	Leicester City Women (h)	W 1-0
13.11	West Bromwich Albion (a)	L 1-2
27.11	Nottingham Forest (a)	L 1-5
11.12	Bradford City (a)	D 0-0
18.12	West Bromwich Albion (h)	L 0-5
15.01	Bradford City (h)+	L 1-5
12.02	Huddersfield Town (a)	L 0-2
19.02	Blackburn Rovers (a)	L 0-3
05.03	Derby County (a)	L 0-2
26.03	Fylde (a)	L 0-3
09.04	Stoke City (h)*	L 1-4
23.04	Derby County (h)	L 1-4
14.05	Leicester City Women (a)	L 0-6

2016/17 WPL CUP RESULTS

04.09	DR	Leicester City Women (h)	W 2-1 (aet)
	R1	Bye	
23.10	R2	Blackburn Rovers (h)+	L 0-1

2016/17 FA CUP RESULTS

04.12	R1	RACA Tynedale (a)	W 3-0
08.01	R2	Liverpool Feds (a)	L 0-1

*played at Morpeth Town

+played at Sport Northumbria

2016/17 WPL NORTHERN DIVISION

	GD	Pts
1. Blackburn Rovers	39	54
2. Middlesbrough	29	43
3. Leicester City Women	7	34
4. Stoke City	6	30
5. Derby County	4	29
6. West Bromwich Albion	-4	27
7. Fylde	6	26*
8. Bradford City	0	22
9. Huddersfield Town	-16	20
10. Nottingham Forest	-22	18
11. Newcastle United	**-49**	**7 (R)**

*Fylde docked 3 points for (ineligible player)

Newcastle United Women formed a partnership with the men's Newcastle United FC in 2016.

In 1996 the club played a Manchester United women's team at Wembley before the men's Community Shield match (then known as the Charity Shield) between the same two clubs.

The Lady Magpies reached the FA Cup quarter-finals for the first time in

2006/07 where they lost to Liverpool 9-8 on penalties after a 2-2 draw.

NORWICH CITY

WPL SOUTH EAST DIVISION ONE (TIER 4)

Founded: 1998
Nickname: The Canaries
Ground: Plantation Park, (Norwich United FC)

SEASON 2016/17

WPL South East Division One: 10th
WPL Cup: R1
FA Cup: R1

2016/17 WPL SOUTH EAST DIVISION ONE

21.08	Lowestoft Town (a)	W 5-1
11.09	Cambridge United (h)	L 1-3
18.09	AFC Wimbledon (a)	L 0-3
02.10	Actonians (a)	L 4-5
30.10	Enfield Town (a)	L 1-2
11.12	AFC Wimbledon (h)	D 1-1
18.12	Enfield Town (h)	D 2-2
08.01	Stevenage (a)	L 0-1
29.01	Milton Keynes Dons (a)	L 0-7
19.02	Gillingham (h)	L 0-9
26.02	Luton Town (a)	L 1-3
26.03	Ipswich Town (h)	D 1-1
02.04	Denham United (h)	L 0-2
09.04	Stevenage (h)	D 0-0
16.04	Cambridge United (a)	L 4-5
23.04	Milton Keynes Dons (h)	L 0-2
30.04	Gillingham (a)	L 0-13
02.05	Ipswich Town (a)	L 1-5
07.05	Denham United (a)	W 4-2
14.05	Actonians (h)	L 0-11
17.05	Lowestoft Town (h)	W 4-2
21.05	Luton Town (h)	W 2-1

2016/17 WPL CUP RESULTS

04.09	DR	QPR (a)	W 3-2
25.09	R1	Gillingham (a)	L 2-8

2016/17 FA CUP RESULTS

09.10	RQ3	Riverside Rovers (h)	W 10-0
20.11	RQ4	Lowestoft Town (h)	D 3-3
			(W 4-3p)
04.12	R1	AFC Wimbledon (h)	L 1-4

2016/17 WPL SOUTH EAST DIVISION ONE

	GD	Pts
1. Gillingham	90	57 (P)
2. Milton Keynes Dons	42	49
3. AFC Wimbledon	29	44
4. Cambridge United	20	41
5. Luton Town	5	37
6. Actonians	14	36
7. Enfield Town	-20	25
8. Denham United	-21	25
9. Ipswich Town	-22	25
10. Norwich City	**-50**	**16**
11. Stevenage	-26	15
12. Lowestoft Town	-61	6 (R)

Norwich City Ladies officially has a partnership with men's professional club Norwich City. However, they groundshare with non-League team Norwich United at Plantation Park.

The club proudly claims that 90% of its players have progressed through its youth ranks.

The Canaries are previous winners of the South East Combination League Cup and Norfolk County Cup. They won the FA WPL Respect Award Club of the Year for 2015/16.

Norwich are three-time winners of the Suffolk FA Cup. They beat Ipswich on penalties in the 2007 final, were 5-0 winners over West Lynn in 2009 and defeated Ipswich 1-0 in 2010. They have also been runners-up seven times.

NOTTINGHAM FOREST

WPL NORTHERN DIVISION (TIER 3)

Founded: 1990
Nickname: The Reds
Ground: Mill Street, (Basford United FC)

SEASON 2016/17

WPL Northern Division: 10th
WPL Cup: R1
FA Cup: R4

2016/17 WPL NORTHERN DIVISION

21.08	Newcastle United (a)	W 1-0
28.08	Derby County (h)	L 0-2
18.09	Middlesbrough (a)	W 1-0
02.10	Huddersfield Town (h)	L 2-5
05.10	Stoke City (a)	D 1-1
09.10	Blackburn Rovers (a)	L 1-4
16.10	West Bromwich Albion (a)	L 0-2
23.10	Bradford City (a)	L 0-6
27.10	Stoke City (h)	L 1-5
13.11	Huddersfield Town (a)	D 3-3
27.11	Newcastle United (h)	W 5-1
11.12	Middlesbrough (h)	L 3-8
29.01	Blackburn Rovers (h)	L 1-2
12.02	Leicester City Women (h)	D 2-2
12.03	Fylde (a)	L 0-1
19.03	Bradford City (h)	W 2-1
09.04	Leicester City Women (a)	L 1-2
23.04	Fylde (h)	W 1-0
07.05	West Bromwich Albion (h)	L 1-2
14.05	Derby County (a)	L 1-2

2016/17 WPL CUP RESULTS

04.09	DR	Chorley (h)	W 3-1 (aet)
25.09	R1	Blackburn Rovers (a)	L 1-3

2016/17 FA CUP RESULTS

04.12	R1	Guiseley Vivens (a)	W 1-0
08.01	R2	Wolverhampton W.(h)	W 4-0
05.02	R3	Derby County (a)	W 1-0
19.02	R4	Millwall (a)	L 1-3

2016/17 WPL NORTHERN DIVISION

	GD	Pts
1. Blackburn Rovers	39	54
2. Middlesbrough	29	43
3. Leicester City Women	7	34
4. Stoke City	6	30
5. Derby County	4	29
6. West Bromwich Albion	-4	27
7. Fylde	6	26*
8. Bradford City	0	22
9. Huddersfield Town	-16	20
10. Nottingham Forest	**-22**	**18**
11. Newcastle United	-49	7 (R)

*Fylde docked 3points (ineligible player)

Forest reached the WPL Cup final in 2010/11 but had to settle for the runners-up spot after losing on penalties to Barnet.

When the club was founded in 1990 they advertised for players in the men's official matchday programme against Everton.

Forest were among the teams who applied to join the WSL2 for the first season of competition at that level in 2014, but they were unsuccessful.

PLYMOUTH ARGYLE

WPL SW DIVISION ONE (TIER 4)

Founded: 1975 (as Plymouth Pilgrims)
Nickname: The Pilgrims
Ground: Haye Road, (Elburton Villa FC)

SEASON 2016/17

WPL South West Division One: 2nd
WPL Cup: DR **WPL Plate: R2**
FA Cup: R2

2016/17 WPL SOUTH WEST DIVISION ONE

21.08	*Shanklin (a)*	*W 6-1 (ex)*
18.09	Cheltenham Town (a)	W 5-2
22.09	Exeter City (h)	W 4-1
25.09	St Nicholas (h)	W 4-1
02.10	Brislington (h)	W 5-1
05.10	Exeter City (a)	W 6-0
23.10	Chichester City (h)	L 4-5
30.10	Maidenhead United (a)	W 8-0
18.12	St Nicholas (a)	W 4-1
12.02	Larkhall Athletic (a)	W 4-0
19.02	Keynsham Town (h)	W 5-2
19.03	Maidenhead United (h)++	W 6-0
26.03	Basingstoke Town (h)	W 4-1
09.04	Chichester City (a)	L 0-3
16.04	Southampton Saints (h)	W 1-0+
16.04	Southampton Saints (a)	W 3-0+
23.04	Brislington (a)	W 8-0
30.04	Larkhall Athletic (h)	W 7-1
07.05	Keynshham Town (a)	W 3-1
09.05	Cheltenham Town (h)*	W 17-0
21.05	Basingstoke Town (a)	W 6-0

(ex) Shanklin withdrew from League: result expunged

+Matches played over 60 minutes on same day

*Played at The Tannery, (Street FC)

++Played at Mill Marsh Park, (Bovey Tracey)

2016/17 WPL CUP RESULTS

04.09	DR	AFC Wimbledon (a)	L 2-3

2016/17 WPL PLATE RESULTS

16.10	R2	Luton Town (h)**	L 2-4

**Played at University of St Mark & St John

2016/17 FA CUP RESULTS

09.10	RQ3	Ilminster Town (a)	W 4-0
20.11	RQ4	Basingstoke Town (h)	W 3-1
04.12	R1	Forest Green Rovers (h)	W w/o
08.01	R2	AFC Wimbledon (h)	L 0-3

2016/17 WPL SOUTH WEST DIVISION ONE

	GD	Pts
1. Chichester City	92	58 (P)
2. Plymouth Argyle	**85**	**54**
3. Southampton Saints	20	41
4. Keynsham Town	39	38
5. Larkhall Athletic	3	36
6. Brislington	-19	22
7. Maidenhead United	-28	16*
8. St Nicholas	-43	15
9. Basingstoke Town	-28	14
10. Cheltenham Town	-49	13
11. Exeter City	-72	4 (R)

*Maidenhead docked 1 point

NB: Shanklin withdrew from League, all results expunged

Following a five-a-side competition at the Mayflower Leisure Centre, two teams joined forces in 1975 to create an 11-a-side team called Plymouth Pilgrims.

With the team at the time playing their home matches at Saltash United's Kimberly Stadium, they changed their name to Saltash Pilgrims in the late 1990s. In 2001/02 they were invited to compete as part of the men's professional club, Plymouth Argyle, and changed their name to the same.

POOLE TOWN

WPL SW DIVISION ONE (TIER 4)

Founded: 1980s
Nickname: Dolphins
Ground: Stanley Green Road in 2016/17, moving to Milborne St Andrew for 2017/18

SEASON 2016/17

SW Regional Premier: 3rd (P)
FA Cup: RQ4

2016/17 SW REGIONAL PREMIER

04.09	Middlezoy Rovers (h)	W 3-1
11.09	Torquay United (a)	D 0-0
25.09	Bishops Lydeard (a)	L 0-1
02.10	Charlestown (h)	W 1-0
23.10	Frome Town (h)	W 6-0
30.10	Marine Academy Plymouth (a)	L 0-7
11.12	Torquay United (h)	L 0-1
08.01	Yeovil Town Intermediate (h)	D 2-2
22.01	Charlestown (a)	W 4-1
05.02	Downend Flyers (h)	D 2-2
12.02	Frome Town (a)	W 8-0
12.03	Bishops Lydeard (h)	W 3-2
26.03	Middlezoy Rovers (a)	W 3-1
02.04	Keynsham Town Development (a)	W 4-0
09.04	Yeovil Town Intermediate (a)	L 1-5
23.04	Keynsham Town Development (h)	W 4-0
30.04	Marine Academy Plymouth (h)	Ww/o
07.05	Downend Flyers (a)	W 3-0

2016/17 FA CUP RESULTS

18.09	RQ2	Warsash Wasps (a)	W 2-1
09.10	RQ3	AEK Boco (h)	W 3-0
13.11	RQ4	Brislington (a)	L 0-8

2016/17 SW REGIONAL PREMIER

	GD	Pts
1. Yeovil Town Intermediate	43	45
2. Marine Academy Plymouth	45	40
3. Poole Town	**21**	**36 (P)**
4. Bishops Lydeard	13	35
5. Torquay United	10	31
6. Downend Flyers	-4	19
7. Middlezoy Rovers	-14	17*
8. Charlestown	-23	16
9. Keysnham Town Development	-16	15
10. Frome Town	-75	6

*Middlezoy Rovers awarded 3 points for abandoned game against Downend Flyers

Back-to-back promotions have carried Poole Town into WPL South West Division One (Tier 4) for the 2017/18 season.

Poole finished third in the South West Regional Division in 2016/17 but they were promoted because champions Yeovil Town Intermediate were not eligible to go up and Marine Academy Plymouth decided to continue competing at their current level.

The Dolphins are reigning Dorset County Cup champions and have won it for the last four seasons in a row.

PORTSMOUTH

WPL SOUTHERN DIVISION (TIER 3)

Founded: 1987
Nickname: Pompey
Ground: Privett Park, (Gosport Borough FC) in 2016/17. Westleigh Park, (Havant & Waterlooville FC) in 2017/18

SEASON 2016/17

WPL Southern Division: 8th
WPL Cup: R3
FA Cup: R2

WPL SOUTHERN DIVISION RESULTS

21.08	C&K Basildon (a)	L 0-2
28.08	West Ham United (h)	W 3-1
11.09	Swindon Town (a)	L 3-4
14.09	Lewes (h)	W 4-3
18.09	Coventry United (a)	L 1-8
05.10	Lewes (a)	W 2-1
09.10	C&K Basildon (h)	L 1-3
30.10	QPR (a)	D 1-1
13.11	Swindon Town (h)	W 5-0
27.11	Charlton Athletic (a)	L 2-4
18.12	Tottenham Hotspur (a)	L 0-4
05.02	Cardiff City (a)	L 0-5
12.02	West Ham United (a)	D 1-1
26.03	Cardiff City (h)	L 1-5
02.04	Charlton Athletic (h)	L 0-3
09.04	Tottenham Hotspur (h)	L 1-4
16.04	Crystal Palace (h)	L 2-5
30.04	Crystal Palace (a)+	L 0-7
07.05	QPR (h)*	W 3-2
14.05	Coventry United (h)	L 1-3

+Played at Palmerston Drive, (Fareham Town FC)

*Played at Fratton Park, (Portsmouth FC)

2016/17 WPL CUP RESULTS

04.09	DR	Lowestoft Town (h)	W 8-2
	R1	Bye	
23.10	R2	Cambridge United (h)	W 3-2
06.11	R3	Charlton Athletic (a)	L 2-4

2016/17 FA CUP RESULTS

04.12	R1	Luton Town (a)	W 4-1
08.01	R2	Charlton Athletic (a)	L 0-5

2016/17 WPL SOUTHERN DIVISION

	GD	Pts
1. Tottenham Hotspur	45	52 (P)
2. Coventry United	40	48
3. Cardiff City	53	44
4. Charlton Athletic	30	42
5. Crystal Palace	25	33
6. C&K Basildon	-13	27
7. Lewes	-5	25
8. Portsmouth	**-35**	**17**
9. West Ham United	-47	9
10. Swindon Town	-40	8
11. QPR	-53	8

Portsmouth have twice won the WPL Southern Division, doing so in 2011/12 and 2014/15.

Their first silverware arrived in 2002/03 when they won the South West Combination League and South West Combination League Cup.

In 2014/15, Ini Umotong became the first Portsmouth player to be capped at senior level when she made her debut for Nigeria in a 2-2 draw with Mali.

QUEENS PARK RANGERS

WPL SOUTHERN DIVISION (TIER 3)

Founded: 2001
Nickname: Rangers
Ground: Honeycroft, (Uxbridge FC)

SEASON 2016/17

WPL Southern Division: 11th
WPL Cup: DR WPL Plate: R3
FA Cup: R1

2016/17 WPL SOUTHERN DIVISION

28.08	Crystal Palace (h)	L 0-1
11.09	C&K Basildon (a)	L 0-4
14.09	Tottenham Hotspur (h)	L 0-4
02.10	Cardiff City (h)	L 1-4
05.10	Tottenham Hotspur (a)	L 0-3
09.10	Coventry United (a)	L 0-5
16.10	Swindon Town (h)	L 0-7
30.10	Portsmouth (h)	D 1-1
13.11	Charlton Athletic (a)	L 0-2
27.11	West Ham United (h)	D 1-1
18.12	West Ham United (a)	W 2-1
29.01	Crystal Palace (a)	L 0-1
12.02	Coventry United (h)	L 0-2
19.02	Lewes (h)	L 0-2
26.02	Charlton Athletic (h)	L 0-6
19.03	Lewes (a)	L 0-1
23.04	Cardiff City (a)	L 1-12
30.04	C&K Basildon (h)	L 1-4
07.05	Portsmouth (a)	L 2-3
14.05	Swindon Town (a)	W 2-0

2016/17 WPL CUP RESULTS

04.09	DR	Norwich City (h)	L 2-3

2016/17 WPL PLATE RESULTS

23.10	R2	Lowestoft Town (a)	W 4-2
06.11	R3	Actonians (a)	L 1-2

2016/17 FA CUP RESULTS

04.12	R1	Cambridge United (a)	L 1-3

2016/17 WPL SOUTHERN DIVISION

	GD	Pts
1. Tottenham Hotspur	45	52 (P)
2. Coventry United	40	48
3. Cardiff City	53	44
4. Charlton Athletic	30	42
5. Crystal Palace	25	33
6. C&K Basildon	-13	27
7. Lewes	-5	25
8. Portsmouth	-35	17
9. West Ham United	-47	9
10. Swindon Town	-40	8
11. QPR	**-53**	**8**

QPR Ladies were formed out of the merger of Wembley Mill Hill and QPR Women's in May 2001.

They were relegated from the WPL at the end of 2001/02 but finally returned to that level when they were promoted at the end of 2008/09.

The team has twice collected silverware: the Middlesex County FA Women's Senior Cup in 2009/10 and the South West Combination League Cup in 2006/07. Their best League season position-wise came in 2002/03 when they were runners-up in the South East Combination League.

RADCLIFFE OLYMPIC

WPL MIDLANDS DIVISION ONE (TIER 4)

Founded: 1999 (as Dayncourt Ladies)
Nickname: None
Ground: The Rec, (Radcliffe Olympic FC)

SEASON 2016/17

WPL Midlands Division One: 4th
WPL Cup: DR **WPL Plate: QF**
FA Cup: R2

2016/17 WPL MIDLANDS DIVISION ONE

21.08	Steel City Wanderers (h)	W 1-0
28.08	The New Saints (h)	W 4-0
11.09	Sporting Khalsa (a)	L 1-4
14.09	Long Eaton United (h)	L 1-2
18.09	Solihull (a)	L 0-3
02.10	Birmingham & WM (h)	W 2-1
05.10	Long Eaton United (a)	W 4-1
30.10	Leicester City Ladies (h)	W 13-0
27.11	Steel City Wanderers (a)	W 5-3
22.01	Solihull (h)	W 3-2
29.01	Sporting Khalsa (h)	L 0-1
05.02	Loughborough Students (h)	W 5-3
26.02	Leicester City Ladies (a)	W 3-1
26.03	Rotherham United (a)	W 2-0
02.04	Wolverhampton Wanderers (a)	L 2-3
16.04	The New Saints (a)	L 0-5
23.04	Loughborough Foxes (a)	L 2-3
30.04	Wolverhampton Wanderers (h)	L 0-2
04.05	Loughborough Foxes (h)	W 3-1
07.05	Birmingham & WM (a)	D 1-1
09.05	Loughborough Students (a)	W 5-0
14.05	Rotherham United (h)	W 1-0

2016/17 WPL CUP RESULTS

04.09	DR	Wolverhampton W. (a)	L 2-3

2016/17 WPL PLATE RESULTS

23.10	R2	Birmingham & WM (a)	W 1-0
06.11	R3	Leicester City Ladies (a)	W 5-0
11.12	QF	Actonians (a)	L 0-3

2016/17 FA CUP RESULTS

09.10	RQ3	Wyrley (a)	W 6-1
13.11	RQ4	Gornall (h)	W 8-0
04.12	R1	Sheffield Wednesday (h)	W 6-0
08.01	R2	West Bromwich Albion (a)	L 0-4

2016/17 WPL MIDLANDS DIVISION ONE

	GD	Pts
1. Wolverhampton Wanderers	39	56 (P)
2. Loughborough Foxes	80	54
3. Sporting Khalsa	24	41
4. Radcliffe Olympic	**22**	**40**
5. Birmingham & WM	14	40
6. The New Saints	21	39
7. Long Eaton United	9	30
8. Steel City Wanderers	-16	28
9. Solihull	-14	23
10. Leicester City Ladies	-61	17
11. Rotherham United	-25	16
12. Loughborough Students	-93	-1* (R)

*Loughborough Students docked 2 points

It was while having a kickabout on Bingham Road in Radcliffe that founder Kate Tinsley and friends came up with the idea of forming a ladies football team.

Ex-Notts County player Mick Vinter was also among those who founded the club, then known as Daynscourt Ladies, in August 1999. The club started life playing in the Third Division of the East Midlands Unison Women's Football League. They have enjoyed many Cup finals and promotions on their route up to the FA WPL Division One.

Kate Tinsley, and other volunteers, have played a key role in the development of the club which has gone from strength to strength since merging with Radcliffe Olympic. The women's team groundshare with Radcliffe Olympic men's at The Rec.

ROTHERHAM UNITED

WPL MIDLANDS DIVISION ONE (TIER 4)

Founded: 1969 (as Kilnhurst Shooting Stars)
Nickname: The Millers
Ground: Roundwood Sports Complex, (Parkgate FC)

SEASON 2016/17:

WPL Midlands Division One: 11th
WPL Cup: DR **WPL Plate: R2**
FA Cup: RQ3

2016/17 WPL MIDLANDS DIVISION ONE

21.08	Birmingham & WM (h)	W 5-1
28.08	Wolverhampton Wanderers (h)	L 2-3
13.09	Steel City Wanderers (a)	L 1-3
18.09	Sporting Khalsa (h)	L 0-4
25.09	Loughborough Students (a)	W 4-3
05.10	Steel City Wanderers (h)	L 0-2
23.10	Leicester City Ladies (h)	W 6-0
30.10	Solihull (a)	L 0-4
13.11	Loughborough Students (h)	W 6-1
27.11	Loughborough Foxes (a)	L 1-7
04.12	Long Eaton United (a)	D 3-3
11.12	Birmingham & WM (a)	L 1-5
08.01	Sporting Khalsa (a)	L 2-4
15.01	Leicester City Ladies (a)	W 6-1
26.02	Long Eaton United (h)	L 0-2
19.03	Solihull (h)	L 2-3
26.03	Radcliffe Olympic (h)	L 0-2
02.04	The New Saints (a)	L 3-4
09.04	Loughborough Foxes (h)	L 1-9
23.04	Wolverhampton Wanderers (a)	L 1-4
30.04	The New Saints (h)	L 1-4
14.05	Radcliffe Olympic (a)	L 0-1

2016/17 WPL CUP RESULTS

04.09	DR	Blackburn Rovers (a)	L 0-19

2016/17 WPL PLATE RESULTS

16.10	R2	Leicester City Women (a)	L 1-6

2016/17 FA CUP RESULTS

09.10	RQ3	Guiseley Vixens (a)	L 2-7

2016/17 WPL MIDLANDS DIVISION ONE

	GD	Pts
1. Wolverhampton Wanderers	39	56 (P)
2. Loughborough Foxes	80	54
3. Sporting Khalsa	24	41
4. Radcliffe Olympic	22	40
5. Birmingham & West Midlands	14	40
6. The New Saints	21	39
7. Long Eaton United	9	30
8. Steel City Wanderers	-16	28
9. Solihull	-14	23
10. Leicester City Ladies	-61	17
11. Rotherham United	**-25**	**16**
12. Loughborough Students	-93	-1* (R)

*Loughborough Students docked 2 points

The team originated out of Kilnhurst Shooting Stars youth club in 1969 where football was one of a number of sports played. In the early 1970s the name was changed to Kilnhurst Ladies and then to Millmoor Ladies in 1989 when they formed their first links with men's professional club Rotherham United.

A further change of name followed when the FA devised the current pyramid system in 1999. The team competed as Parkgate Ladies in the Midland Combination League.

In 2003 they renewed their links with Rotherham United men's club and took the same name.

Current chair Val Hoyle has been with the club since it was formed. In the past she has served as a player, worked on the management committee, and even stood in as caretaker manager in 2016/17.

SHANKLIN

SOUTHERN REGIONAL PREMIER (TIER 5)

Founded: 2000
Nickname: None
Ground: County Ground, (Shanklin FC)

SEASON 2016/17

WPL South West Division One: Withdrew
WPL Cup: DR **WPL Plate: R2**
FA Cup: RQ4

2016/17 WPL SOUTH WEST DIVISION ONE

21.08	*Plymouth Argyle (h)*	*L 1-6*
28.08	*Brislington (a)*	*L 0-1*
18.09	*St Nicholas (h)*	*D 1-1*
02.10	*Basingstoke Town (a)*	*L 2-7*
30.10	*Brislington (h)*	*L 1-3*
08.01	*Chichester City (a)*	*L 0-14*
22.01	*Cheltenham Town (a)*	*L 1-4*
29.01	*Chichester City (h)*	*L 0-6*
12.02	*St Nicholas (a)*	*L 1-3*
19.02	*Basingstoke Town (h)*	*L 0-2*
26.02	*Keynsham Town (h)*	*L 0-7*
12.03	*Exeter City (h)*	*W 3-2*
19.03	*Cheltenham Town (h)*	*L 0-4*
26.03	*Maidenhead United (a)*	*L 0-1*
09.04	*Southampton Saints (a)*	*L 0-5*
16.04	*Keynsham Town (a)*	*L 0-7*
23.04	*Larkhall Athletic (a)*	*P-P*
30.04	*Maidenhead United (h)*	*L 1-2*
05.05	*Southampton Saints (h)*	*P-P*
14.05	*Plymouth Argyle (a)*	*P-P*
20.05	*Larkhall Athletic (h)*	*P-P*

All above results expunged from the records following Shanklin's withdrawal from the League.

2016/17 WPL CUP RESULTS

04.09	DR	Charlton Athletic (a)	L 1-8

2016/17 WPL PLATE RESULTS

16.10	R2	St Nicholas (a)	L 2-7

2016/17 FA CUP RESULTS

09.10	RQ3	St Nicholas (h)	W 3-2
13.11	RQ4	Southampton (h)	L 0-3

2016/17 WPL SOUTH WEST DIVISION ONE FINAL TABLE

	GD	Pts
1. Chichester City	92	58 (P)
2. Plymouth Argyle	85	54
3. Southampton Saints	20	41
4. Keynsham Town	39	38
5. Larkhall Athletic	3	36
6. Brislington	-19	22
7. Maidenhead United	-28	16*
8. St Nicholas	-43	15
9. Basingstoke Town	-28	14
10. Cheltenham Town	-49	13
11. Exeter City	-72	4 (R)

*Maidenhead docked 1 point

NB: Shanklin withdrew from League, all results expunged

Shanklin are based on the Isle of Wight and play their home games at Shanklin men's County Ground.

Shanklin Ladies were Southern Premier League champions in 2012/13 and have won the Hampshire County League on three occasions in 2003/04, 2004/05 and 2005/06. They also won the Hampshire Invitation Cup in 2011/12.

On 17 May 2017, Shanklin withdrew from the WPL South West Division One having been unable to fulfil a number of their fixtures. They were bottom of the League at the time. All of their results were expunged from the records.

SHEFFIELD UNITED

WPL MIDLANDS DIVISION ONE (TIER 4)

Founded: Circa 1988
Nickname: None
Ground: Swallownest Miners Welfare in 2016/17, SteelPhalt Sheffield United Academy in 2017/18

SEASON 2016/17

East Midlands Regional Premier: 1st (P)
FA Cup: R2

2016/17 EAST MIDLANDS REGIONAL PREMIER

04.09	Nettleham (h)	W 4-3
07.09	Mansfield Town (a)	D 1-1
28.09	Mansfield Hosiery Mills (h)	W 5-0
02.10	Rise Park (a)	W 2-0
19.10	Mansfield Town (h)	W 3-2
23.10	Kettering Town (a)	W 4-0
30.10	Bedworth United (h)	L 2-3
06.11	Ruddington Village (h)	W 14-1
11.12	Rise Park (h)	W 4-2
22.01	Notts County Development (h)	W 10-0
05.02	Mansfield Hosiery Mills (a)	W 5-0
12.02	Notts County Development (a)	W 7-0
19.02	Arnold Town (h)	W 5-0
19.03	Bedworth United (a)	W 5-0
09.04	Peterborough Northern Star (a)	W 2-1
13.04	Nettleham (a)	W 2-0
16.04	Arnold Town (a)	W 8-0
30.04	Ruddington Village (a)	W 6-1
14.05	Peterborough Northern Star (h)	W 6-3
16.05	Kettering Town (h)*	D 0-0

*Played at Calverton Miners Welfare, Nottinghamshire

2016/17 FA CUP RESULTS

18.09	R2Q	Bradford Park Av. (a)	W 8-1
09.10	R3Q	Chester-le-Street T. (a)	W 1-0
13.11	R4Q	Merseyrail Bootle (h)	W 3-1
04.12	R1	Leicester City W. Dev. (h)	W 2-0
08.01	R2	Derby County (a)	L 2-3 (aet)

2016/17 EAST MIDLANDS REGIONAL PREMIER

	GD	Pts
1. Sheffield United	**78**	**53 (P)**
2. Bedworth United	62	46
3. Mansfield Town	35	43
4. Peterborough Northern Star	66	42
5. Nettleham	31	36*
6. Rise Park	4	31
7. Kettering Town	-1	24
8. Mansfield Hosiery Mills	-33	19
9. Arnold Town	-29	17
10. Notts County Development	-100	7
11. Ruddington Village	-113	3

*Nettleham docked 3 points (no-show)

Sheffield United became formally affiliated with the men's professional team of the same name in September 2016.

United's Centre of Excellence helped develop England internationals Hannah Cain and Millie Bright.

SOLIHULL MOORS

WPL MIDLANDS DIVISION ONE (TIER 4)

Founded: 1994 (as Shirley Town)
Nickname: None
Ground: Field Lane, (Hampton FC) in 2016/17, West Midlands Sports and Social Club in 2017/18

SEASON 2016/17

WPL Midlands Division One: 9th
WPL Cup: DR **WPL Plate: R2**
FA Cup: R1

2016/17 WPL MIDLANDS DIVISION ONE

28.08	Loughborough Foxes (h)	L 1-7
11.09	Steel City Wanderers (h)	L 1-3
18.09	Radcliffe Olympic (h)	W 3-0
02.10	Wolverhampton Wanderers (a)	L 1-6
23.10	Loughborough Students (h)	W 6-0
30.10	Rotherham United (h)	W 4-0
06.11	Long Eaton United (a)	L 1-2
11.12	Loughborough Foxes (a)	L 0-9
18.12	Birmingham & WM (h)*	L 0-4
22.01	Radcliffe Olympic (a)	L 2-3
05.02	The New Saints (a)	D 3-3
19.02	Sporting Khalsa (a)	D 1-1
26.02	Birmingham & WM (a)	L 2-4
12.03	Wolverhampton Wanderers (h)	D 0-0
19.03	Rotherham United (a)	W 3-2
26.03	Long Eaton United (h)	W 2-0
02.04	Steel City Wanderers (a)	L 3-4
09.04	Sporting Khalsa (h)	L 1-2
23.04	Leicester City Ladies (h)	D 0-0
30.04	Loughborough Students (a)	W 4-1
07.05	Leicester City Ladies (a)	L 1-2
14.05	The New Saints (h)	D 2-2

*Played at Damson Park, (Solihull Moors FC)

2016/17 WPL CUP RESULTS

04.09	DR	The New Saints (a)	L 0-3

2016/17 WPL PLATE RESULTS

16.10	R2	Tranmere Rovers (h)	L 0-2

2016/17 FA CUP RESULTS

09.10	RQ3	Oadby & Wigston (a)	W 6-0
13.11	RQ4	Burton Albion (h)	W 3-0
04.12	R1	Wolverhampton W. (a)	L 0-4

2016/17 WPL MIDLANDS DIVISION ONE

	GD	Pts
1. Wolverhampton Wanderers	39	56 (P)
2. Loughborough Foxes	80	54
3. Sporting Khalsa	24	41
4. Radcliffe Olympic	22	40
5. Birmingham & WM	14	40
6. The New Saints	21	39
7. Long Eaton United	9	30
8. Steel City Wanderers	-16	28
9. Solihull Moors	**-14**	**23**
10. Leicester City Ladies	-61	17
11. Rotherham United	-25	16
12. Loughborough Students	-93	-1* (R)

*Loughborough Students docked 2 points

The club was founded as Shirley Town in 1994. Ground relocations saw them change their name to Woodbourne United in 1996, Billesley United in 1998 and Solihull Glades in 2003 before becoming Solihull in 2005.

In December 2016, Solihull announced they would be partnering with men's National League side Solihull Moors from the start of the 2017/18 season.

The club's top scorer in 2016/17 was Carly Davies who hit 10 goals in 17 appearances in all competitions.

They have won two League titles, finishing top of the West Midlands Division One Central during their days as Solihull Glades in 2003/04 and of the West Midlands Premier Division as Solihull in 2012/13.

SOUTHAMPTON SAINTS

WPL SW DIVISION ONE (TIER 4)

Founded: 1979 (as Red Star Southampton)
Nickname: Saints
Ground: Universal Stadium, (Sholing FC)

SEASON 2016/17

WPL South West Division One: 3rd
WPL Cup: DR WPL Plate: R2
FA Cup: R1

2016/17 WPL SOUTH WEST DIVISION ONE

21.08	Brislington (a)	D 2-2
28.08	Basingstoke Town (a)	W 4-2
11.09	Keynsham Town (h)	W 3-2
15.09	Chichester City (h)	D 1-1
18.09	Exeter City (a)	W 1-0
16.10	Brislington (h)	W 5-3
30.10	Keynsham Town (a)	D 0-0
08.01	Larkhall Athletic (h)	W 6-2
05.02	Exeter City (h)	W 2-0
09.02	Chichester City (a)	L 0-8
12.02	Cheltenham Town (h)	W 3-2
12.03	Maidenhead United (h)	W 4-2
26.03	Larkhall Athletic (a)	D 2-2
02.04	Maidenhead United (a)	D 1-1
09.04	*Shanklin (h)*	*W 5-0 (ex)*
13.04	Basingstoke Town (h)	W 3-1
16.04	Plymouth Argyle (a)*	L 0-1
16.04	Plymouth Argyle (h)*	L 0-3
23.04	St Nicholas (h)	W 2-0
30.04	St Nicholas (a)	W 10-0
07.05	Cheltenham Town (a)	W 3-0

(ex) Shanklin withdrew from League: result expunged

*Played two 60-minute matches on same day

2016/17 WPL CUP RESULTS

04.09	DR	Gillingham (h)	L 0-4

2016/17 WPL PLATE RESULTS

23.10	R2	Keynsham Town (h)	L 2-3

2016/17 FA CUP RESULTS

09.10	RQ3	Downend Flyers (h)	W 8-2

2016/17 FA Cup Results cont.

13.11	RQ4	Exeter City (h)	W 10-0
04.12	R1	Gillingham (h)+	L 1-7

+Played at Maidstone Road, (Chatham Town FC)

2016/17 WPL SOUTH WEST DIVISION ONE

	GD	Pts
1. Chichester City	92	58 (P)
2. Plymouth Argyle	85	54
3. Southampton Saints	**20**	**41**
4. Keynsham Town	39	38
5. Larkhall Athletic	3	36
6. Brislington	-19	22
7. Maidenhead United	-28	16*
8. St Nicholas	-43	15
9. Basingstoke Town	-28	14
10. Cheltenham Town	-49	13
11. Exeter City	-72	4 (R)

*Maidenhead docked 1 point
NB: Shanklin withdrew from League, all results expunged

The first club in the region – Southampton Women's – was founded in 1970 and went on to win the FA Cup eight times. Only Arsenal have won the famous trophy more often – 14 times.

In 1976 the city of Southampton achieved a notable first by winning both the men's and women's FA Cups. The original Southampton Women beat QPR in the final while the men shocked Manchester United. Arsenal are the only club to repeat the feat, doing so in 1993, 1998 and 2014.

Southampton Women folded in 1985/86 and are a separate entity from the current Southampton Women (founded in 2003) and Southampton Saints.

Southampton Saints began life as Red Star Southampton in 1979, and many of the original Southampton Women's players did start to play for Saints when their club folded in 1985/86.

Red Star Southampton later became Southampton Saints. In 1995 Saints formed an affiliation with men's professional outfit Southampton. Southampton men's withdrew their support when they were relegated from the Premier League in 2005.

SOUTHAMPTON WOMEN'S

WPL SW DIVISION ONE (TIER 4)

Founded: 2003
Nickname: None
Ground: Testwood Stadium, (AFC Totton)

SEASON 2016/17

Southern Regional Premier: 1st (P)
FA Cup: R2

2016/17 SOUTHERN REGIONAL PREMIER

04.09	Oxford City (a)	W 3-2
11.09	Newbury (h)	W 5-1
02.10	Chesham United (h)	W 3-2
16.10	Winchester City Flyers (a)	W 3-0
30.10	Bracknell Town (h)	W 13-0
06.11	Milton Keynes City (a)	W 7-0
05.02	Bracknell Town (a)	W 6-0
26.02	Team Solent (a)	W 9-0
05.03	Oxford City (h)	L 2-3
12.03	Marlow (h)	W 11-1
19.03	Newbury (a)	W 8-0
26.03	Milton Keynes City (h)	Ww/o
02.04	Marlow (a)	W 7-1
09.04	Team Solent (h)	Ww/o
16.04	Chesham United (a)	W 1-0
23.04	Winchester City Flyers (h)	W 5-1

2016/17 FA CUP RESULTS

Date	Round	Opponent	Result
18.09	R2Q	Bournemouth Sports (a)	W 12-0
09.10	R3Q	Fleet Town (h)	W 5-1
13.11	R4Q	Shanklin (a)	W 3-0
11.12	R1	Swindon Town (h)	W 2-0
08.01	R2	Cambridge United (a)	L 0-4

2016/17 SOUTHERN REGIONAL PREMIER LEAGUE

	GD	Pts
1. Southampton Women's	**72**	**45 (P)**
2. Oxford City	41	38
3. Chesham United	56	37
4. Winchester City Flyers	21	26
5. Marlow	-2	26
6. Newbury	-50	12
7. Milton Keynes City	-18	10*
8. Team Solent	-58	8**
9. Bracknell Town	-70	3

*Milton Keynes City docked 1 point

**Team Solent docked 2 points

The modern day Southampton Women's are a separate entity to the original Southampton Women who were founded in 1970 and went on to win the FA Cup eight times. Only Arsenal have won the famous trophy more often – 14 times.

In 1976 the city of Southampton was the first to see both its primary men's and women's club win the FA Cup. The original Southampton Women got the better of QPR in the final while the men surprisingly beat Manchester United. Arsenal are the only club to repeat the feat, doing so in 1993, 1998 and 2014.

The original Southampton Women's folded in 1985/86 with the current club not being set up until 2003.

Southampton Women's have never been formally affiliated with the professional men's Southampton Football Club.

Southampton Women's achieved two successive promotions to start the 2017/18 season in the WPL South West Division One (Tier 4).

SPORTING KHALSA

WPL MIDLANDS DIVISION ONE (TIER 4)

Founded: 2004 (as FC Reedswood)
Nickname: None
Ground: Aspray Arena in 2016/17, moving to University of Wolverhampton for 2017/18

SEASON 2016/17

WPL Midlands Division One: 3rd
WPL Cup: DR **WPL Plate: R1**
FA Cup: RQ4

2016/17 WPL MIDLANDS DIVISION ONE

21.08	Loughborough Foxes (a)	L 1-5
11.09	Radcliffe Olympic (h)	W 4-1
15.09	The New Saints (a)	L 2-4
18.09	Rotherham United (a)	W 4-0
02.10	Leicester City Ladies (a)	W 2-0
06.10	The New Saints (h)	W 5-1
16.10	Long Eaton United (h)	W 4-1
23.10	Wolverhampton Wanderers (h)	L 0-3
06.11	Loughborough Students (a)	W 2-0
27.11	Leicester City Ladies (h)	W 8-0
04.12	Steel City Wanderers (a)	D 2-2
11.12	Long Eaton United (a)	L 0-3
18.12	Wolverhampton Wanderers (h)	L 0-2
08.01	Rotherham United (h)	W 4-2
29.01	Radcliffe Olympic (a)	W 1-0
05.02	Birmingham & WM (a)	L 1-4
19.02	Solihull (h)	D 1-1
12.03	Birmingham & WM (h)	W 5-1
19.03	Loughborough Students (h)	W 4-0
09.04	Solihull (a)	W 2-1
23.04	Steel City Wanderers (h)	W 4-0
14.05	Loughborough Foxes (h)	L 1-2

2016/17 WPL CUP RESULTS

04.09	DR	Chester-le-Street Town (h)	L 2-4

2016/17 WPL PLATE RESULTS

25.09	R1	Huddersfield Town (h)	L 2-6

2016/17 FA CUP RESULTS

09.10	RQ3	Coundon Court (h)	W 7-0
13.11	RQ4	Wolverhampton W. (h)	L 2-4 (aet)

2016/17 WPL MIDLANDS DIVISION ONE

	GD	Pts
1. Wolverhampton Wanderers	39	56 (P)
2. Loughborough Foxes	80	54
3. Sporting Khalsa	**24**	**41**
4. Radcliffe Olympic	22	40
5. Birmingham & WM	14	40
6. The New Saints	21	39
7. Long Eaton United	9	30
8. Steel City Wanderers	-16	28
9. Solihull	-14	23
10. Leicester City Ladies	-61	17
11. Rotherham United	-25	16
12. Loughborough Students	-93	-1* (R)

*Loughborough Students docked 2 points

Sporting Khalsa men's club was formed as a grassroots team in 1991 and began life in the Walsall & District Sunday Leagues. They quickly grew and between 1995 and 1997 they were playing at semi-professional level.

FC Reedswood Ladies team was founded in 2004 and was integrated into Sporting Khalsa men's club in 2015.

They have shared the Aspray Arena in Willenhall with the men throughout 2015/16 and 2016/17. With the pitch being removed to make way for a 3G surface in 2017/18, Sporting Khalsa Ladies will play their home matches on the Walsall Campus at the University of Wolverhampton for one season.

ST NICHOLAS

WPL SW DIVISION ONE (TIER 4)

Founded: 2009
Nickname: St Nicks
Ground: Lodge Road, (Yate Town FC)

SEASON 2016/17

WPL South West Division One: 8th
WPL Cup: DR **WPL Plate: R3**
FA Cup: RQ3

2016/17 WPL SOUTH WEST DIVISION ONE

14.09	Larkhall Athletic (a)	L 1-3
18.09	*Shanklin (a)*	*D 1-1 (ex)*
25.09	Plymouth Argyle (a)	L 1-4
02.10	Chichester City (h)	L 0-9
05.10	Larkhall Athletic (h)	W 3-0
30.10	Cheltenham Town (a)	L 1-2
04.12	Cheltenham Town (h)	W 5-2
11.12	Exeter City (h)	D 2-2
18.12	Plymouth Argyle (h)	L 1-4
22.01	Keynsham Town (h)	L 0-7
12.02	*Shanklin (h)*	*W 3-1 (ex)*
26.02	Exeter City (a)	W 5-2
12.03	Keynsham Town (a)	L 2-5
23.03	Brislington (h)	W 5-2
02.04	Brislington (a)	D 0-0
09.04	Maidenhead United (h)	L 1-2
16.04	Basingstoke Town (h)	D 4-4+
23.04	Southampton Saints (a)	L 0-2
30.04	Southampton Saints (h)*	L 0-10
04.05	Chichester City (a)	L 0-10
07.05	Basingstoke Town (a)	L 0-2
10.05	Maidenhead United (a)	L 0-2

(ex) Shanklin withdrew from League: results expunged

*Played at The Ridings, (Chipping Sodbury Town FC)

+Played at AJN Stadium, (Keynsham Town FC)

2016/17 WPL CUP RESULTS

04.09	DR	C&K Basildon (a)	L 0-8

2016/17 WPL PLATE RESULTS

16.10	R2	Shanklin (h)	W 7-2
06.11	R3	Lewes (a)	L w/o

2016/17 FA CUP RESULTS

09.10	RQ3	Shanklin (a)	L 2-3

2016/17 WPL SOUTH WEST DIVISION ONE

	GD	Pts
1. Chichester City	92	58 (P)
2. Plymouth Argyle	85	54
3. Southampton Saints	20	41
4. Keynsham Town	39	38
5. Larkhall Athletic	3	36
6. Brislington	-19	22
7. Maidenhead United	-28	16*
8. St Nicholas	**-43**	**15**
9. Basingstoke Town	-28	14
10. Cheltenham Town	-49	13
11. Exeter City	-72	4 (R)

*Maidenhead docked 1 point

NB: Shanklin withdrew from League, all results expunged

St Nicholas FC was founded as a boys' club in 1974 to provide the chance to play for those aged 9–18yrs in the Yate and Chipping Sodbury region.

A girls' team was introduced in 2008 with a women's team then incorporated in 2009. The club now runs 21 teams for men, women, boys and girls.

Jodie Arkell was the club's top scorer in 2016/17 notching 16 goals in 21 appearances in all competitions.

STEEL CITY WANDERERS

WPL MIDLANDS DIVISION ONE (TIER 4)

Founded: 1993 (as Loxley Girls)
Nickname: Steels
Ground: SGP Thorncliffe, High Green

SEASON 2016/17

WPL Midlands Division One: 8th
WPL Cup: DR **WPL Plate: R2**
FA Cup: RQ3

2016/17 WPL MIDLANDS DIVISION ONE

21.08	Radcliffe Olympic (a)	L 0-1
28.08	Leicester City Ladies (a)	W 3-1
11.09	Solihull (a)	W 3-1
13.09	Rotherham United (h)	W 3-1
18.09	Loughborough Foxes (a)	L 1-6
02.10	The New Saints (a)	L 0-2
05.10	Rotherham United (a)	W 2-0
30.10	Birmingham & WM (h)	L 3-4
27.11	Radcliffe Olympic (h)	L 3-5
04.12	Sporting Khalsa (h)	D 2-2
11.12	Loughborough Students (h)	W 6-1
08.01	Loughborough Foxes (h)	L 4-10
05.02	Wolverhampton Wanderers (a)	L 0-4
26.02	The New Saints (h)	L 1-3
05.03	Long Eaton United (h)	W 3-2
12.03	Long Eaton United (a)	L 1-3
26.03	Birmingham & WM (a)	L 0-1
02.04	Solihull (h)	W 4-3
09.04	Leicester City Ladies (h)	W 4-2
23.04	Sporting Khalsa (a)	L 0-4
07.05	Wolverhampton Wanderers (h)	L 1-5
14.05	Loughborough Students (a)	W 2-1

2016/17 WPL CUP RESULTS

04.09	DR	Derby County (a)	L 0-7

2016/17 WPL PLATE RESULTS

16.10	R2	Leicester City Ladies (a)	L 1-2

2016/17 FA CUP RESULTS

09.10	RQ3	Sheffield Wednesday (h)	L 1-4

2016/17 WPL MIDLANDS DIVISION ONE

	GD	Pts
1. Wolverhampton Wanderers	39	56 (P)
2. Loughborough Foxes	80	54
3. Sporting Khalsa	24	41
4. Radcliffe Olympic	22	40
5. Birmingham & West Midlands	14	40
6. The New Saints	21	39
7. Long Eaton United	9	30
8. Steel City Wanderers	**-16**	**28**
9. Solihull	-14	23
10. Leicester City Ladies	-61	17
11. Rotherham United	-25	16
12. Loughborough Students	-93	-1* (R)

*Loughborough Students docked 2 points

The Sheffield-based club took the name Steel City Wanderers in 1995, two years after forming as Loxley Girls.

The club was founded by Steve and Sue Odams who wanted their triplet daughters Cheryl, Johanna and Selina to be able to play football.

Millie Kenyon was the team's top scorer in 2016/17 with 15 goals in 25 appearances in all competitions.

STEVENAGE

WPL SOUTH EAST DIVISION ONE (TIER 4)

Founded: 2001
Nickname: Boro
Ground: Hertingfordbury Park (Hertford Town FC)

SEASON 2016/17

WPL South East Division One: 11th
WPL Cup: DR **WPL Plate: R3**
FA Cup: RQ4

2016/17 WPL SOUTH EAST DIVISION ONE

21.08	Enfield Town (h)	L 1-2
28.08	Denham United (a)	L 0-5
11.09	Actonians (h)	D 3-3
14.09	Cambridge United (a)	L 2-3
18.09	Ipswich Town (a)	L 1-2
02.10	AFC Wimbledon (a)	L 0-4
05.10	Cambridge United (h)	L 1-3
30.10	Milton Keynes Dons (h)	L 0-4
27.11	Luton Town (h)	D 1-1
04.12	Enfield Town (a)	D 0-0
18.12	Milton Keynes Dons (a)	L 0-2
08.01	Norwich City (h)	W 1-0
12.02	Lowestoft Town (h)	L 0-1
26.02	Lowestoft Town (a)	W 1-0
05.03	AFC Wimbledon (h)	L 1-5
19.03	Ipswich Town (h)	L 2-3
26.03	Denham United (h)	W 4-1
02.04	Gillingham (a)	L 1-5
09.04	Norwich City (a)	D 0-0
16.04	Gillingham (h)	L 0-1
30.04	Actonians (a)	D 0-0
14.05	Luton Town (a)	D 0-0

2016/17 WPL CUP RESULTS

04.09	DR	Larkhall Athletic (h)	L 0-3

2016/17 WPL PLATE RESULTS

23.10	R2	Exeter City (a)	W 4-0
06.11	R3	Luton Town (h)	L 0-2

2016/17 FA CUP RESULTS

09.10	RQ3	Worthing Town (a)	W 15-0
13.11	RQ4	Cambridge United (a)	L 0-3

2016/17 WPL SOUTH EAST DIVISION ONE

	GD	Pts
1. Gillingham	90	57 (P)
2. Milton Keynes Dons	42	49
3. AFC Wimbledon	29	44
4. Cambridge United	20	41
5. Luton Town	5	37
6. Actonians	14	36
7. Enfield Town	-20	25
8. Denham United	-21	25
9. Ipswich Town	-22	25
10. Norwich City	-50	16
11. Stevenage	**-26**	**15**
12. Lowestoft Town	-61	6 (R)

Stevenage Ladies were officially formed as Stevenage Borough Ladies in 2001 but moved under the umbrella of the men's professional outfit in 2014. Like the men's team the club's nickname remains Boro, despite the fact the 'Borough' part of the club's name was dropped in 2010.

Although they have support from the men's club, they continue to fund themselves fully with player subs and fundraising.

Boro won the County Cup for the first time in their history in 2015 and have reached the final in the last three years. They were runners-up in 2016 and winners again in 2017.

In 2015/16 they won the Eastern Region Premier Division to secure promotion to the WPL South East Division One. They achieved their aim of staying up in 2016/17.

STOKE CITY

WPL NORTHERN DIVISION (TIER 3)

Founded: 2001
Nickname: The Potters
Ground: Community Drive, (Norton United FC)

SEASON 2016/17

WPL Northern Division: 4th
WPL Cup: R2
FA Cup: R1

2016/17 WPL NORTHERN DIVISION

21.08	Blackburn Rovers (h)	L 0-2
28.08	Leicester City Women (a)	L 3-5
11.09	Newcastle United (h)	W 2-1
25.09	Bradford City (a)	L 1-5
02.10	Fylde (h)	D 3-3
05.10	Nottingham Forest (h)*	D 1-1
09.10	Middlesbrough (a)	D 1-1
23.10	Leicester City Women (h)	L 1-2
27.10	Nottingham Forest (a)	W 5-1
30.10	Fylde (a)	W 2-0
27.11	Bradford City (h)	L 1-3
18.12	Middlesbrough (h)	W 5-1
12.02	Derby County (h)	W 2-1
26.02	Huddersfield Town (a)	D 2-2
12.03	Derby County (a)	L 3-4
26.03	Huddersfield Town (h)	W 2-0
09.04	Newcastle United (a)	W 4-1
26.04	West Bromwich Albion (h)	D 1-1
30.04	West Bromwich Albion (a)	W 2-1
14.05	Blackburn Rovers (a)	D 2-2

*played at bet365 Stadium, (Stoke City FC)

2016/17 WPL CUP RESULTS

04.09	DR	Birmingham & West Midlands (h)	W 13-0
	R1	Bye	
16.10	R2	Derby County (h)	L 1-2 (aet)

2016/17 FA CUP RESULTS

04.12	R1	Liverpool Feds (h)	D 1-1 (L 2-4 p)

2016/17 WPL NORTHERN DIVISION

	GD	Pts
1. Blackburn Rovers	39	54
2. Middlesbrough	29	43
3. Leicester City Women	7	34
4. Stoke City	**6**	**30**
5. Derby County	4	29
6. West Bromwich Albion	-4	27
7. Fylde	6	26*
8. Bradford City	0	22
9. Huddersfield Town	-16	20
10. Nottingham Forest	-22	18
11. Newcastle United	-49	7 (R)

*Fylde docked 3 points (ineligible player)

The first known women's team in Stoke was founded in 1921 by Led Bridgett, a director at Stoke City men's team. They were known as Stoke United.

They played against the legendary Dick, Kerr's Ladies side from Preston twice in April 1921 and also beat French side Les Sportives de Paris in two exhibition matches played in Barcelona.

The modern Stoke City Ladies team was formed in 2001 and enjoyed their most successful season in 2012/13 when they won a treble of trophies and gained promotion to the Premier League Northern Division.

Stoke City Ladies are now formally affiliated with men's professional Premier League club Stoke City and played one match at the bet365 Stadium during the 2016/17 season – a League fixture against Nottingham Forest which ended in a 1-1 draw.

SWINDON TOWN

WPL SOUTHERN DIVISION (TIER 3)

Founded: 1993
Nickname: The Robins
Ground: Barrington Park, (Shrivenham FC) in 2016/17, Cinder Lane, (Fairford Town FC) in 2017/18

SEASON 2016/17

WPL Southern Division: 10th
WPL Cup: DR **WPL Plate: R1**
FA Cup: R1

2016/17 WPL SOUTHERN DIVISION

21.08	Charlton Athletic (a)	L 0-4
28.08	Tottenham Hotspur (a)	L 1-4
11.09	Portsmouth (h)	W 4-3
18.09	Charlton Athletic (h)	L 0-3
02.10	Coventry United (a)	L 1-2
06.10	Cardiff City (h)	L 0-4
09.10	Crystal Palace (h)	L 0-1
16.10	QPR (a)	W 7-0
23.10	C&K Basildon (a)	L 0-2
30.10	Lewes (h)	L 1-2
13.11	Portsmouth (a)	L 0-5
27.11	Tottenham Hotspur (h)	L 0-4
18.12	Crystal Palace (a)	L 0-3
29.01	Lewes (a)	L 1-3
19.02	Cardiff City (a)	L 0-8
26.02	West Ham United (h)	D 2-2
12.03	West Ham United (a)	D 2-2
23.04	C&K Basildon (h)	L 0-3
26.04	Coventry United (h)	L 1-3
14.05	QPR (h)*	L 0-2

*Played at County Ground, (Swindon Town FC)

2016/17 WPL CUP RESULTS

04.09	DR	Denham United (a)	L 1-2 (aet)

2016/17 WPL PLATE RESULTS

25.09	R1	West Ham United (a)	D 2-2 (L 2-3p)

2016/17 FA CUP RESULTS

11.12	R1	Southampton Women (a)	L 0-2

2016/17 WPL SOUTHERN DIVISION

	GD	Pts
1. Tottenham Hotspur	45	52 (P)
2. Coventry United	40	48
3. Cardiff City	53	44
4. Charlton Athletic	30	42
5. Crystal Palace	25	33
6. C&K Basildon	-13	27
7. Lewes	-5	25
8. Portsmouth	-35	17
9. West Ham United	-47	9
10. Swindon Town	**-40**	**8**
11. QPR	-53	8

The first club to be established in the region were the Swindon Spitfires who were formed in 1967.

Several players broke away from the Spitfires to help set up Swindon Town in 1993. The club started life in the South West Regional League.

The team would have won the inaugural FA WPL South West Division One title in 2014/15 but for a three-point deduction for fielding an ineligible player.

THE NEW SAINTS

WPL MIDLANDS DIVISION ONE (TIER 4)

Founded: 2002
Nickname: The Saints
Ground: Park Hall Stadium

SEASON 2016/17

WPL Midlands Division One: 6th
WPL Cup: R2
FA Cup: RQ4

2016/17 WPL MIDLANDS DIVISION ONE

21.08	Long Eaton United (h)	W 5-2
28.08	Radcliffe Olympic (a)	L 0-4
11.09	Loughborough Foxes (a)	L 0-4
15.09	Sporting Khalsa (h)*	W 4-2
18.09	Wolverhampton W (a)	W 3-0
02.10	Steel City Wanderers (h)	W 2-0
06.10	Sporting Khalsa (a)	L 1-5
30.10	Loughborough Students (a)	W 6-0
06.11	Birmingham & WM (a)	L 2-4
27.11	Birmingham & WM (h)+	L 0-2
04.12	Loughborough Students (h)	W 3-1
18.12	Long Eaton United (a)	D 2-2
08.01	Leicester City Ladies (h)	W 8-2
29.01	Wolverhampton Wanderers (h)*	L 0-1
05.02	Solihull (h)	D 3-3
26.02	Steel City Wanderers (a)	W 3-1
19.03	Leicester City Ladies (a)	W 5-0
02.04	Rotherham United (h)	W 4-3
16.04	Radcliffe Olympic (h)	W 5-0
30.04	Rotherham United (a)	W 4-1
07.05	Loughborough Foxes (h)	L 3-5
14.05	Solihull (a)	D 2-2

*Played at Beech Grove, (Ellesmere FC)

+Played at Foxen Manor, (Four Crosses FC)

2016/17 WPL CUP RESULTS

04.09	DR	Solihull (h)	W 3-0
	R1	Bye	
16.10	R2	Loughborough Foxes (a)	L 1-10

2016/17 FA CUP RESULTS

09.10	RQ3	Shrewsbury Juniors (a)	W 6-2 (aet)
13.11	RQ4	Birmingham & WM (h)	L 2-5

2016/17 WPL MIDLANDS DIVISION ONE

	GD	Pts
1. Wolverhampton Wanderers	39	56 (P)
2. Loughborough Foxes	80	54
3. Sporting Khalsa	24	41
4. Radcliffe Olympic	22	40
5. Birmingham & WM	14	40
6. The New Saints	**21**	**39**
7. Long Eaton United	9	30
8. Steel City Wanderers	-16	28
9. Solihull	-14	23
10. Leicester City Ladies	-61	17
11. Rotherham United	-25	16
12. Loughborough Students	-93	-1* (R)

*Loughborough Students docked 2 points

The New Saints were promoted to WPL Midlands Division One by finishing 2015/16 as West Midlands Regional Premier League Champions in a season in which they also won the West Midlands Regional League Cup.

In 2013 The New Saints Ladies Under-16s became FA National Futsal champions. In 2015, the Under-10s did likewise beating Crystal Palace on penalties in the final.

The club's best FA Cup run to date came in 2005/06 when they made it to the third round proper where they narrowly lost 2-1 away to Northampton Town.

The Shropshire Women's Cup – now called the Tom Farmer's Cup – has been won 11 times by The New Saints.

TRANMERE ROVERS

NW REGIONAL PREMIER LEAGUE (TIER 5)

Founded: 1990
Nickname: Rovers
Ground: Ellesmere Port for 2016/17, moving to Solar Campus for 2017/18

SEASON 2016/17

WPL Northern Division One: 12th (R)
WPL Cup: DR **WPL Plate: QF**
FA Cup: RQ3

2016/17 WPL NORTHERN DIVISION ONE

21.08	Leeds United (h)	L 3-5
28.08	Blackpool Wren Rovers (a)	D 0-0
11.09	Chorley (a)	L 1-5
14.09	Crewe Alexandra (h)	W 4-1
18.09	Brighouse Town (h)	L 0-6
02.10	Leeds United (a)	D 1-1
05.10	Crewe Alexandra (a)	D 1-1
23.10	Hull City (a)	L 1-5
30.10	Blackpool Wren Rovers (h)	L 0-4
13.11	Chorley (h)	D 1-1
27.11	Guiseley Vixens (h)	L 1-4
04.12	Mossley Hill Athletic (a)	L 2-5
18.12	Hull City (h)	L 2-3
08.01	Morecambe (h)	L 0-1
15.01	Mossley Hill Athletic (h)	L 0-4
22.01	Chester-le-Street Town (a)	L 0-5
29.01	Morecambe (a)	L 1-3
26.02	Chester-le-Street Town (h)	L 0-2
12.03	Guiseley Vixens (a)	L 0-4
02.04	Liverpool Feds (a)	L 0-3
09.04	Brighouse Town (a)	L 0-1
26.04	Liverpool Feds (h)	L 1-6

2016/17 WPL CUP RESULTS

04.09	DR	Liverpool Feds (h)	L 0-5

2016/17 WPL PLATE RESULTS

16.10	R2	Solihull (a)	W 2-0
06.11	R3	Mossley Hill A. (a)	W 2-1
11.12	QF	Huddersfield Town (h)	L 0-7

2016/17 FA CUP RESULTS

09.10	RQ3	Accrington (a)	L 0-3

WPL NORTHERN DIVISION ONE

	GD	Pts
1. Guiseley Vixens	52	59 (P)
2. Liverpool Feds	37	44
3. Hull City	16	43
4. Chester-le-Street Town	16	41
5. Chorley	7	38
6. Brighouse Town	16	37
7. Morecambe	1	29*
8. Leeds United	-8	23
9. Mossley Hill Athletic	-27	19
10. Crewe Alexandra	-28	18
11. Blackpool Wren Rovers	-31	18 (R)
12. Tranmere Rovers	**-51**	**7 (R)**

*Morecambe docked 3 points (unregistered player)

The club has been linked to Tranmere Rovers men ever since being formed in 1990.

They played on 3G at Ellesmere Port Sports Village in 2016/17 but will be based on grass at Tranmere Rovers men's Solar Campus training ground from 2017/18.

The most successful period in the club's history came when they spent eight successive seasons in the FA Premier League National Division – the top-flight in England at the time – from 1996/97 to 2003/04. They reached the FA Cup semi-finals in 1999 and 2002 and lost the 2001 Premier League Cup final to Arsenal.

In 2000 Tranmere players featured in a television advert for Daz washing powder alongside TV celebrity Julian Clary. Rovers winger Sue Smith said at the time, 'We've had some terrible stick. The week after we had to go to Southampton. As soon as we walked through the door they were asking us if our colours had run.'

WEST BROMWICH ALBION

WPL NORTHERN DIVISION (TIER 3)

Founded: 1989
Nickname: Albion
Ground: Dales Lane, (Rushall Olympic FC) in 2016/17, Church Road, (Boldmere St Michael's FC) in 2017/18

SEASON 2016/17

WPL Northern Division: 6th
WPL Cup: R4
FA Cup: R5

2016/17 WPL NORTHERN DIVISION

21.08	Middlesbrough (a)	L 0-6
28.08	Fylde (h)	L 0-2
11.09	Blackburn Rovers (a)	L 1-5
18.09	Leicester City Women (a)	L 1-2
25.09	Derby County (a)	W 2-0
09.10	Fylde (a)	D 2-2
16.10	Nottingham Forest (h)	W 2-0
13.11	Newcastle United (h)	W 2-1
18.12	Newcastle United (a)	W 5-0
26.02	Middlesbrough (h)	L 0-4
12.03	Blackburn Rovers (h)	L 2-3
02.04	Huddersfield Town (h)	W 3-1
09.04	Bradford City (a)	L 1-2
16.04	Leicester City Women (h)	W 1-0
23.04	Bradford City (h)	W 4-1
26.04	Stoke City (a)	D 1-1
30.04	Stoke City (h)	L 1-2
07.05	Nottingham Forest (a)	W 2-1
09.05	Derby County (h)*	D 2-2
14.05	Huddersfield Town (a)	L 1-2

*Played at Derby University

2016/17 WPL CUP RESULTS

04.09	DR	Bradford City (h)	W 2-1
	R1	Bye	
23.10	R2	Fylde (h)	W 2-1 (aet)
06.11	R3	Wolverhampton W.(h)	W 1-0 (aet)
11.12	R4	Charlton Athletic (a)	D 1-1 (L 2-4p)

2016/17 FA CUP RESULTS

04.12	R1	Fylde (h)	W 4-1
08.01	R2	Radcliffe Olympic (h)	W 4-0
05.02	R3	Lewes (h)	W 3-1
19.02	R4	Leicester City W (h)	W 2-1
19.03	R5	Birmingham City (a)	L 0-2

2016/17 WPL NORTHERN DIVISION

	GD	Pts
1. Blackburn Rovers	39	54
2. Middlesbrough	29	43
3. Leicester City Women	7	34
4. Stoke City	6	30
5. Derby County	4	29
6. West Bromwich Albion	**-4**	**27**
7. Fylde	6	26*
8. Bradford City	0	22
9. Huddersfield Town	-16	20
10. Nottingham Forest	-22	18
11. Newcastle United	-49	7 (R)

*Fylde docked 3 points (ineligible player)

West Bromwich Albion FC Women competed under the name Sporting Club Albion between 2009 and 2016.

It was as Sporting Club Albion that they won the WPL Northern Division title in 2015/16 for the first time in their history.

Having claimed the title they met WPL Southern Division Champions Brighton & Hove Albion in a one-off play off for promotion to the WSL, but they were beaten 4-2 at Adams Park.

WEST HAM UNITED

WPL SOUTHERN DIVISION (TIER 3)

Founded: 1991
Nickname: The Hammers
Ground: Ship Lane, (Thurrock FC) in 2016/17, moving to London Stadium Community Track for 2017/18

SEASON 2016/17

WPL Southern Division: 9th
WPL Cup: DR **WPL Plate: R3**
FA Cup: R1

2016/17 WPL SOUTHERN DIVISION

21.08	Lewes (a)	L 2-7
28.08	Portsmouth (a)	L 1-3
11.09	Coventry United (a)	L 0-1
14.09	C&K Basildon (h)*	D 0-0
18.09	Crystal Palace (h)	L 0-4
02.10	Charlton Athletic (h)	L 0-2
05.10	C&K Basildon (a)	W 1-0
09.10	Cardiff City (a)	L 0-3
30.10	Coventry United (h)	L 0-5
13.11	Cardiff City (h)	L 0-4
27.11	QPR (a)	D 1-1
18.12	QPR (h)	L 1-2
08.01	Crystal Palace (a)	L 1-6
29.01	Charlton Athletic (a)	L 0-5
12.02	Portsmouth (h)	D 1-1
26.02	Swindon Town (a)	D 2-2
12.03	Swindon Town (h)	D 2-2
16.04	Lewes (h)	D 0-0
19.04	Tottenham Hotspur (a)	L 0-4
14.05	Tottenham Hotspur (h)	L 0-7

WPL CUP RESULTS

04.09	DR	Tottenham Hotspur (h)*	L 0-10

WPL PLATE RESULTS

25.09	R1	Swindon Town (h)	D 2-2 (W 3-2p)
23.10	R2	Cheltenham Town (a)	W 2-1
06.11	R3	Keynsham Town (a)	L 2-3

FA CUP RESULTS

04.12	R1	Coventry United (h)	L 0-3

*played at Bridge Avenue, (AFC Hornchurch)

2016/17 WPL SOUTHERN DIVISION

	GD	Pts
1. Tottenham Hotspur	45	52 (P)
2. Coventry United	40	48
3. Cardiff City	53	44
4. Charlton Athletic	30	42
5. Crystal Palace	25	33
6. C&K Basildon	-13	27
7. Lewes	-5	25
8. Portsmouth	-35	17
9. West Ham United	**-47**	**9**
10. Swindon Town	-40	8
11. QPR	-53	8

Goalkeeper Claire Lacey became the first West Ham Ladies player to be awarded an England cap when, aged 20, she came on as an 81st-minute substitute in a 5-0 win away to Portugal in February 1996.

Former West Ham and Liverpool men's left-back Julian Dicks served as West Ham Ladies manager for the 2014/15 season.

West Ham have twice won the Essex FA County Cup, doing so in 2008/09 and 2010/11. They were South East Combination League champions in 2004/05.

WOLVERHAMPTON WANDERERS

WPL NORTHERN DIVISION (TIER 3)

Founded: 1975 (as Heathfield Rovers)
Nickname: Wolfettes
Ground: Keys Park, (Hednesford Town FC)

SEASON 2016/17

WPL Midlands Division One: 1st (P)
WPL Cup: R3
FA Cup: R2

2016/17 WPL MIDLANDS DIVISION ONE

28.08	Rotherham United (a)	W 3-2
14.09	Birmingham & WM (a)	W 3-1
18.09	The New Saints (h)	L 0-3
25.09	Leicester City Ladies (h)	W 5-0
02.10	Solihull (h)	W 6-1
05.10	Birmingham & WM (h)	W 5-2
23.10	Sporting Khalsa (h)	W 3-0
30.10	Loughborough Foxes (a)	W 2-1
18.12	Sporting Khalsa (a)	W 2-0
29.01	The New Saints (a)	W 1-0
05.02	Steel City Wanderers (h)	W 4-0
12.03	Solihull (a)	D 0-0
26.03	Loughborough Students (h)	D 1-1
02.04	Radcliffe Olympic (h)	W 3-2
09.04	Long Eaton United (h)	W 1-0
16.04	Long Eaton United (a)	L 0-1
23.04	Rotherham United (h)	W 4-1
26.04	Loughborough Foxes (h)	W 3-2
30.04	Radcliffe Olympic (a)	W 2-0
07.05	Steel City Wanderers (a)	W 5-1
11.05	Loughborough Students (a)	W 3-0
14.05	Leicester City Ladies (a)	W 1-0

2016/17 WPL CUP RESULTS

04.09	DR	Radcliffe Olympic (h)	W 3-2
	R1	Bye	
16.10	R2	Brighouse Town (h)	D 2-2 (W 4-2p)
06.11	R3	West Bromwich Albion (a)	L 0-1 (aet)

2016/17 FA CUP RESULTS

09.10	RQ3	Loughborough Foxes (a)	W 3-2
13.11	RQ4	Sporting Khalsa (a)	W 4-2 (aet)
04.12	R1	Solihull (h)	W 4-0
08.01	R2	Nottingham Forest (a)	L 0-4

2016/17 WPL MIDLANDS DIVISION ONE

	GD	Pts
1. Wolverhampton Wanderers	**39**	**56 (P)**
2. Loughborough Foxes	80	54
3. Sporting Khalsa	24	41
4. Radcliffe Olympic	22	40
5. Birmingham & West Midlands	14	40
6. The New Saints	21	39
7. Long Eaton United	9	30
8. Steel City Wanderers	-16	28
9. Solihull	-14	23
10. Leicester City Ladies	-61	17
11. Rotherham United	-25	16
12. Loughborough Students	-93	-1* (R)

*Loughborough Students docked 2 pts

Wolves started out as Heathfield Rovers in 1975 and have also been known in the past as Wolverhampton & Wednesbury Tube and Wolverhampton Ladies. In 1993 they were granted permission from Wolverhampton Wanderers men's club to call themselves by the same name. Today they are officially affiliated to the men's club.

At the end of 1993/94 they were promoted to the top-flight – which was then the FA Women's Premier League National Division – where they spent two years before being relegated.

In 1999 they were incorporated under the Companies Act with several influential people joining the board including BBC presenter Jenny Wilkes and former England women's cricket captain, the late Baroness Rachael Heyhoe Flint.

Aston Villa's 1982 European Cup-winning captain Dennis Mortimer was appointed manager in 2000 and narrowly missed out on promotion to the top-flight during his three seasons in charge.

EURO *2017*

Hosts: Netherlands **Dates:** 16 July – 6 August 2017

Germany's dominance of the continental competition was ended in dramatic style as their quest for a seventh consecutive (and ninth overall) title faltered at the quarter-final stage. A waterlogged pitch in Rotterdam led to the postponement of their match with Denmark and its immediate rescheduling for the following day. When kick-off finally arrived, everything appeared to be going as expected when the 2016 Olympic champions went ahead through Isabel Kerschowski's searing drive in the third minute. A second-half comeback saw Denmark through to the semi-finals courtesy of Nadia Nadim's equaliser and Theresa Nielsen's winner seven minutes from time.

With the Germans out, England – who had managed a 100% record in the group stage before beating France (for the first time since 1974) in the quarter-finals – were installed as the new bookmakers' favourites. However, the 2015 World Cup bronze medallists slumped to a hugely disappointing 3-0 semi-final defeat to the Netherlands. Widely regarded as a missed opportunity by the English media, there were nevertheless some positives to take from the tournament. A peak television audience of more than four million watched Channel 4's coverage of the semi-final and Arsenal's Jodie Taylor claimed the Golden Boot thanks to her five goals. Taylor, along with Manchester City defensive duo Lucy Bronze (who joined 2017 Champions League winners Lyon after the tournament) and Steph Houghton, were included in UEFA's team of the tournament.

The hosts went on to claim their first major title in thrilling style. A crowd of 28,182 was present for the match with Denmark in Enschede, but the home support was silenced when Nadim gave Denmark the lead with a sixth-minute penalty. Arsenal's Vivianne Miedema tucked in an equaliser four minutes later before Lieke Martens put the hosts ahead from 20 yards just before the half-hour mark. Within six minutes Denmark captain Pernille Harder had levelled things up at 2-2. Dutch skipper Sherida Spitse fired in a free-kick to put her side 3-2 ahead just after half-time. The Danes pushed hard for another equaliser, but Miedema's second of the game with a minute to play completed the scoring as the Netherlands triumphed 4-2 to became only the fourth team to win the European Championship.

GROUP A

16.07	Netherlands 1-0 Norway	Stadion Galgenwaard, Utrecht	21,731
16.07	Denmark 1-0 Belgium	De Vijverberg, Doetinchem	4,565
20.07	Norway 0-2 Belgium	Rat Verlegh Stadion, Breda	8,477
20.07	Netherlands 1-0 Denmark	Sparta Stadion Het Kasteel, Rotterdam	10,078
24.07	Belgium 1-2 Netherlands	Koning Willem II Stadion, Tilburg	12,697
24.07	Norway 0-1 Denmark	De Adelaarshorst, Deventer	5,885

GROUP A – FINAL TABLE

	P	W	D	L	F	A	Pts
Netherlands	3	3	0	0	4	1	9
Denmark	3	2	0	1	2	1	6
Belgium	3	1	0	2	3	3	3
Norway	3	0	0	3	0	4	0

GROUP B

17.07	Italy 1-2 Russia	Sparta Stadion Het Kasteel, Rotterdam	1,100
17.07	Germany 0-0 Sweden	Rat Verlegh Stadion, Breda	9,267
21.07	Sweden 2-0 Russia	De Adelaarshorst, Deventer	5,764
21.07	Germany 2-1 Italy	Koning Willem II Stadion, Tilburg	7,108
25.07	Russia 0-2 Germany	Stadion Galgenwaard, Utrecht	6,458
25.07	Sweden 2-3 Italy	De Vijverberg, Doetinchem	3,776

GROUP B – FINAL TABLE

	P	W	D	L	F	A	Pts
Germany	3	2	1	0	4	1	7
Sweden	3	1	1	1	4	3	4
Russia	3	1	0	2	2	5	3
Italy	3	1	0	2	5	6	3

GROUP C

18.07	Austria 1-0 Switzerland	De Adelaarshorst, Deventer	4,781
18.07	France 1-0 Iceland	Koning Willem II Stadion, Tilburg	4,894
22.07	Iceland 1-2 Switzerland	De Vijverberg, Doetinchem	5,647
22.07	France 1-1 Austria	Stadion Galgenwaard, Utrecht	4,387
26.07	Switzerland 1-1 France	Rat Verlegh Stadion, Breda	3,545
26.07	Iceland 0-3 Austria	Sparta Stadion Het Kasteel, Rotterdam	4,120

GROUP C – FINAL TABLE

	P	W	D	L	F	A	Pts
Austria	3	2	1	0	5	1	7
France	3	1	2	0	3	2	5
Switzerland	3	1	1	1	3	3	4
Iceland	3	0	0	3	1	6	0

GROUP D

19.07	Spain 2-0 Portugal	De Vijverberg, Doetinchem	2,424
19.07	England 6-0 Scotland	Stadion Galgenwaard, Utrecht	5,587
23.07	Scotland 1-2 Portugal	Sparta Stadion Het Kasteel, Rotterdam	3,123
23.07	England 2-0 Spain	Rat Verlegh Stadion, Breda	4,879
27.07	Portugal 1-2 England	Koning Willem II Stadion, Tilburg	3,335
27.07	Scotland 1–0 Spain	De Adelaarshorst, Deventer	4,840

GROUP D – FINAL TABLE

	P	W	D	L	F	A	Pts
England	3	3	0	0	10	1	9
Spain	3	1	0	2	2	3	3
Scotland	3	1	0	2	2	8	3
Portugal	3	1	0	2	3	5	3

QUARTER-FINALS

29.07	Netherlands 2-0 Sweden	De Vijverberg, Doetinchem	11,106
29.07	Germany P-P Denmark*	Sparta Stadion Het Kasteel, Rotterdam	-
30.07	Germany 1-2 Denmark	Sparta Stadion Het Kasteel, Rotterdam	5,251
30.07	Austria 0–0 Spain	Koning Willem II Stadion, Tilburg	3,488
	Austria win 5-3 pens (aet)		
30.07	England 1-0 France	De Adelaarshorst, Deventer	6,283

*Postponed due to waterlogged pitch

SEMI-FINALS

03.08	Denmark 0-0 Austria	Rat Verlegh Stadion, Breda	11,312
	Denmark win 3-0 pens (aet)		
03.08	Netherlands 3-0 England	De Grolsch Veste, Enschede	27,093

FINAL

06.08	Netherlands 4-2 Denmark	De Grolsch Veste, Enschede	28,182

Goals: (NED) Miedema 10, 89, Martens 28, Spitse 51; (DEN) Nadim (pen) 6, Harder 33

Ned: 1.Sari van Veenendaal, 2.Desiree van Lunteren (20.Dominique Janssen 57), 3.Stephanie van der Gragt, 5.Kika van Es (4.Mandy van den Berg 90+4), 6.Anouk Dekker, 7.Shanice van de Sanden (13.Renate Jansen 90), 8.Sherida Spitse, 9.Vivianne Miedema, 10.Danielle van de Donk, 11.Lieke Martens, 14.Jackie Groenen

Unused: 16.Angela Christ (GK), 23.Loes Geurts (GK), 12.Jill Roord, 15.Sisca Folkertsma, 17.Kelly Zeeman, 18.Vanity Lewerissa, 19. Sheila van den Bulk, 21.Lineth Beerensteyn, 22. Liza van der Most **Coach:** Sarina Wiegman

Den: 1.Stina Lykke Petersen, 4.Maja Kildemoes (15.Frederikke Thogersen 61), 5.Simone Boye Sorensen (2.Line Roddik 77), 7.Sanne Troelsgaard, 8.Theresa Nielsen, 9.Nadia Nadim, 10.Pernille Harder, 11.Katrine Veje, 12.Stine Larsen, 13.Sofie Pedersen (6.Nanna Christiansen 82), 19.Cecilie Sandvej

Unused: 16.Maria Christensen (GK), 22.Line Johansen (GK), 14.Nicoline Sorensen, 20.Stine Pedersen, 21.Sarah Hansen, 23. Luna Gewitz **Coach:** Nils Nielsen

Booked: (NED) Jackie Groenen (21), Anouk Dekker (43), Stephanie van der Gragt (72) (DEN) Nadia Nadim (45)

Referee: Esther Staubli (SUI)

ENGLAND'S EURO 2017 LINE-UPS

19.07.17 Group D: Stadion Galgenwaard, Utrecht
W 6-0 Scotland (Jodie Taylor 11, 26, 53, Ellen White 32, Jordan Nobbs 87, Toni Duggan 90+3)

1.Karen Bardsley, 2.Lucy Bronze, 3.Demi Stokes, 4.Jill Scott, 5.Steph Houghton, 7.Jordan Nobbs, 9.Jodie Taylor (19.Toni Duggan 59), 11.Jade Moore, 16.Millie Bright, 18.Ellen White (14.Karen Carney 74), 23.Fran Kirby (17.Nikita Parris 65)

Booked: Steph Houghton (55), Jill Scott (62)

Unused: 13.Siobhan Chamberlain (GK), 21.Carly Telford (GK), 6.Jo Potter, 8.Izzy Christiansen, 10.Fara Williams, 15.Laura Bassett, 20.Alex Greenwood, 22.Alex Scott

23.07.17 Group D: Rat Verlegh Stadion, Breda
W 2-0 Spain (Fran Kirby 2, Jodie Taylor 85)

1.Karen Bardsley, 2.Lucy Bronze, 3.Demi Stokes, 4.Jill Scott, 5.Steph Houghton, 7.Jordan Nobbs, 9.Jodie Taylor (6.Jo Potter 89), 11.Jade Moore, 16.Millie Bright, 18.Ellen White (19.Toni Duggan 79), 23.Fran Kirby (8.Izzy Christiansen 69)

Unused: 13.Siobhan Chamberlain (GK), 21.Carly Telford (GK), 10.Fara Williams, 14.Karen Carney, 15.Laura Bassett, 17.Nikita Parris, 20.Alex Greenwood, 22.Alex Scott

27.07.17 Group D: Willem II Stadion, Tilburg
W 2-1 Portugal (Toni Duggan 7, Nikita Parris 48)

13.Siobhan Chamberlain, 6.Jo Potter, 8.Izzy Christiansen, 10.Fara Williams, 14.Karen Carney, 15.Laura Bassett, 16.Millie Bright (7.Jordan Nobbs 60), 17.Nikita Parris, 19.Toni Duggan (3.Demi Stokes 81), 20.Alex Greenwood, 22.Alex Scott

Booked: Fara Williams (5), Izzy Christiansen (27)

Unused: 1.Karen Bardsley (GK), 21.Carly Telford (GK), 2.Lucy Bronze, 4.Jill Scott, 5.Steph Houghton, 9.Jodie Taylor, 11.Jade Moore, 12.Casey Stoney, 18.Ellen White, 23.Fran Kirby

30.07.17 Quarter-final: Stadion De Adelaarshorst, Deventer
W 1-0 France (Jodie Taylor 60)

1.Karen Bardsley (13.Siobhan Chamberlain 75), 2.Lucy Bronze, 3.Demi Stokes, 4.Jill Scott, 5.Steph Houghton, 7.Jordan Nobbs, 9.Jodie Taylor, 11.Jade Moore, 16.Millie Bright, 18.Ellen White, 23.Fran Kirby

Booked: Jill Scott (33), Jodie Taylor (62)

Unused: 21.Carly Telford (GK), 6.Jo Potter, 8.Izzy Christiansen, 10.Fara Williams, 12.Casey Stoney, 14.Karen Carney, 15.Laura Bassett, 17.Nikita Parris, 19.Toni Duggan, 20.Alex Greenwood, 22.Alex Scott

03.08.17 Semi-final: FC Twente Stadion, Enschede
L 0-3 Netherlands

13.Siobhan Chamberlain, 2.Lucy Bronze, 3.Demi Stokes, 5.Steph Houghton, 7.Jordan Nobbs, 9.Jodie Taylor, 10.Fara Williams (19.Toni Duggan 67), 11.Jade Moore (14.Karen Carney 76), 16.Millie Bright, 18.Ellen White, 23.Fran Kirby

Booked: Millie Bright (16), Jade Moore (47)

Unused: 21.Carly Telford (GK), 6.Jo Potter, 8.Izzy Christiansen, 12.Casey Stoney, 15.Laura Bassett, 17.Nikita Parris, 20.Alex Greenwood, 22.Alex Scott

EURO 2017 TOP GOAL SCORERS

Player	Country	Goals	Assists
Jodie Taylor	England	5	0
Vivianne Miedema	Netherlands	4	0
Lieke Martens	Netherlands	3	2
Sherida Spitse	Netherlands	3	1

LIST OF EUROPEAN CHAMPIONS (official UEFA tournaments only)

2017	Netherlands
2013	Germany
2009	Germany
2005	Germany
2001	Germany
1997	Germany

1995	Germany
1993	Norway
1991	Germany
1989	West Germany
1987	Norway
1984	Sweden

NUMBER OF EUROPEAN CHAMPIONSHIP TITLES BY NATION (official UEFA tournaments only)

Germany/West Germany	8
Norway	2
Netherlands	1
Sweden	1

ENGLAND 2016/17

ECQu = European Championship Qualifier

ECGr = European Championship Group Stage

ECQF = European Championship Quarter-final

ECSF = European Championship Semi-final

Fr = Friendly

SBC = SheBelieves Cup

15.09.16	ECQu	Estonia (h)	W 5-0	D.Carter (3), J.Scott, K.Carney (pen)
20.09.16	ECQu	Belgium (a)	W 2-0	N.Parris, K.Carney
21.10.16	Fr	France (h)	D 0-0	
25.10.16	Fr	Spain (a)	W 2-1	M.Torrejon (og), S.Houghton
29.11.16	Fr	Netherlands (a)	W 1-0	J.Taylor
22.01.17	Fr	Norway (n)	L 0-1	
24.01.17	Fr	Sweden (n)	D 0-0	
01.03.17	SBC	France (n)	L 1-2	J.Nobbs
04.03.17	SBC	USA (a)	W 1-0	E.White
07.03.17	SBC	Germany (n)	L 0-1	
07.04.17	Fr	Italy (h)	D 1-1	J.Taylor
10.04.17	Fr	Austria (h)	W 3-0	E.White, L.Bronze, I.Christiansen
10.06.17	Fr	Switzerland (a)	W 4-0	J.Nobbs, F.Kirby, J.Taylor (2)
01.07.17	Fr	Denmark (a)	W 2-1	E.White (2)
19.07.17	ECGr	Scotland (n)	W 6-0	J.Taylor (3), E.White, J.Nobbs, T.Duggan
23.07.17	ECGr	Spain (n)	W 2-0	F.Kirby, J.Taylor
27.07.17	ECGr	Portugal (n)	W 2-1	T.Duggan, N.Parris
30.07.17	ECQF	France (n)	W 1-0	J.Taylor
03.08.17	ECSF	Netherlands (a)	L 0-3	

Head Coach: Mark Sampson (appointed December 2013)

2016/17 All matches	P19	W12	D3	L4	F33	A11
2016/17 Competition matches	P10	W7	D0	L3	F20	A7

2016/17 GOAL SCORERS

Jodie Taylor (Arsenal)	9
Ellen White (Notts County/Birmingham City)	5
Danielle Carter (Arsenal)	3
Jordan Nobbs (Arsenal)	3
Karen Carney (Chelsea)	2
Toni Duggan (Manchester City)	2
Fran Kirby (Chelsea)	2
Nikita Parris (Manchester City)	2
Lucy Bronze (Manchester City)	1
Izzy Christiansen (Manchester City)	1
Steph Houghton (Manchester City)	1
Jill Scott (Manchester City)	1
Own goals	1

The 2016/17 Barnsley squad which won promotion to WPL Northern One as North East Regional Premier Division champions. © Barnsley FC Ladies

Bolton Wanderers are crowned North West Premier League Champions 2016/17. © Bolton Wanderers Community Trust

Chichester City uncork the champagne following their WPL South West One title triumph. © Chichester City Ladies

Durham celebrate a WSL2 2017 Spring Series goal en masse. © Durham Women's

WPL South East One champions Gillingham. © Gillingham Ladies

Lewes get to grips with the WPL Plate after beating Huddersfield 4-0 in the 2017 final. © Lewes FC

Rinsola Babajide in action for WSL2 side Watford. © Ed Henderson

Mai Butler scores for eventual WPL Midlands One champions Wolves v Radcliffe Olympic. © Simon Faulkner

Millwall Lionesses celebrate a goal during the WSL2 Spring Series.
© Millwall Lionesses

The party begins for Haringey Borough after they seal promotion to WPL South East One. © Haringey Borough

Lightning Source UK Ltd.
Milton Keynes UK
UKOW07n1932111017
310835UK00003B/6/P

9 781783 240722